WITHDRAWN FROM
GVSU LIBRARIES

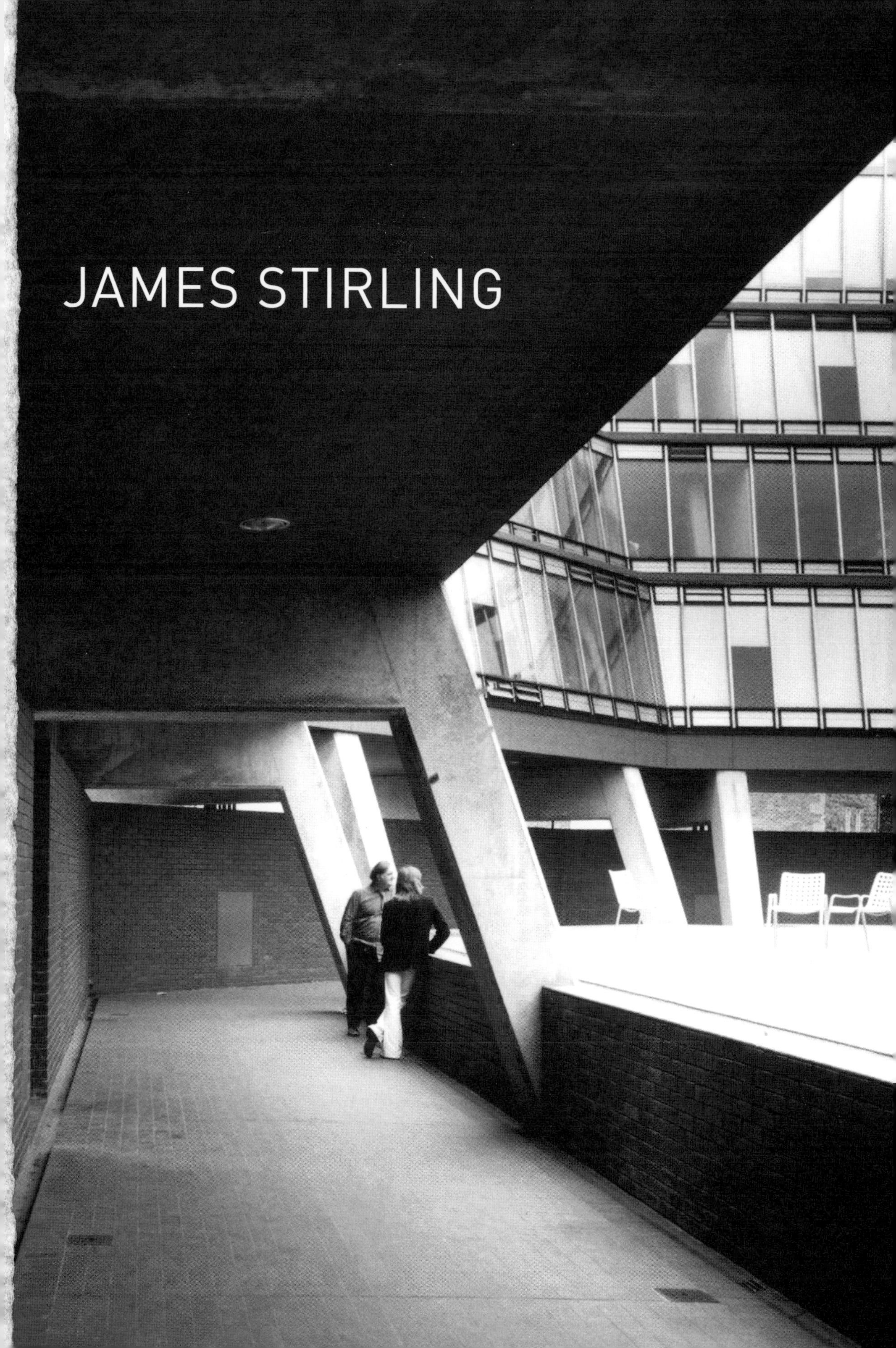
JAMES STIRLING

JAMES STIRLING
REVISIONARY MODERNIST

Amanda Reeser Lawrence

Yale University Press
New Haven and London

Published with assistance from the Graham Foundation for Advanced Studies in the Fine Arts and the Paul Mellon Centre for Studies in British Art.

Yale University Press books may be purchased in quantity for educational, business, or promotional use. For information, please e-mail sales.press@yale.edu (U.S. office) or sales@yaleup.co.uk (U.K. office).

Designed by Jena Sher
Set in Prensa and Din type by Jena Sher
Printed in China by Regent Publishing Services Limited

Library of Congress Cataloging-in-Publication Data
Lawrence, Amanda Reeser.
James Stirling : revisionary modernist / Amanda Reeser Lawrence.
pages cm
Includes bibliographical references and index.
ISBN 978-0-300-17005-4 (cloth : alk. paper) 1. Stirling, James (James Frazer)—Criticism and interpretation.
2. Modern movement (Architecture) I. Stirling, James (James Frazer) Works. Selections. 2012. II. Title.
NA997.S78L39 2012
720.92—dc23 2012003771

A catalogue record for this book is available from the British Library.

This paper meets the requirements of ANSI/NISO Z39.48-1992 (Permanence of Paper).

10 9 8 7 6 5 4 3 2 1

Jacket illustrations: *(front)* James Stirling, Florey Building, detail of fig. 98; *(back)* Stirling and Partner, Düsseldorf, model, fig. 118

Title page: James Stirling, Florey Building, detail of fig. 82

ACKNOWLEDGMENTS

This book would have been inconceivable without the still relatively unexplored archival riches of the James Stirling/Michael Wilford Fonds at the Canadian Centre for Architecture (CCA). It was through the generosity of both the Advanced Studies Program at Harvard's Graduate School of Design (GSD) and the CCA that I was able to make multiple trips to the archive, including a month-long stay working with Anthony Vidler on the Stirling portion of the 2003 exhibition "Out of the Box." At the GSD I am grateful to Mimi Truslow, Barbara Elfman, and Antoine Picon for their stewardship of my travels. The CCA staff was con-

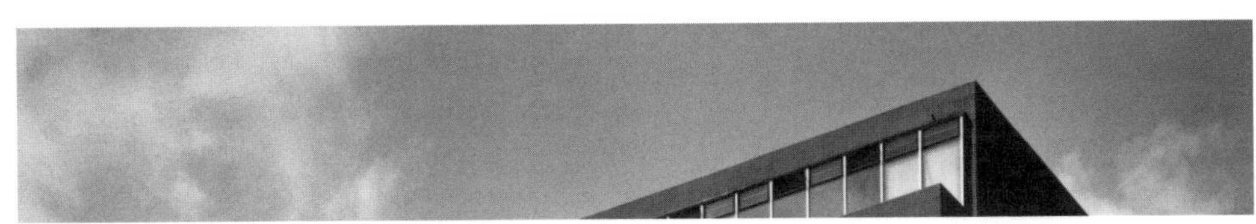

CONTENTS

For Abbott

sistently patient and knowledgeable; Alexis Sornin, Andrea Kuchembuck, and Anne-Marie Sigouin provided invaluable assistance, and I must especially thank Howard Shubert for years of guidance through the often murky world of the archive. For their help with image selection and permissions I thank Renata Gutman and, especially, Julia Dawson.

In the fall of 2005 a grant from the Paul Mellon Centre for Studies in British Art enabled me to visit many of Stirling's buildings. While in England I consulted a number of archives and am grateful to Michael Riordan, archivist at St. Johns and Queens, Justine Sambrook at the V&A Archive, the RIBA British Architectural Library's Drawings and Archives Collections, and the Preston City Archives. I would also thank Geoffrey Tyack for an informative tour of the Oxford University campus and for facilitating my trip to the Queens College archive, as well as Oscar Van Nooijen, Old Members Officer at Queens College, for his tour of the Florey Building. Both Nicola Reid at the Branksome Conference Center and Maureen Strange, departmental secretary for the Department of Engineering at the University of Leicester, were extremely helpful on my visits there, as was Tony Forryan. During this trip I was able to visit the Staatsgalerie at Stuttgart, and I thank Heike Kotzurek for her assistance at the library.

In the course of my research I have consulted many libraries and archives, and I am particularly grateful to the staff at Harvard University's Loeb Library, especially Desiree Goodwin and Barbara Mitchell. I would also like to thank Sophie Bridges, archivist, Churchill Archives Centre, and Adrian Allan, university archivist, University of Liverpool, for their assistance in locating material, especially given the difficulties of transatlantic communication. I am indebted to the work of innumerable scholars, but in particular I would like to thank Mark Crinson, Claire Zimmerman, and Emmanuel Petit for sharing invaluable information at various stages of the project. My gratitude is also extended to George Baird, Neil Levine, and Sarah Williams Goldhagen, all of whom read the manuscript in its dissertation form and were pivotal in helping to frame the subsequent book.

Completion of the manuscript would not have been possible without grants from the Paul Mellon Centre and the Graham Foundation for Advanced Studies in the Fine Arts. Most recently a Junior Research Grant from the Northeastern University School of Architecture sponsored a critical final trip to the CCA, and gave me the opportunity to teach a graduate seminar on the topic, which enriched the manuscript greatly. I would particularly like to thank my chair, George Thrush, for his support and encouragement of the project.

I am honored to publish this book with Yale University Press, whose recent coverage of the postwar period has proved exemplary. Michelle Komie stewarded the manuscript through the submission and review process, and a talented team of editors and designers brought it to completion: Katherine Boller, Heidi Downey, Sarah Henry, and Jena Sher.

Finally, K. Michael Hays first suggested James Stirling as a potential topic, and for this, as well as nearly ten years of sustained intellectual mentorship, I owe him the greatest acknowledgment.

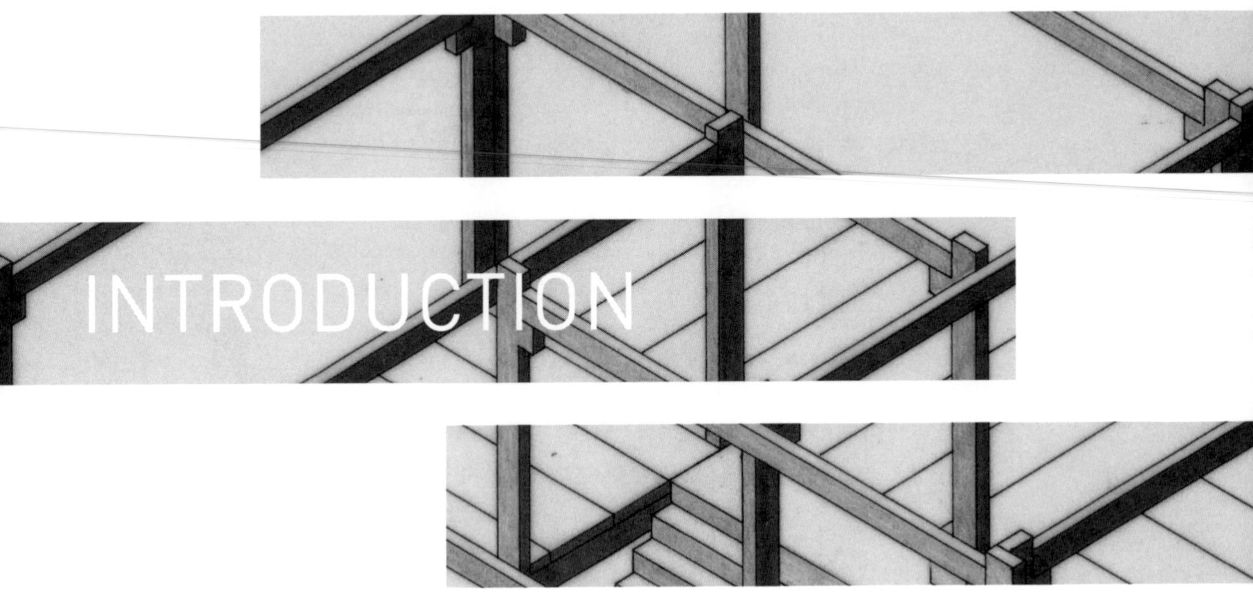

INTRODUCTION

The revisionist strives to *see* again, so as to *esteem* and estimate differently, so as then to *aim* "correctively."
Harold Bloom, *A Map of Misreading*

History is our only guide to the future.
Reyner Banham

Was James Stirling modernism's last great prophet, or postmodernism's original poster child?

This book is an extended response to that question—one that predictably arises when Stirling's work is discussed and that produces heated disagreement among practitioners and theorists alike. The diversity in Stirling's architectural work, which spans from the early 1950s until his premature death in 1992, both prompts the question and obscures its answer. Stirling built some of postwar modernism's most celebrated buildings in the 1950s and 1960s, notably the series of "red brick" university buildings that began with the Leicester Engineering Building (1963) and continued with the History Faculty and Library at Cambridge (1968) and the Florey Building at Oxford (1971). With their clever mixture of machine-age vocabulary and British industrial vernacular, they marked Stirling as the wunderkind of postwar modernism. In the later 1970s, however, his projects began to incorporate overtly classical references—centralized rotundas, columns, and pediments—and seemed to herald a new sensibility marked by a return to architectural tradition. The Neue Staatsgallerie in Stuttgart (1984) embodied Stirling's apparent "turn" from "high-tech modernism to a kind of post-modern classicism."[1] Further muddying the ideological waters are projects sprinkled in and around these seminal works in which Stirling (both alone and in partnership with James Gowan and then Michael Wilford) explored a range of architectural techniques and ideas across the modern/postmodern spectrum, including prefabrication, contextual urbanism, regionalism, and collage. Perhaps the most succinct embodiment of the generally accepted stylistic split in Stirling's architecture is his dual placement in nearly all architectural textbooks: Leicester renders a triumphant conclusion to the "Modern" section, while Stuttgart floats somewhere toward the beginning of the "Postmodern" one.

Despite the "convulsions" in his style (to borrow Reyner Banham's description of Le Corbusier's similarly varied oeuvre) and in deliberate contrast to the widely held belief in a mid-career postmodern "turn," the core argument of this book is that Stirling remained unequivocally and undeniably modern throughout his career. That argument is advanced not by refuting his use of historical reference but by challenging the presumed association of historical reference with the postmodern. My argument is that, from the beginning, Stirling understood modernism as a set of principles that transcended association with the contemporary or even with the twentieth century; they had nothing to do with any stylistic language, modern or remote. As Stirling was fond of saying, "There's nothing fundamentally new about modern architecture," by which he meant that modern qualities could be found in buildings throughout all of history.[2]

By the mid-1950s, when Stirling began to practice and develop his own intellectual preoccupations and positions, there was another truth to his wry statement—modernism was indeed old, or at least aging. As Harold Rosenberg wrote in *The Tradition of the New* in 1959, "The famous 'modern break with tradition' has lasted long enough to produce its own tradition."[3] For Stirling and his peers coming of age in Britain after the war, both the International Style and the Machine Aesthetic were considered important in their time but inadequate for their own era. Certainly what Stirling termed the "white architecture of the thirties" (a deliberate reference to the "latecomer" modernism of the 1930s, rather than the 1920s "original") could not be resuscitated unquestioned in a postwar guise: he referred to himself as a "post-white" architect.[4] And while the British prewar interpretations of continental modernism by figures such as Berthold Lubetkin or Welles Coates still exerted some influence on Stirling's generation, there was also a sense that these architects had simply coopted the streamlined aesthetic of 1920s "revolutionary" modernism without the revolution. To borrow a phrase from William Jordy's well-known analysis of this era, their architecture had become the "mere manipulation of pretty shapes" and had lost its original ideological charge.[5] Penguin pools and gorilla houses done up in white stucco—the earliest incarnations of a British modernism—hardly seemed adequate statements for postwar life among its young architects, many of whom, including Stirling, were newly returned from the war.

And yet even with this mounting critique of modernism's stylization, there persisted a belief in modernism as a set of ideals. The "core" modernist values of functionalism, rationalism, standardization, and economy were, in Stirling's mind, still relevant. Throughout his writings he returns to these concepts again and again; functionalism in particular would maintain a stronghold in Stirling's thinking. For Stirling, functionalism as a "principle"—in other words, functionalism with a small "f"—stood outside stylistic categorization and ensured its endurance. This is not to say, however, that Stirling accepted modernism's principles unchallenged. Even as he subscribed to modernism's "original" aims, Stirling deliberately worked to challenge and expand them, often exploiting their inherent and inherited contradictions, among them rationalism vs. expressionism, subjectivity vs. universalism, abstraction vs. representation, and art vs. technology.

More important than his critique of the stylization of prewar modernism, however, or even his allegiance to modernism's core principles, was Stirling's belief in modernism's fundamental relationship with history. In a 1988 interview, when asked to define the greatest architectural achievement of the century, he replied that while the "achievements of the modernists before the second world war, the revolution of modernism," were important, equally significant was "the de-revolutionizing period following the war, the democratization of modernism, the creation of a pluralist architecture in dialogue with architectural tradition."[6] This willingness to see modernism as engaged with "tradition" was remarkable insofar as proscriptions against reference to the past had constituted a foundational aspect of the modernism of the earlier part of the century. The central argument of this book is that in all of Stirling's work—including projects that are considered canonically "modern," as well as those deemed more historically referential—there was both a reliance on and a critique of history. Because he understood modernism as a set of principles—not forms—he was able to locate those principles throughout history. An investigation into architecture's past thus became a means to advance modernism's fundamental ideals, rather than a betrayal of them. This seemingly contradictory notion of an historically dependent modernism defines his singular contribution to twentieth-century architecture and will be the focus of this book.

Stirling's understanding of architectural history and its relationship to the present was distinct from such earlier architectural movements as the Renaissance or Neoclassicism or even the nineteenth century, in that he didn't see it as part of an organic or evolutionary continuum, or as a kind of "revival." He recalled precedents not as naturalized and inviolable moments in architectural history, rooted to their specific time and place, but as free-floating elements to be reconfigured. As evidenced by the diverse list of precedents for his early projects—the Liverpool docks, Le Corbusier's villas, medieval walled cities, eighteenth-century brick warehouse buildings, and vernacular farmhouses, for instance—the notion of what constituted history had become, for Stirling, much more inclusive and comprehensive than in earlier architectural eras. That list would expand to include additional "high" and "low," as well as contemporary and ancient, examples: Karl Friedrich Schinkel, Nicholas Hawksmoor, and Louis Kahn, to name a few. This expanded historical playing field challenged appropriateness as an idea both typological and formal.

But it wasn't simply the broad range of historical allusions that distinguished his architecture, it was the *way* he appropriated history. Stirling's abstracted, compositional game of typological recombination remains unique within architectural history. He layered and recombined references, stripping away their specificity and legibility. He created single forms that evoked not one but many precedents. And he mined history for projects that embodied modern "principles" (a term with deliberate Wittkowerian associations, as will be developed)—from the "functional" layout of medieval castles to the "rational" expression of eighteenth-century warehouses. Although Stirling's use of the past has been long acknowledged, there has been no attempt to theorize the *specific* design strategies that he employed to manipulate precedent, nor to relate them, however paradoxical it may seem, to modernism. As this book will demonstrate, Stirling didn't simply string together a series of direct quotations; he interrogated precedent based on a discovered or desired connection between the original and his own project, often citing a continued functional or programmatic use.

Understanding that he was manipulating and reconfiguring precedent from his earliest commissions allows us to see his later work as an evolution of, rather than a break from, his early work. This interpretation challenges the conventionally held assumption that Stirling's work was fundamentally transformed by a more overt use of historical references in the 1970s—in other words, that it became postmodern—and argues instead that Stirling's architecture was always dependent upon and deeply embedded with history. As someone who refused the term postmodernism, Stirling found that modernism was elastic enough to encapsulate a more direct and deliberate use of history without betraying its fundamental ideals. In fact, the inclusion of history represented yet another possibility for modernism's continued development. For Stirling, the past and the future were interconnected and mutually dependent. Was that a critical postmodernism? Or an historically informed modernism? His work challenges the very terms and concepts that we use to define it, destabilizing the relationship of the past and the present, between tradition and the new, and ultimately between modern and postmodern.

EARLY INFLUENCES, AND THE DOMINANT PRECURSOR OF LE CORBUSIER

The group of teachers and influences that Stirling encountered in his early training and career goes some way toward explaining his willingness to contaminate modernism with history. While a student at the Liverpool School of Architecture, beginning in 1946, the Beaux-Arts influence of its former head Sir Charles Reilly was still palpable, although the school had also begun to accept modernism, with some reservation, under the new leadership of Lionel Budden.[7] Stirling's teacher Colin Rowe, who came to the school in 1947, would recall a program less polemical than neutral, with an atmosphere of "inane, stable and liberal bureaucracy," which, he acknowledged, provided the "manure" for revolt as much as a highly polemical program.[8] Swedish modernism and "New Empiricism," as advocated by the *Architectural Review,* were thought by some to be more acceptable forms of modernism. Added to the mix was a Polish architectural community of teachers and scholars who brought a "minimalist precision" to the school during their stay from 1942 to 1946, and a penchant for Corbusian tower blocks (often with an "expressive" element) rendered in hard-lined ink drawings. Stirling's self-described response to this debate over the "validity of the modern movement," at least as he remembered it in later years, was a "deep conviction of the moral rightness of the New Architecture."[9]

In a 1948 letter Stirling listed the most important books to him while in architecture school, ranked in order of influence:

1. Fritz Saxl and Rudolf Wittkower's *British Art and the Mediterranean* (1948);
2. Le Corbusier's *Towards a New Architecture* (1927);
3. A. E. Richardson's *Monumental Classic Architecture in Britain and Ireland* (1914);
4. Alberto Sartoris's *Encyclopédie de l'Architecture Nouvelle* (1948);
5. Le Corbusier's *Oeuvre Complète,* vols. 1 and 2.[10]

The list is remarkable for its diversity, and in a compact form it suggests the dual preoccupations that would guide Stirling's early career: British vernacular and high modernism.

The book he singled out as having been the most important—Saxl and Wittkower's *British Art and the Mediterranean*—is a surprising choice for a burgeoning modernist. In a later lecture Stirling would again emphasize its importance: "In addition to *Towards a New Architecture,* the book which influenced me most at this time was Saxl and Wittkower's atlas-like *British Art and the Mediterranean,* this much more so than Wittkower's later *Architectural Principles.*" Through it, he continued, he "developed obsessions through the entire history of architecture though at certain times I'm more interested in some aspects than others."[11] Saxl and Wittkower's 1947 tome, now largely forgotten, is a photographic survey tracing the Mediterranean influence on English art, from prehistory through the nineteenth century. The book is large. Stirling would write that "it just lay around on the floor and got looked at," because it didn't fit on any bookshelf, something Robert Maxwell referred to as the "Rowe method."[12] In the text accompanying the photographs, Saxl and Wittkower describe how various continental artistic motifs were brought to the island and incorporated into local and indigenous artistic movements, resulting in work that was particularly British, even as it reflected the influence of exogenous cultures. Richardson's *Monumental Classic Architecture in Britain and Ireland,* number three on the list, similarly addresses Britain's adoption of external influences. The text is a survey of what Richardson terms "Neo-Classic" architecture from the beginning of the seventeenth century until the second half of the nineteenth, which he characterizes broadly as a "desire to transplant to England part of the warmth of character of antique culture," first Rome and then Greece. Stirling's embrace of both *British Art and the Mediterranean* and *Monumental Classic Architecture* can be linked to his search for a uniquely British architecture, as well as an expanded or at least expanding historical consciousness in this early period of his career. Both texts are descriptions of how Britain imported and made her own various architectural styles; both legitimize the practice of architectural contamination and hybridization. Importantly, Stirling's unapologetic interest in history via these two texts—British history in particular—predated the use of recognizable classical forms in his architecture and held no connection to any specific period of style. The unifying context was geographic, not stylistic.

There is no question that the writings of Le Corbusier—two and five on the list, and undoubtedly undervalued—as well as his seemingly inexhaustible repertoire of projects, both built and unbuilt, would exert the most profound and sustained influence on Stirling. Harold Bloom writes that we can't choose a predecessor any more than we can choose a father, and indeed, the inevitability of Le Corbusier as Stirling's first and most enduring predecessor seems, if not a foregone conclusion, one that would have taken considerable intellectual work to escape.[13] In a 1986 BBC interview Stirling described his "immediate rapport" with *Towards a New Architecture* when he encountered it his first year in architecture school, in particular because of its "play of the form of ships as against that of conventional buildings," which spoke to his own history, and to a childhood spent on the Liverpool docks.[14] Describing his time at Liverpool, Stirling wrote: "We pored through the pages of Corb's *Oeuvre Complète.* . . . The books of Corbusier were thus utilized as catalogues, as had been previously the books of Alberti and Palladio in the Renaissance."[15]

The *Oeuvre Complète* in particular, he writes, was a "vast source of plastic invention to stimulate succeeding architecture."[16] His "black notebook" from the early 1950s is filled with impressions of the Le Corbusier buildings he visited—Maisons Jaoul, Pavillon Suisse, Villa Stein at Garches, the Salvation Army Building—as well as notes from Le Corbusier texts, including the *Modular* (1952) and the lesser-known *New World of Space* (1948), with references to *Towards a New Architecture* sprinkled throughout. The importance of Le Corbusier as a polemicist is worth mentioning, and the fact that Stirling, like most of his peers, knew his work principally through his publications, largely because of the difficulty and cost of visiting the majority of his buildings. In the same black notebook Stirling writes of his time at Liverpool: "One's first acquaintance with Corb's buildings, and also the work of Gropius and Mies and the other masters, was through the medium of the printed page. The formative process was an intellectual one."[17]

Of course, Le Corbusier's significance and impact within postwar European architectural culture were not specific to Stirling, and can hardly be overstated. The British in particular were voracious consumers of his writings and projects and eager to adopt Le Corbusier's ideas and forms on their own soil.[18] By the mid-1950s dozens, if not hundreds, of projects in Britain deliberately manipulated Corbusian precedents—in particular the Unité d'Habitation in Marseilles, completed in 1952 and published widely in England, which represented an antidote to the institutionalized, corporate modernism of Mies van der Rohe's concurrent work in America. The London County Council's enormously influential Alton Estate Roehampton (1958), with its array of Corbusian towers, was perhaps the most visible and publicized Corbusian knock-off, but Le Corbusier's influence wasn't confined to governmental or large-scale firms; the younger, avant-gardist groups of Team X and the Independent Group (Stirling was a loosely affiliated and a self-described "social" member of both groups) took Le Corbusier as a principal source of invention and inspiration.

This is not to say that Le Corbusier's prewar oeuvre had been forgotten, nor that the postwar work was universally accepted. Le Corbusier's seminal works, such as the Villa Savoye and the Villa Stein, remained influential. Stirling's first published essay, discussed in Chapter 1, demonstrates his continued allegiance to the latter. Even with their doubts about the simplistic regurgitation of modernist aesthetics, Stirling's generation still held the prewar work of Le Corbusier as the unquestioned pinnacle of high modernism. The fact that they came into professional practice at the moment of Le Corbusier's seeming *volte-face*—from the "white walls" of the prewar to the rough brick and concrete of the postwar—led to Stirling's understandable "disorientation" about Le Corbusier's "new direction."[19] As Stirling's writing and projects of the early to mid-1950s make clear, he was both intrigued but also dismayed by the more "regional" and "primitive" aesthetic embodied by projects like the Chapel at Ronchamp and the Maisons Jaoul, as opposed to the prewar "rational" work.

Many of Stirling's reactions to Le Corbusier were inflected by Colin Rowe, Stirling's mentor and teacher at Liverpool (though only a few years older than Stirling). Although Rowe's influence can be argued for an entire generation of architects, his impact on Stirling was more immediate and more personal, and he was the most significant figure in determining the way that Stirling "read" history vis-à-vis modernism. Rowe's early analyses of Le Corbusier in relation to Palladio would inform Stirling's own interpretation of Le Corbusier, and of modernism more broadly, as imbricated with history, and a strong scent of Rowe is discernable in Stirling's writings of the early 1950s. His influence would continue into Stirling's later work as well, particularly his writings on collage of the 1970s, as will be discussed in Chapter 5.

It is important, however, to distinguish Stirling's position from Rowe's. Anthony Vidler has described Rowe's understanding of history as a set of "paradigmatic formal *procedures*" that enabled him to see beyond superficial distinctions across historical time periods—modern villas and Palladian ones, for example—and locate a "deeper interpretation of difference and similarity."[20] This sense of history as a set of "procedures" was shared (or perhaps inherited) by Stirling; but if Rowe was an "impassioned observer of the modern in light of the past," as Vidler argues, Stirling was instead an impassioned observer of the past in light of the present.[21] Stirling looked to history for modern principles that could be applied to his own work, that could be made modern. In other words, Rowe historicized the modern while Stirling modernized history. And although this distinction could be said to represent the differing viewpoints of the theorist and the practitioner, I would argue that it also reflected a more fundamental difference in their attitudes toward modernism. Joan Ockman has described Rowe's conceptual position as one in which the "present may be read as a series of strategic efforts to exorcise and overcome the utopian spirit of modernism," which followed from the "revelation" that the "great achievement of the modern movement was not a better world but a new formal style."[22] Although Stirling, like Rowe, may no longer have held fast to, or at least not accepted completely, modernism's "utopian spirit," he remained committed to modernism as an idea whose "achievement" was more than simply a "formal style." He sought to locate its original principles outside the narrow confines of the modern movement, as will be developed throughout the book.

Select examples from Stirling's early career as a student and young architect—before the official "beginning" of this study in 1955—support his interest in Le Corbusier and offer the first articulations of Stirling's wrestling with influence. His thesis project at Liverpool, a "Plan of Town Centre and Community Centre for Newton Aycliffe, England," comprises both a plan for the new town of 10,000 and the development of one specific building in its cultural district—the community center (fig. 1). Accompanying the large-format drawings—plans, sections, and perspectives—is a bound red-leather book that contains a written description of the program, site analyses, bibliography, and a list of buildings visited in preparation for the design. First on

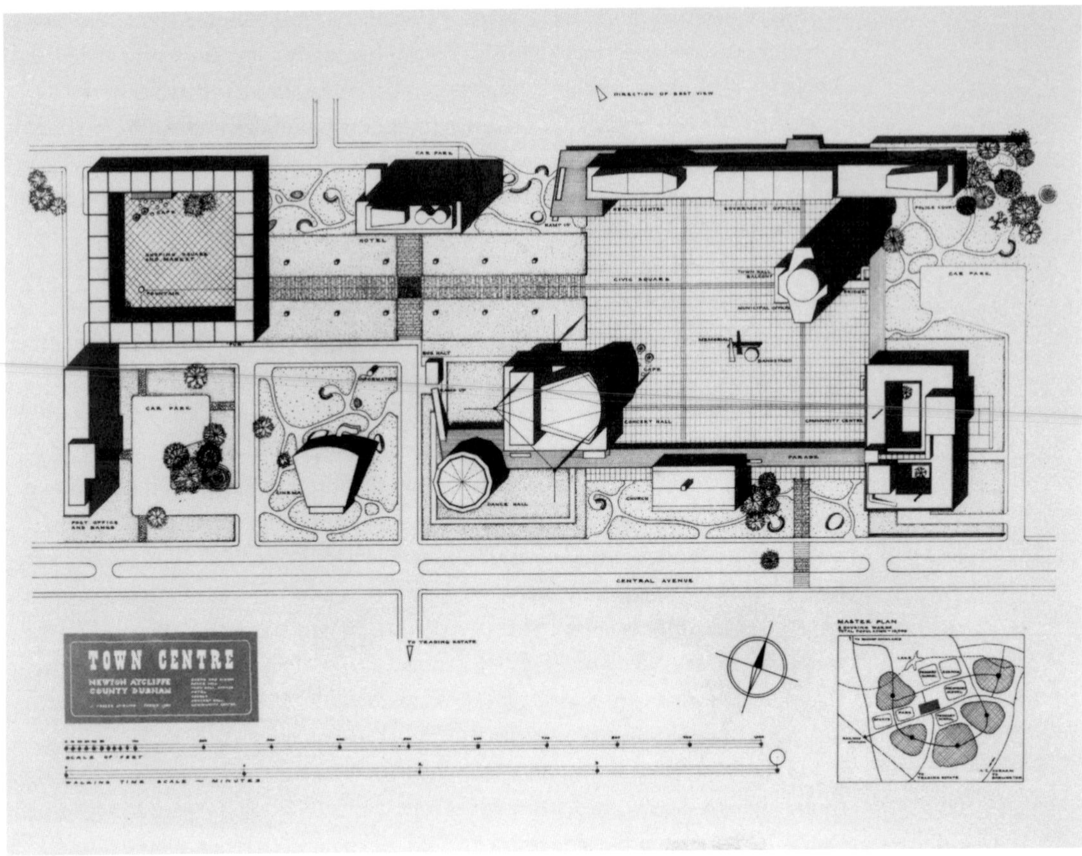

Figure 1
James Stirling, "Plan of Town Centre and Community Centre for Newton Aycliffe, England," thesis, Liverpool School of Architecture, 1950. Site plan with Community Centre at lower right.

Figure 2
James Stirling, thesis. Elevation and sections for the Community Centre show the building elevated on pilotis, with program inserted on the ground floor.

the list of buildings visited is Le Corbusier's Unité at Marseilles, and second is the Pavillon Suisse.[23]

Stirling's design for the Community Centre is a reinforced concrete structure elevated on *pilotis*. Two open courtyards of differing sizes occupy the interior of the building, asymmetrically placed within the column grid (figs. 2, 3). Rather than leaving the ground floor, now liberated by the pilotis, as an open and newly reclaimed terrain, as Le Corbusier decreed in his "five points" and as he achieves to some degree at both the Unité and Pavillon Suisse, Stirling infills it with program, including a coffee shop and lounge. He then encircles this ground floor with rusticated stone walls that move independently of the column structure. Stopping short of the concrete structure, these stone walls act as a strangely nonsensical base, detached from the floating building above. Challenging another of the five points, Stirling expresses doubts about the *plan libre*, noting that it leads to rooms and circulation that are "intermixed and no doubt compromised each other functionally," as well as to excessive circulation in which various programs are "compressed" into the "constricting box."[24] In fact, the free plan truly operates only on the ground floor—in the upper floors nearly all interior walls align with the column grid (prompting Rowe to demand, "Just *where* is the 'free plan'?").[25]

EAST ELEVATION

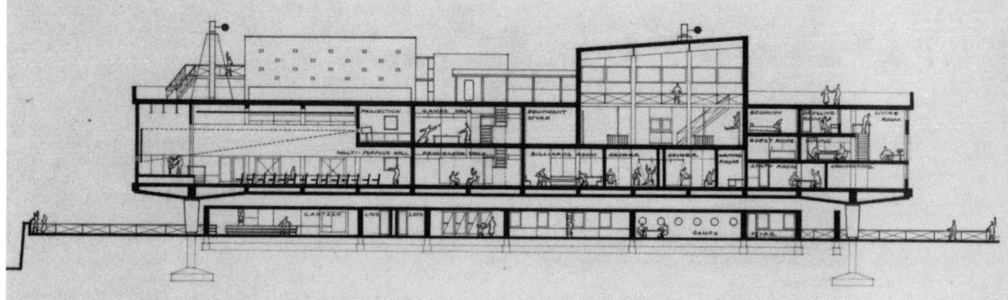
PROJECTION
EQUIPMENT STORE
BEDROOM
LIVING ROOM
GUEST ROOM
DINING
MULTI-PURPOSE HALL
BILLIARDS ROOM
SHOWER
SHOWER
WAITING ROOM
STAFF ROOM
CONSULTING
CANTEEN
LAVS
LAVS
GAMES
STORE
SECTION 1

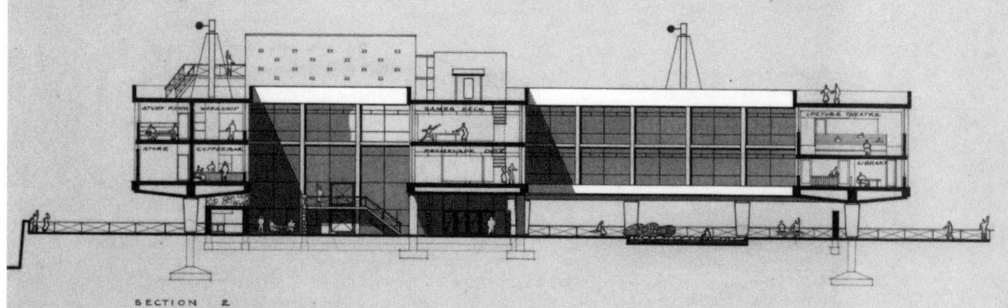
STUDY ROOM
WORKSHOP
STORE
COFFEE BAR
GAMES DECK
PROMENADE DECK
LECTURE THEATRE
LIBRARY
SECTION 2

COMMUNITY CENTRE
NEWTON AYCLIFFE
COUNTY DURHAM

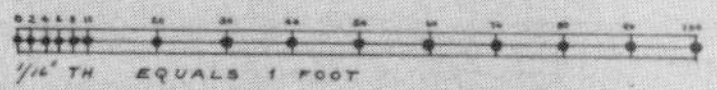
1/16" TH EQUALS 1 FOOT

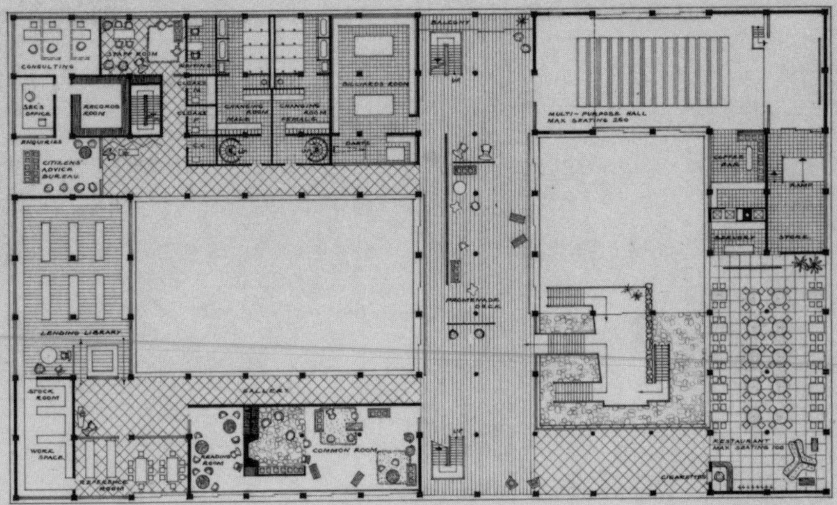

FIRST FLOOR

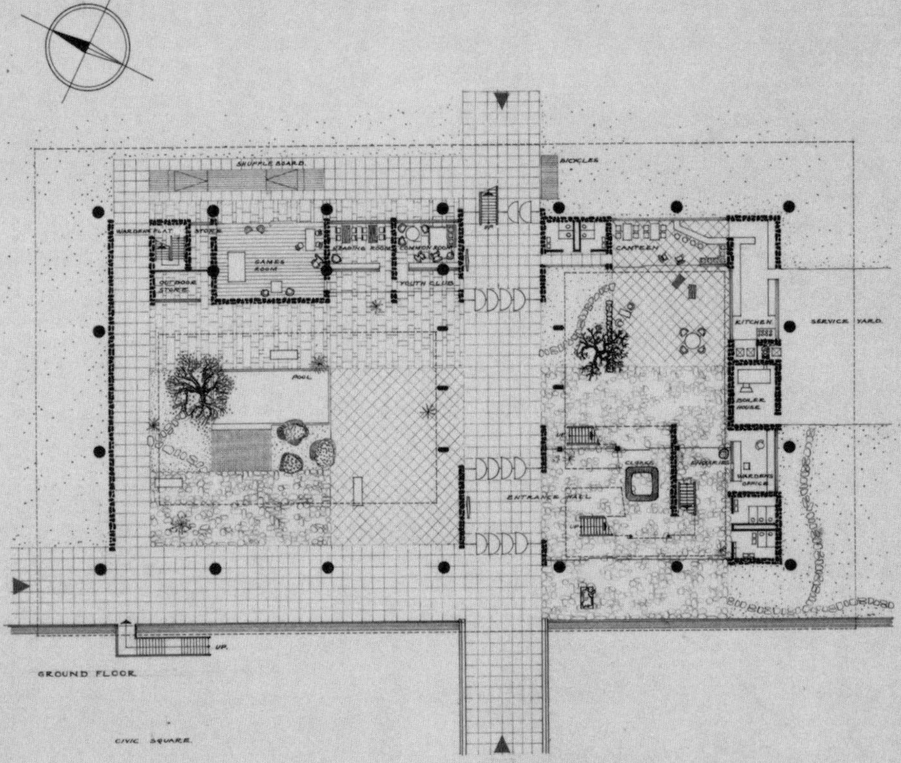

1/16" TH EQUALS 1 FOOT

Figure 3
James Stirling, thesis. Ground-floor and first-floor plans. Note the lack of free plan on the upper floor.

Though with his thesis Stirling undoubtedly references Le Corbusier, it was by no means a purely derivative work; as others have noted, the influence of Mies is perhaps equally strong. Rowe writes, "We are here presented with an asymmetrical rendition of the unbuilt Library and Administration Building at I.I.T," referring to Mies's well-known and highly publicized project of 1945.[26] And according to Stirling's own description, the thesis represented a "return to Greco-Roman principles (e.g., The Acropolis and Forum)"[27] while also alluding to the classical colonnades of Liverpool's nineteenth-century docks—Stirling's own photographs of the docks are pasted on the competition boards (fig. 4).

Two analytical studies from 1951, the year after he completed his thesis, offer even clearer illustrations of Stirling's deliberate response to Le Corbusier and his early struggles to differentiate himself. With its clean, white, cubic form and its use of regulating lines, the Core and Crosswall House makes a direct nod to Le Corbusier's purist villas of the 1920s. Comparisons are most often made with Maison Cook (1926), although the Villa Stein at Garches (1927) was equally at play, particularly in the exterior landing and stair that pull away from the building, touching the ground plane just past the building's

Figure 4
James Stirling, photographer, view of Liverpool industrial buildings pasted to the back of a page from the thesis.

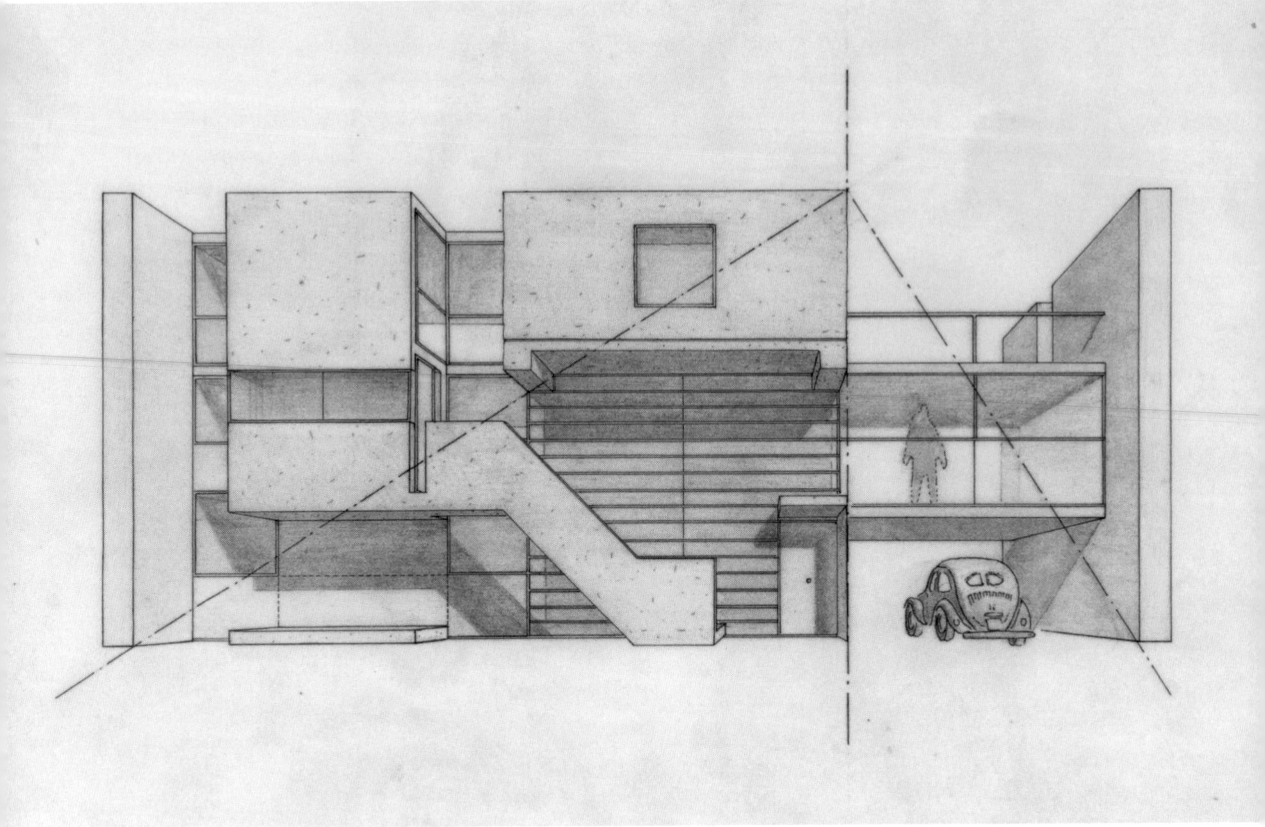

Figure 5
James Stirling, Core and Crosswall House, United Kingdom, 1951.

Figure 6
Le Corbusier, Villa Stein de Monzie, Garches, France, 1927.

center line (figs. 5, 6). Stirling's study focuses on the prosaic construction technique of load-bearing, crosswall construction—generating two distinctive, structural end walls—and replaces the planar façade at Garches with a volumetrically complex, highly three-dimensional, and "deep" façade—in effect, bringing the "back" of Garches to the "front." Like the garden façade at Garches, the front façade of Core and Crosswall introduces large voids into the overall rectangular volume, though Stirling dematerializes the building even more dramatically and begins to flip the reading from one in which space is subtracted, as at Garches, to one in which solids are added. This is another way of saying that the dominance of the singular shape at Garches gives way to a building that is instead an accumulation of various volumetric components, a strategy that would become increasingly important in Stirling's work, particularly at Leicester.

The Stiff Dom-ino Housing project was an even more explicit development of a Corbusian precedent—in this case reconfiguring the Dom-ino House project of 1914 (figs. 7, 8). Like Le Corbusier's prototype it was meant to be mass-produced and modular, strung together to form larger housing blocks. Rather than using a simple column-and-slab structure, with a poured monolithic concrete slab, Stirling employs a pinwheeling structure with a panelized, prefabricated system. In addition to its alleged increased structural stiffness, as well as the possibility for total offsite prefabrication, Stirling's modified domino system creates radically different spatial possibilities: the internal stair destroys the free plan, and the notched perimeter columns, supporting the slabs, are no longer pulled in from the building edge, thus eliminating the possibility for the free façade.

Even as they fortify the depth of Stirling's preoccupation with Le Corbusier at this early moment, these two projects also demonstrate his willingness to dismantle some of the core precepts underlying Le Corbusier's ideas, notably some of his five points. These early appropriations of Le Corbusier are noteworthy, and distinguished from other British Corbusian work by Tecton or Lubetkin or more contemporaneous projects such as Roehampton, in that they engage in a highly self-conscious critique of Le Corbusier's prewar "rational" work, using it as a springboard for the development of his own projects. These are some of the first of Stirling's registrations of influence, and they demonstrate his early desire not simply to copy or imitate but to "revision" his predecessors.

THEORIZING INFLUENCE

The question of influence remains one of the least studied and frankly one of the few taboo subjects remaining in architectural history, particularly as it relates to modernism. In the field of architectural criticism we have arguably made little advancement to the "original" notion of influence, with its astral etymological roots—the affects "attributed to the stars, upon the destiny of men."[28] Stated more forcefully, influence continues to be seen as a lingering and unfortunate aftertaste of postmodernism, an era defined by its seemingly

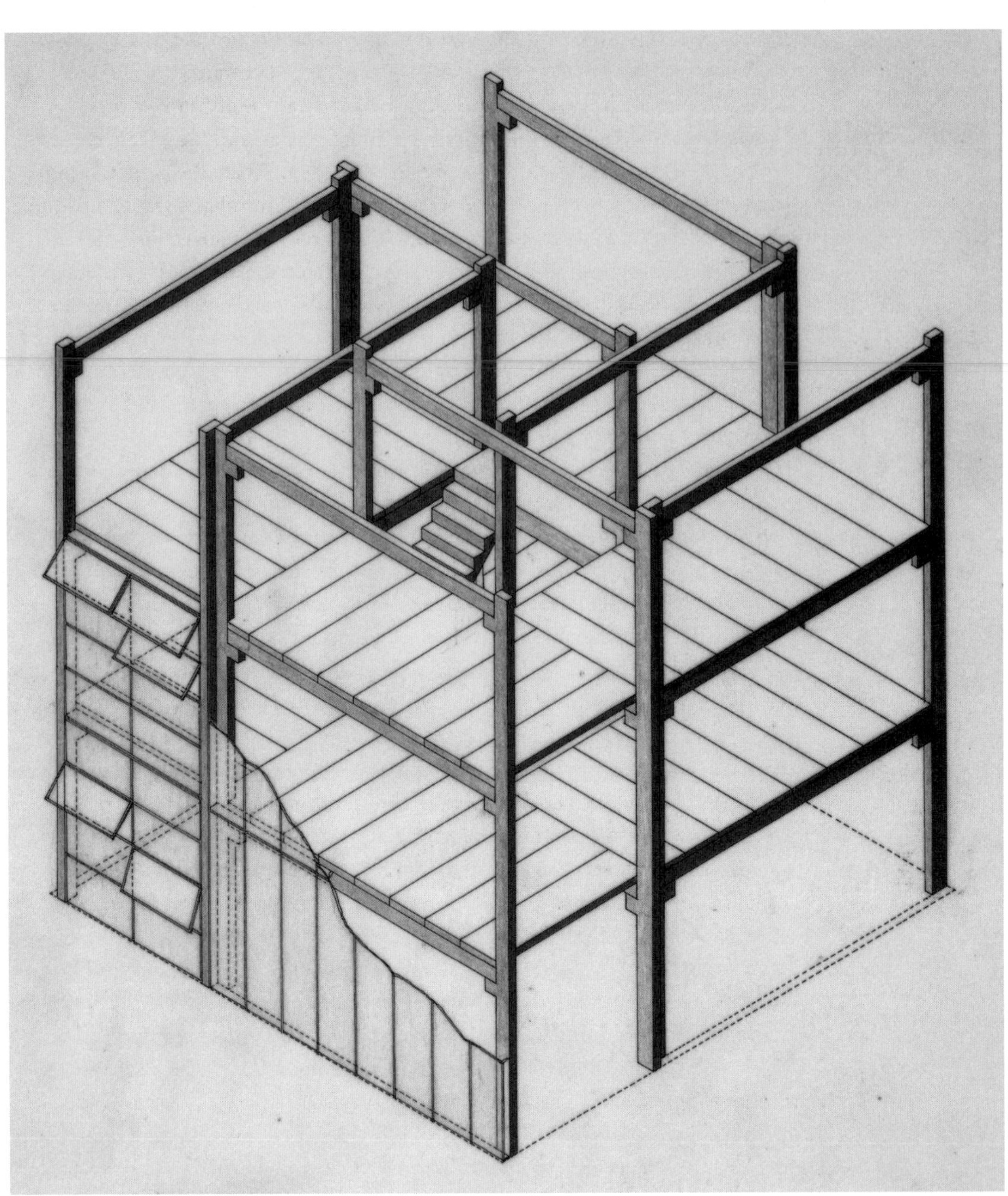

Figure 7
James Stirling, Stiff Dom-ino Housing, 1951.

facile and pastiche historical appropriations. The etymological link between "influence" and "influenza" is telling; both share the notion of an "infection," an unwanted pathogen that invades unwittingly.

By contrast, the 1970s writings of literary critic Harold Bloom (themselves quite influential) offer a theoretical model for analyzing influence, in particular the awareness and deliberate manipulation of precedent within an artistic work.[29] In *The Anxiety of Influence* (1973) and his follow-up text *A Map of Misreading* (1975), Bloom offers a series of strategies for understanding how "strong poets" misread or, in his term, "misprision" their predecessors. These strategies articulate the specific means by which poets generate new aesthetic utterances by "transforming their blindness towards their precursors into the revisionary insights of their own work."[30] Although Bloom's theory is articulated in relation to poets, its precepts serve equally well for any creative discipline, including architecture, and particularly ones in which there are not only seminal "masters" but also seminal works that constitute a disciplinary history. Bloom's theory investigates how "one poet helps to form another" and brings to the forefront an acceptance of the fact that poets, "strong poets" even, are profoundly indebted to their predecessors.

Rather than trying to comprehensively delineate a broader context, Bloom's critical framework instead generates a context of "intra-poetic relationships," providing a means to evaluate an architect's work against that of his peers, who are wrestling with the same predecessors. By acknowledging an engagement with the past as a legitimate part of the creative act, Bloom's framework not only enacts a powerful reversal that locates possible sources of modernism's "newness" within the past, it also removes from the notion of influence the impossibility of originality—"poetic influence need not make poets less original; as often it makes them more original."[31] By analyzing Stirling's "misreadings" of his predecessors—particularly Le Corbusier—along with his engagement with his peers, who are simultaneously battling the same forefathers, his own "revisionary insights" emerge.

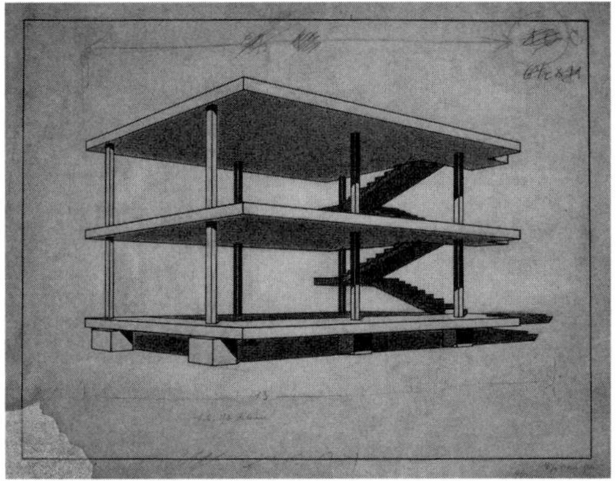

Figure 8
Le Corbusier, Maison Dom-ino, 1914.

Particularly relevant in the case of Stirling is the importance that Bloom places on the individual artifact—the poem in his case, the architectural project in Stirling's—as a source of influence, rather than a more abstract idea of the precursor: "Influence-anxiety does not so much concern the forerunner but rather is an anxiety achieved in and by the story, novel, play, poem, or essay." In other words, Shakespeare is less important than Hamlet. When thinking about Stirling's engagement with his predecessors, and even more particularly with the dominating influence of Le Corbusier, we might say, then, that Le Corbusier is less important than the Unité or Garches. This is especially true in Stirling's early work, when he is not yet, in Bloom's terms, a "strong poet." Although in his later projects Stirling engages a range of precedents and predecessors more fully, his early works (particularly Ham Common) are almost singlemindedly directed at one precedent. This focus on the "artifact" rather than the artist is substantiated by Stirling's consistent fascination with individual buildings. In the black notebook, Stirling compiled a list of twenty or so buildings, by Frank Lloyd Wright, Mies van der Rohe, and Le Corbusier, from which he felt the entire "vocabulary of modern architecture" had "descended." More important than his particular choice of buildings is his belief in the power of the building itself rather than in the more generalized influence of the architect.[32]

Throughout this book I use Bloom's writings as an analytical framework through which to understand Stirling's own meditations and preoccupations with precedent and the past.[33] More specifically, his notion of "revisioning" underlies the entirety of this book and it is worth fleshing out not only its meaning as Bloom employs it but also its distinction from related terms such as reference, quotation, or copy. To revision something is, as Bloom notes, to literally "see" it "again." This is a distinct idea from referencing, a more neutral act in which the element brought forward from the past is acknowledged as complete and left more or less intact. The Latin root of "reference" defines an origin point—in other words, a fixed and knowable beginning. Copying similarly implies that the original element is unmodified; the later version simply a repetition of the earlier incarnation. Revisioning, on the other hand, acts more violently and more decisively on the precedent, violating its initial terms. The act of revision necessitates some kind of change—a "correction," to use Bloom's term. Here we are reminded of T. S. Eliot's famous quote, "Immature poets imitate; mature poets steal," which, like Bloom's theory of influence, acknowledges that all poets are indebted to their predecessors—the distinction, in other words, is not between those who are and those who are not influenced by the past, but between those who make the past into something new and those who simply repeat it.

Stirling looked to the past in order to reinvent the present. A source wasn't simply reconfigured, it was revisioned into something new. While not a revolutionary modernist—an ideologically untenable term in the postwar period—Stirling was a revisionary modernist, searching for ways to generate novelty while maintaining a connection to history. To use Bloom's terminology,

Stirling looked back to "esteem differently" and ultimately to "aim correctively." The means by which he did so mark his singular contribution to the history of postwar modernism and forms the driving investigation of this book.

A CLOSE READING

This book is structured as a "close reading" of six of Stirling's architectural projects, both built and unbuilt. It begins with his first commissioned work, the Flats at Ham Common, the design of which began in 1955, and ends with his exhibition entry for Roma Interrotta from 1978. Each chapter centers on one project, chosen because it marks a significant moment not only in Stirling's career but in his revisionings of the past. Chapter 1 analyzes Stirling's early struggle with the "crisis" provoked by the postwar work of Le Corbusier in the 1950s, which would lead Stirling to his first attempt to misread his predecessor and to "rationalize" Maisons Jaoul at Ham Common. In the second chapter I look at Stirling's Churchill College Competition project of 1959, a national competition for a new college at Cambridge in which Stirling first investigated an expanded range of historical precedents. Chapter 3 closely studies Leicester, Stirling's most celebrated building and also one of his clearest articulations of a revisionary attitude, particularly in relation to high modernist and Constructivist sources. At the Florey Building at Oxford, the focus of Chapter 4, the revisioned sources become both more myriad and more embedded, the result of which is arguably Stirling's most singular and idiosyncratic project. Chapter 5 considers the incorporation of a more classical language at his project for the North Rhine–Westphalia Museum, Düsseldorf, of 1975 as a development of rather than a break from these revisionary strategies. And finally, Chapter 6 explores Stirling's contribution to the Roma Interrotta exhibition, in which he reconfigured eighteenth-century Rome using his own projects as "precedents."

In addition to these six projects, Stirling's writings offer an equally important piece of evidence in my analysis. Beginning with his essay "Garches to Jaoul: Le Corbusier as a Domestic Architect," which appeared in the September 1955 issue of the *Architectural Review,* Stirling wrote a series of articles throughout the 1950s and 1960s, followed largely by lectures and short project descriptions in later decades.[34] Stirling claimed that writing was always difficult for him—"intelligent writing . . . takes me much longer than designing buildings"[35]—and never considered himself a theorist or polemicist, unlike many of his contemporaries, chief among them Alison and Peter Smithson. As Robert Maxwell wrote in his introduction to the only collection of Stirling's writings: "If the writings of James Stirling have any interest for us today, it is not because he was a great writer, but because he was quite possibly a great architect." Nevertheless, Stirling's writings—which predominantly take the form of an architect explicating design methods—provide more than simply perfunctory project descriptions; they elucidate key aspects of his thinking while also articulating many significant dilemmas of the period.

In choosing to consider these projects and writings dating from 1955 to 1978, I am tracing the best-known or at least the most celebrated portion of Stirling's career. In his review of the first Stirling monograph, *James Stirling: Buildings and Projects, 1950–74,* Rafael Moneo noted that Stirling's work, when seen retrospectively, no longer seemed the achievement of a singular architect, but rather a "documentation" of architectural history itself: "It is, in fact, the history of the architecture of these last twenty-five years which can be called the real protagonist of the work. We are in this sense confronted more with the history of recent modern architecture than with Stirling's own career in particular."[36] And indeed these six projects seem to echo or mirror the dominant architectural themes and discourses during this period—from New Brutalism to Neo-Palladianism, a burgeoning High-Tech, and ultimately a resurgent Neoclassicism that would come to be known as postmodernism.

But Stirling's architecture was in no way a facile mirror of the times; and there is an equally prevalent commentary running through the literature on Stirling's work that describes a seemingly opposite tendency, highlighting the formal brilliance of Stirling's unprecedented solutions and his ability to transcend given stylistic norms.[37] These two contradictory interpretations of Stirling's architecture, while to some extent reflecting the bias of certain critics or historians (particularly a Hegelian quest for a zeitgeist), also suggest the very thing that distinguishes Stirling from his contemporaries; his work embodies the larger discourses of the period while remaining resolutely idiosyncratic. This dialectic has intrigued critics for decades, and it is what makes his architecture such a powerful register of the interplay between the distinct manifestation of an individual artistic will and a broader historical context.

It is worth noting what this book is not. It is not a comprehensive survey of Stirling's career; it does not include every project within this period, nor does it include the last fifteen years of Stirling's career. The two monographs on Stirling's work—one of which covers his work from 1950–74, the other from 1975 through Stirling's death in 1992, and which were meant as an oeuvre complète—provide a competent overview of his career as a whole, though with little analytical material.[38] It is not a monograph—not because it doesn't focus on a singular architect (it does) but because it treats the architectural artifacts, rather than the architect himself, as the primary subject. It is not primarily an attempt to uncover formerly unknown archival material—although there are instances of such—nor is it an historical survey. It does not attempt to place Stirling's projects into a stylistic succession, as past historians have done—especially in the memorializing that occurred following his death in 1992—or to call attention to the undeniable differences in his extensive range of work.[39] And finally, it is not a biography; Mark Girouard's highly readable 1998 *Big Jim,* the result of years of research, including interviews with friends, family, and colleagues of Stirling's, ably covers the details of his life.

Within this nearly twenty-five-year span there are many projects not discussed and there are of course many other possible histories to be written about Stirling's career, during this period and beyond: particularly ones that explore the design impact of his two partners—James Gowan and Michael Wilford—as well as the myriad collaborators, employees, peers, and mentors with whom he worked and studied and argued over the years.[40] Rather than attempt to parse out any exact understanding of who did what, or aspire to any overarching understanding of Stirling's oeuvre, I have chosen to analyze the six projects herein because they articulate a specific intellectual arc, one focused on Stirling's investigation of historical sources and their relationship to modernism. Like Walter Benjamin's "surgeon," whose vantage point refuses the totalizing view of the "magician," the reading of these select projects enables an understanding of Stirling's architecture as a series of "multiple fragments" that nevertheless constitute a new whole.[41]

But why end in 1978? Stirling would continue to practice for almost another fifteen years, until his death at sixty-six in 1992. Am I suggesting that 1978 was a kind of endpoint for Stirling (as many other commentators have suggested previously), the culmination of his modern "period" before his fall into perhaps less interesting or what Craig Hodgetts has described as his "less adventurous" work.[42] Not exactly. While there is no doubt that much of the later work indeed became "less adventurous," attributable partly to the increase in the scale and number of projects, as well as to their international scope, there were still many genuinely innovative works—the Wissenschaftszentrum Berlin (1988), the Braun AG Headquarters (1992), and the Venice Biennale bookshop (1989) all come to mind, probably because each has been singled out by critics as works that seemed to suggest that the "old" Stirling was back. Regardless of what followed, however, 1978 is a fitting endpoint for a couple of reasons.

The first is that Roma Interrotta offers a neat encapsulation of his work up that point, given that it anthologizes his oeuvre in one retrospective project. Beyond this convenient self-summarizing, Roma Interrotta represents a culmination of the strategies of influence and quotation that had been evident from his earliest projects. Second, 1978 is the year that work began in earnest on the Staatsgallerie, a project that is often and rightfully called Stirling's masterpiece. Many of the techniques of appropriation and revisioning at Stuttgart are borrowed directly from Düsseldorf, as will be developed in Chapter 5. Nevertheless, Stuttgart does demarcate a new phase of Stirling's work—a phase in which his work would become much more international and in which his commissions were often large-scale museum or university projects. Importantly, I do not suggest that Stuttgart marked his "turn" to history, as is often suggested, for, as I will show throughout this book, Stirling had been facing it from the beginning. But to evaluate Stuttgart and the projects following it would necessitate a consideration of an entirely different set of questions, not to mention many more pages.

The choice of Stirling as a topic bears mention, even as his significance within the architectural profession appears, at the moment, seemingly self-evident. The second decade of the twenty-first century is starting out as the beginning of a Stirling renaissance. There are exhibitions of his own and his students' work, catalogues, essays, conferences, and forthcoming books. The most significant of these is the exhibition "James Stirling: Notes from the Archive," mounted at the Yale Center for British Art, New Haven, in 2010, which then traveled to the Tate Britain, London, the Neue Staatsgallerie, Stuttgart (both Stirling-designed buildings), and finally to the CCA, home of the Stirling archive. The show was curated by Anthony Vidler, with an accompanying publication.[43]

On the one hand this current interest in Stirling can be explained by the *lack* of scholarship up to this point. Many contemporary essays begin by pointing out this seeming oversight, though in fact a review of the literature on Stirling over the past two or three decades yields a seeming abundance of material. Upon a more detailed inspection, however, much of this work reveals little of considered historical or theoretical content. Countless essays, project descriptions, and features on Stirling's work were published in both the British and international architectural presses, beginning with a five-page article on his House in the Isle of Wight in April 1954 in the *Architectural Review,* and increasing exponentially as his career advanced. Nearly all of the most important architectural critics and historians—including Rowe, Manfredo Tafuri, Alan Colquhoun, Robert Maxwell, and John Summerson, as well as Vidler, Charles Jencks, Peter Eisenman, and Kenneth Frampton—wrote on Stirling's work at some point. But most of these articles are either hagiographic, highly personal, and anecdotal, or simply project descriptions, with the buildings left to speak for themselves. With very few exceptions, none attempted any larger theorization of the work.

To explain the spike in Stirling interest, one must also consider that enough temporal distance has accumulated to allow for a reading of Stirling's architecture as "history." Beyond the inevitability of the expanding historical lens, however, the recent Stirling "turn," I would argue, results from a recognition of his significance as one of the most influential figures of the postwar period, whose absence represents a glaring omission in the larger reconceptualization of that era currently being developed in architectural scholarship. In particular, a new generation of scholars has begun to render more complex the postwar period—no longer simply portraying it as an "interregnum" between modernism and postmodernism.[44] And although one outcome of this reevaluation has been specific and much-needed scholarship dedicated to British postwar architecture—on both the larger cultural and architectural climate as well as individual figures—Stirling has remained conspicuously absent from these writings. Philip Johnson had prophesied that "in the future looking back to this period . . . Jim's place is going to be extraordinarily high," but, until perhaps quite recently, his prediction has remained unfulfilled.[45]

One could also argue that the current interest in Stirling's work is a result of contemporary interests rather than historical ones. Moneo began his recent survey of contemporary architectural practice with Stirling, writing: "Though he is less discussed nowadays, it is obligatory to begin any study of the evolution of contemporary architecture with Stirling."[46] Perhaps even more speculatively, I would suggest that an interest in Stirling's idiosyncratic, resolutely innovative architectural language and in particular his reuse and reinvention of architecture's own history and traditions reflects a resurgent desire to understand the role of influence and reference outside the narrow confines of postmodernism. Claire Zimmerman has suggested that Stirling's astounding absence from architectural historiography is a result of architectural culture's still deep-seated fear that his postmodernist operations are, in fact, still at work.[47] Perhaps we are ready to embrace a more complex postmodernism, and Stirling' architecture, with all of its complex and shifting allusions and revisionary strategies, as a productive and ongoing response to modernism. Stirling's projects are neither avant-garde ex novo invention nor arrière-garde reiterative traditionalism, but instead a deliberate and daring interplay between the two—a position that still resonates today.

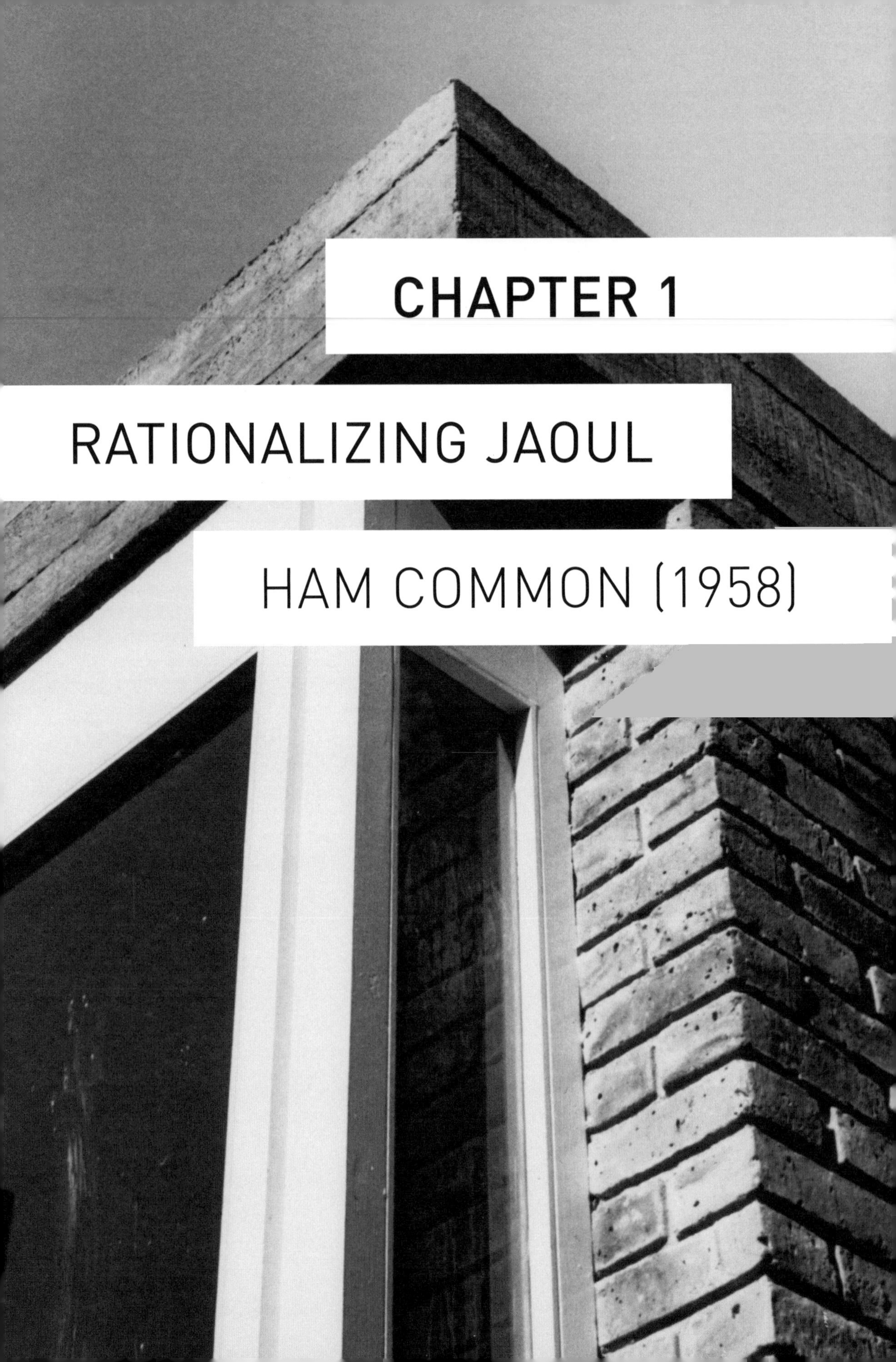

CHAPTER 1

RATIONALIZING JAOUL

HAM COMMON (1958)

James Stirling's first commissioned project—the Flats at Ham Common, completed in partnership with James Gowan in 1958—is frankly derivative. With its horizontal banding of exposed concrete infilled with load-bearing brick walls; its arrangement of low-rise, detached cubic buildings on a long, narrow site; and even such specific details such as the U-shaped precast concrete gargoyles, Ham Common is clearly indebted to Le Corbusier's Maisons Jaoul, completed the year before (figs. 9, 10). Stirling made little attempt to disguise the reference and even publicly emphasized the link—in lecture notes, under the heading Ham Common, Stirling typically wrote "Jaoul" or "Corb" as a reminder to himself. Critics and historians have noted the connection many times—none more succinctly, if perhaps unfairly, than Reyner Banham, who described Ham Common as a "tidying" up of the "casual and untidy" Jaoul.[1]

Ham Common was not a copy, however. While undeniably indebted to Le Corbusier's earlier project, it nevertheless enacted a fundamental critique of Jaoul—a project that, at least on the surface, seemed to abandon modernism's core values and certainly its whitewashed aesthetic in favor of more expressive language and primitive construction techniques. Stirling publicly and vociferously criticized Jaoul and other of Le Corbusier's postwar projects as "irrational" in two essays published at the very moment Ham Common was under development. This seeming contradiction between Stirling's written critique of Jaoul and his clear adoption of its aesthetic can be explained by the fact that with Ham Common Stirling was attempting to overlay the principles associated with the modern movement—principles that Stirling had found lacking at Jaoul—onto the "crude" postwar architectural language being developed by Le Corbusier. Revisioning Jaoul as a "rational" project (in both material and ideal terms) while also engaging a novel set of programmatic and site constraints gave Stirling an opportunity to explore, within a postwar material idiom, what he found to be the still operative and relevant modern ideals.

The clear reference to Maisons Jaoul at Ham Common reflected Le Corbusier's powerful influence at this early stage of Stirling's career, but by no means was the master swallowed whole, nor was he the only notable precursor. Mies, the Smithsons, de Stijl, as well as British industrial vernacular all appear in the constellation of references surrounding Ham Common. Understanding how Stirling and Gowan reconfigured Jaoul, as well as the various other influences and sources embedded in and suggested by the work, serves as a starting point for considering the role of influence in Stirling's career, and how it tracked against his evolving definition of architectural modernism.

POSTWAR LE CORBUSIER AND "THE CRISIS OF RATIONALISM"

Sometime in 1954, Stirling visited a number of Le Corbusier buildings in France. While he found the Paris projects—Maisons Cook, Porte Molitor, and La Roche/Jeanneret—"disappointing" (La Roche/Jeanneret the least so) he was overwhelmed by the Villa Stein at Garches, "magnificent beyond expec-

Figure 9
Stirling and Gowan, Flats at Ham Common, London, 1958.

Figure 10
Le Corbusier, Maisons Jaoul, Neuilly-sur-Seine, France, 1956. Photograph by James Stirling.

tation."[2] Soon after, he visited the Maisons Jaoul; a plan sketch and extensive notes in his black notebook attest to the significance of the encounter (fig. 11). For a young architect raised on a steady diet of whitewashed "heroic" buildings of the interwar and prewar period, particularly from Le Corbusier, the apparent volte-face in Le Corbusier's postwar work came as nothing short of an architectural cardiac arrest; by and large, Stirling was discouraged if not dismayed. In stark contrast to his lavish praise for Garches, his reaction to Jaoul was mixed; though he found aspects of the project "exciting"—particularly the interior spaces—he also found them "against the machine" and "arty-crafty" (despite, he notes, a large budget).[3] Stirling would later write that he was "disoriented" by the seeming shift in Le Corbusier's direction to a more regionally inflected, "primitive" language, but this retroactive characterization pales in contrast to his contemporaneous remarks and hardly captures the anxiety he and others felt at the time.[4]

Stirling went public with his anxiety in a September 1955 article published in the *Architectural Review*. "Garches to Jaoul: Le Corbusier as Domestic Architect in 1927 and 1953," the first English-language review of Maisons Jaoul, was largely critical not only of Jaoul but of Le Corbusier's postwar projects more generally, and expressed admiration, if not reverence, for his prewar work (fig. 12).[5] In the essay, more or less a one-to-one comparison between the Villa Stein at Garches and the Maisons Jaoul, Stirling lauds Garches as the pinnacle of Le Corbusier's "particular expression of the machine aesthetic," arguing that the building is the "standard by which Le Corbusier's genius is measured." The Maisons Jaoul, on the other hand, he deplores as "primitive" and "antimechanistic," a structure whose construction techniques—cross-wall construction, exposed, load-bearing brick, Catalan vaults, and earth-covered roofs—"make no advance on medieval building."[6] Many of his remarks are copied wholesale

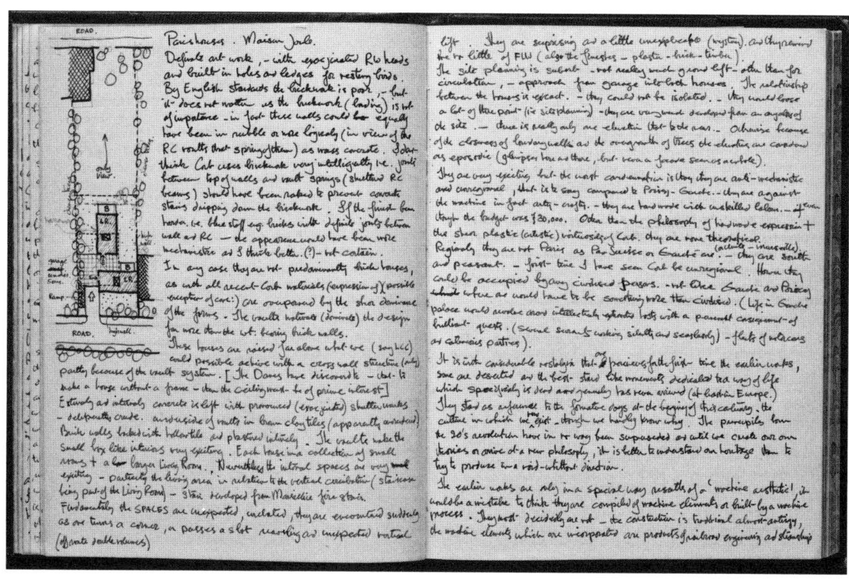

Figure 11
James Stirling, Black Notebook, 1954. Plan and comments on Le Corbusier's Maisons Jaoul.

from the black notebook. As Mark Crinson has pointed out, Stirling chose to publish his own photographs of Jaoul under construction in the "Garches to Jaoul" essay, complete with site debris, construction ladders, and exposed wires: "Stirling clearly enjoyed this unpolished and ad hoc state."[7] These photographs highlight the unfinished, "primitive" quality of the project, allowing Garches to appear more "sophisticated" and "rational" by comparison.

A second essay, "Ronchamp: Le Corbusier's Chapel and the Crisis of Rationalism," which was published only six months later, and also in the *Architectural Review,* is even more explicitly critical of Le Corbusier's postwar projects (fig. 13).[8] Though Stirling lauds the building's formal masterstrokes, he finds it even less "rational" than Jaoul, a reflection of a singular and idiosyncratic "artistic" approach to building, which, while clearly having a "sensational impact," is ultimately fleeting and superficial since it is not based on any "appeal to the intellect."[9] While acknowledging the need to find an adequate language for the postwar period, Stirling concludes that the "flight from the 'academism' of pre-war modern is questionable when it produces an architecture of the irrational."[10] He includes a photograph of Jaoul as further illustration of this "trend toward the arbitrary," reinforcing his earlier critique of the project and conjoining Jaoul and Ronchamp as examples of Le Corbusier's "irrational" postwar tendencies.

Despite his clear advocacy for the prewar projects and criticism of the "irrational" postwar work, in both texts Stirling equivocates. Even as he derides the "primitive" quality of Jaoul, for example, he acknowledges that the stuccoed white walls at Garches, although geometrically precise and "suggestive" of the Machine Aesthetic, are, in the end, equally primitive in their construction technique, with concrete block construction concealed beneath the plaster.[11] His critique of Jaoul as "anti-mechanistic" does not preclude him from praising the building as "magnificent" art with "sheer plastic virtuosity," and he admires the site planning, particularly the division of vehicular and pedestrian circulation onto two levels.[12] Similarly, he describes the "overpowering virtuosity in moulding the contours of the solid masses" at Ronchamp, the "ingenuity" and "precision" of Le Corbusier's concrete work at the Ronchamp altar, as well as the building's "superb acoustics."[13]

As in Colin Rowe's seminal essay "The Mathematics of the Ideal Villa" of 1947, which pairs Garches with Andrea Palladio's Villa Malcontenta, Stirling's "Garches to Jaoul" essay capitalizes on the comparative framework. Though the two projects under consideration in Stirling's article are separated by only a few decades, while Rowe's comparison of Corbusian and Palladian villas span centuries, in both cases the pairing reinforces similarity as well as difference. In coupling the garden façade at Garches, for example, with an exterior shot of Jaoul, Stirling emphasizes the horizontal banding controlling both projects—one a result of the layers of *fenêtre en longueur* and white plaster, the other a result of the stacking of the exposed concrete floor slabs. Similarly, Stirling juxtaposes an image of the projecting cantilevered balcony at Jaoul with a similar entry canopy at Garches. This is not to invert Stirling's desire to estab-

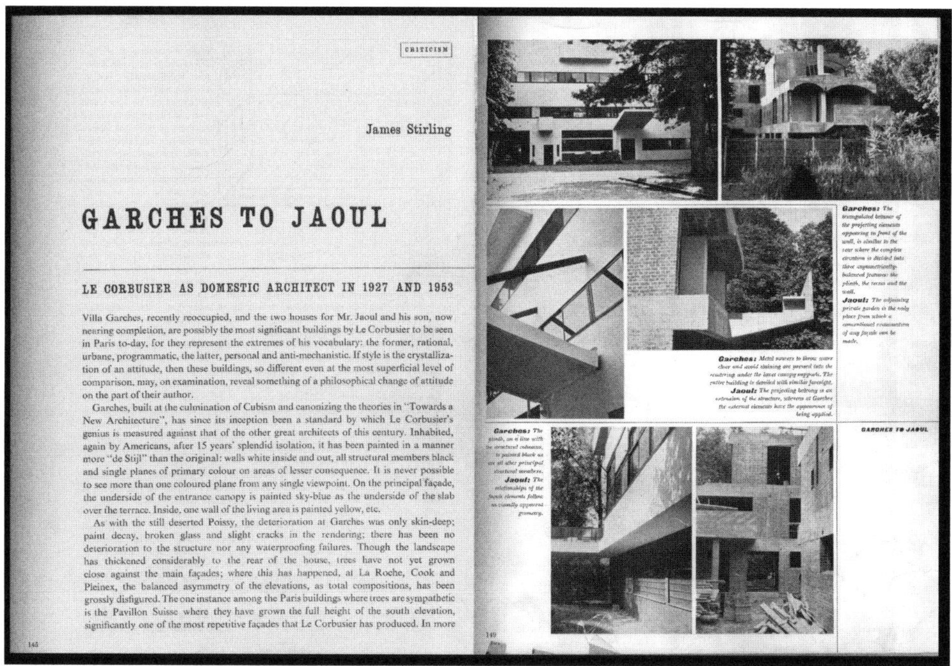

CRITICISM

James Stirling

GARCHES TO JAOUL

LE CORBUSIER AS DOMESTIC ARCHITECT IN 1927 AND 1953

Villa Garches, recently reoccupied, and the two houses for Mr. Jaoul and his son, now nearing completion, are possibly the most significant buildings by Le Corbusier to be seen in Paris to-day, for they represent the extremes of his vocabulary: the former, rational, urbane, programmatic, the latter, personal and anti-mechanistic. If style is the crystallization of an attitude, then these buildings, so different even at the most superficial level of comparison, may, on examination, reveal something of a philosophical change of attitude on the part of their author.

Garches, built at the culmination of Cubism and canonizing the theories in "Towards a New Architecture", has since its inception been a standard by which Le Corbusier's genius is measured against that of the other great architects of this century. Inhabited, again by Americans, after 15 years' splendid isolation, it has been painted in a manner more "de Stijl" than the original: walls white inside and out, all structural members black and single planes of primary colour on areas of lesser consequence. It is never possible to see more than one coloured plane from any single viewpoint. On the principal façade, the underside of the entrance canopy is painted sky-blue as the underside of the slab over the terrace. Inside, one wall of the living area is painted yellow, etc.

As with the still deserted Poissy, the deterioration at Garches was only skin-deep; paint decay, broken glass and slight cracks in the rendering; there has been no deterioration to the structure nor any waterproofing failures. Though the landscape has thickened considerably to the rear of the house, trees have not yet grown close against the main façades; where this has happened, at La Roche, Cook and Pleinex, the balanced asymmetry of the elevations, as total compositions, has been grossly disfigured. The one instance among the Paris buildings where trees are sympathetic is the Pavillon Suisse where they have grown the full height of the south elevation, significantly one of the most repetitive façades that Le Corbusier has produced. In more

GARCHES TO JAOUL

James Stirling

RONCHAMP

LE CORBUSIER'S CHAPEL AND THE CRISIS OF RATIONALISM

With the simultaneous appearance of Lever House in New York and the Unité in Marseilles, it had become obvious that the stylistic schism between Europe and the New World had entered on a decisive phase. The issue of art or technology had divided the ideological basis of the modern movement, and the diverging styles apparent since Constructivism probably have their origin in the attempt to fuse Art Nouveau and late 19th century engineering. In the U.S.A., functionalism now means the adaptation to building of industrial processes and products, but in Europe it remains the essentially humanist method of designing to a specific use. The post-war architecture of America may appear brittle to Europeans and, by obviating the hierarchical disposition of elements, anonymous; however, this academic method of criticism may no longer be adequate in considering technological products of the 20th century. Yet this method would still appear valid in criticizing recent European architecture where the elaboration of space and form has continued without abatement; and the chapel by Le Corbusier may possibly be the most plastic building ever erected in the name of modern architecture.

The south tower of the chapel, emerging as a white thumb above the landscape, can be seen for many miles as one approaches the Swiss border. The rolling hills and green woodlands of the Haute-Saône are reminiscent of many parts of England and Wales, and the village of Ronchamp spreads along either side of the Dijon-Basle road. After climbing a steep and winding dirt-track, leading from the village through dense woodland,

Figure 12
James Stirling, "Garches to Jaoul: Le Corbusier as Domestic Architect in 1927 and 1953," *Architectural Review*, September 1955.

Figure 13
James Stirling, "Ronchamp: Le Corbusier's Chapel and the Crisis of Rationalism," *Architectural Review*, March 1956.

lish difference between the two projects, only to say that, like Rowe's comparison of Garches and Malcontenta, Stirling's pairing of Garches and Jaoul highlights similarities between the two projects even as it calls out their distinctions. Put more simply, in both essays the Wölfflinian comparative method invites both contrast and comparison between the works in question, an inevitable byproduct of the intimate and deliberate relationship set up between them. And although their stated aims and choice of examples are distinct, both Stirling's and Rowe's essays expanded the received understanding of Le Corbusier at the time—Rowe's highlighting classical resonances within Le Corbusier's work, Stirling's bringing prewar and postwar Le Corbusier into direct confrontation. Both begin with Garches, but Rowe's juxtaposition with Malcontenta reinforces a shared classical ideal, while Stirling's comparison with Jaoul highlights Garches's role as an emblem of a modern, "rational" building.

RATIONALISM: ETHICS VS. AESTHETICS

Of all the arts, architecture is the one in which it is least possible to exclude the idea of rationality.

Alan Colquhoun, "Rationalism: A Philosophical Concept in Architecture"

Concluding his "Garches to Jaoul" essay, Stirling writes that in the latest work of Le Corbusier there is "little reference to the rational principles which are the basis of the modern movement."[14] Though Jaoul was the more recent building, it was Le Corbusier's architecture of 1927, not 1953, Stirling insists, to which contemporary architects "must aspire if modern architecture is to retain its vitality." Stirling's critiques of Jaoul and Ronchamp, then, are predicated on the apparent abandonment of the "rational principles" of the modern movement in this postwar work—but what did rationalism mean for Stirling? To a large extent, the term was employed by Stirling and others during this period as a stand-in, though not necessarily a synonym, for "modernism." More pointedly, rationalism was a way to refer to the principles—a term with explicitly Wittkowerian associations—aligned with the practices of the early twentieth-century avant-garde but without its attendant formal vocabulary. It is significant that Stirling subtitled his "Ronchamp" essay "Le Corbusier's Chapel and the Crisis of Rationalism," not the "Crisis of Modernism" or the "Crisis of Functionalism." Both of the latter terms had, by the 1950s, taken on specific stylistic and aesthetic connotations, while rationalism still largely connoted a conceptual notion.[15] Rationalism, then, was modern but not—to use Stirling's slightly wry terminology—"white." To simply equate rationalism with a nonstylized modernism, however, does acknowledge the complexity inherent to both terms. Moreover, it prefaces the definition of the former on the later, a binary that ultimately proves about as useful as defining post-modernism as the opposite of modernism. As an idea, rationalism carried its own history , separate from but related to that of modernism, which is critical in understanding Stirling's critique of Jaoul and his subsequent response at Ham Common.

Foremost among the defining aspects of rationalism as it emerged in the early twentieth century was a relationship with the machine, a relationship articulated through the writings of Le Corbusier, among others, and one which became institutionalized by the use of the phrase "Machine Aesthetic" as a stand-in for "modern movement." The problem of the "stylization" of the machine was identified as early as 1935 by J. M. Richards, the British architectural historian and editor of the *Architectural Review,* in his article "Towards a Rational Aesthetic." His influential essay offers one of the clearest attempts to define rationalism, linking it directly to the machine (made clear by the subtitle of the article: "An Examination of the Characteristics of Modern Design with Particular Reference to the Influence of the Machine"). Richards warns against adopting the purely aesthetic components of the machine, emphasizing rationalism as not simply tied to "abstract aesthetic virtues of machines themselves"—"exactness," "cleanness," "precision," and "simplicity"—but also to the *qualities* of the machine.[16] "The distinction has to be maintained between the machine as an aesthetic object and the machine as a source of aesthetic form."[17]

From this early moment, then, a struggle was established between a rational *aesthetic* and a rational *logic*—even though for Richards the former predominated. In both his "Garches to Jaoul" and "Ronchamp" essays Stirling struggles with the logic vs. the aesthetics of the machine as key components of rationalism, even as he evokes the machine as a primary criterion through which to evaluate Le Corbusier's projects. Garches, he writes, embodies the "essence of machine power" (even as he acknowledges that it is not the "product of any high-powered mechanization"), whereas Jaoul holds "no reference to any aspect of the machine . . . either in construction or aesthetic."[18] Stirling is even more explicit—and poetic—in his notes in the black notebook documenting his first visit to Jaoul, where he writes that Le Corbusier's early works are neither "compiled of machine elements" nor "built by a machine process"—the construction is in fact "traditional almost antiquy" [*sic*]. But this literalist interpretation is less important for him than the fact that they represent the "spiritual presence of machine power. The whole atmosphere is charged with a silent dynamism (the silent machine perpetually in motion)."[19]

The struggle between these two aspects of rationalism underlies Stirling's critique of prewar and postwar Le Corbusier; he describes the postwar work in the same machinelike terms—the "precision" in the concrete at Ronchamp, for example—when referencing a quality or principle embodied in the work, despite his criticism of its anti-machinelike aesthetic. Perhaps it was these machinelike—that is, rational—qualities in the postwar work, despite the fact that they lacked an aesthetic relationship to the machine, that led to his equivocation. Or perhaps he was searching for redeeming qualities in the postwar work, which came in the form of machinelike praise.

A related component in the understanding of rationalism focused on its alleged objectivity. This positivist legacy, with its close link to functionalism, was an important aspect of modernism in its earlier years. Equally important, however, was its inverse—the notion that a nonobjective or subjective architecture was irrational. Undoubtedly the most important figure in this eliding of irrationality and subjectivity during the postwar period was Nikolaus Pevsner, who singled out Le Corbusier's postwar projects as particularly egregious offenders. In the 1960 revised edition of his *Outline of European Architecture* he attacks Ronchamp as an "escape out of reality into a fairy world"; he finds the project inexcusable and a singularly egotistical effort because it ignores the architect's fundamental responsibility to society: "The whims of individual architects, the strokes of genius of others cannot be accepted as an answer to the serious questions which it is the responsibility of the architect to answer."[20]

Pevsner's disdain for "subjectivity," or what he would elsewhere call "expression," was undeniably a reflection of his personal anti-Corbusian and pro-Gropius leanings. It also reflected a larger cultural bias and was a notion substantiated by the economic and professional reality after the Second World War. Until 1954 no private construction was allowed in England, and even once the ban was repealed a sense of responsibility to the welfare state prevailed. The role of the architect was one of public servant. By 1957, 48 percent of all architects were working for the government.[21] Stirling himself had worked for the London County Council, though only briefly, and cannot have escaped this sense of civic duty.[22] An individualistic architecture betrayed not only the cause of the modern movement but the responsibility toward a collective postwar society. Although the intensity of this sentiment subsided once the immediate demands of the war were over, it was still a principal concern for postwar architects.[23]

Stirling's condemnation of Le Corbusier's postwar projects as "irrational"—as well as his identification of a more general "crisis of rationalism"—can thus be seen as a response to this perceived rise of subjectivity as a general cultural condition in postwar England. Although Stirling's general ideological position was decidedly unaligned with Pevsner's—the two would famously and publicly quarrel ten years later when Pevsner attacked Stirling and Gowan's Leicester as "expressionistic"—his "Ronchamp" text suggests a similar disdain for subjectivity, and in particular the conjoining of subjectivity and irrationality. When Stirling concedes in "Ronchamp" that the building is a masterpiece, but of a "most personal order," a reflection of a singular and idiosyncratic "artistic" approach to building, he was, in effect, condemning it with misplaced praise. Its "lack of appeal to the intellect" and its "personal" qualities were yet more ways in which it had strayed from the "rational principles" of modernism.

Common to both Pevsner's and Richards's ideas about rationalism—whether tied to the functionalist work of Gropius or the streamlined forms of the prewar era—was an underlying assumption that rationalism was more or less the sole property of the modern movement. Rationalism, in their terms, was intextricably tied to twentieth-century values of industrialization and standardization. John Summerson's well-read and influential 1957 essay "The Case for a Theory of Modern Architecture" put forth an important modification to this notion by debunking the presumed allegiance between modernism and rationalism, emphasizing instead rationalism's history and tracing its roots to the eighteenth and nineteenth centuries. Summerson describes an intellectual trajectory that moves from Perrault's critique of Vitruvius through Durand, Viollet-le-Duc, and Pugin, and ultimately winds its way to Le Corbusier. Common to each of these authors, Summerson writes, is an attempt to replace the "absolute authority" of antiquity with the "new" authority of rationalism.[24] Unlike Richardson, Summerson is neither attempting to define an aesthetic of rationalism (there are no illustrations in his "Case for a Theory of Modern Architecture") nor trying to assert its significance as a moral imperative against a seeming resurgence of expressionism, à la Pevsner, but instead to theorize and, most importantly, historicize its key logic or ideas.

His conclusion that program could effectively supplant the "authority" of antiquity as a new form of unity in modern architecture was perhaps the most durable aspect of the article. But Summerson also expanded the discourse on rationalism in the 1950s by resuscitating the importance and legacy of French rationalism.[25] More broadly, the article suggested that rationalism could be used as a gauge against which to measure *any* work, a constant to counteract the loss of a universally agreed-upon aesthetic or a reliance on historical form. This devotion to a universalizing concept of rationalism is clear in both "Ronchamp" and "Garches to Jaoul," in which Stirling searches for a criterion through which to judge Le Corbusier's contemporary work, foregrounding the "rational principles" of modernism as a kind of benchmark. The critical distinction between Stirling's position and Pevsner's is the former's understanding of modernism itself as constituted of ahistorical, universally applicable, and, crucially, still relevant principles—rationalism chief among them.

Stirling's "crisis of rationalism" vis-à-vis postwar Le Corbusier can thus be seen to demonstrate his continuing faith in the concept, and, by extension, his willingness to expand the notion outside the stylistic confines of high modernism. And while Summerson was an important figure in this continuing reevaluation of the term, a more significant influence can be traced to the writings of Rudolf Wittkower. As Alina Payne has demonstrated, Wittkower's analysis in his cataclysmically influential 1950 book *Architectural Principles in the Age of Humanism,* based on mathematical structural analyses of Renaissance design practices, ultimately enabled him "to situate Renaissance formal practices within the objective and rational rather than subjective realm," echoing the discourses of modernist historiography at the time and ultimately enabling modern architects themselves a way to access history. "Wittkower ultimately rescues the Renaissance and hence classical architecture as a viable thinking ground for the further development of contemporary discourse."[26] *Architectural Principles* indeed enabled Stirling's generation to understand classicism as something akin to modernism in its rational basis. As Banham described this period in Britain: "The importance of that [Classical] tradition lay in its abstract intellectual disciplines (proportion, symmetry) and habits of mind (clarity, rationalism) far more than matters of detailed style."[27]

Although Stirling singled out Wittkower's *British Art and the Mediterranean* as a more significant text for him in his early years than was *Architectural Principles*, the import of the latter cannot be ignored.[28] I would extend Payne's argument to say that in Stirling's case the lessons of *Architectural Principles*—channeled through Rowe—provided an interpretive framework through which *any* precedent—whether from the twentieth century or the fifteenth—could thereafter be understood not as a set of historical motifs, or even as formal gestures, but as something that embodied an abstract set of principles. In other words, any precedent, including but not limited to classical ones, could be engaged at the level of the ideas behind the production of the artifact—its "architectural principles." This would become a foundational concept for Stirling, particularly in his later work, since historical sources could be seen as repositories of properties or principles—like functionalism—rather than "merely" forms.

With this understanding of "rationalism" as it was constituted in the mid-1950s via the legacy of Pevsner, Summerson, and Wittkower, the "crisis of rationalism" that Stirling describes in his "Garches to Jaoul" and "Ronchamp" essays can be seen as more than simply a personal reaction to the expressive language of Le Corbusier's postwar buildings, and instead as a response to the complex and multiple meanings of "rationalism" itself. Stirling remained committed to the possibility of a "machinelike" architecture even as he acknowledged the problematics of an aesthetic associated with or derived from the machine, and he seemed to desire within the architectural object a kind of objectivity, or at least something that appealed to the "intellect," and which embodied a set of principles consistent with modernism's original aims.

However, this still leaves unexplained why Stirling and Gowan chose Jaoul as a precedent for Ham Common, particularly after Stirling's highly visible critique of Jaoul at the same moment that he and Gowan received the commission. A few general answers come easily. Clearly there was a generational desire among Stirling and his peers to differentiate themselves not only from the prewar "high" modernists but also from the work of Lubetkin and others, which had been so reliant on the high modernist work of the twenties and thirties; turning to Le Corbusier's postwar work as a source represented something of a shift. Along the same lines was an interest in Le Corbusier's postwar work purely for its novelty, as the latest works available from the master. A more considered answer, however, emerges through a close reading of Ham Common and the discovery that while it is explicitly referencing certain tectonic and stylistic characteristics of Jaoul, it is also a more "rational" version of the precursor's work.

SYSTEMATIZATION, REGIONALISM, AND "MODERN DESIGN"

Stirling was a senior design assistant in the London office of Lyons Israel Ellis when he was approached by developer Leonard Manousso to develop a group of flats at Langham House, Ham Common, in 1955.[29] The site was in the wealthy London suburb of Richmond-sur-Thames and had originally been the garden

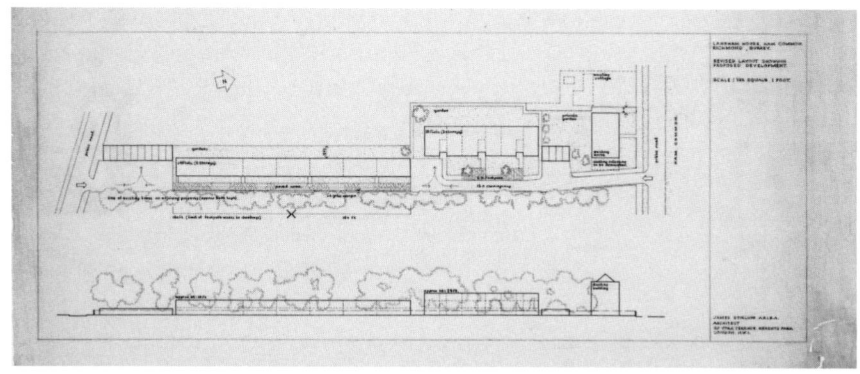

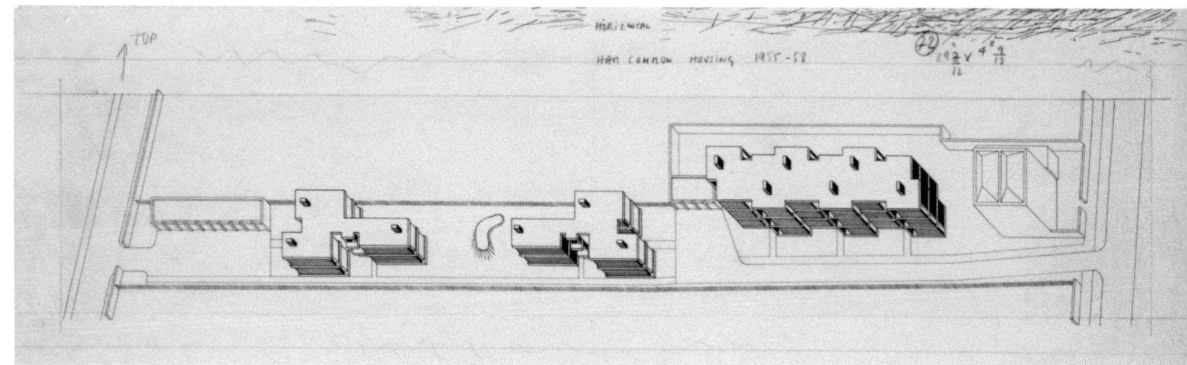

Figure 14
Stirling and Gowan, Ham Common. This early site plan, with two rather than three structures, was rejected for its lack of proper access across the site.

Figure 15
Stirling and Gowan, Ham Common. Final site plan, with pair of two-story buildings at left and three-story building at right.

of a large Georgian house, which was to remain on the northern edge of the site and which prevented the project from having any real "front" or relationship to the common. The almost prohibitively narrow site extended perpendicularly to the common, behind the existing house, widening at the northern half, and with a heavy band of trees along the eastern edge.

An early undated site plan—the only working document pertaining to the project in the archive—shows that Stirling and Gowan had originally conceived a pair of two-story structures to accommodate the thirty units on the site, an arrangement that would have given the project an even closer relation to Jaoul (although the two buildings at Ham Common were parallel to one another, not perpendicular, as at Jaoul) (fig. 14). After the proposal was rejected by the planning authority for not providing proper access roads across the length of the site, Stirling and Gowan divided the program among three rather than two buildings—a three-story block on the north end and a pair of two-story structures aligned at the south end (fig. 15).[30]

Although the two- and three-story blocks contain the same program—a mix of one-, two-, and three-bedroom apartments—they vary in their layout and structural system. In the three-story building, the six units on each floor are organized along a central structural and programmatic spine, with interlocking units that alternately flip across this central axis (fig. 16). The living and dining spaces occupy one side of this spine, facing either east or west, with bedrooms on the opposite side. By offsetting and alternately flipping units, Stirling and Gowan create an undulating plan in which the living/dining volume of each unit projects slightly beyond the bedroom block of the adjacent apartment, which is tucked back into the building profile. The structural system for the three-story block is a continuous load-bearing brick wall supported on poured-in-place concrete slabs. Select concrete elements are precast (including concrete gargoyles and drainspouts, as well as some interior features), as are the window frame units (fig. 17). In the two-story buildings, identical save for their "handedness," units are arranged along a short internal corridor—one unit at its end, and two at intervals along its edge (fig. 18). Rather than an undulating plan arrangement, as in the three-story building, here units pinwheel around the circulation core. The structural system is also distinct from that in the three-story buildings; although it is composed of load-bearing brick walls and concrete floor slabs, here Stirling and Gowan employ the core and crosswall system that Stirling had explored in his 1951 Core and Crosswall House study. Unlike in his earlier study, the structural crosswalls now occupy the long side of the buildings rather than the short—a more logical (and traditional) arrangement that more closely mimics the structural system at Maisons Jaoul and that also frees up the north and south façades entirely from any structural requirements.

Each façade at Ham Common comprises a series of repeating window patterns, which correspond to interior plan conditions—a more systematic treatment than the haphazard and seemingly arbitrary patterning at Jaoul that reflects Stirling and Gowan's desire to make more a "rational" version of the precedent. The north and south façades of the living spaces in the two-story buildings, for example, are opened up through large windows to reflect their more public program (and their lack of structural restraints). By contrast, the east and west elevations contain only a few select openings, reflecting the more private aspect of the bedroom and bathroom spaces while also signifying that these are the structural crosswalls—and therefore less available for dematerializing—as well as their proximity to the edge of the site (fig. 19). The long east and west façades of the three-story building are perhaps the best illustration of this more systematic treatment, if only because they are the most repetitive, with vertical bands of window shapes keyed to the various rooms behind (fig. 20). Stirling and Gowan chose to scale *up* the Maisons Jaoul rather than try to scale *down* the Unité; in so doing they were able to introduce aspects of a more rationalized construction method while avoiding some of the more monotonous Corbusian derivatives of the immediate postwar that had been based on the Unité. Somewhere between the totalizing system of the Unité and the more "painterly" and singular composition at Jaoul (or even Garches), Ham Common negotiates individuality and community while eliminating the more "subjective" quality of the wall surface that Stirling had found at Jaoul.

This more systematic façade logic also operates at a smaller scale—notably in the L-shaped windows cribbed more or less directly from Le Corbusier

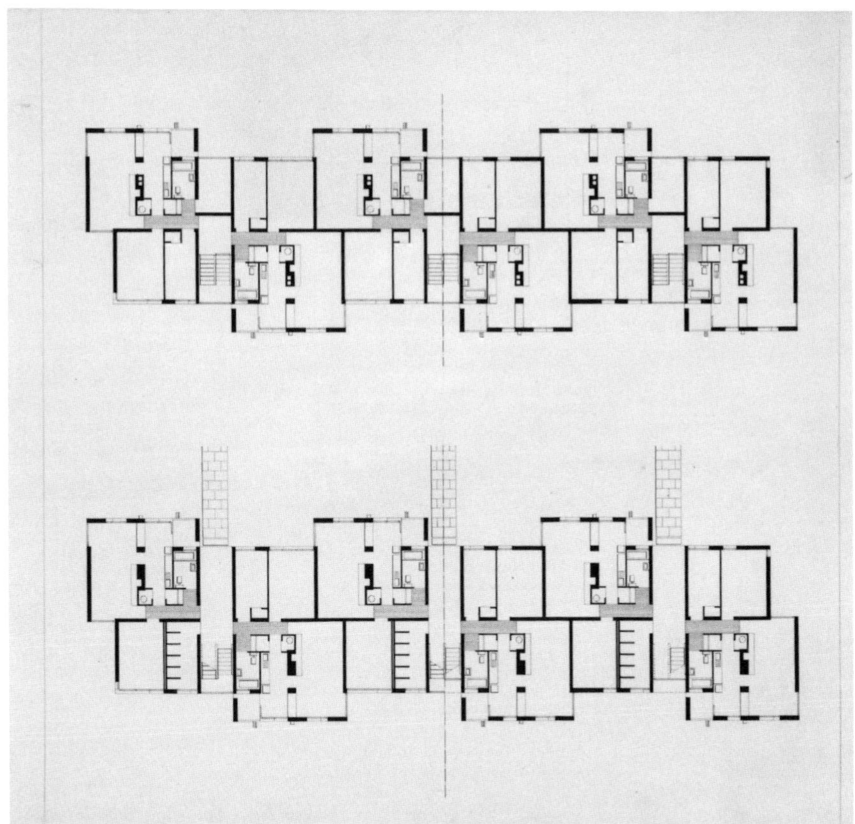

Figure 16
Stirling and Gowan, Ham Common. Ground-floor and upper-floor plans of three-story building.

Figure 17
Stirling and Gowan, Ham Common. Construction photo of three-story building. Note the prefabricated wooden window units and the continuous brick load-bearing walls.

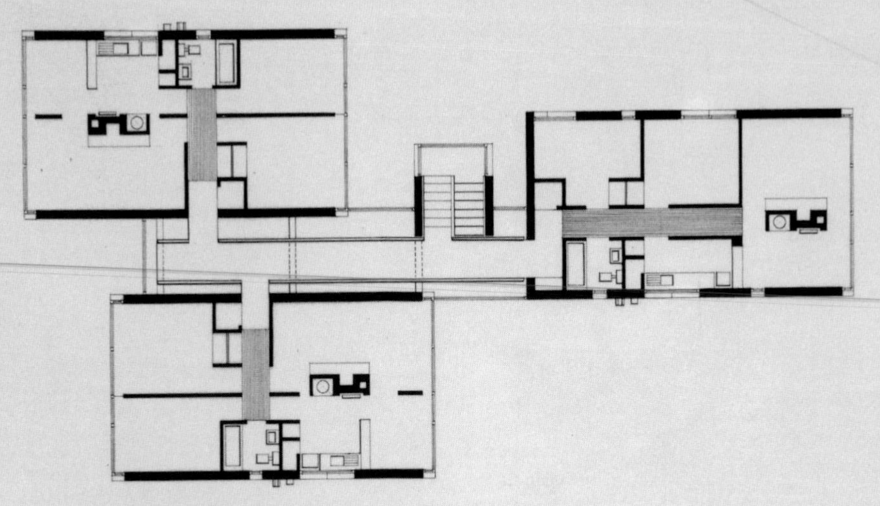

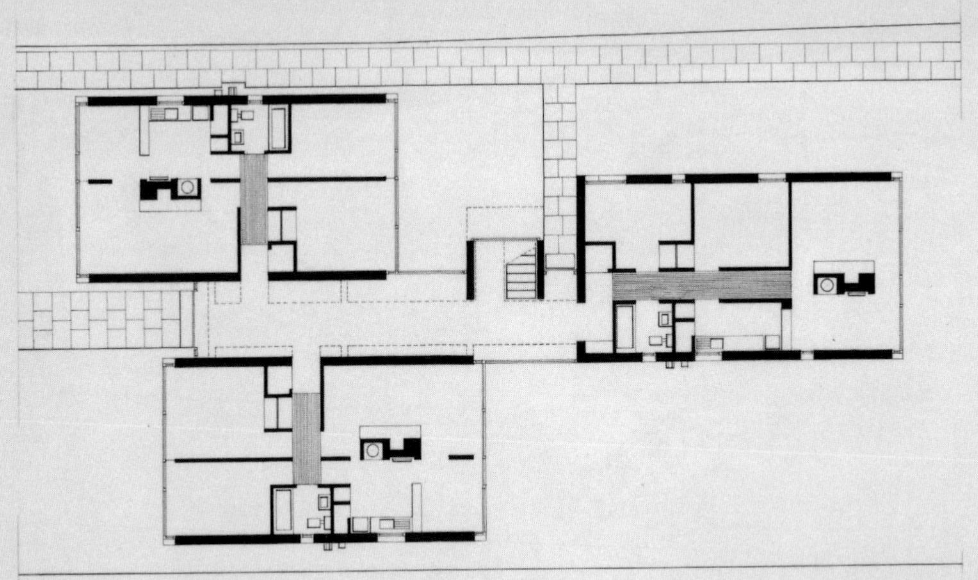

Figure 18
Stirling and Gowan, Ham Common. Ground-floor and upper-floor plans of the two-story buildings, with core and crosswall construction.

Figure 19
Stirling and Gowan, Ham Common. West façade of two-story building.

Figure 20
Stirling and Gowan, Ham Common. East façade of three-story building.

(figs. 21, 22).[31] Although Caroline Benton argues that the L-shaped windows at Ham Common are "part of an arbitrary, autonomous design vocabulary," in contrast to those at Jaoul, in fact Stirling and Gowan deploy them in a calculated way; they correspond to specific programs (bedrooms and kitchens) and serve as external markers for the more "private" spaces, as opposed to the larger windows on the east and west elevations. Often the top portion of the "L" is extended as a clerestory to the edge of the building. Stirling and Gowan also employ various proportional versions of the "L"—in some the top horizontal band is narrow, while in others the "L" becomes more squat, with the top window square instead of rectangular. In unabashedly employing this distinctive Corbusian motif they were unafraid not only to acknowledge influence but, as we saw in Stirling's early projects such as Core and Crosswall and Stiff Dom-ino, to reconfigure the original precedent. In the updated "L" window the glass no longer reads as a single piece, but is everywhere broken into two distinct windows, outlined by white wood framing, which also enabled them to be operable.

Although this desire for a more systematic, "rationalized" Jaoul dictated many of the design choices at Ham Common, there was an equal desire to maintain a focus on the individual unit. In both building types at Ham Common the plan arrangement—"pushed" and "pulled" units in the three-story building,

Figure 21
Stirling and Gowan, Ham Common. Various iterations of the L-shaped window on the façade of the three-story building.

Figure 22
Le Corbusier, Maisons Jaoul. Le Corbusier's L-shaped windows at Jaoul, a clear precedent for those at Ham Common.

atomized units pinwheeling around a central hallway in the two-story ones—breaks down the overall scale of the structure,[31] emphasizing the single dwelling. This exterior legibility of the individual unit, as well as the overall scale of the project, suggests an affinity with the traditional English "maisonette" or townhouse, though of course rendered in a very different material and decorative language, and a scalar contextualism with the adjacent Georgian townhouse. The scaling of the project was also in line with a resurgence of low-rise housing models in the postwar period, which had been discredited in the interwar years as a social and architectural type tied to the urban slums but which saw a renaissance in the postwar years, particularly as it provided a density close to that recommended by the London County Plan.[32] Though many of the low-rise housing developments in the late forties and early fifties employed a "modern" vocabulary of brick and concrete, they were typically mediated by more traditional massing, pitched roofs, and nods to British terrace housing tradition. The modern aesthetic was largely still reserved for the high-rise slab or "point-block" housing.[33]

In a 1958 article describing Ham Common, Stirling and Gowan credited Manousso with a willingness to forgo this "retrogressive" standard and instead experiment with "modern design"—a notion that clearly still provoked anxiety among prospective suburban clients.[34] Mannousso also requested a low-cost development—approximately 1,900 pounds per dwelling—which meant using "simple and everyday materials" that would offer "similar construction and selling price to the nearby 'Span' housing."[35] The material palette of poured-in-place concrete foundations and floor slabs, load-bearing brick infill walls, and wood framed windows can be explained to some degree, then, as reflecting Mannouso's desire for low-cost, everyday materials. Certainly the choice of a concrete structure was in keeping with postwar material availability, as steel was prohibitively expensive and a majority of steel manufacturers had turned to producing reinforcements over structural steel.[36] And in these terms, brick too was a natural choice. In a lecture describing the project Stirling singled out the use of bricks as the "cheapest form of structure," representing "cheap labor."[37] Significantly, Stirling and Gowan did not employ prefabricated systems similar to those at the Hertfordshire schools, which had been so successful and lauded in the immediate postwar years, and which Stirling had called "our best postwar effort," or even the Span housing model that Mannouso mentions, both of which would have certainly been means to keep the cost down.[38]

Beyond its cost-saving measures, the material language at Ham Common—particularly the use of brick—was related more immediately and recognizably to a resurgent interest in regionalism. When the project was published in the *Architectural Review* the editor highlighted the no-nonsense approach of the project as indicative of a broader "attempt to face the economic realities of dwelling construction in England today.[39] Equally important, the *Review* finds it indicative of the "younger generation's rejection of international style modernism, and toward a 'sophisticated regionalism.'"[40] Pevsner would echo the description in his assessment of the project as a "landmark in the emerging style of the late 1950s in England, in reaction against all-glass façades and thin, precise detailing."[41] At Ham Common we see the influence of the British industrial vernacular, in particular the Liverpool dock buildings and the brick façades of the nineteenth century, that would come to characterize Stirling's work. As Kenneth Frampton described both Ham Common and the Preston housing project (1961), "The vernacular of the industrial north is returned to its roots."[42] Stirling himself would make the comparison explicit in a later article by pairing an image of the L-shaped windows at Ham Common with his photo of a surprisingly similar window in a Liverpool dock building (fig. 23). The L-shaped window, then, while clearly indebted to Le Corbusier, was also a more generalized motif, and Stirling capitalized on the lack of fixity in its "origin." Ham Common incorporated both "direct" appropriations of regional precedents, largely from British industrial vernacular, as well as "second-hand" interpretations of regional motifs.

This leads to the larger point that Stirling's understanding of regionalism must be situated in relation to Le Corbusier's "shift" to the vernacular more broadly and the Maisons Jaoul specifically. Although this shift had in fact begun to appear in the 1930s—in projects such as his Errazurus House of 1930 and the Villa Mandrot of 1932, both of which incorporated a vernacular language of stone walls, Catalan vault roofs, and a more generalized return to a "Mediterranean prototype"—Maisons Jaoul became a watershed moment in Le Corbusier's postwar regionalism. The Smithsons dubbed Jaoul a "master-work on the knife edge of peasantism," and their response epitomized the recognition of as well as an ambivalence toward the vernacular or regional qualities of the work.[43]

In "Garches to Jaoul," Stirling describes Jaoul as resonant with vernacular prototypes, particularly those "recalling the Provençal farmhouse community," and calls Le Corbusier the "most regional of architects."[44] He singles out the earth roof at Jaoul as one of the most "primitive" elements of the project. Among the most significant changes Stirling and Gowan make in revisioning

Figure 23
James Stirling, photographer, view of the façade of a Liverpool dock building, also with L-shaped windows.

Jaoul at Ham Common are to remove the earth roof and the Catalan vault. This is notable not only because the Catalan vault would become a kind of leitmotif of Le Corbusier's postwar projects—widely aped by British architects, including Richard Sheppard, Robson and Partners in their competition-winning design for Churchill College, and Farmler Jouse at the University of Sussex by Sir Basil Spence—but also for the deliberate jettisoning of its vernacular associations.[45] Rather than focus on the signature visual element of Jaoul, Stirling and Gowan's reinterpretation focuses instead on its material language of brick and concrete.

Aside from its associations with more a more "primitive" construction method, in the 1950s brick also embodied a national identity—in explaining the use of brick at Ham Common Stirling emphasized "English know-how."[46] This was tied to the brick warehouses of Liverpool and the industrial vernacular of factories, along with the anonymous structures of the British countryside, such as oast houses or kilns, all of which would soon come to be termed the Functional Tradition, as will be developed in the next chapter. But brick had also been an important aspect of Britain's modern movement of the 1920s and 1930s. As evidenced by its traditional use in both "high" and "low" precedents, brick was well suited to the English climate, and offered significant advantages over the white stucco surfaces that predominated in prewar modernist buildings, or even of the exposed concrete of the postwar. As Henry-Russell Hitchcock wrote in his essay accompanying the 1937 exhibition "Modern Architecture in England" at the Museum of Modern Art, the English climate "soon reduces all natural materials . . . to an excessively romantic patina."[47] Even in 1937, Hitchcock extolled the virtues of brick, tile, and stone surfaces, which, while "less effective as propaganda than those covered with light-colored rendering," would "probably grow old more gracefully."[48] Stirling and Gowan's material choice was, therefore, in line with prewar British versions of continental modernism, Le Corbusier's postwar language, as well as an unselfconscious, vernacular brick of the Liverpool docks—all "regional" ideas.

A "MORE MECHANISTIC" JAOUL

After visiting Jaoul for the first time, Stirling wrote in his black notebook: "If the finish had been harder i.e. blue Staffordshire English bricks with definite joints between the wall and RC—the appearance would have been more mechanistic and I think that better."[49] Importantly, he does not question the material itself—he doesn't say, for example, that the "appearance" would have been "better" if he'd used stucco. There is an implicit acceptance of the brick, even as he asks for the "brute" surfaces of Jaoul to be made more "mechanistic." Here the *quality* of the machine, to return to Richards's distinction, rather than the look of the machine, is evoked as a means to define a more "modern" or rational architecture.

Rather than switch to a "harder" brick, however, at Ham Common Stirling and Gowan employ the relatively messy, uneven, and inexpensive cheap London stock brick. The "mechanistic" is introduced in other ways. The most immediately visible material correction to the bricks at Jaoul is the introduction of the "definite joints" that Stirling found lacking between the brick wall and the reinforced concrete horizontal floor slabs. More specifically, Stirling and Gowan introduce a reveal beneath the concrete slab, calling attention to the gap in the materials while also rendering their respective edges more precise. At some locations, clerestory windows further separate the two materials and isolate the slab from the walls to resemble exaggerated reveals in and of them selves (fig. 24). These reveals inscribe a gridded armature over the structure, articulating more fully the logic of the material choices—brick walls, concrete floor slabs—by distancing them, if only slightly, from one another. This material distinction is extended to the corners, where the wood, brick, and concrete are all held off the corner such that the edge of each material is revealed (fig. 25). Here, too, we have a development from Maisons Jaoul, where

Figure 24
Stirling and Gowan, Ham Common. The clerestory window creates an exaggerated "reveal" between the brick wall and concrete floor slab.

the concrete and brickwork are coplanar within the façade and abut directly—and much more crudely—at each floor (fig. 26).

It wasn't only the lack of joints but the brickwork itself that Stirling found to be of "poor" quality at Jaoul, writing that it was "considered a surface and not a pattern," and that the brick could have very well been replaced with another material—rubble or concrete—and still the "principle of design" would have remained.[50] The brick walls at Maisons Jaoul could even be read as the sublayer over which Le Corbusier placed his plaster coating at Garches—in other words, the same façade as Garches but with the "machinelike" plaster coating peeled away to reveal the "primitive" construction beneath. As a reaction to the undifferentiated brick surface at Jaoul, the bricks at Ham Common are arrayed in a deliberate and regular gridded pattern, with horizontal banding defined by the running bond, and are calculated to maximize efficiency and minimize material use. Further, the pointing in the bricks is recessed, creating an "oblique shadow" that calls into relief the outlines of each brick.[51] The intent, as Stirling makes clear in his reactions to Jaoul in the black notebook, wasn't simply to "tidy up" Jaoul, to use Banham's terminology, but instead to use the brick more precisely—to give it the "mechanistic" qualities that Richards had outlined in the 1930s and which Stirling found lacking in Le Corbusier's postwar projects.

In this insistence on a more machinelike brickwork, Stirling was perhaps more indebted to Mies than to Le Corbusier.[52] Although Mies never exerted the same influence on Stirling as did Le Corbusier, Stirling was nevertheless intimately familiar with his work, and the precision and order of Mies's brickwork offered a powerful antidote to Le Corbusier's "untidy" and "primitive" brick surfaces of the time. As with Mies's architecture, there was a desire at Ham Common to harness the brick as a modular element—Stirling would later say that "bricks are a 9-inch-by-4 ½-inch pre-cast system."[53] But Stirling's bricks never achieve the pure rationality of the Miesian bricks; even as he desires a "more mechanistic" treatment, the rough, slightly uneven profile of the London stock brick maintains a residual messiness, a slight bit of disorder. The London stock brick is the equivalent of the ready-made; it is the plywood of bricks, a deliberately common material. It inserts a surreptitious untidiness within the overall tidiness of Jaoul that acts as a foil against the desire for mechanistic appearance and precision articulated in the reveals.

In addition to brick, a more "mechanistic" treatment of materials at Ham Common is achieved in the *béton brut*.[54] Though completed after Banham's first essay of 1955, Ham Common would become an oft-cited New Brutalist work (a label that Stirling and Gowan summarily rejected): it was featured prominently in Banham's 1966 book, and in his early review of Ham Common Banham described the project as "about the most accessible example there is of the New Brutalism."[55] The concrete work at Ham Common, however, differs significantly from some of the canonical brutalist projects, particularly the work of Le Corbusier that marked the brutalist onset. In both the Maisons Jaoul and the Unité, which pioneered and popularized the use of the fair-

Figure 25
Stirling and Gowan, Ham Common. A "more mechanistic" treatment of materials is demonstrated in the "definite joints" around each brick and the precise shutter-board patterning in the concrete.

Figure 26
Le Corbusier, Maisons Jaoul. Stirling found the brickwork at Maisons Jaoul of "poor" quality. Photograph by James Stirling.

faced concrete, the markings of the wood formwork are left visible rather than sanded off, the shutterboards laid out as alternating horizontal and vertical bands. The resultant concrete surface is rough and uneven; the béton brut refuses the machinelike, uniform surface of Garches and offers instead a handmade, artisanal finish. Conversely, at Ham Common the shutterboard pattern is decidedly precise, composed of a series of consistently horizontal bands that traverse all concrete surfaces of the project, including the exposed floor slabs and "upstands"—concrete panels beneath selected windows—where each band corresponds to the width of two adjacent brick courses. Here the shutterboard pattern is still exposed but meant to be understood not as an "arty-crafty " product but as a horizontal system applied across the entire building. The use of the shutterboard patterning diminishes rather than enhances the material "crudity" of the concrete. Although not an inherently "mechanistic" material, concrete is essentially made more "mechanistic" through its casting procedures. As with the bricks, Stirling and Gowan rationalize the irrational, and make the "primitive" material more "modern."

A final instance of this rationalizing instinct at Ham Common manifests itself in the concrete upstands that appear beneath vertical windows in the three-story buildings. In their text accompanying the publication of Ham Common in 1958 in the *Architectural Review,* Stirling and Gowan write that the project expressed the "duality of the principal materials, brick and concrete."[56] These two materials are both exposed on the building's exterior, where the continuous horizontal edges of the concrete floor slab as well as the load-bearing brick walls are laid bare. But this exterior expression, Stirling and Gowan felt, did not accurately represent the volumetric proportion of concrete to brick throughout the project—approximately 50/50. To remedy the disparity between the material ratio suggested by the exterior and the actual brick-to-concrete ratio in the building, they insert concrete upstands—nonstructural concrete panels beneath the windows. These applied concrete panels, which appear as part of the same concrete structural system as the floor slabs but are in fact attached over brick spur walls, demonstrate a desire for structural "truth." Though not structurally necessary, the upstands became *conceptually* necessary to achieve "visual balance."[57]

Each of these gestures—regularizing brick, organizing béton brut, optimizing structural efficiency, making a more "honest" visual expression of the structural condition—were indebted to prewar modernist discourse and its emphasis on "rationalism," but they were all performed on a distinctly postwar material vocabulary of brick and exposed concrete. Was Ham Common, then, a pure hybridizing of prewar principles and postwar aesthetics? In other words, did they completely abandon the look of the "white architecture" of the 1930s while trying to recapture its ideals?

The façade-length windows along the east and west sides of the two-story buildings, composed primarily of white wood, offer one example of a "high" modernist reference, with a flat, taut quality closer to the Le Corbusier of 1927 than 1955 (fig. 27). Like the fenêtre en longueur, these windows trespass

Figure 27
Stirling and Gowan, Ham Common.
The updated fenêtre en longueur at the south façade of the two-story buildings.

over any number of spaces and programs behind, although they occupy the entire wall, not simply a horizontal slice. Rather than acknowledging the individual spaces behind, as in a traditional punched window, they instead express the integrity of the individual unit. They also go some way toward masking the crosswall construction behind, since the interior brick crosswall is intentionally held back from the building's edge to allow for the uninterrupted span of the window, which in the two-story buildings takes up the entire façade.[58]

Although visually resonant with the work of the 1920s and 1930s, these white window walls also reference the floor-to-ceiling windows, or the "fourth wall" as Stirling referred to it, at Jaoul, which were infilled with bookshelves or other opaque materials. By breaking their window walls with

Figure 28
Stirling and Gowan, Ham Common. The de Stijl–influenced stair volume of the two-story buildings.

three twelve-inch-thick wooden transoms—one at top, one at bottom, and one at waist height, the last of which acts as a balustrade when the top window is opened—Stirling and Gowan create a "deliberate wall/window ambiguity."[59] They highlight the transom's multiple functions: it provides a feeling of greater security on the relatively urban side; it offers additional thermal insulation; and its thickness helps diminish "curtaining chaos."[60]

There are other prewar modernist references as well. The stair in the two-story building, in which the glass volume, lined in white-painted wood, emerges from the building in a prismatic collection of planes and rectilinear collision, has been compared to de Stijl, and indeed the composition is undoubtedly more Schröder than Jaoul (fig. 28). Stirling's lecture notes on Ham Common in 1959 or 1960 read: "Jaoul/De Stijl."[61] Banham noted Ham Common's de Stijl resonance as well, particularly in the glazed ends of the two-story blocks, where "one can appreciate the floor-slabs as planes in space," as well as in the strip windows under the slabs, which give "visual independence to the horizontal and vertical planes."[62] Alan Colquhoun wrote that at Ham

Common "Corbusian parallel brick structural walls are cross-fertilized with a combinatory play of volumes recalling van Doesburg."[63]

Both of these "high" modernist references—the fenêtre en longueur and de Stijl—were concentrated in the two-story block, the portion of the project that appears to have been more Gowan's focus than Stirling's.[64] Although it is impossible to parse out specific individual contributions, it is nevertheless worth noting this predominance of prewar modernist references in the two-story blocks (particularly de Stijl), while in the three-story block the focus is material precision within the postwar language of concrete and fair-faced concrete (with a heavy nod to Maisons Jaoul). Stirling, then, already seems to be moving farther away from the canonical modernist language, willing to experiment with a postwar vocabulary and, most importantly, thinking through modernism's principles as operations to be performed on any material language.

FIRST NOTES ON INFLUENCE AND THE "EPHEBE"

Even with these multiple references clearly at play—including de Stijl, Mies, and British industrial vernacular—Ham Common is overwhelmingly a meditation on one precedent: Maisons Jaoul. As such, it is instructive to compare Stirling and Gowan's project with another "first" work that was highly derivative—at least on first glance. Like Ham Common, the Smithsons' Hunstanton Secondary School, begun in 1949 and completed in 1954 (just one year before Stirling and Gowan began their design of Ham Common), was more or less an interpretation of a single precedent—the steel frames, glass, and brick infill of the walls of Mies's campus for IIT. Both projects are almost uncomfortably derivative, and both launched their respective authors to international acclaim. Although Stirling and the Smithsons would later publicly quarrel, they came up among the same groups in London, were members of the Independent Group, and spent Sundays together at the Banhams'. The Smithsons' reworking of IIT parallels Stirling and Gowan's own reinterpretation of Jaoul, inasmuch as it represents a generation actively modifying a vocabulary defined by the previous generation, as well as the willingness to engage a specific architectural precedent. Both buildings were held up as early examples of the New Brutalism school—a label the Smithsons not only relished but claimed to have invented (at least partially), while Stirling wholeheartedly rejected it. Banham wrote that Hunstanton was "almost unique among modern buildings in being made of what it appears to be made of," and we could apply the same description to Ham Common—its structural "truth" is written all over its brick and concrete façade.[65] Of course, the two differed in materials—Hunstanton was brick infill in a steel frame rather than a concrete one—scale, and program.

At these early stages of both the Smithsons' and Stirling's careers—their "ephebe" period, if you will—the use of reference is highly literal and less mediated than it would later become, and, importantly, it is also singular. In their first publicly recognized projects they both look back to one specific modern precedent to offer a clear reinterpretation. In both cases the singular building (Maisons Jaoul, IIT) emerges as more important than the figure (Le Corbusier, Mies). Both interrogated their predecessors to "rewrite" the work in their terms. Peter Smithson would later write that at Hunstanton they were trying to "use Mies's methods without any mannerisms," distilling the essence of Mies to get past the aesthetics to the "ethics"—to use Banham's terminology.[66] Like Stirling, who desired to return rational "principles" to Le Corbusier's work, the Smithsons were similarly trying to drill down to the core "methods" at work in Mies's work.

Here Bloom's theory of influence, in particular his elaboration of the "swerve," offers a compelling analytical framework. In performing a swerve a predecessor introduces a "corrective" to the original work. The suggestion is that the precursor was on the right track but didn't go quite far enough and "should have swerved, precisely in the direction that the new poem moves."[67] In Bloom's terms, the younger version of the precursor is often easier to deal with since it is less formed, less perfect. Vincent Scully cleverly illustrates this notion in his comparison of Richard Meier with Robert Venturi and their respective revisionings of Le Corbusier; by choosing Le Corbusier's later more "complete" work as his model, Scully writes, Meier never convinces us that his work is advancing the original, whereas Venturi, in choosing Le Corbusier's early work as his precedent—the Schwob Villa and the theater in La Chaux-de-Fonds, both of 1916—achieves more successful revisions. Perhaps, as Scully suggested vis-à-vis Venturi, Stirling had a "keener sense for the precursor's jugular."[68] Although Jaoul was a "late" project of Le Corbusier's, it was in fact the beginning of a new system not yet fully formed. Stirling, then, can convince us that Jaoul was, at least in some respects, a less mature, or certainly a less "rational," version of his own work.

In his "rationalizing" of Jaoul, Stirling was in effect "correcting" Le Corbusier by making him more "Corbusian"; he understood Le Corbusier as embodying modernism more broadly—as rational, precise, systematic, orderly, objective, machinelike—and was attempting to reintroduce those terms into his postwar work. Stirling and Gowan's choice of Jaoul over Garches as a precedent for Ham Common takes on particular significance insofar as they rejected the aesthetic of Garches but capitalized on the principles that it embodied—the "source" of the aesthetic, to use Richards's terminology, rather than the aesthetic itself. The modifications at Ham Common to make "more mechanistic" what Stirling termed the "primitive" aspects of Jaoul (introducing material reveals, inscribing individual bricks, regularizing the béton brut formwork, systematizing elevations in response to their orientation) all employed "qualities" of the machine (exactness, cleanness, precision, and simplicity) as a means to rationalize, or modernize, Jaoul. Though this first built project remained highly derivative and did not yet possess the "plastic invention" that would come to characterize Stirling's later projects, it was more than simply a copy.

Significantly, neither Stirling and Gowan nor the Smithsons explain their projects in terms of influence—unlike Philip Johnson, for example, who carefully delineates the set of references behind his "frankly derivative" glass house of 1949.[69] For the most part, the connections were made by others—Banham linking the "untidy" Jaoul to the "tidy" Ham Common, or Colin Rowe writing that in the 1950s Stirling was "prone to think about Le Corbusier's Maisons Jaoul as almost a revelation from on high."[70] If anything, the Smithsons and Stirling were quick to *deny* influence in any form; in a report submitted with their initial competition entry for the project, the Smithsons wrote that the form of Hunstanton was based on "close study of educational needs and purely formal requirements rather than by precedent."[71] Denial, of course, is often the clearest admission of guilt, and undoubtedly a hallmark of youth—the desire for a "pure" and unmediated creative expression. Later in their careers both architects were able to openly acknowledge influence and embrace its impact. For Stirling, influence would become not simply an after-the-fact descriptive trope but a definitive and generative aspect of his work.

CHAPTER 2

DISCOVERING HISTORY

CHURCHILL COLLEGE (1959)

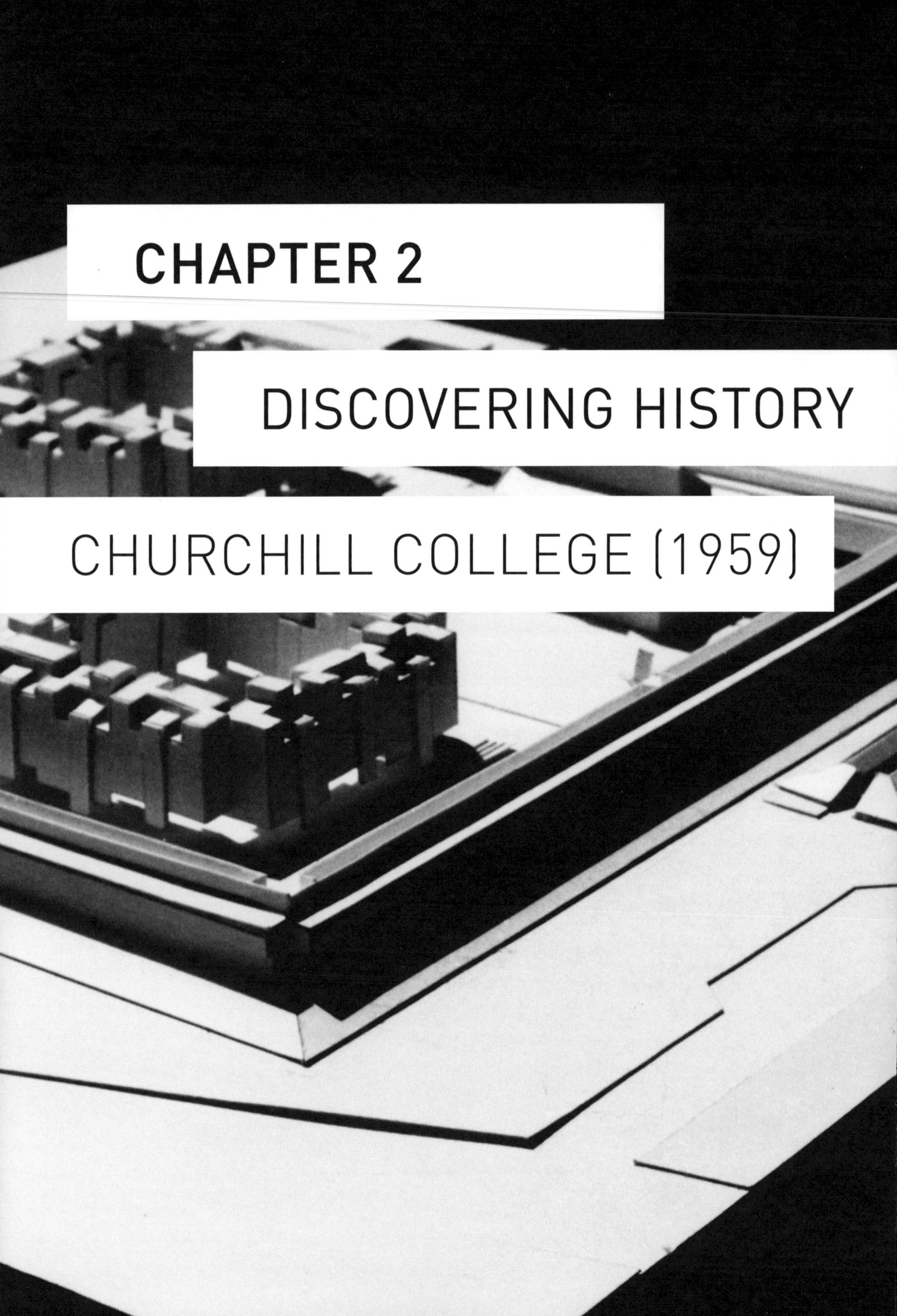

Just a few years after his essay "Ronchamp: Le Corbusier and the Crisis of Rationalism" appeared in the *Architectural Review,* Stirling, it seems, had changed his mind about Le Corbusier's "irrational" building. In the 1960 issue of the Yale student journal *Perspecta* Stirling published "'The Functional Tradition' and Expression," which begins with a pair of images: Ronchamp and an anonymous Ischian peasant tower.[1] In the accompanying text Stirling compares the two projects, writing that both are representative of "direct and undecorated volumes evolved from building usage and particularly from the functions of their major elements."[2] Though he finds the connection "disquieting," he nevertheless acknowledges that the form of the ventilation and light towers in the two projects, separated by centuries, remains more or less the same because the "function they are serving has not changed."[3] No longer exemplifying a "crisis of rationalism," Ronchamp is now seen to represent perhaps the most "rational" of all modernism's principles—function (fig. 29).

This revision in Stirling's interpretation of Ronchamp reflected both a changing personal attitude as well as developments in architectural discourse during the late 1950s and early 1960s in Britain. Stirling's *Perspecta* article was written in response to growing historicization of functionalism—thus the willingness to see Ischian peasant towers as "functional"—as a means to expand the language of modernism in the postwar period. At the same time, Stirling's inclusion of the Ischian peasant towers reflected a developing interest in regionalism, first seen at Ham Common, which, like the search for a Functional Tradition, was an attempt to supplant the by-then formulaic language of both the Machine Aesthetic and the International Style by reconsidering vernacular and anonymous architecture as a model for a reinvigorated modernism. On a more personal level, Stirling's inclusion of the peasant towers—along with a range of other sources, both "high" and "low," contemporary and historical, that appear in the article—reflected a dramatic increase in his repertoire of references. If his projects of the early 1950s—including his thesis

"THE FUNCTIONAL TRADITION" AND EXPRESSION

Figure 29
James Stirling, "'The Functional Tradition' and Expression," *Perspecta* 6, 1960.

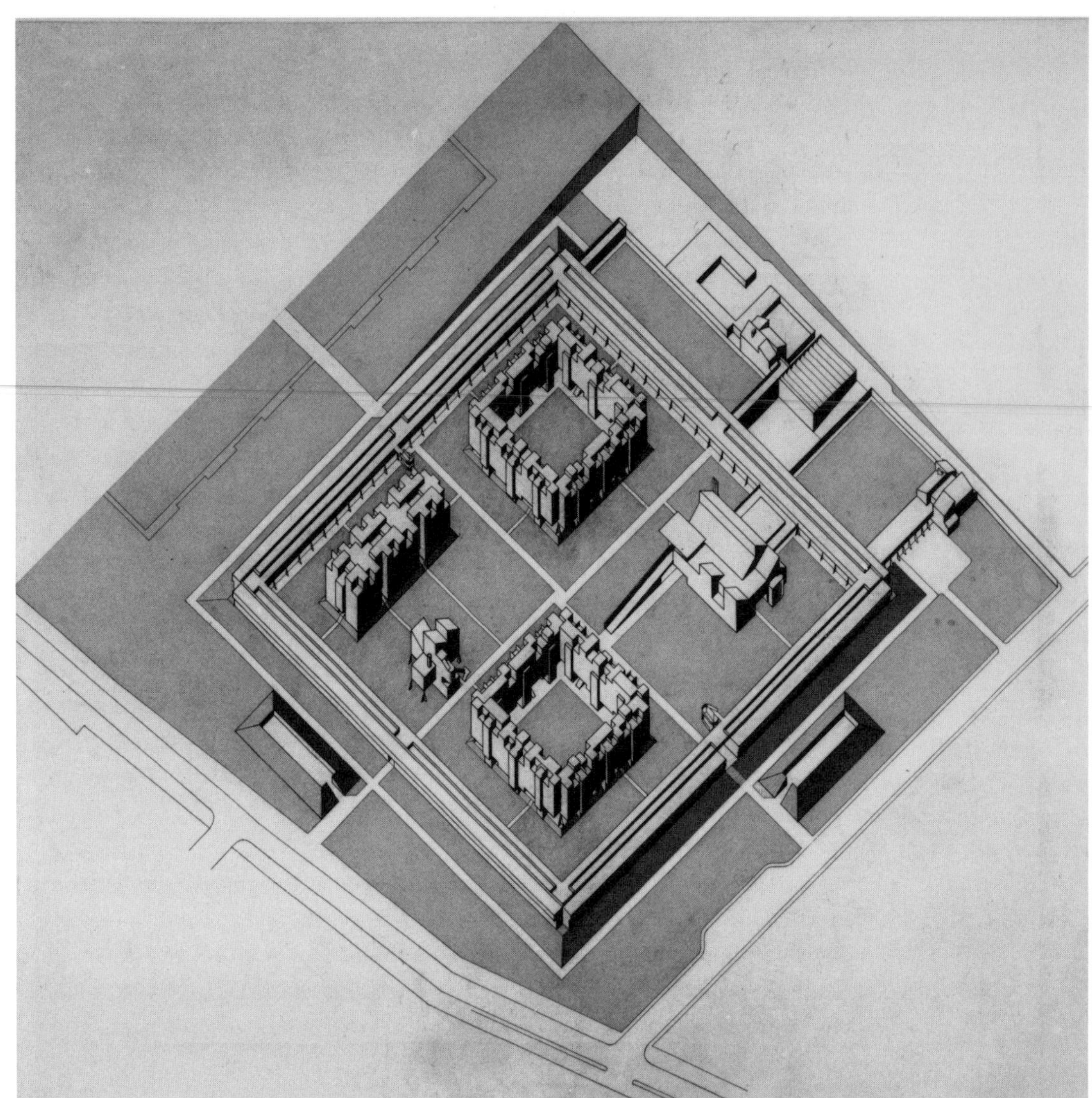

at Liverpool, the Core and Crosswall House, the Stiff Dom-Ino project, and, of course, Ham Common—were indebted largely to his modernist predecessors (even as they articulated a "crisis" in modernism's principles), by the late 1950s Stirling had moved away from a strictly modern pedigree to incorporate a range of historical precedents into his work, an expansion that can be linked directly to the search for "functional" qualities in regional, vernacular architectures. It is at this moment, then, that Stirling "discovers" history in its broadest sense, unlocking a whole set of previously unavailable architectural sources. Locating modern qualities, particularly functionalism, in historical precedents, irrespective of their time period, style, or author, allowed Stirling to mine history with relative freedom and modernist abandon a full twenty years before his alleged postmodern "turn."

Figure 30
Stirling and Gowan, Churchill College, University of Cambridge, England, 1959. Axonometric.

The architectural project that marks the moment of this expanded historical consciousness, and the focus of this chapter, is one of Stirling's least studied works, the Churchill College competition of 1959 (fig. 30).[4] While Ham Common was largely a meditation on one precedent—Le Corbusier's Maisons Jaoul—Churchill College looked to a range of sources, from medieval fortifications to the most recent work of Louis Kahn, all of which were held together through an investigation into and critique of the courtyard type. Churchill represented Stirling's first attempt to incorporate a broader range of historical references, as well as an early attempt at "generalizing away the uniqueness" of earlier precedents.

A COLLEGE "ARRANGED AROUND COURTS"

The idea for a new college at Cambridge University to be named in honor of Sir Winston Churchill was first suggested in 1957, arising from an acknowledged need to train scientists in the postwar period as well as provide for the general growth in British universities in the mid- to late 1950s.[5] As Britain anticipated a postwar bulge in student populations, existing universities expanded their capacity while a number of entirely new campuses were planned, notably the seven New Universities (dubbed the Shakespearean Seven) constructed during the 1960s.[6] Cambridge began to plan for its own expansion following a 1950 report by Sir William Holford that foresaw major growth in the University as well as in the town of Cambridge itself.[7] One outcome of the Holford report was the new Arts Faculties Campus on Sidgwick Road, awarded to Sir Hugh Casson, Neville Conder and Partners in 1953, a thirteen-acre development that represented the first large-scale postwar university planning effort at Cambridge.[8] The new arts campus created the first development west of the "backs," the formerly rural area west of the Cam River in which most of the postwar expansion would take place, and which was also the setting for the Churchill College competition.

As outlined in the competition brief of January 1959, Churchill College was to be located on forty-one acres of agricultural land situated to the north and west of the campus center.[9] The program called for the accommodation of five hundred fellows or students, both graduate and undergraduate—making it the largest college at Cambridge—as well as guest lodging, a master's and tutor's house, a dining hall, a chapel, a library, a reading room, kitchen and administrative buildings, and extensive provisions for athletic spaces.[10] Unlike the rest of the densely knit Cambridge campus, Churchill College would stand as an independent entity, removed both physically and conceptually from the rest of the university, on a relatively isolated and disconnected site.

Twenty-one firms were invited to compete in the two-stage competition, with twenty submitting designs.[11] Stirling and Gowan's inclusion among the group is a testament to their growing profile on the London architectural scene, and a result of their connection to the head of Cambridge's architecture school and former director of the London County Council architects department, Leslie Martin. Martin was responsible for the original list of invitees, as well as the program brief and initial cost estimate.[12] The highly publicized competition was one of the most important in the development of the postwar university. It offered architects a rare chance to conceptualize an entirely new college plan, and it served as a testing ground for some of the best-known architects of the era—many of whom would go on to design and build university buildings of the 1960s, at Cambridge as well as at the Shakespearean Seven.[13]

Four of the initial twenty firms—Stirling and Gowan; Chamberlin, Powell and Bon; Howell, Killick and Partridge; and Richard Sheppard, Robson and Partners—were invited to a second stage, paid a nominal fee of 500 pounds, and given about two and a half months to devise the first phase, a tight schedule that, one reviewer noted, surely favored the larger firms with "more manpower."[14] Though predictably diverse, the four schemes share important similarities: all place the principal student residences at the east end of the site, with athletic fields to the west, and, perhaps most importantly, all are based on some version of a courtyard plan. Adherence to the collegiate courtyard model was strongly hinted at by the competition brief, which described the traditional aspects of a Cambridge College as "arranged around courts and related to major rooms like Hall, Chapel, etc."[15] Nevertheless, it is striking that none of the entrants resisted this courtyard model. As one reviewer questioned, if this was really a "scientific" college, shouldn't there be a more "scientific" inquiry into the best form the college should take? "Most people seem to think of colleges as essentially inward-looking, and therefore con-

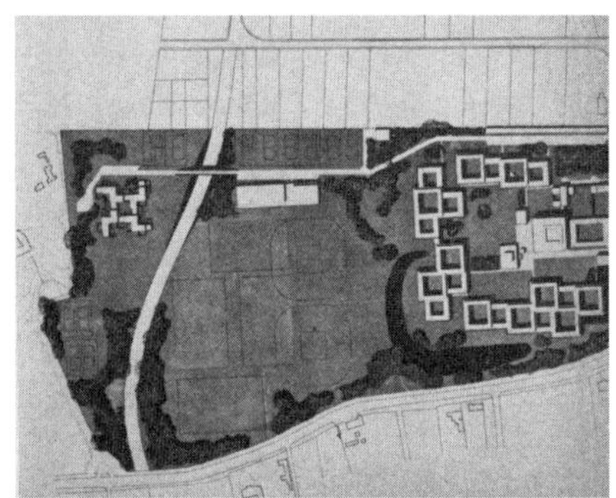

31

Figure 31
Richard Sheppard, Robson and Partners, Churchill College. Site plan.

32

Figure 32
Howell, Killick and Partridge, Churchill College. Site plan.

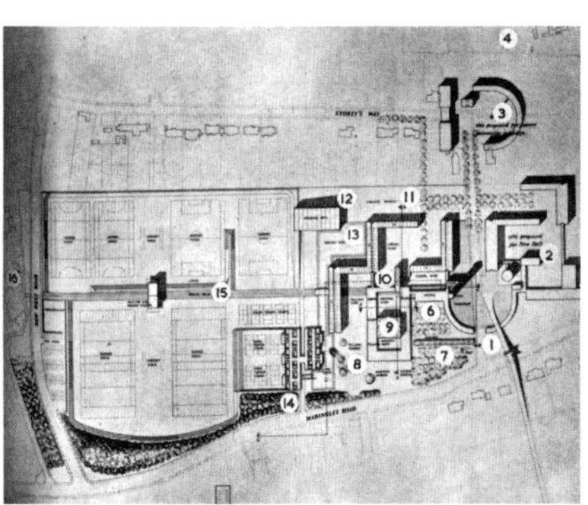

33

Figure 33
Chamberlin, Powell and Bon, Churchill College. Site plan.

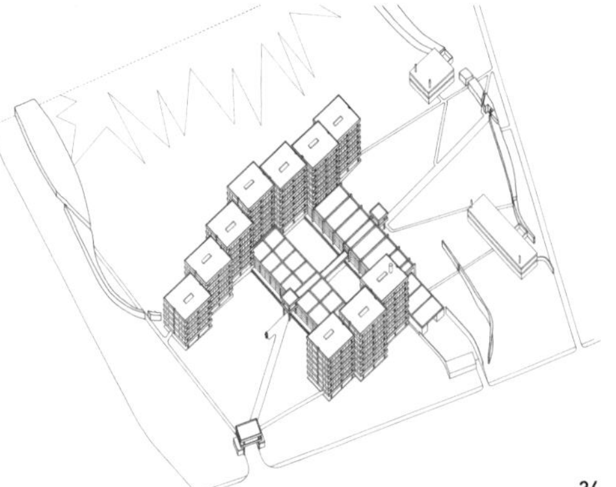

34

Figure 34
Alison and Peter Smithson, Churchill College. Axonometric.

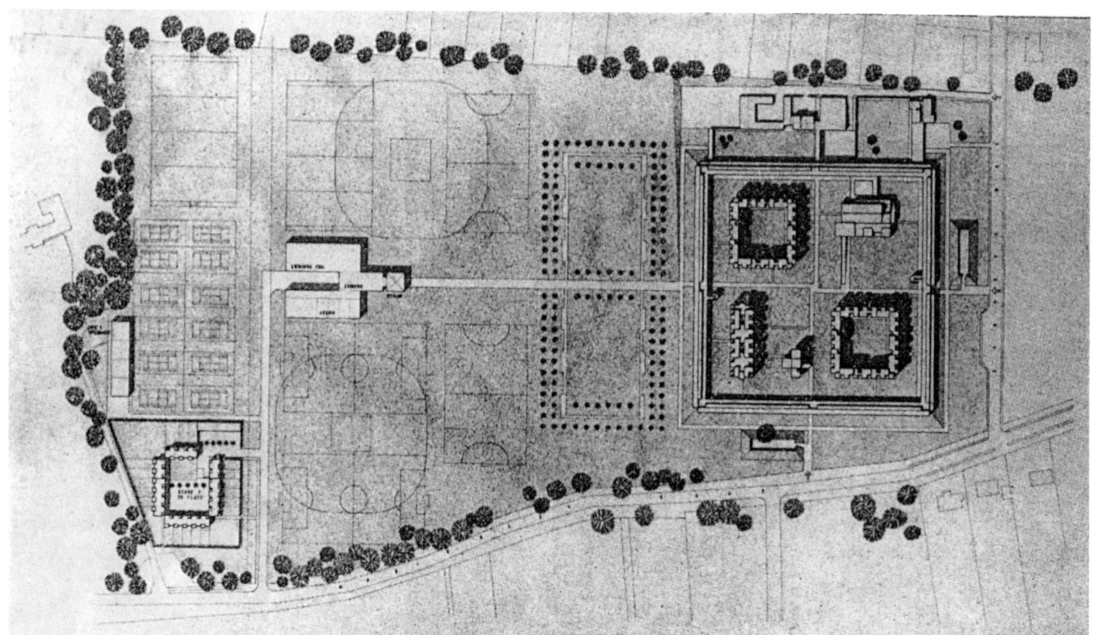

Figure 35
Stirling and Gowan, Churchill College. Site plan. Like those of the other finalists, Stirling and Gowan's scheme was based on the traditional courtyard model, though they proposed one enormous "great court" in lieu of a series of aggregated or implied courtyards.

templative and corporate, but this only occurs at Oxford and Cambridge. . . . Is there any evidence that courtyard planning improves the life and efficiency of Cambridge students?"[16]

Colin Rowe, in his 1964 review of the Churchill Competition, "The Blenheim of the Welfare State," commented wryly on the courtyard predominance, noting that most of the competitors seemed to feel "that a college implies a courtyard, and that the more courtyards a college possessed, the more collegiate it is likely to become."[17] Rowe's remark was no doubt directed at the winning scheme from Richard Sheppard, Robson and Partners, which contained more than twenty smaller residential courtyards grouped around larger "informal" courtyard spaces meant to "correspond to the quadrangles of a typical college" (fig. 31).[18] Unlike Rowe, the committee found the scheme an "interesting variant on the traditional college plan" and recommended its acceptance.[19]

The two other nonwinning schemes were less obsessive in their courtyard deployment. Howell, Killick and Partridge's design, loosely organized around two open courts, focused largely on material exploration, with a system of molded, precast concrete panels that generate a highly articulated and deeply shadowed skin (fig. 32). The scheme won praise from the committee for its "distinctive" and "imaginative" solution. With the highest cost estimate of the four (at 1.3 million pounds, nearly one third over the given budget of 1 million) and 25 percent more space than the other schemes, the committee rejected the proposal—though the cost overrun might simply have offered a convenient excuse for what many viewed as the committee's inherent conservatism.[20] The submission by Chamberlin, Powell and Bon adopts a looser courtyard arrangement, similar to the Miesian open-campus model of Arne

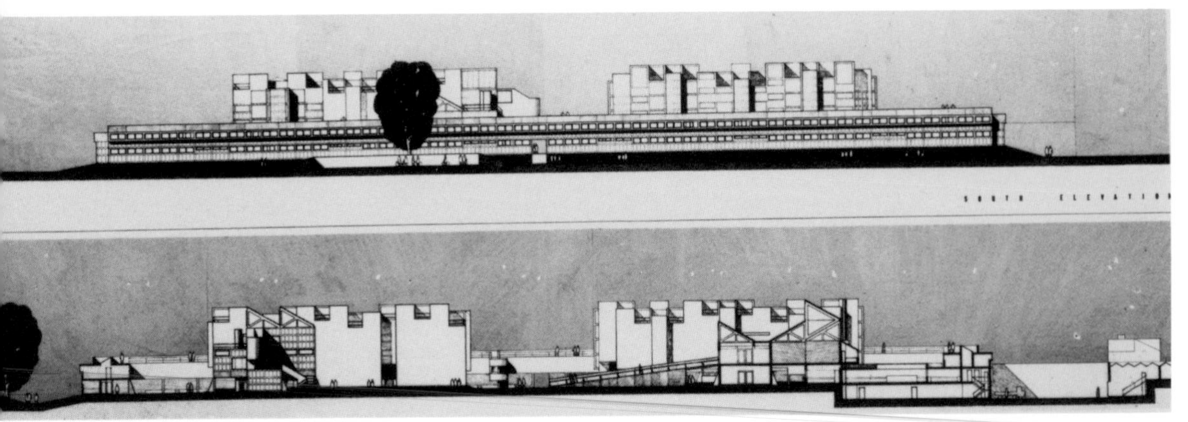

Figure 36
Stirling and Gowan, Churchill College. Elevation and section.

Jacobsen's St. Catherine's College at Oxford, begun the same year, with vaulted roofs derived from Le Corbusier's Maisons Jaoul, but it was dismissed by the committee as "hardly more than outline drawings" (fig. 33).[21] The Smithsons also submitted an entry that, though it didn't place in the top four, offered a counterpoint to the courtyard focus with its use of aggregated towers (fig. 34).

Like the other three finalists, Stirling and Gowan employed the courtyard as an organizing device; rather than a series of aggregated or open courtyards, however, their scheme proposes one enormous courtyard at the eastern edge of the site (fig. 35). This "great court" is defined by a continuous two-story wall of dormitory rooms (what Stirling would also term the "stockade") that traces its perimeter. Inside are five freestanding buildings—three additional dormitory buildings, a library, and a multipurpose building—all visible above the perimeter wall (fig. 36). The entire scheme is raised on an enormous earth platform that serves not only to level the uneven terrain but also to create the sense of what Stirling and Gowan termed a "protected" environment.[22]

The project was designed to be built in four phases, in direct response to the committee's requirements, with the necessary condition that the project be viable and "complete" at each stage; first the married student housing complex, at the southeastern corner of the site; then the outer ring of dormitory rooms, the chapel, and multipurpose building; and finally the three interior dormitory buildings. All buildings are concrete frame, with either Portland stone cladding or exposed shuttered-concrete exterior finishes, and wood window frames. In the library and multipurpose buildings Stirling and Gowan employ precast concrete trusses and triangular frames, distinguishing them from the dormitory buildings, all of which are column and slab concrete frame.

Although the assessors found the scheme "impressive," they concluded that it didn't seem to be "deriving from college use."[23] A contemporary reviewer seconded the opinion: "The court is too large and the scheme ran completely against the genius loci of Cambridge."[24] But it was precisely the traditional Cambridge courtyard model—the "genius loci of Cambridge"—that Stirling and Gowan sought to engage, albeit in more radical terms. In their competition report Stirling and Gowan wrote, "The working of a residential college has changed only slightly in the last few centuries." Their scheme, they added, was a deliberate attempt to interrogate—and update—the core tenets of the courtyard type.[25]

GENERALIZING AWAY UNIQUENESS

The first aspect of the traditional Cambridge courtyard that Stirling and Gowan's scheme challenges is scale. Unlike their competitors, who take pains to break down the scale of the project through the use of multiple low-rise buildings and faceted and stepped plans, Stirling and Gowan intentionally exaggerate the magnitude of the project through its massive courtyard—a 580-foot square, three times the size of the courtyard at Trinity College. This enormous courtyard is evident from the earliest version of the scheme, a single image of which survives in the archive (fig. 37). The undated drawing (presumably submitted for the first round of the competition in early 1959) depicts a square courtyard surrounded by a band of student rooms, with four freestanding buildings placed within the courtyard. Although the configuration of the interior buildings differs from the final scheme, and the project is, predictably, less developed than their final entry, the emphatic image of the square courtyard, ringed by the two-story "wall" of student rooms and containing a group of detached structures, is consistent. Undoubtedly the enormity of the courtyard was the aspect that contributed most to both the reviewers' and assessors' disapproval of the project, making it seem "against the genius loci" of Cambridge.

The inflated scale gives the scheme a decidedly monumental air. In his analysis of the project years later, Kenneth Frampton described it, somewhat disparagingly, as a "classical reversion to new monumentality."[26] But the "monumental" was something that Stirling saw as inherent in, rather than antithetical to, a Cambridge college, and as appropriate to both the project and the time period. Rowe wrote in his "Blenheim" article that the "building of a Churchill College should be in some way Churchillian—building perhaps big in scale, exuberant, simple, pugnacious, uncompromising and, to a degree, rhetorical. . . . Churchill College, a training ground for a scientific elite, is also in some sense a monument."[27] Stirling echoes Rowe's description; he writes that raising the Churchill scheme on the earth platform gave it a "degree of monumentality," and he describes Churchill College as a "monument" to Winston Churchill.[28]

Both Rowe's and Stirling's comments reflect the lineage of the New Monumentality debates of a decade previous. Certainly the desire for buildings to "represent their social and community life to give more than functional fulfillment," articulated by Sert, Léger, and Giedion in their 1943 essay "Nine Points on Monumentality," resonates in Stirling and Gowan's enclosed scheme, and particularly in the courtyard space that serves as the focal point.[29] The sheer scale and "totalizing" gesture of the project must be seen as a statement of the possibility to return to some kind of monumental expression. Of course

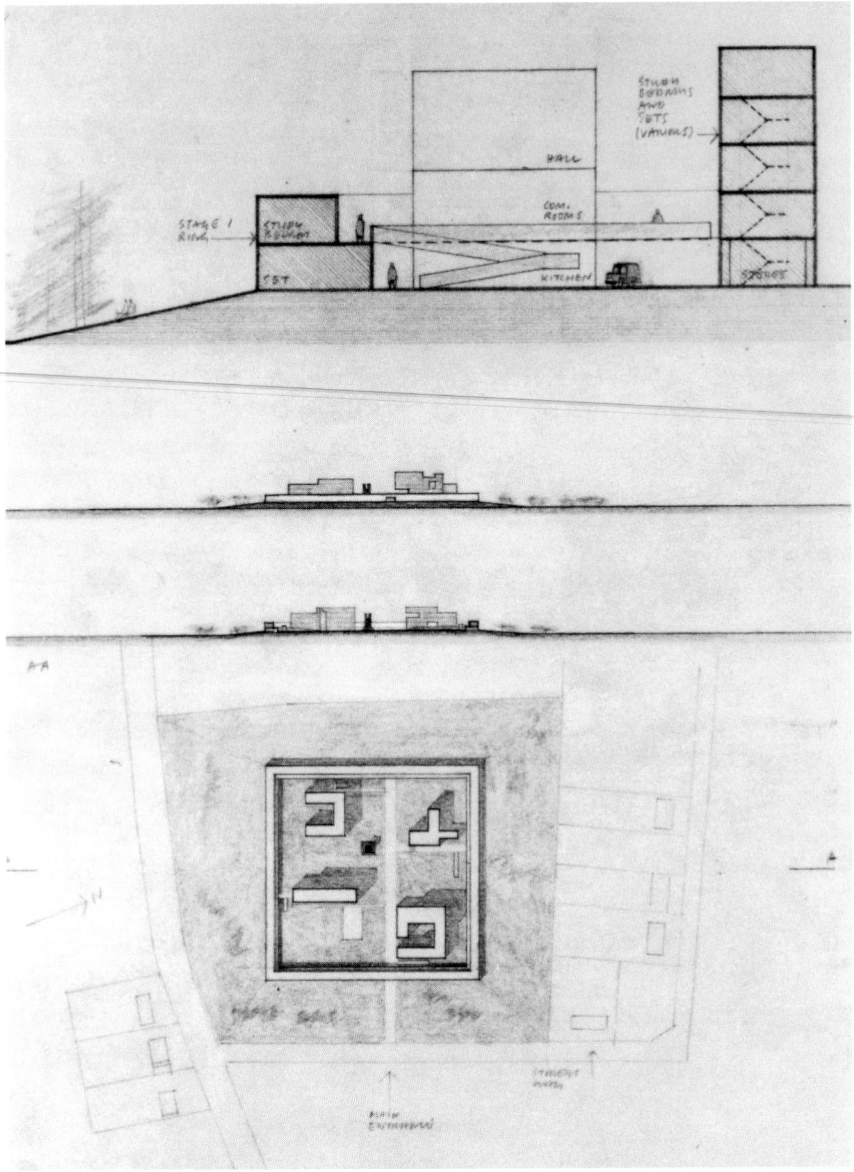
STAGE / RING
SET
HALL
COM. ROOMS
KITCHEN
MAIN ENTRANCE

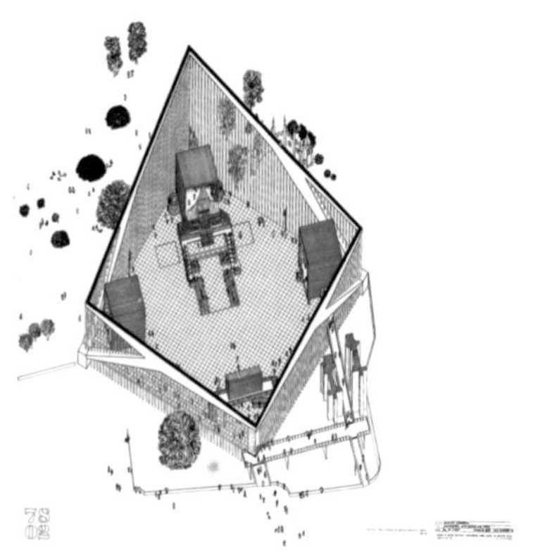

Figure 37
Stirling and Gowan, Churchill College. This early development drawing shows a large square courtyard with freestanding interior buildings.

Figure 38
Alison and Peter Smithson, Coventry Cathedral, 1951. An example of what Stirling termed a "one idea" project.

theirs was a very different monumentality than had been suggested by Sert et al., who advocated mobility, color, "light metal structures," and projection as methods to achieve this new symbolic expression.[30] Churchill's monumentality was more in line with the term's traditional meaning of "solidity, steadiness, and simplicity of effect"—the definition given by A. E. Richardson in his *Monumental Classic Architecture in Britain and Ireland,* the text Stirling listed as third most influential during his student years. Monumentality in this more traditional sense was meant to impress upon the viewer a sense of the building's significance, to provoke a degree of wonder, and, perhaps, to suggest a kind of foreboding, a restrictive quality. Along these lines, Richardson described the necessity for a monumental building to "impress the mind at once with one great idea."[31] The exaggerated scale and singular form of the great court at Churchill, as well as the elevated earth mound, thus become a clear manifestation of Richardson's "one great idea"—the monumental gesture.

This notion of the "one idea" project was something that had preoccupied Stirling at least since the early 1950s. In his black notebook he resolves to design "essential one idea buildings," calling it the "next step in my development."[32] And later he records another "resolution for 1954": to do a "competition which is of the 'one dominating space' species."[33] He uses the "one idea" criterion as a means to judge other projects as well; he finds the Smithsons' Coventry Cathedral of 1951 acceptable as a one-idea approach because it contained complexity and multiplicity within its singular form, with "one element" (the structural system) "dominating a number of minors" (fig. 38).[34] Churchill College, with its "dominating" figure of the great court, was clearly articulated as a one-idea scheme, but, like in the Smithsons' Coventry project, there were "minors" in the design as well—notably the freestanding interior buildings—that lent depth to an otherwise totalizing design.

Certainly the one-idea quality of Churchill is reinforced, if not enabled, by its symmetry. The great court is divided into four quadrants by paved walkways, which form the conceptual cardo and decumanus of the scheme (figs. 39, 40). Entry to the courtyard is at the midpoint of each of the four perimeter walls, leading directly onto the walkways. The symmetry of Stirling and Gowan's scheme is in clear contrast to the more ad hoc, asymmetrical model of a traditional Cambridge college like Trinity, which represented an aggregation of buildings over time, as well as to a prevailing neopicturesque tendency in England. A number of the other Churchill College submissions, including the Howell, Killick and Partridge scheme and the Smithsons', exemplify this tendency toward studied "informality," marked by seemingly haphazard angles and "picturesque" elements. Instead, Stirling and Gowan's use of symmetry coincided with contemporary "Neo-Palladian" interests, evidenced in schemes such as the Smithsons' Coventry Cathedral. Distinguished by the use of axiality, proportional schemes, and an explicit reaction to the "usual asymmetry of Modern Architecture," as Stirling described it, Neo-Palladianism was distinguished from its eighteenth-century counterpart, the Neo-Palladianism of Lord Burlington and others, in that it was not specifically indebted to Palladio but to a more general notion of Renaissance "principles" put forth by Wittkower in *Architectural Principles in the Age of Humanism.*[35]

Stirling and Gowan's use of symmetry at Churchill is distinct not only from Palladio but from other contemporaneous Wittkowerian, Neo-Palladian projects in that it operates principally in plan rather than elevation. Morever, although a symmetry seems to control the plan, particularly in the great court, it is in fact incomplete; it breaks down in the interior courtyard with the library and multipurpose buildings, which are not only asymmetrical themselves, but also placed asymmetrically within the scheme. Even the seemingly symmetrical is in fact slightly out of sync: the two principal walkways bisecting the great court do not meet directly at the center of the courtyard but instead arrive just slightly off-center, a slip in the otherwise symmetrical, axial plan. More broadly, symmetry at Churchill was put in the service of a very different ideological goal than it had been for the Neo-Palladians. Rather than operating as any kind of idealizing or historicizing impulse, it instead became a means to distill the core attributes of the courtyard type into a pure form, to reduce the courtyard model to its essence. For example, the idiosyncratic outer walls of a typical Cambridge college that must respond to existing structures or site constraints are here, in the absence of any context, made rectilinear; the "quadrangle," more often than not a five- or six-sided shape, with randomly angled sides of uneven lengths, is taken to its logical endpoint of a perfect square; the usually erratic paths across the courtyard are now straightened and evenly spaced. Symmetry, then, as employed at Churchill College, abstracts and "corrects" the typical features of the Cambridge college. This idea is demonstrated most clearly in a drawing in which the Churchill plan is overlaid onto plans of the historic Cambridge colleges Downing and Pembroke; the irregularities and idiosyncrasies of the extant colleges are highlighted against the regular geometry of the Churchill plan (fig. 41).[36]

This desire to abstract the core principles of the courtyard, evidenced in the exaggerated scale and regularized form of the overall quadrangle, appear elsewhere in the project as well, in some instances through attributes that at first appear to violate key tenets of Cambridge tradition. The freestanding structures in the middle of the courtyard, for example, run counter to the longstanding Cambridge tradition of leaving the courtyards open, as seen in the image of Trinity College that Stirling pairs with Churchill in his "'Functional Tradition' and Expression" article (fig. 42). Each of the other three finalists' schemes respect this tradition by placing all rooms (both the dormitories and the public programs) in sequence surrounding the court, or as another "wall" to frame a new courtyard. But these illicit buildings within the courtyard are a key aspect in Stirling and Gowan's reinterpretation of the Cambridge college. First, they break down the great court into a series of smaller interstitial spaces—essentially smaller courtyards—between the various buildings, bringing the scale of the spaces back into alignment with those of the traditional Cambridge college. In other words, they enable the simultaneous possibility for both the grand gesture of the great court, as well as the familiar

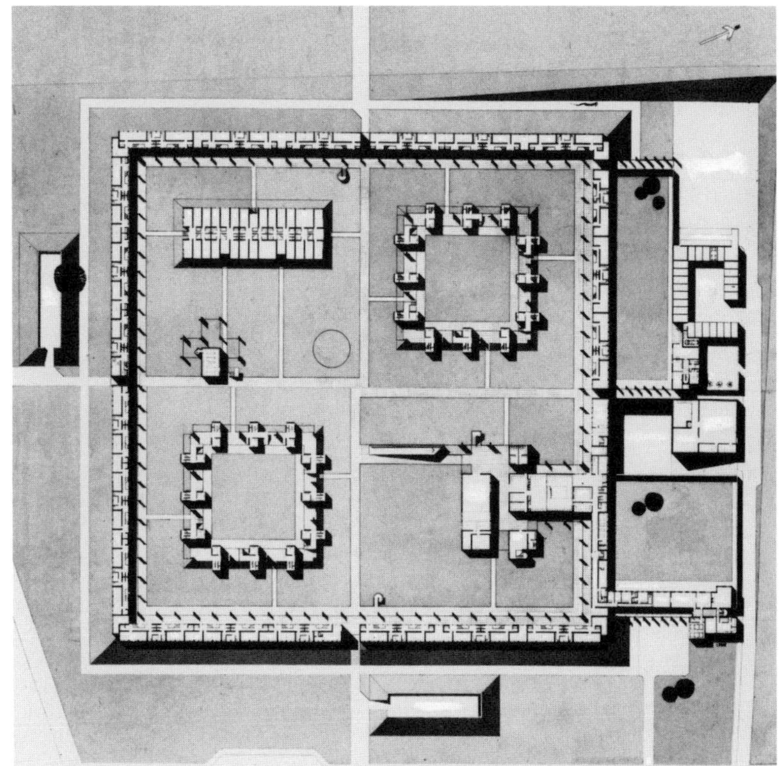

Figure 39
Stirling and Gowan, Churchill College. Ground-floor plan.

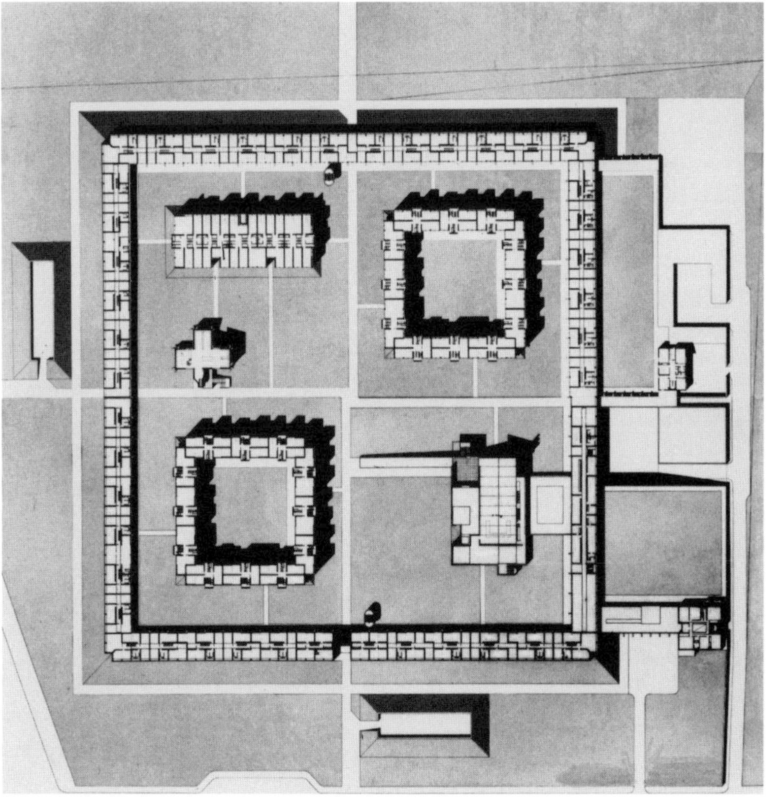

Figure 40
Stirling and Gowan, Churchill College. Second-floor plan.

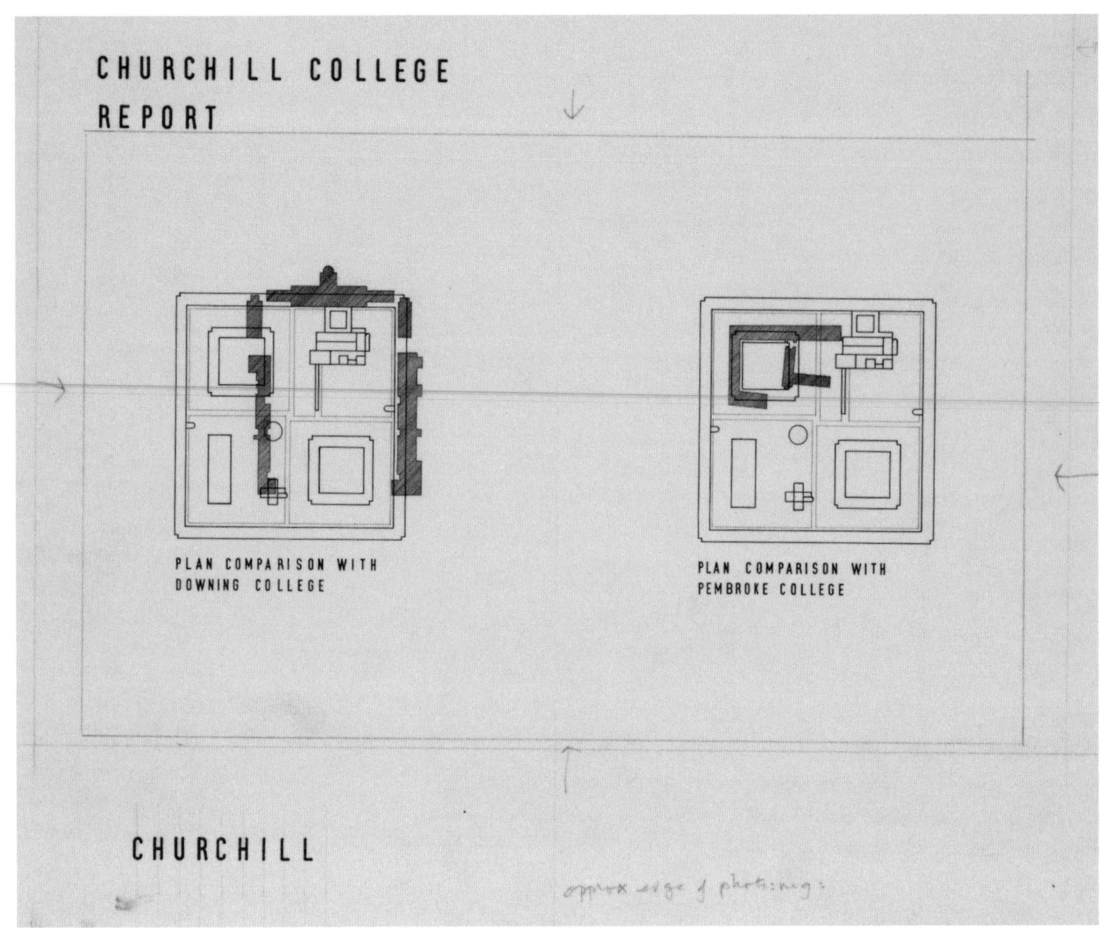

Figure 41
Stirling and Gowan, Churchill College Report. Plan comparisons of Churchill College with Downing and Pembroke Colleges reveal the former's massive scale and geometric regularity.

scale of the traditional court, preserving, at least to some degree, the genius loci of the courtyard idea. On a more pragmatic level, the freestanding buildings provide a clever solution to the phased construction mandated by the competition; the outer ring could be built first and would stand as complete, per the committee's requirements, and the inner buildings could then be built in sequence without disrupting the outer ring.

Most importantly, these inner buildings clarify programmatic distinctions in a way that the traditional courtyard typology does not. The shared public spaces, which are typically located in the "ring" of buildings around the courtyard, are now ejected into the middle of the courtyard. This programmatic separation is a foundational aspect of the scheme—evident from the first competition plan, with its four irregularly shaped buildings within the rigid exterior square—and offers a more "functional" answer to the programmatic differentiation of spaces within a traditional college. Each public program is housed in an independent building. Here perhaps was an answer to the call for a more "scientific inquiry" into the form a college should like—one that might in fact "improve the life and efficiency of Cambridge students"—

though its scientific merit was compromised by the inclusion of the additional dormitory buildings in the courtyard as well.[37] The model would have been more "pure" had only the public programs (library, multipurpose hall) populated the courtyard's interior with the private student rooms along the exterior ring, but the interior dormitory buildings were necessary for the phased construction mandate.

Two of the dormitory buildings inside the courtyard offer a more specific reinterpretation of the courtyard type. Both are miniature versions of the overall scheme—four-square buildings, with a courtyard at the center—though they are elevated on pilotis (allowing access to the courtyard at the center), unlike the outer ring, which rests on the earth podium. These two smaller courtyard buildings offer a novel alternative to the traditional courtyard circulation pattern; rather than moving from one adjacent court to another, movement is from a larger court to a smaller court-within-a-court. These interior courtyard buildings also invert the interiority of the overall courtyard, which now becomes "exterior" to these smaller courtyard buildings. Finally, and perhaps most importantly, they further reinforce the overall *idea* of courtyard—like a fractal, repeating the figure at multiple scales. Unlike the Richard Sheppard, Robson scheme, in which courtyards are aggregated in self-same form, Stirling and Gowan's project employs multiple scalar versions of the courtyard: the overall great court and the two inner courtyard buildings. There is another, even smaller "courtyard" (really just a few square feet) suggested by the static space at the very center of the scheme, created by the offset intersection of the two crisscrossing paths.

In aggregate, these formal manipulations of the courtyard—regularizing the plan, segregating functional programs into distinct buildings, exploding

Figure 42
James Stirling, "'The Functional Tradition' and Expression." Stirling juxtaposes his Churchill College scheme with the traditional courtyard model exemplified by Trinity College.

the scale of the overall courtyard and repeating the courtyard figure at various scales—distill the foundational ideas of the type. Enabled by the relatively unencumbered, rural site and ex novo construction, Stirling and Gowan's project becomes an idealized courtyard plan, what a Cambridge college *would* look like were it not for the burdens of site and accumulated history. Like Rowe's "ideal villa," their "ideal college" is an ahistorical formal conception. The project is removed from any specific historical referent yet undeniably references a general typological idea, what Quatremère de Quincy referred to as the "common root form"—that which has no particular formal manifestation, though it is indebted to any number of previous forms.[38]

This understanding of type, though it relies on past examples, in fact *dehistoricizes* historical precedent. The symmetrical, enclosed, elevated form of Churchill College is immediately recognizable yet historically indeterminate. One of Bloom's strategies—what he termed "Daemonization"—describes a way of operating in which the "later poet" looks back to the work of the "parent poet" for meaning that extends beyond the specifics of the original work of art. In other words, the later poet attempts to "generalize away the uniqueness of the earlier work."[39] At Churchill, Stirling and Gowan indeed generalize away the uniqueness of past examples—stripping the historical model of its exigencies, exaggerating its characteristics to generate a kind of hyperbole that becomes a generic condition, an "ideogram" representing all courtyard buildings. Rather than providing another iteration of the type, Stirling and Gowan probe more deeply into its history and its general conditions.

REGIONALISM AS A FUNCTIONAL VERNACULAR

Stirling would later recollect that "in the early fifties I developed an interest in all things vernacular from the very small—farms, barns and village housing—to the very large—warehouses, industrial buildings, engineering structures."[40] This interest in regional and anonymous forms was first elucidated in his "Regionalism and Modern Architecture" essay, published in the *Architects Yearbook* in 1957, which features images of anonymous, vernacular buildings—"anything of any period which is unselfconscious and usually anonymous." A large portion of Stirling's article is composed of his own early 1950s photographs: of the English countryside (oast houses, Martello towers, and kilns); of early brick industrial warehouses in Liverpool; of student projects from the Architectural Association that incorporate these regionalist impulses; and of two projects by Alvar Aalto.[41] Also included in the article are a photograph of a model and drawings of Stirling's House near Liverpool of 1954, with pitched roofs and thick masonry walls evoking regional precedents (figs. 43, 44).

Published less than two years before his Churchill project, Stirling's article demonstrates his growing fascination with vernacular architecture. Certainly a number of his projects in the early 1950s demonstrate this interest as well, not least among them Ham Common and its explicit reference to Le Corbusier's own exploration of a more "regional" vocabulary at Maisons Jaoul. Missing from the regionalism article is the most explicitly regional of Stirling's projects from this era: the Village Housing project of 1955 (fig. 45).[42] Of all his projects of the mid-1950s, perhaps the entirety of his career, the Village Housing scheme appears the most aberrant (which might explain its absence from the article)—a project whose seemingly simplistic formal and material language of pitched roofs and load-bearing masonry construction was aligned with local, anonymous architecture in England, and difficult to reconcile as the work of a young modernist. To add to this incongruity, the scheme was presented at the final meeting of the Congrès International d'Architecture Moderne (CIAM), the most important organization of the prewar modern movement, in Dubrovnik in 1956.[43]

Although it features local materials and primitive construction techniques, the project also demonstrates Stirling's interest in creating a systematic building approach in a rural environment and to some degree represents his critique of regionalism. The original CIAM "grille" was titled: "An Attempt at Order with Infinite Flexibility: Traditional Materials and Construction by

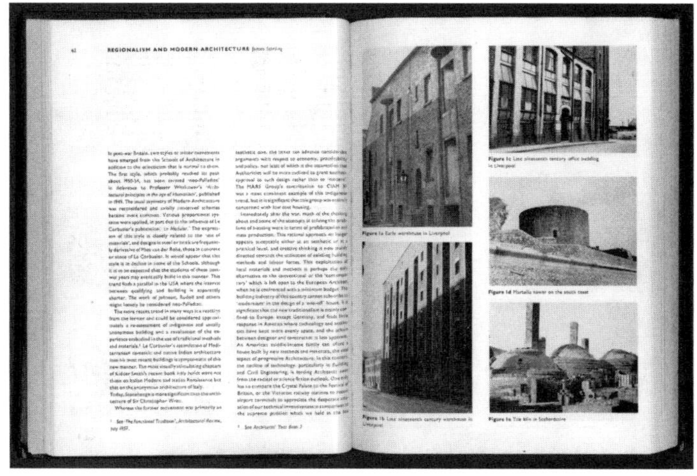

REGIONALISM AND MODERN ARCHITECTURE

Figure 43
James Stirling, "Regionalism and Modern Architecture," *Architects Yearbook*, 1957. The photographs of vernacular structures are Stirling's own.

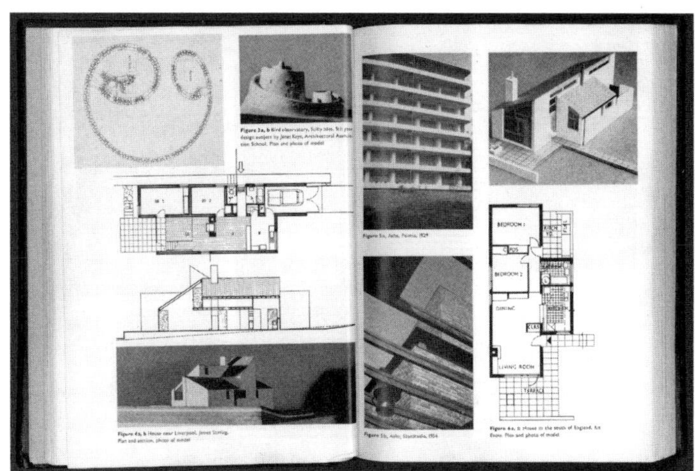

Figure 44
Stirling, "Regionalism and Modern Architecture." Stirling's House near Liverpool, with its monopitched roofs, is among the examples of "regional" architecture.

Local Unskilled Labor"; as the title makes explicit, it was meant to be built by unskilled workers using locally available materials: brick and stone for load-bearing walls; tile, thatch, and slate for roofs; and timber for rafters and floor joists. But as the title also makes clear, Stirling intended to establish some kind of "order," or system, within this regional construction system. The scheme proposes a basic structural frame—three parallel walls "of any load bearing material"—between which timber rafters are angled to create mono-pitched lean-to roofs. The design is based on two geometric modules, employed in both plan and section, as well as standardized roof angles.[44] As Stirling would later describe it, "There is perhaps more system although the building forms and their clustering are quite traditional, even folksy."[45] Even in this most regional work, then, we see his continuing effort to develop the modern ideals of standardization and rationalized building construction systems.

In fact, Stirling remained openly ambivalent about the idea of regionalism as it was understood in 1957. While it offered an antidote to the largely "aesthetic" Neo-Palladian work of the early fifties (which he found "in decline" even as his own Churchill scheme adopted some of its formal tropes) it also represented an admission of technological defeat.[46] A focus on traditional and vernacular materials was, in his mind, largely a result of the failures of rationalization and prefabrication in the immediate postwar years. He acknowledges, too, that often adoption of "indigenous and usually anonymous building" reflected a default condition that was more palatable to the local authorities. He begrudgingly admits that this new regionalism seemed the only alternative to the "conventional" or the "contemporary"—the latter a code word for the watered-down British modernism epitomized by the Festival of Britain of 1951. He questions the validity of this "old world" regionalism, "exploiting, and contorting, traditional ways and means" while the "New World" (America) continues "inventing techniques and developing the appropriate expression of the modern attitude."[47]

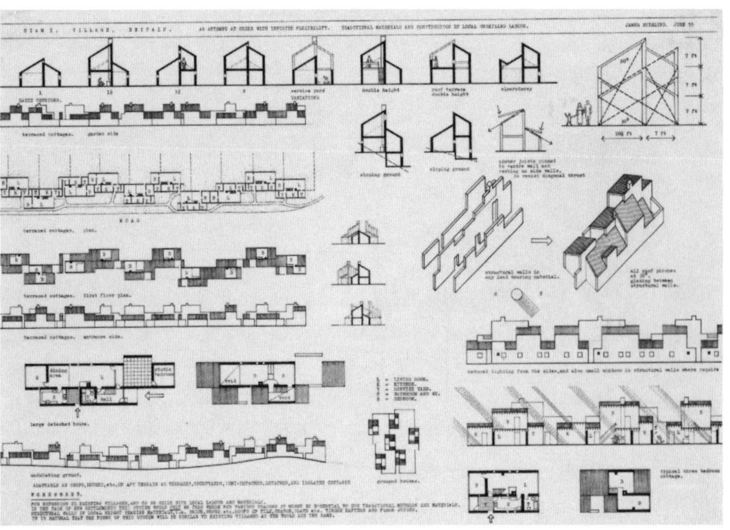

Figure 45
James Stirling, "An Attempt at Order with Infinite Flexibility: Traditional Materials and Construction by Local Unskilled Labor," Village Housing for CIAM 10, 1955.

Stirling's reluctant endorsement of this "new" regionalism was also inflected by a complex situation in which it might be seen to represent the lesser of a number of stylistic evils. He distances it from its immediate postwar antecedents, particularly the New Empiricism of the late 1940s—one of the most important, or at least widely discussed, of Britain's postwar responses to modernism, which espoused Swedish modernism as a means to bring back the "cosiness that we human beings are so dependent upon."[48] Stirling writes that "Swedish architecture has surprisingly little influence on this new movement" (a followup to his more famous retort, "William Morris was a Swede!" reflecting his exasperation with the New Empiricist craze).[49] This distinction was more than simply a matter of taste; it represented what Stirling saw as a fundamental difference between this "new" regionalism and earlier postwar iterations, including not only New Empiricism but also Lewis Mumford's Bay Region Style of the late 1940s, a "native and humane form of modernism" that made an "effort to humanise the aesthetic expression of functionalism," or even Le Corbusier's "regional" work of the 1930s and 1940s, such as Errazuris, or his postwar "primitive," work such as the Maisons Jaoul. All of these earlier regionalisms had reacted *against* functionalism. This "new" regionalism, however—or at least Stirling's version of it—intentionally *recuperated* functionalism by locating it within these anonymous, vernacular buildings: Stirling writes of the warehouses and farmhouses featured in his "Regionalism" article that the "outside appearance of these buildings is an efficient expression of their specific function."[50] This new, "harder" regionalism attempted to articulate a regionalism based not on aesthetics (at least not on the "cozy" and "softer" aesthetic of Swedish modernism) but on the principles of the modern movement.

Stirling further develops this connection between functionalism and vernacular buildings in his "Functional Tradition" essay of 1960, published three years after his "Regionalism" essay and following immediately on the heels of the Churchill College competition. In fact, the term regionalism no longer appears in the essay at all: instead he describes "anonymous" buildings that "express" their functions as part of "The Functional Tradition"—an explicit reference (as the quotes in his title make evident) to the "Functional Tradition" article that occupied the entire July 1957 issue of the *Architectural Review,* and which was later published as a book by J. M. Richards.[51] In this Functional Tradition issue, the editors at the *Architectural Review* argue that functionalism was not the property of the modern movement but rather a part of a larger history. Photographs of eighteenth- and nineteenth-century industrial buildings (remarkably similar to the buildings that Stirling uses to illustrate his "Regionalism" essay of the same year) are organized into categories, including warehouses, docks, factories, water mills, and oast houses, and interlaced with short descriptions meant to demonstrate that the "functional tradition is as old as the styles" and that this industrial vernacular is resolutely "modern."[52] Though Stirling admits to finding the selection of buildings in the article "perhaps a little narrow, faintly Georgian, and too nearly confined to early industrialism," he nevertheless agrees that these industrial buildings have merit and relevance for the contemporary architect. "They are usually composed of direct and undecorated volumes evolved from building usage." Although they predate the official "beginning" of modernism, they are, in Stirling's words, "peculiarly modern."[53]

Not only did the Functional Tradition expand earlier notions of regionalism, it radically repositioned functionalism by distancing it both chronologically and conceptually from the avant-garde of the 1920s and 1930s and placing it somewhat sacrilegiously in the realm of anonymous building. This reevaluation of functionalism reflected a larger questioning of its history and lineage at the time—articulated more broadly in Edward Robert de Zurko's *Origins of Functionalist Theory,* also of 1957, in which he ascribes to functionalism an even "deeper" history, tracing it back to the ancient Greeks.[54] As early as 1947 Colin Rowe exposed the pseudoscientific fallacy of functionalism's claims: "Functionalism was, perhaps, a highly Positivistic attempt to reassert a scientific aesthetic which might possess the objective value of the old, and ultimately Platonic-Aristotelian critique."[55] Functionalism's allegedly empirical status was now up for critique—to the extent that it had never been accepted unquestionably—exposed as a value system arguably no different than classicism. In short, functionalism was in crisis, a crisis that could perhaps be addressed through an investigation of the qualities embodied in regional, anonymous architecture.

For Stirling, the imagery of the Functional Tradition was particularly resonant given his own interest in vernacular structures, documented through his extensive photography and his personal biography; he would later recall visiting his father on the docks in Liverpool and admiring their "vernacular monumental" architecture.[56] He had been photographing the docks since his student days, always drawn to their muscular, straightforward forms—recall the images of the Liverpool docks pasted to the back of his thesis project. Within his archive remains a disproportionate number of photographs of the docks taken throughout his career, in particular a series from the early 1960s; he even saved the permit he obtained on June 9, 1961, granting permission "to take photographs and/or make sketches on the Mersey docks in Liverpool."[57]

Stirling's Village Housing and House near Liverpool were clearly "regional" projects in their informal language and "primitive" construction materials. The monumental, symmetrical, frankly heroic Churchill College, however, seems a more difficult project to reconcile as "regional," particularly given the seemingly obvious Neo-Palladian tendencies—the very "movement" that Stirling opposed to this new regionalism. Churchill was constructed of precast concrete struts rather than brick, thatched roofs or rough masonry. Nevertheless, it is arguably his most "regional" work" because it demonstrates a more fundamental understanding of the vernacular as embodying functional principles. In "'Functional Tradition' and Expression" Stirling compares Churchill College to medieval earthworks and fortifications—truly "anonymous" buildings whose qualities (enclosure, protection, etc.) he finds "functional" and applicable to his own work. Churchill reflects an expanded understanding of regionalism that emphasizes its functional qualities rather than any aesthetic or material language. Francesco Passanti's analysis of Le Corbusier's 1920s work as "regional" is here instructive: Passanti stresses the importance of the vernacular as an open model—unlike classicism—which is connected to the collective identity of a society.[58] Stirling and Gowan's use of the courtyard type offered a "deeper" connection to the vernacular than had they simply imitated the formal vocabulary of the Trinity towers. Stirling's notion of regionalism at Churchill demonstrated a connection to a "collective identity" rather than superficial imitations of local materials or styles.

In his "Regionalism" essay, Stirling includes a lengthy quote from W. R. Lethaby, who writes of the "modern" way of designing as allied with a scientific, analytical approach, rather than a poetic sensibility, and in which farmhouses and cottages are incorporated not as "flavours" but as "things themselves." The Functional Tradition, as an expansion of the regionalism discourse, gave Stirling the tools with which to cull through history and see "things themselves"—whether it was the "high" architecture of a Cambridge college or a "low" building such as a Liverpool warehouse. Stirling writes: "If folk architecture is to re-vitalize the movement, it will first be necessary to determine what it is that is modern in modern architecture."[59] The "economy" and "practicability" of anonymous, vernacular buildings offered, potentially, a way to determine exactly what was "modern in modern architecture." The consideration of these buildings as an "efficient expression of their particular function" suggested an opportunity to bypass stylistic concerns altogether, to investigate the idea of function as an "ideal" before it was co-opted as an "ism." Moreover, unlike the "continental innovations of the twenties and early thirties," which were "foreign" to Stirling's own experience and therefore "no longer valid in our present situation," a regional British architecture of practical, anonymous buildings seemed both functionally and geographically resonant.

THE ENGLISHNESS OF CHURCHILL COLLEGE

In his notebook from the early 1950s, Stirling writes: "Frequently I wake in the morning and consider how it is that I can be an architect and an Englishman at the same time, particularly a modern architect. Since the crystallization of the modern movement around 1920—Britain has not produced one single masterpiece and it must be practically the only European country which has not produced a 'great man.'"[60] In his "Regionalism" article Stirling is openly critical of the current situation in Britain, whose technology he finds lagging behind America's, and he laments the passing of the era of the Crystal Palace and the Victorian railway stations, symbols of Britain at its technological prime. He writes of the era of Voysey and Mackintosh, "when we last held the initiative in Europe."[61] As Murray Fraser and Joe Kerr have shown, British postwar architects had a "special relationship" with America, one in which American influence became the most significant factor in developing a more "modernized and globalized perspective."[62]

British architects battled inferiority in relation to continental Europe as well as America. A galvanizing issue among the younger generation of postwar architects was the recognition that the modern movement had been generated elsewhere—it was an imported phenomenon. This issue seemed particularly pertinent in the postwar years, as there was perhaps a chance to remedy Britain's earlier "outsider" status. Though England wasn't responsible for generating the original modern movement, perhaps it could become a key player in defining a new postwar modernism. This was an urgent issue for Stirling, for whom the desire to respond to and incorporate his own British traditions cannot be underestimated. He wasn't interested simply in the vernacular, then, but in a *British* vernacular. The "region" under consideration, in this sense, was the nation.

This search for a uniquely British architectural language was an undercurrent if not a dominating factor in much of the writings and movements of the postwar. Saxl and Wittkower's *British Art and the Mediterranean* and Richardson's *Monumental Classic Architecture in Britain and Ireland,* as well as the various regionalist movements of the mid-1940s—the "picturesque" (especially in its later incarnation as "Townscape") and the "contemporary style" that emerged from the Festival of Britain and even Banham's New Brutalism—can all be seen in this nationalistic vein. Beginning in 1955, Pevsner's well-known radio series "The Englishness of English Art" explored the "geography of art" and how "national character" was expressed. Continuing in this tradition, a significant part of the motivation behind and appeal of the Functional Tradition was its insistence on Britain as the source of the "original" functional moment. As Stirling's above remark makes clear, there was also a heavy anti-American foundation to the "regionalism as nationalism" discourse, though Stirling's own relationship with America was always complex—a mix of envy, admiration, and antipathy.[63]

But if nationalism was an important aspect of both artistic and architectural inquiry in the 1950s, an investigation into the *local* was equally significant. In his 1955 "Garches to Jaoul" essay Stirling describes Le Corbusier, "frequently accused of being 'internationalist,'" as in fact the "most regional of architects," not because of his use of primitive materials or construction methods, but as a result of his consideration of buildings in relation to their sites: "The difference between the cities of Paris and Marseilles is precisely the difference between the Pavillon Suisse and the Unité d'Habitation."[64] The Maisons Jaoul, continuing this line of reasoning, was "surprising" for its location "within half a mile of the Champs Elysees," and in his black notebook he writes that at Jaoul, for the "first time," he saw "Corb be unregional."[65] With their "arty-crafty" look and "handmade" quality they represented "south and peasant" rather than Paris; in other words, their vocabulary was out of sync with the specific "regional" context.[66]

To see Le Corbusier as a "regional" architect was, of course, nothing new, but Stirling's reasoning as to why he was the "most regional of architects"—because of his understanding of the specificity of place rather than his use of materials—coupled with the fact that he saw the Pavillon Suisse and the

Unité as regional and the Maisons Jaoul as "unregional" are both noteworthy. It was also significant, at least for Stirling, that Le Corbusier, unlike most of the other modern "masters," including Mies and Gropius, had not immigrated to the United States during the war. Since so much of the debate around regionalism centered on the United States vs. Europe, the fact that Le Corbusier was still living in Europe and that he was looking to European examples for this new "regionalism" made him exemplary to young architects. Stirling wrote: "Significantly, the only major architects who are not now resident in the U.S.A.—Le Corbusier and Alvar Aalto—are, of course, the innovators."[67] Le Corbusier legitimized the practice of referencing the vernacular not only because of his stature and sheer formal inventiveness, but also because of his status as a European, as a "local" figure himself.

Stirling's remarks on Le Corbusier as a regional architect mark a subtle but significant shift in Stirling's understanding of regionalism more broadly. By removing an association with local materials or traditional building practices Stirling recenters the debate on the value of place and context—but with a sensibility about general "qualities," not local aesthetics or materials. In this understanding of regionalism as an idea connected to a specific place, Churchill College was exemplary in its indebtedness to the traditions of Cambridge, and in particular the courtyard type. This connection to place wasn't about a facile contextualism or even an easy relationship with the immediate landscape—embedding a project into the landscape, for example, as Frank Lloyd Wright might do. Churchill was deliberately elevated from the ground, seemingly shut out from its surroundings. And yet this attitude was taken precisely from the existing colleges at Cambridge. Churchill then, which had a seeming unease, even hostility, relative to its context—a hostility that had prompted the assessors to accuse it of running counter to the Cambridge genius loci—was arguably more regional in its desire to abstract and idealize the Cambridge courtyard model than was Ham Common, which incorporated a visual language based on a previous Le Corbusier project from another location.

Also noteworthy in this context is Stirling and Gowan's decision to build Churchill out of masonry instead of brick. The associations of the red-brick university, which they would confront head-on the same year at Leicester, are here kept at bay in favor of a material language more in keeping with the university context. While not regional in the sense of a locally sourced material, the choice of stone cladding takes on regional associations in relation to the specific material vocabulary of Cambridge colleges. Here the definition of regionalism becomes slightly slippery, and its meaning veers perhaps perilously close to contextualism, but these were precisely the complexities and even the contradictions that Stirling not only embraced but seemed to want to embody in his architecture. Frampton wrote that Stirling couldn't bring himself to use brick at Churchill because of its "symbolic limitations." "Where the vernacular brick tradition could well serve for residential accommodation, it could not be brought, at this stage of Stirling's career, to express the honorific status of a Cambridge College."[68] But with the design of Leicester, Stirling was clearly able to understand the more "honorific" symbolic status of brick (though Leicester, unlike Cambridge, was in fact a red-brick university). The fact that Stirling was willing to use concrete—an even less "honorific" structure than brick—is also telling. The choice of materials was less about the inappropriateness of brick than it was about the regional appropriateness of stone.

THINKING THROUGH HISTORY

One of the most remarkable aspects of Stirling's "'Functional Tradition' and Expression" essay is the ease and seemingly unselfconscious manner in which he demarcates a series of historical sources for his early projects. Churchill in particular is connected with a range of precedents taken from a wide swath of architectural history. He cites Le Corbusier's La Tourette (1960) as a model of an "internal environment, private, enclosed and protected" and one that "grammatically explains a pattern of cellular repetitive spaces."[69] He notes the "juxtaposition of towers and horizontally stressed laboratories" in Louis Kahn's Richards Medical Building (1961).[70] It is easy to find formal traces of these precedents at Churchill, and indeed they seem to explain many of Stirling and Gowan's design decisions. Echoes of La Tourette are evident in Churchill's enclosed courtyard, with its series of freestanding sculptural buildings, as well as in the exterior elevation, where single dormitory rooms are strung out in horizontal rows to create a monolithic exterior wall (figs. 46, 47). The interior dormitory blocks at Churchill bear a clear relation to Kahn's laboratory building with their vertical stacks of studios and service towers, mixture of horizontal and vertical elements, and variegated roofline (figs. 48, 49).

While these references to Le Corbusier and Kahn were not surprising in light of Stirling's modern allegiances—perhaps they were even predictable—and while we might be tempted to see Churchill College simply as an abstraction of the traditional Cambridge courtyard overlaid with select modern examples, Stirling's essay yields more surprising comparisons than the predictable citations of the two masters' latest works. Stirling in fact places more emphasis on the *non*-modern references at play. He includes a drawing of a motte-and-bailey system (taken from *Castles of the Western World,* published by Armin Tuulse in 1948) typical of English fortress architecture from the eleventh century onward (fig. 50). Its characteristic feature is a mounded hill, or "motte," connected to a lower mound, or "bailey," ringed by a stockade or palisade and with a series of freestanding buildings inside. As well, he includes images of a Lisbon fortress, also from Tuulse's book, photographs of a fortified city, and a drawing of Blenheim Palace, Churchill's ancestral home. Tellingly, there are no images of either Richards Medical Building or La Tourette, but multiple images of medieval fortifications and earthworks.

Stirling's fascination with castle architecture was certainly an extension of his regionalist explorations and was undoubtedly influenced by Gowan, who maintained an interest in castle forms and architecture throughout his career.

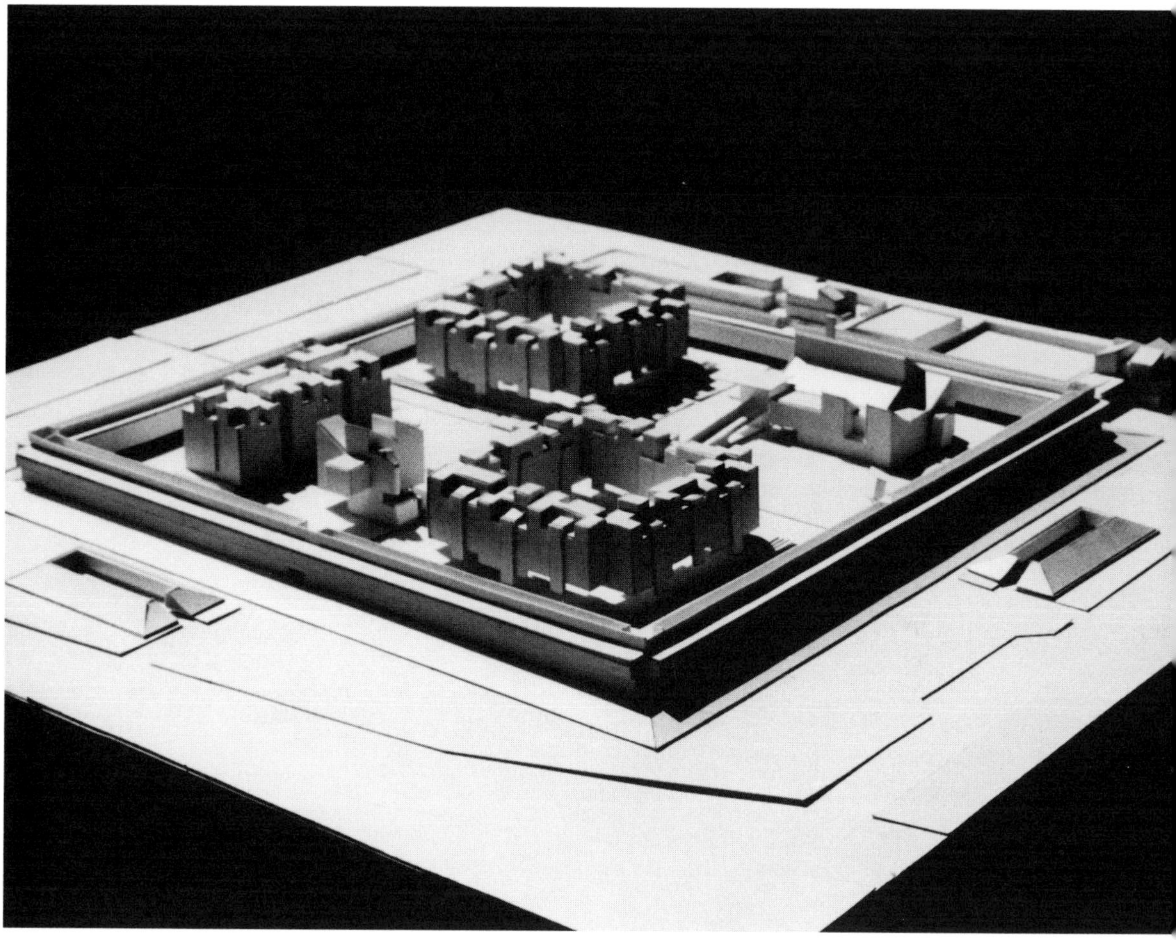

Figure 46
Stirling and Gowan, Churchill College. Model.

Figure 47
Le Corbusier, Dominican Monastery of La Tourette, France, 1960. Model.

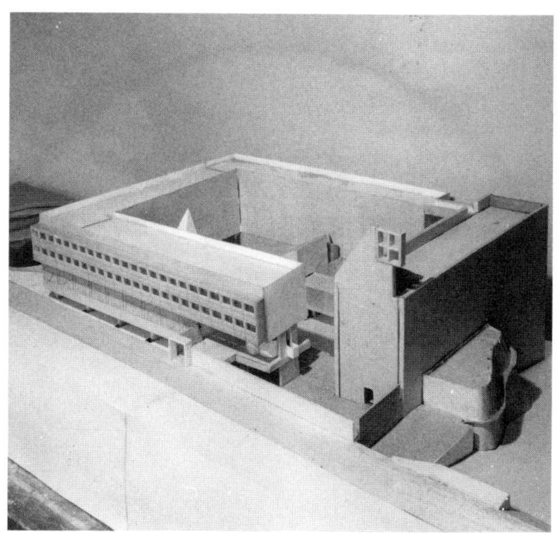

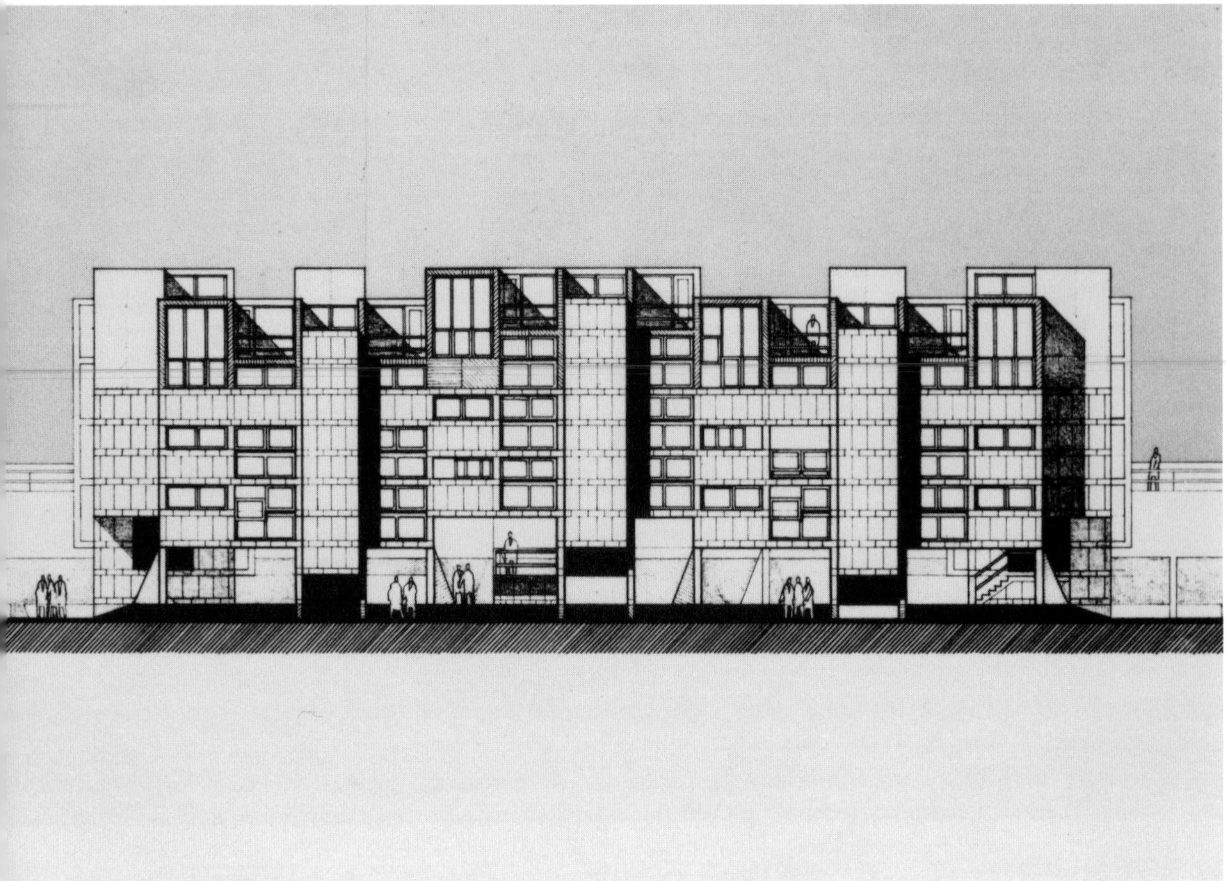

Figure 48
Stirling and Gowan, Churchill College. Elevation of interior dormitory building.

Figure 49
Louis Kahn, Richards Medical Building, Philadelphia, 1961. Elevation.

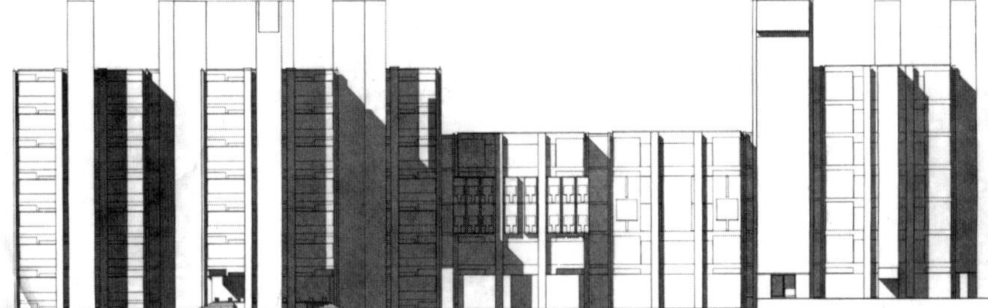

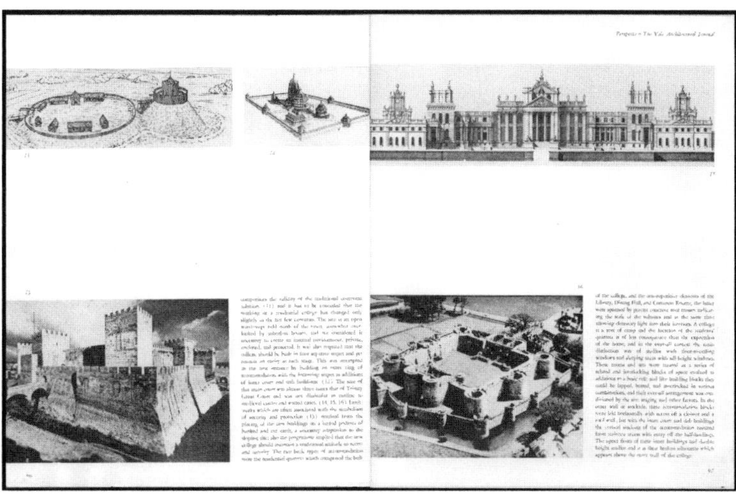

Figure 50
Stirling, "'The Functional Tradition' and Expression." Stirling cites medieval fortresses, motte-and-bailey castles, and Blenheim Palace (Winston Churchill's ancestral home) among the influences on his Churchill scheme.

In a 1959 lecture Stirling listed more castle "sources" for Churchill, each pertaining to a key element of Churchill: the wall (Framlingham), the internal buildings (Castle Acre, Orford Castle Keep), and the mound (Thetford).[71] This interest in castle architecture was shared if not inherited from Kahn, who also maintained books on castles in his library and was particularly fascinated with the "thick walls" of traditional stone castles.[72] Like Kahn, Stirling was interested in the materiality and weight of these traditional structures. Unlike Kahn, however, Stirling's revisioning of castle architecture didn't attempt to re-create the sense of solidity and thickness through the use of folded corners or trompe l'oeil—consider Kahn's First Unitarian Church, the design of which was also begun in 1959, in which the form of the corner towers and simulated thick walls, as well as the more or less impenetrable exterior, are all drawn directly from the Scottish castle plans in Kahn's library. At Churchill, by contrast, Stirling abstracts a planning language—square court, interior buildings, etc.—deleting the corner towers altogether. For Stirling, the sense of protection comes instead from the earth mound and in the elevation of the entire project rather than from the simulated solidity of the corner towers and "thick" wall.

By including these various historical references, to Scottish and medieval castles in particular, Stirling extends the pedigree for Churchill College further into history—past Trinity College and certainly past Le Corbusier or Kahn. This willingness to look at a range of sources was a clear continuation of his self-described "eclecticism," evident from his early student days, in which he passed through changing "obsessions," from Mackintosh and Hoffmann to Hawksmoor, Archer, and Vanbrugh, and later still to Butterfield, Street, and Scott.[73] It should also be remembered that Wittkower and Saxl's panhistoric *British Art and the Mediterranean,* with its sweeping look across architectural history, was, by Stirling's own admission, the most important text in his student years. But this desire to situate his work as part of an historical continuum, and, even more, the willingness to state those precedents openly, is something that bears greater investigation. Put more contentiously, was Churchill College an example of a "return of historicism," to use Pevsner's condemning phrase from his 1961 RIBA address?

In Pevsner's terms, this new historicism was characterized by architects looking not to the classical past but to the recent past, to "styles which had never previously been revived." Pevsner's litany of these various "neos" includes "neo-Liberty" (an idea codified and criticized by Pevsner's student Reyner Banham), "neo-Gaudi," "neo-de Stijl," and "neo-German Expressionism," and he traces their appearance in contemporary projects by Eero Saarinen, Claude Parent, and Vittorio Gregotti, among others. Even Stirling and Gowan make his list; their interior at Ham Common, with its "odd bits, ledges and chunks," recalled, Pevsner felt, the School of Amsterdam. Most of these new styles were invented by Pevsner, and he predictably criticizes the "revival" of these historical sources as "anti-rational" and as a reaction to the modern movement that began with Neo-Empiricism and a kind of "softening" of modernism in the late 1930s.[74]

Even if his position is reactionary in its defense of a frankly outdated notion of modernism as equivalent to the allegedly historically mute language of the International Style—a muteness that many others, including Stirling, had already come to see as a fallacy—Pevsner's article is significant in the context of a burgeoning historical consciousness during the postwar period. On the one hand, there was a growing interest in and professionalization of the architectural historian; the Society of Architectural Historians of Great Britain was founded in 1958, and the society published the first issue of *Architectural History* in 1958/9. On the other hand, there was an awareness

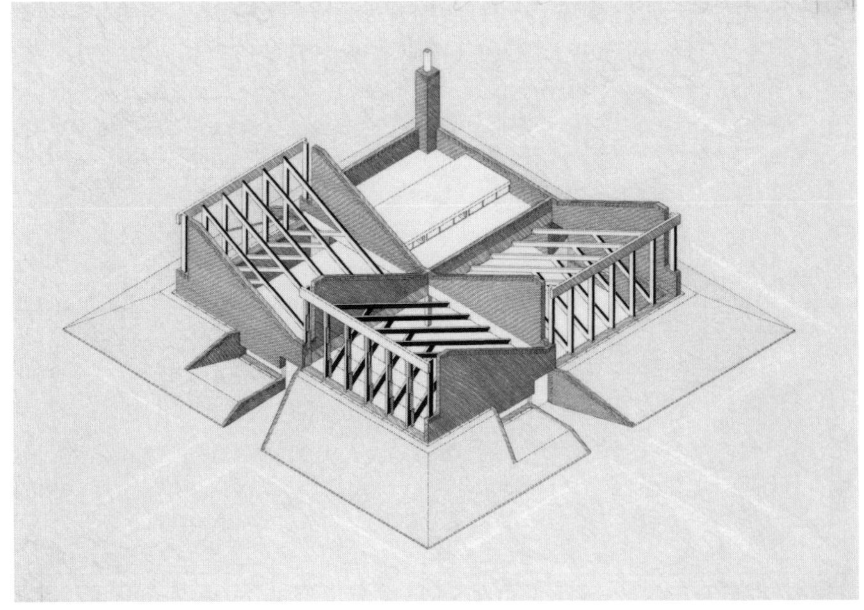

Figure 51
Stirling and Gowan, School Assembly Hall, Brunswick Park Primary School, Camberwell, London, 1959. With its four-square plan and sloped earth embankment, Camberwell miniaturizes the Churchill scheme.

and codification of modernism itself as history: Banham's *Theory and Design in the First Machine Age* was published in 1960. Wittkower and others had opened up new means to interpret history and modernism in tandem. And finally, though not insignificantly, modernism itself was literally becoming history—CIAM was disbanded in 1959.

Although we might be tempted to see Stirling as part of this neo-historicist group, since he clearly and openly elaborates historical sources at Churchill College—both recent and remote—his use of precedent is significantly and materially different from the one that Pevsner identifies in contemporary architectural production. Rather than employing "imitation" or "revivalism," as Pevsner characterized his various "neo" historical styles of the time, Stirling looks to history in search of modernist ideals. As his "'Functional Tradition' and Expression" makes clear, his catholic mining of historical sources was enabled precisely because he was looking for the "modern" qualities wherever and in whatever time period—from the "rational" layout of the traditional Cambridge college to the "functional" property of a sloped earth embankment in a medieval fortified city. Another way to say this is that he was able to sidestep aesthetics to arrive at principles; as Summerson once characterized the work of Viollet-le-Duc, so too Stirling was "man enough to *think his way through* the romantic attraction of style to a philosophic point of view."[75] By "thinking through" history, Stirling was able to translate its forms into a contemporary language. Just as the Ischian peasant towers serve as a model for Ronchamp the traditional Cambridge college is the basis for Churchill College; in both cases the "function they are serving has not changed."

Perhaps the best illustration of a developing attitude toward history was Stirling's willingness to see his *own* work as part of history. Although this strategy of self-quotation wouldn't come fully into play for another twenty years, at this early moment there were nevertheless the seeds of a fascination with folding his own architectural solutions into the available repository of architectural forms. Stirling and Gowan's plan for the Camberwell Primary School, completed in 1959 and designed almost exactly contemporaneously with Churchill, is a scaled-down version of the college (fig. 51). Like Churchill, the square plan is divided into four quadrants. And like Churchill, the project is ringed by a sloped earth embankment, which now rises up to the building on all four sides, and which is similarly cut away to provide entry. A series of single-sloping roofs that angle toward the center and spin around the four-square shape are further reminiscent of those in the library and multipurpose room at Churchill (fig. 52).

The Churchill and Camberwell pairing illustrate the beginnings of a more reflexive practice, one in which Stirling's own projects, or at least elements of them, were used and reused—something that would become a hallmark of his later work and would culminate in the Roma Interrotta project, which consists entirely of references to his own previous works. This willingness to revision himself followed from his willingness to revision others. It represented a continuation of the specific strategies of historical appropriation

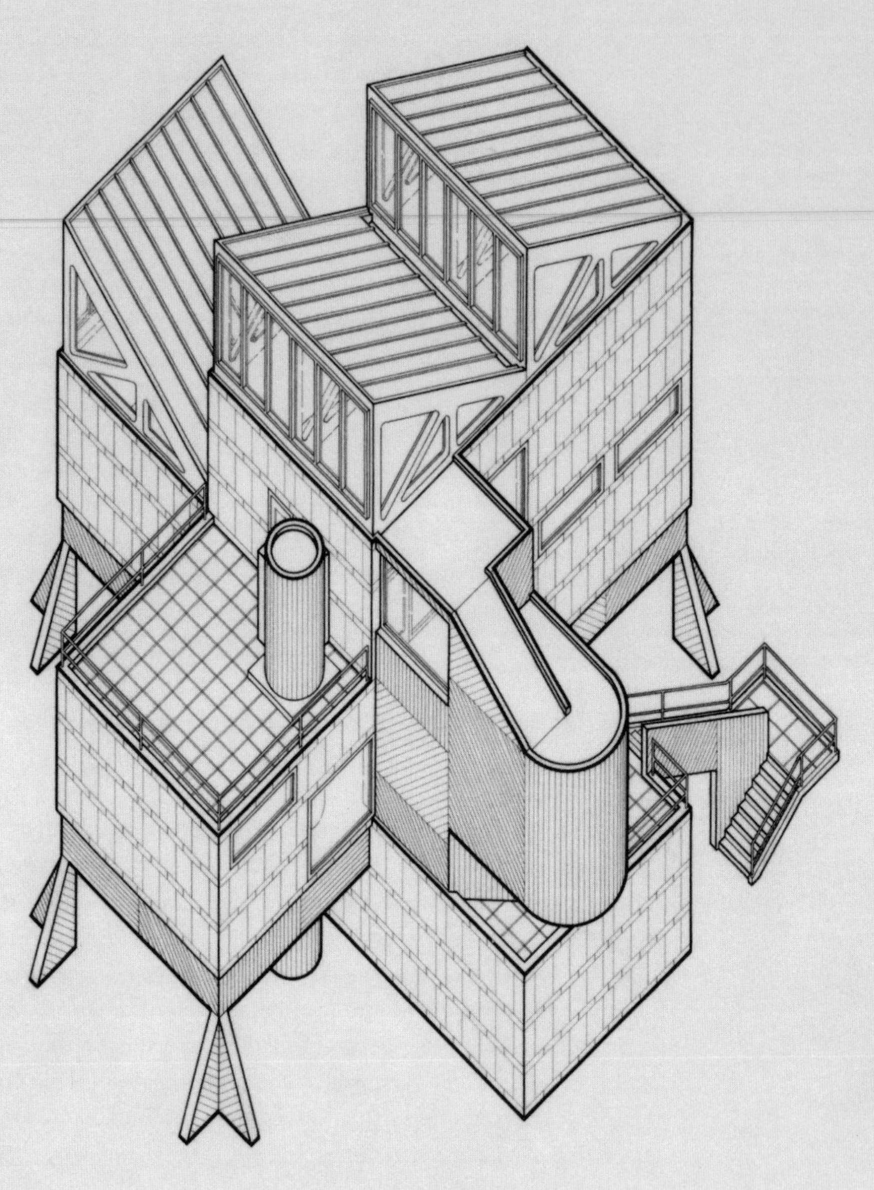

Figure 52
Stirling and Gowan, Churchill College. Axonometric of library building.

evident at Churchill—the willingness to isolate functional principles, to find its core tenets and ideas, to think through history as a set of ideas rather than styles. A natural extension of this approach was not only that all of history became available as a possible precedent, a source to be mined, but that his *own* work entered into the repertoire of sources.

Churchill College illustrates an understanding of history in which the precedent is no longer necessarily modern but in which the principles of modernism still hold fast as the lens through which to evaluate and ultimately reuse historical sources. For Stirling, this was the first project in which he employed this lamination of historical reference, an approach that was indebted to the regionalism and Functional Tradition discourses and their understanding of the past as embedded with modern ideals, but to which Stirling contributed his own interpretation by extending the paradigm beyond local vernacular forms to encapsulate—at least potentially—all of history. At Churchill College history was co-opted but also corrupted, layered into the project to define its own history. On the one hand, history became more deeply connected to place and culture—witness the interrogation of the Cambridge courtyard type at Churchill vs. the geographically displaced referent of Maisons Jaoul at Ham Common. On the other hand, the past was radically rethought and historical sources were mined for their "modern" principles—chief among them functionalism. In this way, the role of precedent could be understood in modern terms.

Rafael Moneo describes Churchill as the end of Stirling's youth, the "summing up of all previous phases."[76] For Moneo it represents a watershed moment, after which Stirling would enter a more mature phase, one that was principally an investigation of section. The subtext of his argument is that Churchill wasn't yet "fully" Stirling and that his unique contribution wasn't altogether formed. Churchill, however, was neither a beginning nor an end, but a continuation and development of Stirling's strategies of appropriation. It was at this moment that Stirling not only began to look to history more synthetically and widely, but also that he first "generalized away the uniqueness" of precedents to define an architecture that was both historically embedded and formally inventive. Stirling and Gowan received the commission for the Leicester Engineering Building just as they completed Churchill, and though the two projects could hardly be more formally dissimilar, the "discovery" of history and the abstraction and manipulation of historical sources evidenced at Churchill would become the driving formal imperative—rendered in more radical terms—at Leicester.

CHAPTER 3

AN "EXPRESSIVE" FUNCTIONALISM

LEICESTER ENGINEERING BUILDING (1963)

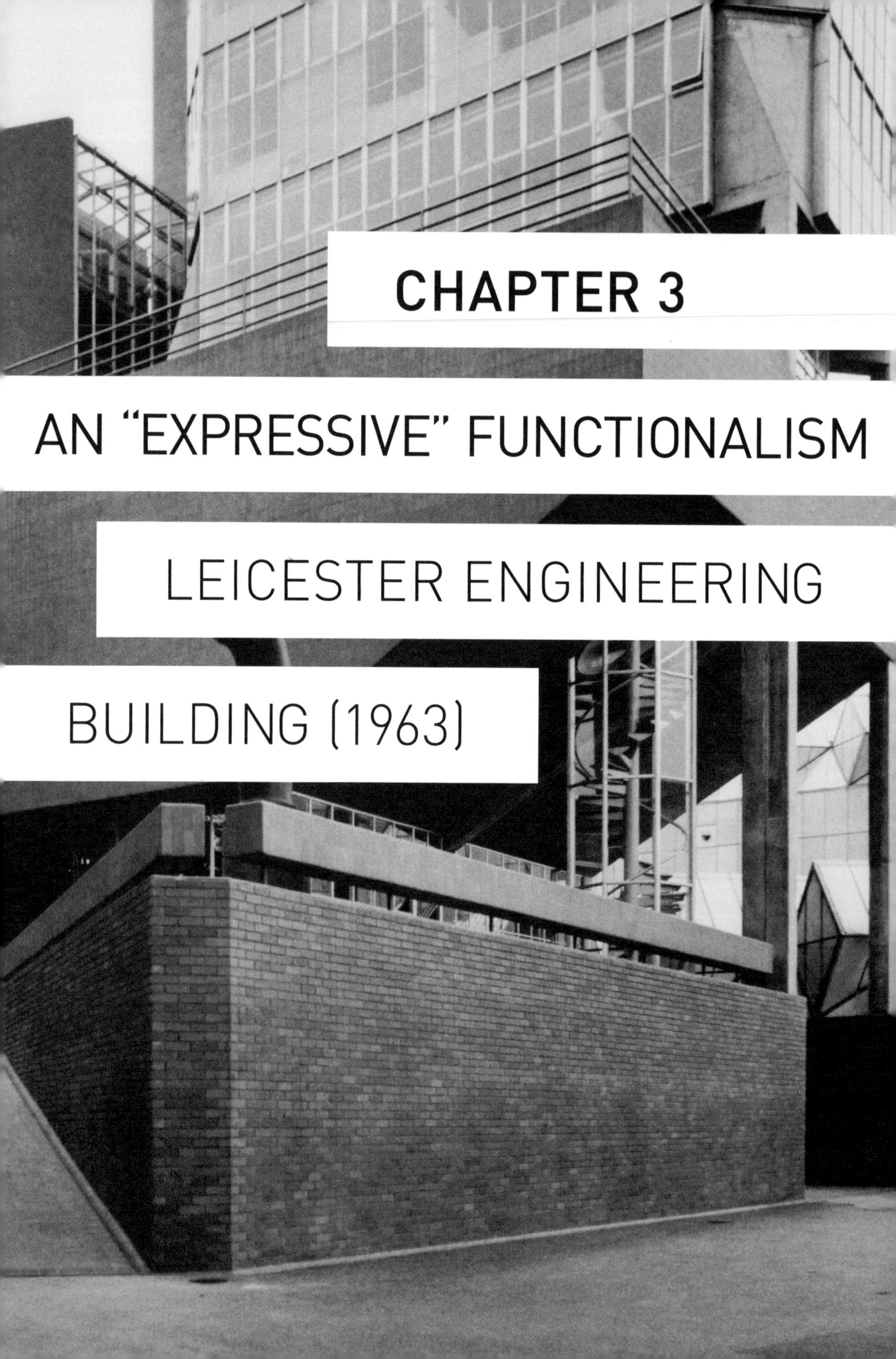

It's nearly impossible to overstate the seismic shift that the Leicester University Engineering Building defined, not only in Stirling's career but in architecture more broadly. Completed in 1963, the building seemed somehow to answer a question that no one knew was even being asked until the answer was upon them: What should postwar modern architecture look like? With its assemblage of red-tile towers and faceted, crystalline glass forms, the Leicester Engineering Building was unprecedented yet familiar (fig. 53). Reyner Banham insisted that it was the first building to approximate the "heroic" architecture of high modernism and that it was "inventing modern architecture all over again."[1] It was hailed by *Fortune* magazine as one of ten buildings that "point

Figure 53
Stirling and Gowan, Leicester University Engineering Building, England, 1963.

to the future," featured on the front page of the *Times* of London, visited by hundreds if not thousands of architecture enthusiasts, and covered in countless architectural publications both in England and elsewhere (Stirling admitted in 1965 that it had been "overdone in the glossies").[2] Its presence even sparked outrage over the mediocrity and banality of postwar British architecture until that point: as John Jacobus wrote in his review of the newly completed building, "Leicester is so complete and integral an architectural solution that at last one is consumed with a paradoxical sense of fury. Why have we been willing for decades to settle for less?"[3] The building also made Stirling and Gowan—particularly Stirling—an international sensation, though its completion effectively coincided with (and perhaps contributed to) the end of the pair's partnership.

There is no doubt that Leicester was groundbreaking—certainly it marked a dramatic shift from the symmetrical, monumental form of Churchill (though both projects were begun in 1959). Yet it was also part of a continuum that had begun with Stirling's earlier projects, reaching as far back as his thesis. In this chapter I aim not to diminish the formal inventiveness or significance of Leicester but to contextualize the mechanisms at work that enabled that invention. Like Ham Common and Churchill College, Leicester's novelty was derived from the past. Unlike these earlier projects, however, it openly referenced a much broader range of recognizable and specific quotations—most famously the Rusakov Workers' Club by Konstantin Melnikov (1929)—while employing strategies derived from art practices and linking more directly with the British Industrial vocabulary through a new material palette of red brick, tile, and patent glazing. As in his earlier works, Stirling was experimenting at Leicester with ways to abstract history in order to make it modern. Unique to Leicester, however, was the volumetric abstraction of historical forms into a "solidified space," Stirling's play with a more "expressive" language, and the development of a three-dimensional massing strategy in which various programmatic pieces were assembled in a kind of suspended equilibrium. As an emerging "strong" architect, Stirling makes a more definitive stance vis-à-vis history, embracing sources without apology and revisioning them into an entirely new form.

BREAKING THE BOX: THE "PARTICULATE APPROACH"

When the University of Leicester hired the relatively untested partnership of Stirling and Gowan in 1959, the university itself was something of a new kid on the block. Founded in 1921, it had broken away from University College London in 1957 to become an independent university. As part of its new status, the university hired Leslie Martin, then head of the architecture division of the London County Council, to design a master plan for the site, and it was Martin who recommended Stirling and Gowan. The site given to Stirling and Gowan was heavily restricted on every side—a road at the northwestern edge, and buildings lining two other sides; on one edge it fronted the expansive Victoria Park (fig. 54).

The program was complex: research and teaching laboratories, office space, lecture halls, staff rooms, and administration space. Despite this complexity, there were few architectural requirements or restrictions, at least in Stirling's mind—he would quip that their brief was indeed brief, as well as highly scientific: "With this particular building you would have needed a degree in about four subjects to have been able to dissect it."[4] In the "First Brief for Architects," dated August 16, 1959, the newly appointed head of the engineering department, E. W. Parks, laid out the overarching requirement: "There is only one essential concept which should be before the architects, and that is flexibility." An engineering building was, at its core, "not a static thing," and its use would change, "often at an alarming rate," he stated. "Anything which limits adaptability for the future is as far as possible to be avoided."[5] There were other requirements. One was to have northern light in the research laboratories. The brief also required a water tower, elevated at least 100 feet off the ground, to provide pressure for hydraulic experiments, and it was suggested that the offices have a view onto Victoria Park. The exceptions to the mandate for flexibility were the two lecture theaters, given that they

Figure 54
Stirling and Gowan, Leicester Engineering Building. Site plan. The tower block faces onto Victoria Park, while the workshop shed occupies the remainder of the site, with its diagonal roof "twisted" to the north.

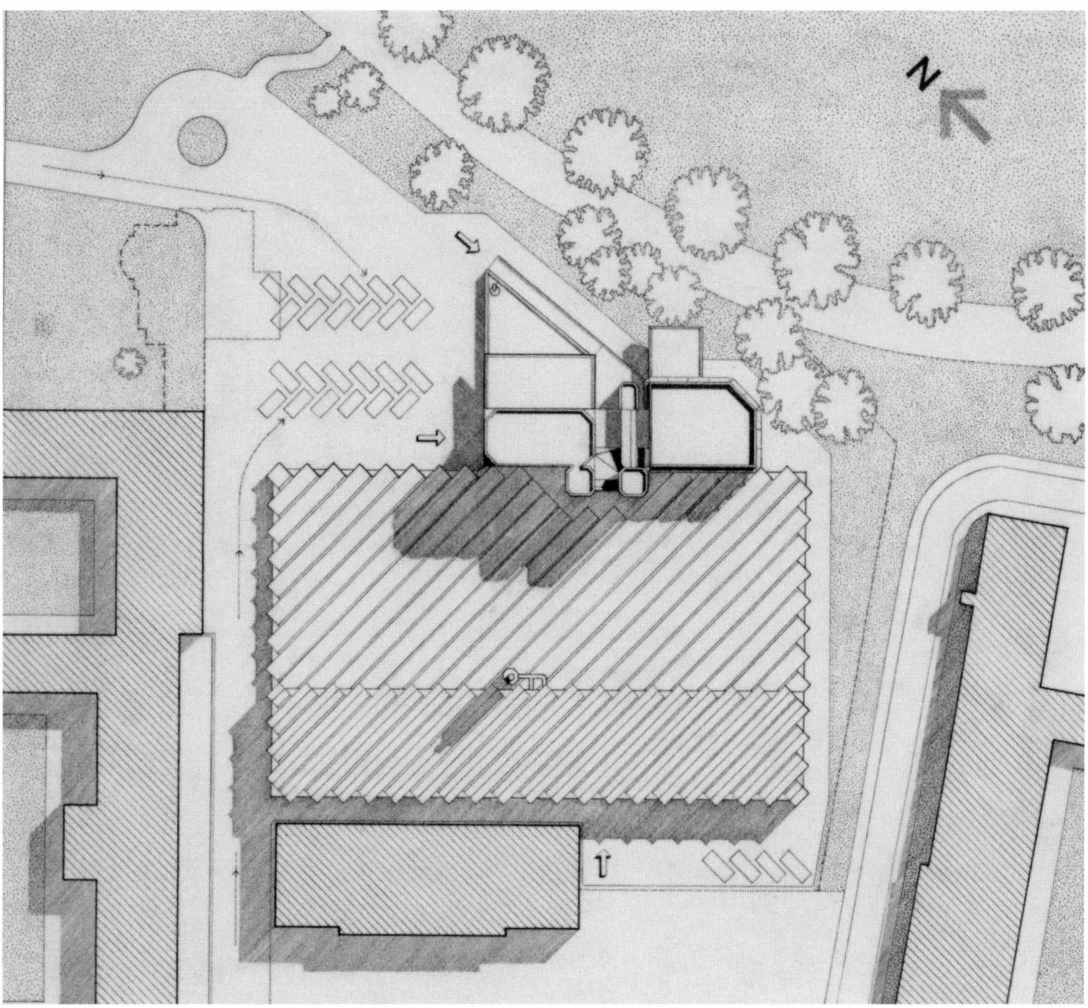

represented a program which, Parks acknowledged, "is not readily adaptable to other purposes." He requested a raked design, a profile he found desirable despite its "one-purpose role."[6]

As a solution to this complex yet cursory brief, Stirling and Gowan broke the building into two chunks: a low-slung workshop "shed" on the southwestern side of the site, and a tower complex on its northeastern end. The workshops blanket more than three-quarters of the site and take to heart Parks's mandate for flexibility: all partitions are able to be removed or repositioned. The workshops are covered with a faceted roof of plyglass—fiberglass sandwiched between clear glass—with an added aluminum sheet inserted into the assembly on the southern-facing portions to restrict light exposure. The striking glass prisms on the workshop roof—the signature visual element of the shed—are consistently explained by the architects in the most rational and functional of terms; the folded steel ribs run diagonally across the structure because

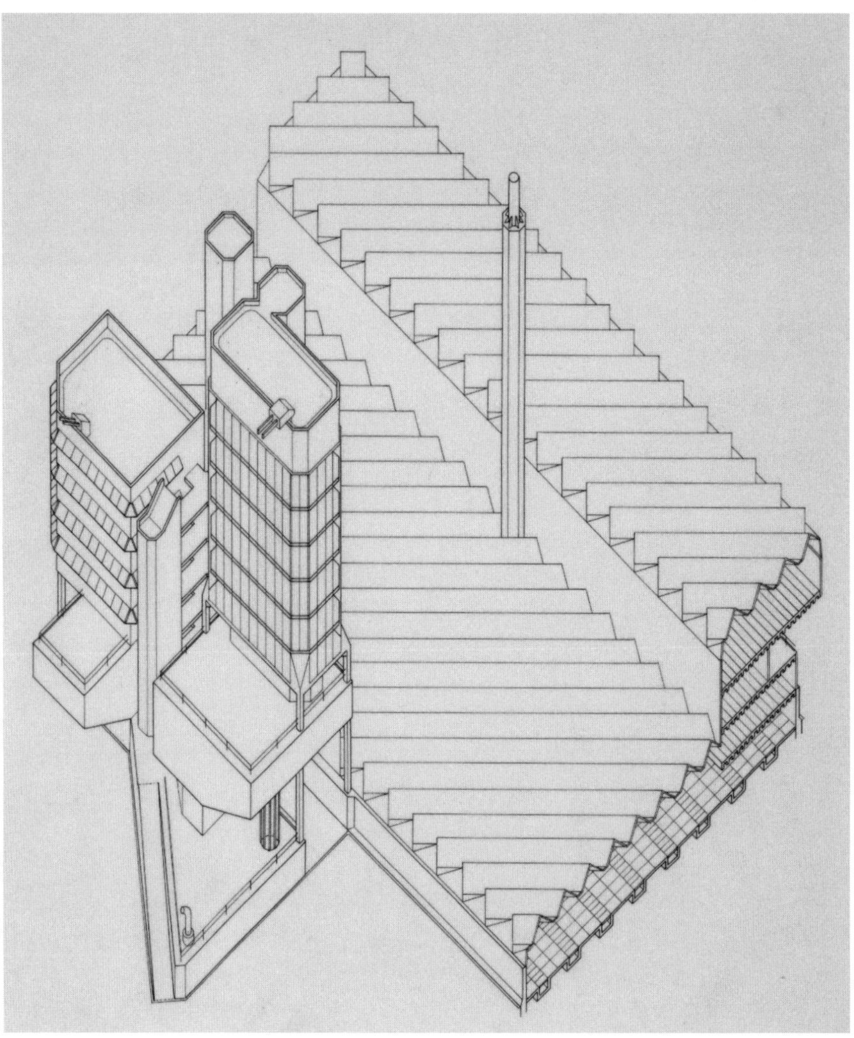

Figure 55
Stirling and Gowan, Leicester Engineering Building. Axonometric.

Figure 56
Stirling and Gowan, Leicester Engineering Building. Patent glazing blankets the roof of the workshop shed.

of their required northern exposure, which is at forty-five degrees to the building orientation, necessitated by the site restrictions (figs. 55, 56). As Stirling describes it in his 1962 Team Ten Royaumont talk, "It was an impossibility to twist the building to the conventional north-south relationship that you got in a factory roof. . . . The building sits in the site bursting at the seams (boundaries). The roof has had to be twisted to a north-south orientation."[7] In other words, there wasn't enough room to twist the building, so they twisted the roof instead. At the southwestern edge of the workshop shed is a four-story workshop block overhanging a service road allowing for equipment to be hauled through openings in the floor.

Unlike the more or less monolithic workshop, the tower portion of the project—which sits at the western edge of the workshop shed and is attached to it through a ground-floor lobby—is composed of a collection of multiple volumetric pieces: a four-story research laboratory tower, a six-story administration tower (with the water tower at its top), and two stair towers with an elevator tower between them. One stair tower stops at the top of the four-story laboratory building, while the elevator and second stair extend to the top of the office tower. Between them is a faceted enclosure of patent glazing that contracts as it scales upward, decreasing along with the size of each stair landing as the circulation requirements diminish (figs. 57, 58). The scale of

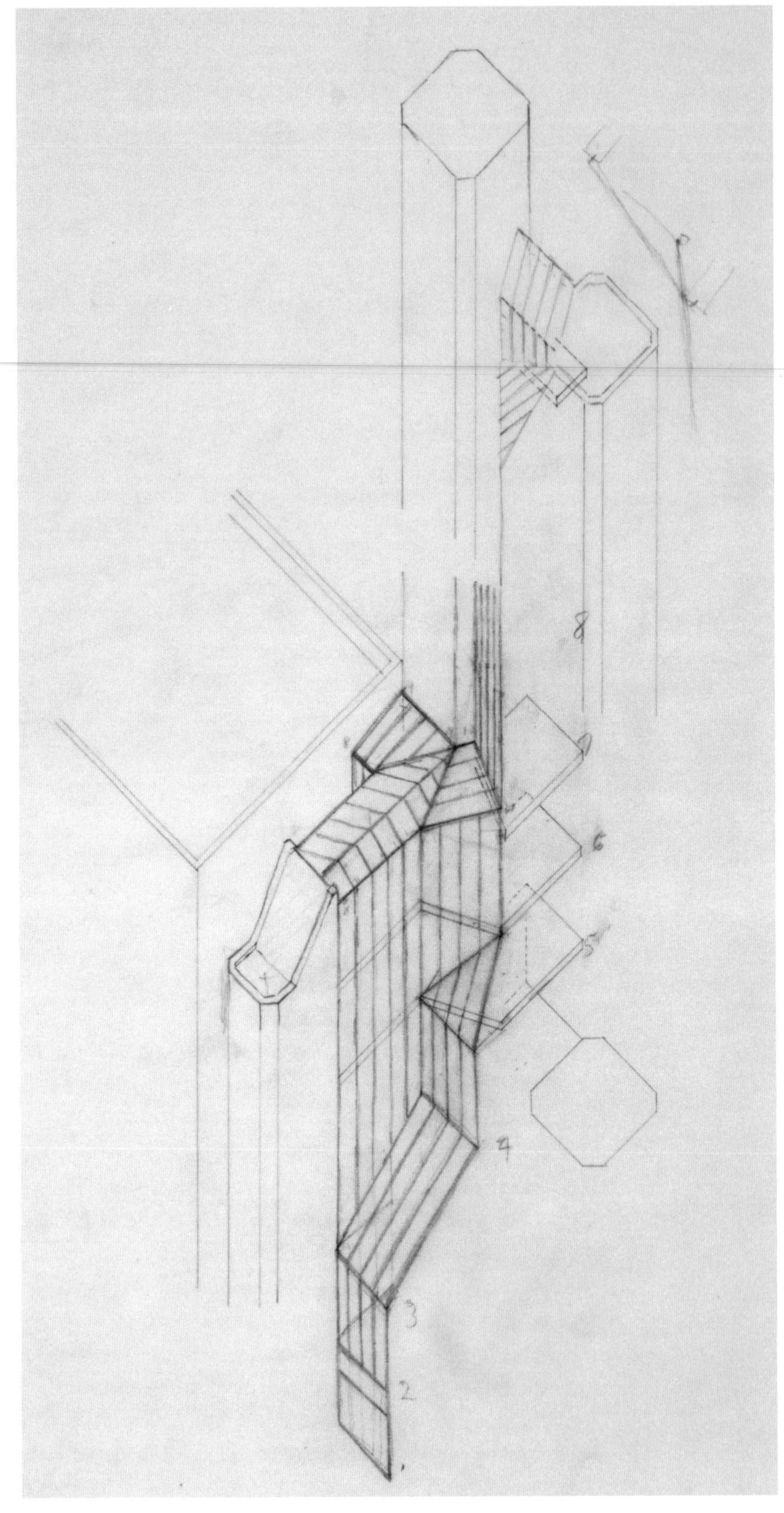

Figure 57
Stirling and Gowan, Leicester Engineering Building. An axonometric sketch depicts the complex geometry of the patent glazing enclosing the landings between the stair and elevator towers.

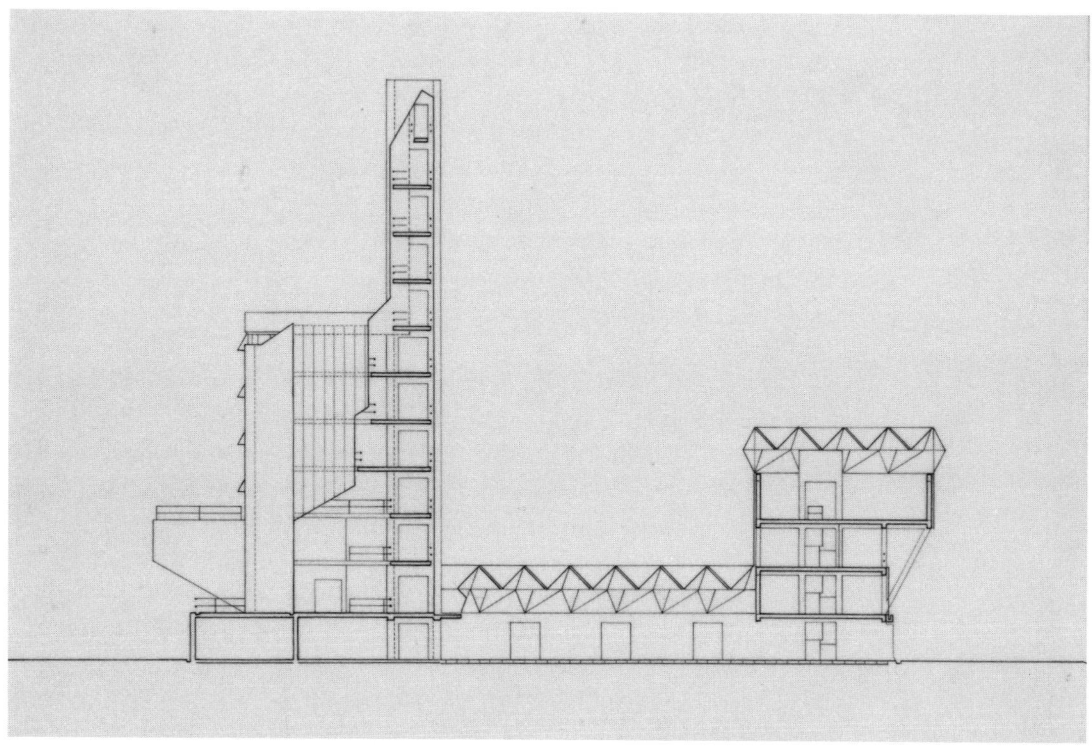

Figure 58
Stirling and Gowan, Leicester Engineering Building. Section through the stair tower and workshop shed. The faceted glass enclosure of the stair tower diminishes along with the circulation requirements as the building rises.

the building, but particularly of this circulation core, is remarkably modest; at the upper three levels the elevator and stair service only four occupants in the tower. This contrasts with the lower sections, which were designed to accommodate the approximately three hundred students moving to and from class each hour. The project, then, is sectionally divided, with students at the bottom and faculty/staff at the top. "In this way," Stirling wrote, "you contrive to keep the staff and the students from colliding."[8]

Both the laboratory and office towers are elevated on tall, thin piers, and "hanging" beneath each tower is a lecture theater hall rendered as a solid red-tile-clad mass: the larger theater, under the office tower, accommodates four hundred students; the smaller, under the laboratory tower, two hundred. The theaters are oriented at right angles to each other and cantilever twenty feet from beneath their respective towers toward the park, the cantilever "tailed down" by the weight of the tower above.[9] The larger of the two lecture halls is pierced by a glass-enclosed staircase at its underbelly; the sculptural stair provides a means for latecoming students to sneak into the upper portion of the lecture hall without disturbing the lecturer.

One of the more striking aspects of the project is its lack of a clearly legible façade or front. Although it wasn't until Stuttgart that Colin Rowe (and later Anthony Vidler) would analyze the lack of a "face" in Stirling's architecture, the faceless quality is here evident already. Entry to the building is bifurcated between the ground-floor entrance, which provides immediate access to the

Figure 59
Stirling and Gowan, Leicester Engineering Building. Study model, 1959.

Figures 60 and 61
Stirling and Gowan, Leicester Engineering Building. Preliminary axonometrics, 1960. In both of these early axonometric studies, the basic arrangement of tower block and workshop shed is in place, as is the forty-five-degree geometry of the workshop roof.

workshop shed, and a second-floor entrance, which is accessed from a diagonal ramp along the park. The diagonal path is clearly the prioritized entrance; it offers a three-quarter view of the volumetric complexity and three-dimensional massing of the structure, whereas the ground-floor entrance is surprisingly flat—the front face of the lecture theater, brick base, and narrow end of the administration tower all flush in one plane—a rare moment of alignment in the project. Tellingly, nearly all of the axonometrics of the scheme are drawn from the angle of the diagonal entry, further prioritizing this entrance and belying its status as the privileged view.

Although the brick podium demarcates a base, the tower and theater volumes elevated above it create many "grounds" specific to each volume. The pieces are intertwined, and each depends on the other for visual and structural support. There is a sense that the whole complex would fall like a house of cards if one piece was removed. In fact, Stirling loved to point out that the giant water tower at the top of the administration tower counterbalanced the cantilever of the theater volume below. "If you removed the top floor the building would collapse."[10] He notes that during construction the theater volumes had to be supported until enough of the building was finished to serve as a counterweight.[11] Evidence of this "piece-by-piece" compositional strategy, to use another of Banham's apt descriptions, is already present in early axonometrics and models of Leicester, the earliest of which—a model from 1959—assembles the various programmatic pieces (fig. 59). Although the components of the tower complex are not yet arranged as they are in the final design, the overall massing of a low structure at the back of the site and a high tower at the front is in place. Two axonometric drawings from the following year show further development of the scheme and a parti more or less consistent with the final scheme: the diagonals have appeared on the workshop roof, and the tower block now comprises a four- and a six-story tower. They assume their final position—taller administration tower in front, shorter laboratory tower in back—in the later scheme (figs. 60, 61). Also in the later drawing Stirling cantilevers the main lecture hall and extends the laboratory tower past the lecture theater, which is now tucked beneath—a more dynamic composition than in the first drawing, where each lecture theater serves as a static "base" for the tower above. Both of these two early drawings suggest that Stirling conceptualized the project as a set of three-dimensional elements to be manipulated, along the lines of Frank Lloyd Wright's famous Froebel blocks.

This volumetric articulation of various programmatic pieces was not unprecedented in Stirling's work—though earlier iterations were decidedly less complex. In his and Gowan's studies from 1956 (a "test" for their new partnership), cubes, cylinders, and bars are assembled into massings that Stirling referred to as "cluster assemblies" (figs. 62, 63).[12] And at Ham Common, the unit as a recognizable, volumetric piece is pulled away from the overall volume and made legible, either connected with a corridor in the two-story block or "pushed and pulled" in the three-story block. In lecture notes from 1963

59

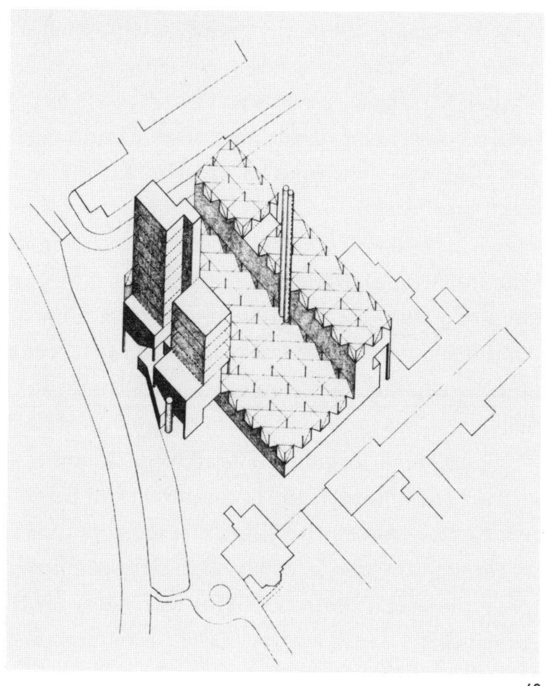

60

61

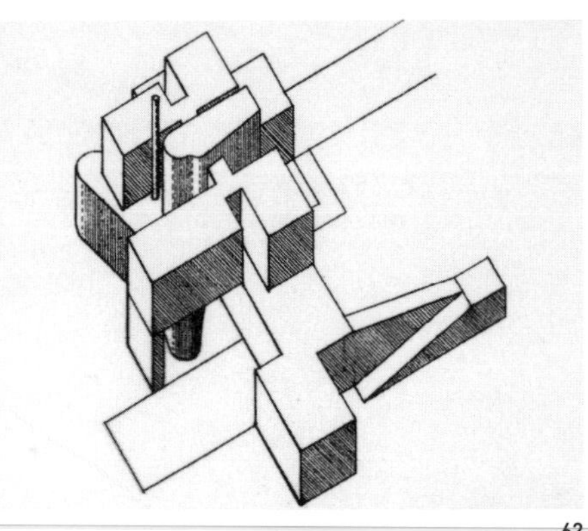

62

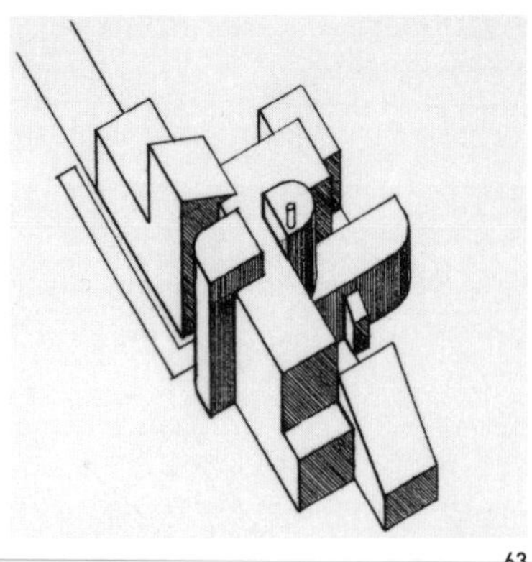

63

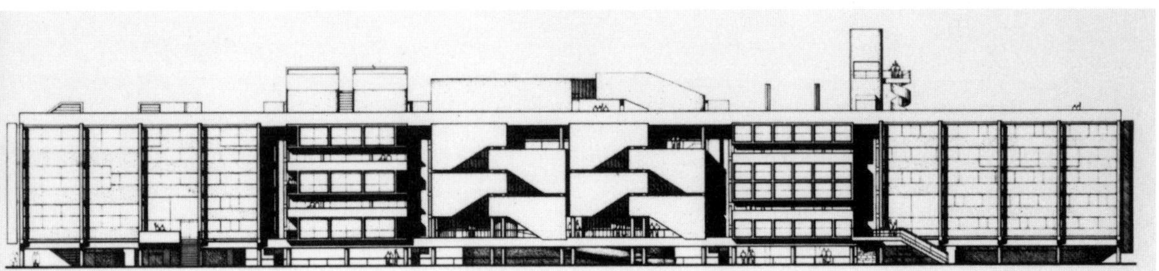

64

Stirling's own critique of Ham Common focuses on the fact that the volumetric articulation of the different units wasn't "evident enough on exterior."[13]

This desire to "break the box" and subdivide the project into programmatic components was evident not only in Stirling's buildings but in his writings and commentary as well. One of Stirling's most frequent criticisms of postwar modern architecture was its placement of diverse programs into discrete, totalizing boxes. As far back as his thesis of 1950 he wrestled with trying to "compress" programs into a "constricting box," and he would later question the fact that, in the project, various diverse programs were all "fitted into a rectangle."[14] For Stirling, the inherent dilemmas of such constriction were the essentially antifunctionalist operations of equalizing distinct programmatic pieces and hiding functions behind a uniform façade or in a characterless box. In notes made regarding the Sheffield University competition of 1953 he faults Sandy Wilson's scheme on the grounds that it condensed everything into one box and put a series of diverse programs behind a continuous curtain wall, "disguising the nature (function) of the accommodation behind."[15] In 1965 he states the same idea more forcefully: "A great amount of modern architecture is banal, partly through the easy accommodation of compressing room accommodation into simple overall forms."[16] In his own entry for the Sheffield competition Stirling boldly expresses the specific programmatic pieces—notably the lecture halls—as individual volumes whose shapes registered their function even as the entire composition was held within a regularized frame—in other words, within the box (fig. 64).

Figures 62 and 63
Stirling and Gowan, house studies, 1956. Axonometrics. In these early "cluster assemblies," program is arranged as a series of volumetric components.

Figure 64
James Stirling and Alan Cordingly, University of Sheffield, England, Arts and Administration Block, 1953. Elevation. Within the confines of the "box," programmatic elements (particularly the lecture halls) are expressed.

At Leicester the box truly explodes. The various volumes are "plastically assembled" as a kind of three-dimensional puzzle; the cantilevered, extruded trapezoids of the lecture halls, the chamfered towers of the offices, the low glass prisms of the workshops, and so forth. The specific architectural strategies with which Stirling and Gowan "break the box" at Leicester are indebted to the "elementarist" work of Le Corbusier, particularly the League of Nations competition of 1927 and the Centrosoyuz project of 1928, as well as his design for the Palace of the Soviets (1931), with its various "organs" brought together to form a "synthetic solution" (fig. 65). Alan Colquhoun identifies this compositional notion of "elementarization" in Le Corbusier's work as one in which "each program element is given its own form and is clearly articulated from its neighbor."[17] The articulated or elementarist composition had other British antecedents as well, largely as Corbusian responses. Denys Lasdun's Hallfield school (1955) and his Bethnal Green "cluster" block in London (1959) were both notable examples of projects in which various functions were clearly separated into distinct volumes (fig. 66). The key distinction between these earlier projects and Leicester was that Le Corbusier's and certainly Lasdun's assemblages were essentially plan-based. The pieces, in other words, were assembled on the ground plane and then extruded vertically. Although the geometry of the pieces was more complex in Le Corbusier's projects than in Lasdun's—particularly at Centrosoyuz—the basic operation of arranging the pieces on a more or less flat plane was the same. At Leicester, by contrast, the assemblage is fully three-dimensional and more sectionally complex; the articulated volumes are arranged centripetally around both vertical and horizontal axes, and most—including the towers and lecture halls—never touch the ground plane.

As Claire Zimmerman notes, this "particulate" compositional strategy at Leicester might well be related to Banham's writings on Julien Guadet in the opening lines of *Theory and Design in the First Machine Age*—a book dedicated to Stirling, among others.[18] Banham points out Guadet's "insistence on com-

Figure 65
Le Corbusier, Centrosoyuz, Moscow, 1928. Model. An example of Le Corbusier's "elementarist" work, in which each program element is a clearly articulated volume.

position, the assembly of a building from its component volumes," as a direct inheritance from Durand, whom he quotes: "Any complete building whatever is not, and cannot be, anything but the result of the assembly and putting together (composition) of a greater or lesser number of parts."[19] Banham's reading of Guadet is decidedly skewed—he admits that Guadet "barely discusses" the "specific mode of putting together the parts"—and his revisionist interpretation serves his own interest in particulate composition and, more specifically, in the use of the technique in the architecture of the 1920s and 1930s. As Banham notes, this "particulate approach" was common to Academics and Moderns alike, but he insists on it as an underlying characteristic of modern architecture "It may be taken as a general characteristic of the progressive architecture of the early twentieth century that it was conceived in terms of a separate and defined volume for each separate and defined function, and composed in such a way that this separation and definition was made plain."[20] Like Stirling, Banham clearly prefers this compositional attitude to the Miesian strategy of "subdividing a bulk volume" into various spaces—in other words, beginning with the "box."

The most thorough analysis of Leicester as a "multi-volumetric composition" is Peter Eisenman's 1974 essay "Real and English."[21] In this protracted, myopic, and intermittently dazzling formal reading of the project, Eisenman argues that at Leicester Stirling groups a series of volumes around a vertical

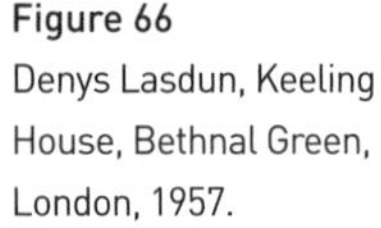

Figure 66
Denys Lasdun, Keeling House, Bethnal Green, London, 1957.

datum, an operation of volumetric assemblage that, to Eisenman's mind, clearly recalls the work of the Russian Constructivists; Eisenman singles out works by Alexander Vesnin, in particular, as exemplifying the Constructivist "compositional attitude" of "solid volumes juxtaposed about a vertical axis (as opposed to a vertical plane), which acts as a fulcrum for these volumes which are seemingly in collision or straining to pull apart from a centralized vortex of dense, centripetal pressure; the whole creating dynamic visual configurations."[22] He contrasts this to the "subtractive" logic of cubism.

This Constructivist compositional technique, Eisenman stresses, runs counter to the strategy of starting with a single box. However, according to Eisenman's dialectical framework, Stirling then erodes these accumulated volumes—by chamfering corners, eating away beneath parapets, and so on—to produce once again the "virtual quality of a single box."[23] For Eisenman, Leicester is a fundamentally a *critique* of Constructivist practice, as it negates its technique of aggregation with a simultaneous dissolution. In other words, it is both additive and subtractive. Furthermore, he argues that Stirling overlays the Corbusian "conception of layered space" and the insistence on a vertical plane (rather than a vertical axis) to further subvert the Constructivist paradigm.

In his essay "Architecture as a Continuous Text," which appeared in the *ANY* memorial issue following Stirling's death in 1992, Alan Colquhoun uses related terminology, finding Leicester emblematic of Stirling's theme of "fragmentation/explosion," which he contrasts with the "unification/implosion" embodied by Churchill College.[24] Colquhoun reads all of Stirling's projects as alternating between an "elementarist dispersion" on the one hand and "classical closure on the other," even as the range of historical precedents recalled becomes more exhaustive in the later work. For both Eisenman and Colquhoun, Leicester exemplifies a compositional strategy of articulation, and while Eisenman offers a more nuanced and dialectical reading, both stress this additive and multivolumetric quality of the scheme.

Stirling's use of the axonometric drawing here bears mention as more than simply an arbitrary choice of representational technique and instead as a reifying of his conceptual strategy of "articulation" or "piece-by-piece" composition. As the early drawings make clear, Stirling designed the project in axonometric drawing. To say that somewhat more forcefully, the drawing technique wasn't an after-the-fact means through which to represent the building as it had been conceived; it was the means through which Stirling arrived at and tested design ideas. Leicester is a built axonometric. Robin Evans famously argued that drawing always precedes building in architecture, and that there is a necessary translation, a gap, between drawing and building. But in Stirling's case, and particularly at Leicester, it's as if that gap is missing. He simply "records" the drawing with the architecture.[25]

As a drawing technique, the axonometric both enables and precludes certain information; by and large it displays exterior objects (unless a cutaway, which Stirling would use to some extent at Leicester and much more extensively in his later work, particularly Düsseldorf), but most importantly it gives a sense of the building as *both* a volumetric totality and a collection or assembly of parts. Banham compares Stirling's axonometrics to the mechanical drawings to which they were exposed during the war—drawings which "intended to make it possible to strip, reassemble and, above all, understand, sophisticated and enigmatic items of machinery."[26] Charles Jencks also emphasizes the explanatory power of Stirling's axonometrics, writing that they show "space, the structure, geometry, function and detail together without distortion."[27] Although Stirling's use of the axonometric will be developed in the following chapters—particularly his use of the Choisy, or worm's-eye axonometric, which is not yet in play at Leicester—here it is important to understand that the reading of Leicester as a singular object composed of various volumes is enabled by the use of the axonometric—both as a design and as a representational tool.

At the same time, however, as there is complexity in the assemblage of programmatic pieces, there is a relative simplicity and purity of each of the volumetric components themselves. Importantly, the various program elements (the lecture theater, the administration tower, the laboratory tower, the workshop shed) are also the primary volumetric components; in other words, there is a one-to-one correspondence between program and form. This is an important distinction from Banham's characterization of the compositional method in which the building begins with the "small structural and functional members," which are then assembled to make "functional volumes," which are then assembled to make the building. Instead, Stirling's "functional volumes" are the primary building blocks—his initial building blocks are much larger and, more importantly, linked with a specific program. The volumes of the tower, in particular, recall Le Corbusier's primitive, Platonic Phileban shapes from *Towards a New Architecture,* in which he "reminds" architects that the "essentials of architecture lie in sphere, cones and cylinders," or what William Jordy called "primal shapes."[28] They also echo the unadorned "primal" volumes that Stirling documents in his myriad photographs of vernacular buildings—Martello towers, oast houses, and so on—taken in the English countryside in the 1950s. The use of these simple volumetric elements allows for their assembly to take precedence over the reading of any individual form. This is distinct from Le Corbusier's Centrosoyuz, in which the pieces themselves—the theater volume, for example, with its exposed exterior trusses—comprise much more complex and articulated forms. At Leicester the volumes are simply volumes. As in Stirling and Gowan's early house studies, the act of accumulation dominates precisely because of the relative simplicity of the forms.

Although Eisenman stresses the unifying quality of the materials, and Zimmerman similarly insists that Stirling "disciplined the elements of a collage aesthetic within a single object, largely through the use of continuous surface," in fact the use of materials at Leicester reinforces the particulate quality of the scheme as much as serves as a continuous coverage for the "exploded" or "collaged" sensibility.[29] Each volumetric piece achieves its singularity within the composition through its particular material combination—the horizontal brick and glass bands on the laboratory tower, the glass prisms of the workshop shed, the wrapped glass façade of the administrative tower, the taut tile skins of the lecture halls. This material singularity is critical to understanding the building as simultaneously "unified" *and* "exploded." Rather than simply breaking the box, Stirling aggregates multiple "boxes," rendering each in a specific material language to clarify and emphasize both its individuality and the act of assembly. No longer "compressed" into a "simple overall form," the scheme becomes instead multiple simple overall forms aggregated into a more complex project. But perhaps most importantly, each volumetric piece is meant to register or "express" a specific programmatic function.

LUIGI MORETTI'S "SOLIDIFIED SPACE"

In the winter 1952–53 issue of the short-lived Italian magazine *Spazio*, Luigi Moretti (also the magazine's editor) published "The Structures and Sequences of Spaces." In the article Moretti features a series of plaster casts made from models that he constructed of the interiors of historical buildings: the long portico and circular natatorium of Hadrian's villa at Tivoli; the nave and side chapels of the Basilica of St. Peter's; the nine intersecting domes of Guarino Guarini's San Filippo Neri and the fluid interior space of his Church of Santa Maria of Divine Providence in Lisbon; a perfectly square cubic mass in the interior of Antonio da Sangallo and Michelangelo's Palazzo Farnese (figs. 67, 68). In each example the smooth, fluid plaster casts represent a highly manipulated abstraction of the original. In a kind of proto–Rachel Whiteread exercise—though at a much smaller scale—he models the negative space of the building's interior. Void becomes solid.

Although little discussed now, Moretti was a key figure in British postwar discourse. His design work was widely admired—particularly the Casa del Girasole, which Banham claims was "discovered by Anglo-Saxons" in 1953 (Banham's own article on the project appeared in 1953). Stirling singles him out as one of the most important architects of the "second generation" (he places Moretti third, after Terragni and Gunnar Asplund, and ahead of Aalto) and calls him one of the great "plasticians of modern architecture," after Le Corbusier.[30] Stirling was exposed to Moretti not only through Banham's writings but also through friends in London in the 1950s, and, as Crinson has shown, Moretti is the fourth most mentioned architect in Stirling's black notebook, following Le Corbusier, Wright, and Mies.[31]

Stirling references Moretti's *Spazio* article in his "'Functional Tradition' and Expression" essay when describing his procedures for abstracting historical buildings: "A few years ago, Luigi Moretti illustrated in *Spazio* the plaster castings taken from inside accurate models of certain historical buildings. By treating the external surface and the inner constructions of a building as a three-dimensional negative or mould, he was able to obtain solidified space. If space can be imagined as a solid mass determined in shape and size by the proportion of a room or the function of a corridor, then an architectural solution could be perceived by the consideration of alternative ways in which the various elements of the programme could be plastically assembled."[32]

Figures 67 and 68
Luigi Moretti,
"The Structures and Sequences of Spaces," *Spazio* (Winter 1952–53).
Moretti's plaster casts made from models of the interiors of historic buildings generate "solidified space."

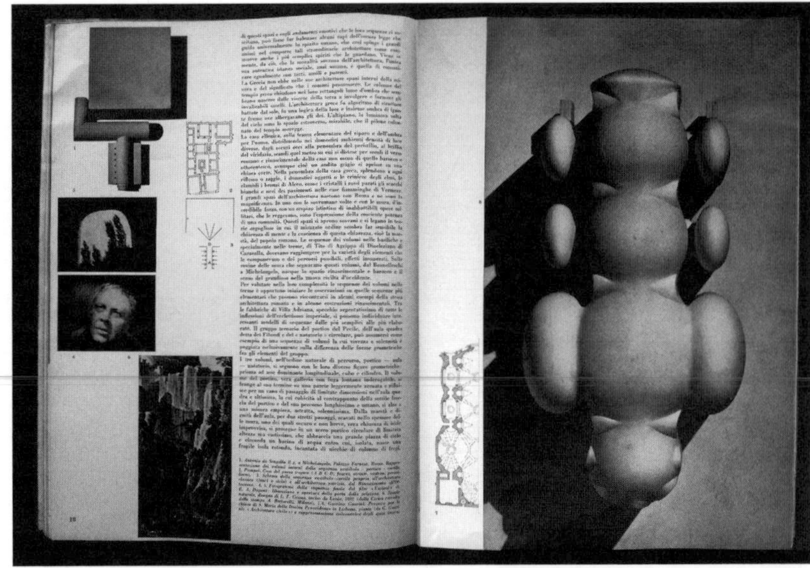

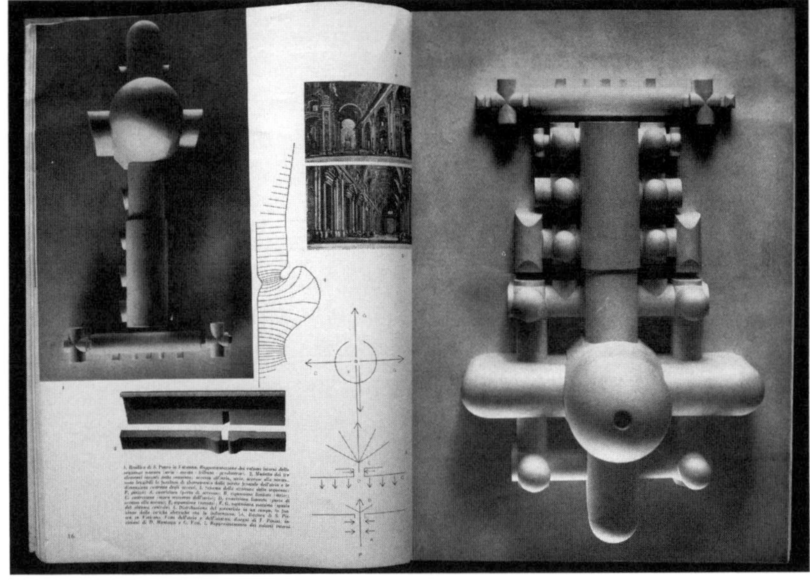

Stirling's synopsis of Moretti reveals two critical misreadings of the text and of Moretti's volumetric casts. First, Stirling equates each "space" with a specific function; each room or corridor is aligned with an element of program. This was not Moretti's intention nor a byproduct of his models—a cast of the interior of the nave at St. Peter's, for example, reveals a highly complex space with multiple volumetric pieces that is in fact a single programmatic "element." Moretti's text emphasizes the sequence and movement between the spaces; for him the volumetric castings enable an understanding of the "modality of their succession" and an investigation into "differences among the volumes" with a decidedly more metaphysical aim—to study the "emotional trends their sequences excite in us" and to "bring to light certain points of the obscure law that universally guides the human spirit."[33] But for Stirling, in a radically different interpretation, each "solidified space," each volumetric solid, is equated with a singular, monovalent program and serves as a registration not only of its dimensions but of its functional distinction from other programmatic pieces.

In a second critical misreading of Moretti's casts, Stirling effectively reverses the procedure—the resultant blocks of "solidified space" become, for Stirling, positive building elements from which to *assemble* a new structure. For Moretti they are meant simply as a tool to help understand the character or sequences and spaces in historical buildings. This is not to say that Moretti wasn't interested in the translation of his ideas into contemporary architecture—in fact, his stated aim is to reinsert the spatial variety evident in these largely baroque forms, since "we moderns have forgotten the laws of the sequences of internal volumes." Later, he is even more explicit, writing that his aim is to "once again reach the lyrical clarity of the classics."[34] But Moretti's search to recapture an "intuitive" internal spatial sequence is decidedly different from Stirling's "plastic assembly" of these various volumetric pieces. For Stirling, the "solidified spaces" are no longer byproducts of existing buildings but generative components of a new one.

Stirling refers to Leicester as an "iceberg," by which he means that it diminishes in size and tapers as it rises.[35] But his metaphor equally suggests the building as a solid, carveable mass, as a malleable, plastic entity, much like Moretti's plaster casts. Eisenman's reading of Leicester's "eroded" solid can be extended through this lens; rather than presenting the project as a giant block to be carved away, Moretti's casts allow us to see it as the result of a molded form that responds to both positive and negative pressures. In his analysis of the workshop tower, for example, Eisenman emphasizes the fact that glass—an inherently two-dimensional material—is made three-dimensional in the projecting windows, which violate the reading of the brick "solid" as a mass. As a continuation of this thesis, and armed with Moretti's negative molds, we can also interpret the glass windows as a kind of frozen, liquid mass oozing from the slits carved in brick mass (fig. 69). The glass offers a visual marker of the interior space literally straining at its limits, as if it can't quite be contained in the given space and therefore escapes the brick envelope.

Figure 69
Stirling and Gowan, Leicester Engineering Building. Laboratory tower with projecting glass windows.

Soon after Leicester was completed, Stirling wrote that he considered glass "rather like polythene, to be pushed in and out enveloping the shape of the rooms, which are considered as always having an ideal shape according to their use."[36] His statement was principally in reference to the glass reading at Cambridge, but it serves equally for the use of glass at Leicester.

Moretti's notion of solidified space became, for Stirling, more than simply a modeling technique since it also offered a novel—and visually stunning—method for misreading historical precedents. Like Rowe, Moretti is interested in formal comparisons between various precedents. Unlike Rowe, however, whose diachronic comparisons (Palladio and Le Corbusier, for example) offer a formal but inherently two-dimensional framework (the plan of Garches vs. the plan of Villa Malcontenta), Moretti provides a specific tectonic and volumetric expression of history and a visual comparison based on three-dimensional rather than two-dimensional forms as a means to emphasize their shared spatial quality (the capped cylindrical forms of Guarini's S. Filippo Neri juxtaposed with the adjoined circles of Wright's McCord House). More broadly, Moretti's analysis opens up an entirely new reading of historical architecture; to see St. Peter's inside out, as a series of bulbous volumes, rather than as an accumulated layering of classical motifs, enables an interpretation of the project based not on a set of formulaic stylistic vocabularies or even semiotic reshufflings but as pure spatial form. This abstract language of volumetric forms offered Stirling a powerful new tool for revisioning historical sources.

Moretti, of course, was not alone in stressing the importance of space as a consideration in architecture during this period—Bruno Zevi's *Architecture as Space,* translated into English in 1957, is but one notable example—and neither was Leicester the first project where Stirling began to think in terms of "solidified space." Stirling describes Churchill as made up of "related and interlocking blocks of space." These blocks occur at the overall scale of the project—the exterior dormitory ring, or the library and multipurpose blocks—but they also occur at the smaller or "functional volume" scale—the library, for example, comprises a series of smaller blocks: the rectangular reading room base, the cylindrical stair volume, the triangular skylight projections. Churchill is "subtracted" space as well as "solidified space," and the modeling of the positive emerges as strongly as the negative. This framework allows for a more complex reading than the scheme initially suggests, since the series of "bars"—the outer ring as well as the interior dormitory courtyard and slab buildings—are not only linear accumulations of cellular entities (along the lines of Le Corbusier's La Tourette) but extruded "solidified space." And of course there is actual empty space: the entire courtyard can be understood as an extracted void, removed from the solid mass of the overall scheme.

While evident at Churchill, this trope of solidified space becomes the central massing technique at Leicester. The two lecture hall volumes are perhaps the clearest example. Moretti's framework allows us to see them as the program *literally* turned inside-out, as if a cast had been made of the interior of the lecture hall and the walls taken away. The smooth, red-tile, featureless

exterior becomes equivalent to a Moretti cast. Although Eisenman argues that the wrapped tile surface on these lecture theaters emphasizes surface rather than the volume, and while a solid mass of concrete would have been a more literal translation of Moretti's "casting" motif, the uniform surface of the tile approximates the monolithic quality of the plaster models. Certainly if Stirling had wanted to emphasize the tile as a surface, to call attention to its role as cladding, he would have somewhere exposed its edge. Instead, the tiles slip seamlessly over the faces and around the folded corners of the trapezoidal volumes.

The fact that the lecture halls are the most distinctively articulated volumetric pieces is significant, since the program of the lecture hall has a more specific set of functional requirements—raked seating, entrances in front and back, a podium at the base, and so on—than a more generic function space. Stirling: "We usually try to keep the ideal specific shape of a room and avoid distorting it to fit a structural module or a preconceived overall shape."[37] The "ideal specific shape" for an office or workshop would arguably be more difficult to define. This is no doubt why the theater volume was often the most precisely elaborated form in earlier modernist projects as well; at Centrosoyuz, for example, the lecture hall stands out as the most highly elaborated and sculpturally distinctive component. Unlike the more "flexible" space of the workshops, which Stirling felt would necessarily change over time—and which were in fact "distorted" within a structural module—there was also a sense that the program of the lecture halls was more fixed and immutable: "The only expressed units of accommodation are those we understood at the level of our own experience and felt reasonably confident would not change—lecture theaters, staircases, etc."[38]

Moretti's casts are at once referential and abstract, both tied to specific architectural precedents and autonomous, at least once the original precedent—the "mold"—is discarded. The cast then takes on a life of its own, no longer associated with the original. With these casts Moretti provides an architectural operation that can be performed on any architectural precedent. Although Moretti's sources remain largely Italian, and predominantly seventeenth century, there was nothing to say that the method couldn't be used on a building from any era. For Stirling, the conceptual power of Moretti's casts—the negative, solidified space—was in their suggestion of a new way to read precedents, to see history. They provided an architecturally specific connection between function and form, but a connection that was removed from the problematic, positivist nature of functionalism, or at least what functionalism had become by the late 1950s.

TOWARD AN "EXPRESSIVE" FUNCTIONALISM

In a 1963 article, "Seven Keys to a Good Architecture," Stirling wrote that he considered himself a "routine functionalist" but that functionalism alone was "not enough." "The building must also be expressive. You ought to be able to look at it and recognize its various component parts where people are doing different things."[39] This statement extended the argument put forth in his

1960 article "'The Functional Tradition' and Expression," in which he suggested that anonymous, regional structures offered a model of an architecture in which "direct and undecorated volumes" directly "expressed" their functions.[40] Stirling also referred to Leicester specifically in terms of its expressiveness: in his Royaumont talk he spoke of the "aesthetic expression" of the tower piece, which was more "expressive of its content" than was the shed.

Stirling's use of the term expression, and particularly in association with functionalism, is, at first, surprising. In the immediate postwar period in Britain, both the curvilinear forms of Erich Mendelsohn and the faceted geometries of Bruno Taut were seen as a deliberate rejection of the rectilinear, rational language of the New Objectivity from which Stirling—an admitted "routine functionalist"—saw himself as descended. "The term expressionist," Reyner Banham wrote in 1954, "has become a dirty word in architectural criticism." But expressionism took on a more complex meaning in postwar Britain, particularly in relation to functionalism. As discussed in relation to the Functional Tradition in the last chapter, by the mid- to late 1950s functionalism had begun to shed its stylistic associations with the International Style and instead to indicate a set of values or operations, a quality that could be found in any historical source—from British castles to industrial warehouse buildings. The antipathy between expressionism and functionalism was also challenged: in a 1951 article Lewis Mumford wrote, "In all systems of architecture, both function and expression have a place."[41] And in Banham's writings of the 1950s—notably his 1954 article "Mendelsohn"—he emphasizes the "functional" considerations behind Mendelsohn's curvilinear forms such as the Einstein tower while also highlighting his angular forms and his use of precast concrete elements—in other words, insisting on the more "rational" aspects of his work. More broadly, an expressive architecture emerged as a means to enrich the stagnant and seemingly exhausted project of functionalism, which, in its Machine Aesthetic and International Style guise, had become stylized as white cubes and glass boxes. Although the core principles of functionalism were still held to be relevant, it had become clear that as an end, rather than a means, functionalism left architects with little direction.

By the early 1960s, expressive buildings were also seen to offer a corrective to the "bleakness" of the early postwar efforts, a recognition of the desires of a less austere time. The low-cost associations of modern architecture, evident at Ham Common, had begun to give way, replaced by the possibility of an inventive, even playful, formal language. This not to say that expressionism was universally accepted as a palliative for functionalism's shortcomings. Banham's teacher Nikolaus Pevsner was deeply critical of 1920s expressionism as well as its contemporary equivalents. "Expressive" became Pevsner's stand-in term for works that he found whimsical or highly subjective. His ire, as we saw in Chapter 1, was principally directly at Le Corbusier, whose postwar projects—particularly Ronchamp—he deemed "inexcusable" and an "escape . . . into a fairy world."[42] Unlike Banham, then, Pevsner wasn't trying to make more relevant or complex the historically calcified and stylistic idea of expressionism, nor to establish its functional parallels, but instead to assert that the "intellectual deviationists" of the 1920s, along with their "self-expressive" contemporary descendents, were fundamentally antimodern.

Pevsner's most famous or perhaps infamous "expressive" attack was directed at Leicester. In a radio broadcast in 1966 Pevsner singled out Leicester as emblematic of the expressive tendencies of the "anti-pioneers." "I see expression in the diagonal undersides of the jutting-out lecture theaters, and the chamfering of the higher tower and the angularly projecting aprons of the lower tower. Indeed, this aggressive angularity repeats all over the building. So to me that Leicester engineering building is Expressionism, as much as Poelzig's Grosses Schauspielhaus and Taut's fantastic Stadtkrone. It is architecture heightened in emotional effects by sharp stabbing angles, and expression not of the character of the building but of the architect."[43]

Others shared his sentiment. After Stirling took a group of students and architects to visit the newly opened building in October 1963, their reactions were published in the *Architectural Association Journal,* and the term expression emerges as a consistent pejorative. A student's reaction is perhaps the most telling in its evocation of the term and the inherently conflicted if not ambiguous deployment of its meaning: "This is a worrying building. Formally it is one of the most exciting modern buildings in this country. Yet its very success in this field calls into doubt the architects' motives and suggests that at times they were only concerned with human function insofar as it provided them with the excuses for formal expression."[44] Banham sums up the widely held dichotomy between an expressive and a functional building in his 1964 review of the building, in which he challenges the idea that "anything that looks like good architecture must be at least 'out of character' with the functions it shelters, if not physically hostile to them."[45] Banham errs in the opposite direction, bending over backward to explain the crystalline roofs and tower forms as purely functional, citing "good technical reasons" for elevating the tower and the fact that the "only way" to fit the workshops onto the site was to fill it completely, necessitating the north-facing windows and therefore the forty-five-degree geometry. Here his language echoes Stirling's own (or perhaps vice-versa).

Unlike Banham and Pevsner, Stirling didn't see expressionism as counter to functionalism. For Stirling, Pevsner's opposition of function and expression and, more importantly, his notion that the "style of the 1930s" was more rational and based on the needs of the client, not the architect, was frankly outdated and misplaced. As with his earlier writings on Le Corbusier, Pevsner insisted on the link between what he saw as a subjective, irresponsible design and a building's "expressive" form. And although this was an idea to which Stirling had subscribed in his earlier writing on Le Corbusier, if in a much less extreme fashion, "expressionistic" was never equivalent to "individualistic" or "subjective" for Stirling, as it was for Pevsner. Like Pevsner, Stirling still held on to the functionalist belief in a correspondence between a building and its form, but he had broadened that understanding to include the notion of an expressive functionalism. And Stirling was never stricken with the puritanical functionalist fervor of Banham. By this point Stirling felt that a pure functionalism was a myth. In a letter responding to Pevsner's attack of Leicester, he wrote, "I agree with Le Corbusier—The purpose of construction is to make things hold together; of architecture to move us."[46] In other words, architecture was more than building, more than simply a response to "'anonymous' users of demand." Banham surely would have shuddered at a "moving" architecture—unless of course "moving" referred to an automated walkway, not a spiritual awakening.

Stirling doesn't employ the term expressionism as a stylistic category but instead speaks of "expressive" or "expression" as conceptual and highly architectonic ideas. Often he uses it as a verb, as in the building "expressing" its functions. For Stirling the term was nearly synonymous with "articulate"—recall "'The Functional Tradition' and Expression," in which he described the "direct and undecorated volumes" that "expressed" their functions. This association of each volumetric piece with a function is restated somewhat more casually in his 1957 article "Seven Keys to a Good Architecture," in which he writes that one "ought to be able to look at [a building] and recognize its various component parts where people are doing different things."[47] Stirling's "expressive functionalism," then, is a kind of updated architecture parlante—the building tells you what it is, what "people are doing inside." It is a strategy for making interior programs or functions legible or "expressed" on the building's exterior. Importantly, expression does not simply mean a subjective appeal to the senses, or a "visible impression," as others used it at the time. For Stirling, expression signaled a specific design strategy to be used in combination with an adherence to a functionalist creed, a specific translation of function into form.[48] Charles Jencks describes Stirling as the "apotheosis of the functional sensibility."[49] But, as Jencks points out, it didn't much matter whether his buildings worked "extraordinarily well": what mattered was that they looked as if they did. The visual "expressive" power of the architecture was as significant as its "actual" function.

MANNERIZING MODERNISM'S "DISCARDED FRAGMENTS"

In his essay "L'Architecture dans le Boudoir" of 1974, Manfredo Tafuri singles out Stirling's work as exemplary of a neo-avant-garde practice engaged in the resuscitation of modernism's "discarded fragments," which remain available for reuse but have been denuded of their ideological charge. "Stirling has 're-written' the 'words' of modern architecture, building a true 'archeology of the present.'"[50] To Tafuri's mind, Stirling is unique among his peers in that he embraces the absurdity and lack of meaning in architectural language, "abandoning the sacred precinct in which the semantic universe of the modern tradition has been enclosed" and therefore uttering a language that is "perversely closed into itself"—in other words, relegated in the "boudoir."[51] Tafuri compares Stirling's operation to the "bricoleur," as does, only slightly later, Peter Eisenman.[52] Zimmerman finds Stirling's operations closer to the montagist, but she distinguishes Stirling's act of montage from earlier avant-gardists: "No longer assembling found objects, like Kurt Schwitters; rather the found objects of industrial modernity are fed through the processing machine of a production aesthetic. They represent montage rather than enact it."[53]

Certainly the reference to Melnikov's lecture theaters is one of the clearest "rewritings" of this historical avant-garde. Stirling and Gowan import the distinctive trapezoidal volume of the earlier work but without its initial revolutionary aims. As Irénée Scalbert rightly points out, Leicester is "far more forbidding than it is heroic," and "it evokes Burke's sublime far more than it does Bolshevik zeal, which did not enter into the architect's preoccupations."[54] Beyond the numerous historical quotations, however, the operations of the bricoleur or montagist occur at the level of materials, all of which are treated both as objets trouvés amassed throughout the building, and as having cultural and disciplinary meaning.

The three principal materials are red tile, red brick, and patent glazing. As a general rule, brick clads the structural frame while tile covers the reinforced concrete walls. Tile encases the stair and lift towers, the concrete boxes of the lecture theaters, and many of the interior surfaces. Because the client requested no fair-faced concrete surfaces, the tile cladding becomes a kind of substitute or marker for what would have been concrete. Brick appears in the podium at the base of the building, on the exterior wall of the workshop shed, as well as in the laboratory tower. Arguably, then, there is a consistent usage of each material, a kind of logic and even an "expression" of the structural material behind. But the use of brick and tile bears more exploration given the attempt to obfuscate the distinction between the two, if not equalize them. On the one hand, their nearly identical hue creates a uniform surface across the building. But this could have been achieved by using all tile or all brick, since both are used as cladding surfaces. Beyond simply providing consistency, the brick/tile verisimilitude offers commentary on the seemingly load-bearing quality of one (brick) vs. the nonstructural property of the other (tile.) By using both as cladding, and by visually blurring their distinction, the structural or non-structural properties of each dissipate in light of their visual similarities.

In Eisenman's meticulous analysis of the brick and glass at Leicester, he stresses Stirling's desire to invert the expected properties of each. Glass appears "solid," and brick becomes "skin." Each, in other words, takes on properties seemingly antithetical to its "true" nature. For Eisenman, Stirling's use of materials was purely about negating expected material signification. To his mind, the two materials are "presented in such a way that their respective load-bearing and surface qualities, while apparently functional, are actually often reversed."[55] As an example, the prismatic, volumetric glass windows in the laboratory tower make the seemingly "solid" brick volume instead become thin. And the brick, "which was first seen as literally solid, positive and horizontal, can now be read as the negative segments or residue of a vertical plane, sliding behind the glass."[56] Further proof of this "iconic" treatment of brick can be seen, in Eisenman's eyes, in the fact that the brick laboratory building is elevated, revealing its status as an applied surface. Eisenman's clever and thorough reading of the building, however, never explores the additional "iconic" material treatment in the visual conflation of brick and tile, which takes on a similar role in calling into question the seeming structural or functional characteristics of each.

Stirling and Gowan's use of brick, however, wasn't simply a means to question material properties or even to insert a critical reading of the avant-garde. Brick—particularly red brick—"meant" more than simply its quality as a light or heavy material, as a skin or a structure. As discussed in Chapter 1, brick had important connotations not only with regional, vernacular architecture but also with the specific tradition of Stirling's beloved nineteenth-century warehouses. Brick was a logical, low-cost material; it was also, at its most basic, a ready-made industrial object—recall Stirling's comment that every brick is a "9-inch-by-4 ½-inch pre-cast system."[57] And within the immediate context of Leicester, brick took on the further association of the "red-brick" universities—the civic universities established in working-class towns (Liverpool among them) that were granted university status before World War I, and which typically taught science or engineering. If they were nothing else, these red-brick universities were distinct from the "white-stone" campuses of Cambridge and Oxford. So the embrace of red brick at Leicester (a decidedly different brick from the rough, yellowish London stock brick used at Ham Common) put forth a deliberate statement relating to its context.

In his seminal article "The Symbolic Essence of Modern European Architecture of the Twenties and Its Continuing Influence," William Jordy refutes Banham's position that modernism didn't adequately embrace cutting-edge technologies, "discard its cultural load," and strive for a pure engineering aesthetic. Jordy argues that, indeed, modern architects were better off for having used the "typical" technology of their time than for attempting to prophesy an unknown future, a future that was in fact already at hand: "The architect did not need to conjure the fantastic. He had only to open his eyes to the laconic facts of modern existence around him."[58] As an example of architects using these "laconic facts," Jordy cites the industrial glazing in Le Corbusier and Pierre Jeanneret's Ozenfant studio; the material fills two walls and extends onto the ceiling to create the distinctive glass corner of the studio (fig. 70). To Jordy's mind, the industrial glazing retains its "plebian essence" while taking on additional significance through its importation into a foreign setting: "Things which started as compliant servants, so flatly factual as to have been all but invisible, suddenly erupt into positive assertion."[59]

Can we, then, compare the patent glazing or the brick at Leicester to the industrial glazing at Ozenfant's studio? Were Stirling and Gowan using "typical" technology to make their progressive statement? And was there a kind of shock to be registered in the translation of materials into a new context? At Leicester, the "flatly factual" brick indeed "erupts into positive assertion" at certain moments through its unexpected treatment as a cladding system—particularly in instances like the brick door at the laboratory where it traverses a

Figure 71
Stirling and Gowan, Leicester Engineering Building. Glass enclosure of the stair tower.

typically forbidden territory. But the brick, unlike the industrial glazing, wasn't brought from a realm "outside" of its immediate context (recall the red-brick university) but from "within." Here perhaps Mies's I-beam is a better example: Jordy writes that the "flat fact" of Mies's I-beam is as a steel construction member, but that it also represents a technology, a tradition, an aesthetic, and an order. "The emanative potential of the object (contributing to Mies' 'more') depends on its remaining very intensely the object that it is (his 'less')."[60] Like Mies's I-beam, Stirling's brick is more than the flat fact as a masonry building component; it represents working-class traditions, "Englishness," directness, thrift.

The patent glazing at Leicester offers perhaps a better example of Stirling and Gowan's operations as bricoleurs, of bringing "everyday" materials from industrial uses into the "high" world of architecture. While for Mies or Le Corbusier the act of exposing the "fact" of the I-beam or industrial glazing was enough to articulate an avant-garde position, for Stirling's generation, that position had already been established. There was no longer any shock in the seeming transgression of boundaries. Stirling's advancement, then, was to consider that "as found" material as something more (or perhaps less) than it had been, as a moldable, pliable, plastic element. More than simply placing an allegedly "industrial" element into an educational building, Stirling treats the patent glazing as a fully plastic form (fig. 71). It cascades down the stair towers, wraps the administration tower, oozes from behind brick in the laboratory tower, and ripples across the workshop shed. When comparing the Leicester glazing to that in the Ozenfant corner, the volumetric complexity of the former emerges as the most apparent distinction, although, not insignificantly, the registration and aggregation of the individual panes remain paramount in both cases; the limits of the material dimensions, its "factness," remain consistent.

This interpretation of the patent glazing at Leicester is an extension of Tafuri's argument that the "battle remnants" of modernity had been emptied of their ideological charge and were now available as denuded, formal elements. Patent glazing had become yet another of modernism's "discarded frag-

Figure 70
Le Corbusier and Pierre Jeanneret, Ozenfant studio, Paris, 1922. Like Stirling and Gowan's later example at Leicester, the industrial glazing at the Ozenfant studio becomes more than its material "factness."

ments." That emptying allowed it to become pure material again—a reversal to its "original" industrial use but with the necessary memory of its avant-gardist position as a residue. According to Peter Bürger's classic definition, the avant-garde artist "kills the life" of the material, "tears it out of its functional context that gives it meaning": for the avant-gardist, "material is just material," an "empty sign" with no meaning.[61] The avant-garde work is put together from fragments; it "proclaims itself as an artificial construct, an artifact."[62] As someone antecedent to the "original" avant-garde, Stirling occupies a different position than Burger's framework allows. For Stirling, the act of emptying has already occurred—and as Tafuri rightly notes, the material is no longer ideologically charged. But neither is it purely mute. The industrial glazing of Leicester may well have been the same industrial glazing used at the Ozenfant studio, but with the intervening generation it had become a codified gesture. Banham argues that the use of patent glazing at Leicester is "unaffectedly crude," that Stirling and Gowan "took their glazing as they found it, and left it to detail itself."[63] He highlights the "fairly crummy" things that happen as a result—exposed flashings, gaps in panes. Banham desires a purely technocratic appropriation, but tellingly Stirling had originally lobbied for plate glass on the tower buildings because he found it superior. The molding of patent glazing is a more complex operation of using "as found"; Stirling is performing the operations of a mannerist using the vocabulary of a modernist. Patent glazing wasn't simply an appropriated "flat fact" of industrial production, to be used as a pure signifier for its "machinelike" qualities, it was also an established trope of the modern movement.

STANDING ON PRECEDENT: AN "ART HISTORICAL FIELD DAY"?

Leicester seems to invite style-spotting and source hunting. Nearly every architectural critic commenting on the building, particularly when it was first completed, couldn't escape speculating on various antecedents and alleged influences. Kenneth Frampton found clear connections to Frank Lloyd Wright, particularly to the combination of tower and low prisms of Wright's Johnson Wax Building. Frampton also lists as precedents Joseph Paxton's Crystal Palace, Isambard Brunel's Paddington Station, Peter Ellis's Cook Street Building in Liverpool, as well as Antonio Sant'Elia's Città Nuova and Hans Poelzig's water tower at Posen.[64] In his review of the building John Jacobus similarly cites the influence of Johnson Wax and Città Nuova, along with the Van Nelle factory in Rotterdam.[65] In addition to the inevitable Melnikov reference, Peter Eisenman includes Le Corbusier's Salvation Army Building, Aalto's Civic Center at Saynatsalo, and Ilya Golosov's Zuyez Workers' Club in Moscow. Rowe compares the structural expression to the work of Viollet-le-Duc, particularly the exposed concrete supports that transfer the octagonal geometry of the office tower down to the four square pillars—which Rowe also links to William Butterfield and Frank Furness.[66] A number of critics mention the fourth-year AA project of Edward Reynolds designed under Frank Newby—a warehouse building with a tower and crystal-like roof geometry capping a horizontal workshop—that seems to prefigure the workshop roof at Leicester.

Of course there are more general associations and evocations as well. Frampton notes its resonance with "late nineteenth century marine and civil engineering," and Rowe calls this work "High Victorian with perhaps a little bit of Old Russia."[67] Joseph Rykwert finds it an attempt to "graft" Wright onto "earlier constructivist stock," with Louis Kahn as a "catalyst" rather than a "direct influence."[68] Even Tafuri can't resist "fishing for references." He cites the example of the exhaust tower jutting out from the base of the brick podium at Leicester as an "almost too obvious reference to the 1923 design for the Palace of the Soviets by the Vesnin brothers" (he's right).[69]

Many of these same critics claim to have the inside track on Stirling and Gowan's "true" influences. According to Frampton, the architects "acknowledge" Wright's Johnson Wax Building as the "one dominant influence underlying the conception of the whole work."[70] Stirling's published writings about the building, however, are almost always perfunctory and rarely discuss the building's sources. In a few instances he does attribute direct influence; in a 1974 lecture he links the octagonal glass stair beneath the large lecture hall to Ellis's Cook Street Building, and in a 1974 *Casabella* article he pairs an image of Leicester with Nicholas Hawksmoor's Christ Church. As Scalbert notes, Gowan elaborates on the influence of a house project by Van Doesburg and Van Eesteren of 1923, which features cubic rooms assembled around a central stair.[71]

Against this desire to establish Leicester as an "art historical field day," to use Rowe's memorable phrase, the lone naysayer, at least as it appears in his 1964 review of the building, is Banham, for whom the building "stands on no precedents."[72] He wills it into a pure functionalism, a project that answers only the "honest service of need" but somehow magically returns "beauty" as a byproduct. Banham goes so far as to challenge those sniffing for sources, asserting that the building "rebuffs the attempts of art-historians to identify its sources."[73] In a slightly later essay he reasserts this point more forcefully (and seems to rebuff Frampton directly), writing that "style-spotting" critics are on "shaky ground." He writes, "Stirling and Gowan know their recent architectural history so well that they are long past cribbing."[74]

Here Banham identifies the crux of the matter, which is not whether certain precedents are at play in the building but in what way they are "re-exposed" rather than simply "cribbed." For Banham, history is so embedded as to become invisible—yet he doesn't deny that Stirling and Gowan know their history, that even in this "purely" functional building influence is at work. Frampton—here in rare agreement with Banham—marvels that although the building "almost comprises a compendium of early modern constructional development" there is no "single specific quotation."[75] The building's true distinction, he writes, is precisely that "both its formal and conceptual influences have been fully absorbed into the total abstraction of its final form."[76]

Both Banham and Frampton suggest that Leicester registers influence in a way that exceeds "style-spotting" or "source hunting"—diverting but ultimately trivial exercises that, it might be argued, have no logical conclusion and

Figure 72
Stirling and Gowan, Leicester Engineering Building. The lecture hall volumes suspended beneath the administrative and laboratory towers embody solidified space.

Figure 73
Konstantin Melnikov, Rusakov Workers' Club, Moscow, 1929. The "source" for Stirling and Gowan's volumetrically expressed lecture halls.

potentially open up an endless chain of references. Couldn't we also say that the plan of Leicester, with its juxtaposition of an "expressive" element and a rectangular block, recalls Le Corbusier's Pavillon Suisse? And what about the crystalline glass forms? Don't they derive from Bruno Taut or even Paul Scheerbart? There is no way to measure any greater or lesser truth, or validity to the claim, other than visual similarity. Bloom's call for a more "antithetical" criticism that looks to uncover the revisionary ratios at work offers a more productive analytical frame in that it doesn't propose to "understand" the work or to uncover the "real" sources that were in the minds of the architects, but instead to consider how the work of Stirling and Gowan's predecessors is "revisioned" at Leicester. Put more simply, the focus shifts from a search for the object being reconfigured to the act of reconfiguration itself.

The Rusakov Workers' Club is an apt source to consider in these terms, particularly since it is the most accessible and certainly most discussed "quotation" in the building. Melnikov's influence is unquestionable though perhaps overemphasized and oversimplified. Rather than conjecture on the architects' "preoccupations" or intentions, however, it is useful to consider the specific means through which Leicester's lecture halls allow us to "see again" Melnikov's "original."

The most significant difference between Stirling and Gowan's lecture halls at Leicester and their predecessors by Melnikov is the degree of visual and structural independence they have within the overall scheme. At Rusakov only the upper portions of the theaters emerge from the building envelope; the rest of the theater volumes are buried within the overall building profile. At Leicester, by contrast, the volume of the theater is revealed in its entirety (figs. 72, 73). The lecture halls become more or less autonomous objects, harnessed within the overall building cage. Their independence is reinforced by their dramatic cantilevers, which make them appear to literally escape from the rest of the building, and by the fact that around every edge they are confronted by a contrasting material or a gap and seem to "float" above the brick base. Structurally, the theaters are tied to the stair and elevator cores, but this connection is concealed behind their cantilevered masses so they effectively read as separate.

The volumetric treatment of the lecture halls at Leicester can be contrasted with Stirling's earlier scheme for Sheffield, in which the Melnikovian lecture hall first appears as a compositional element. At Sheffield, Stirling multiplies the number of lecture halls (eight in total), alternately flips them left to right, stacks them, and then encases them within the rectangular structural frame of the building. The original orientation of the Melnikov lecture halls—rotating out from the building's central core—is reconfigured so that the theaters instead align with the rectilinear grid, the sectional outlines of each theater legible as an exaggerated bas-relief in the façade. Here Stirling seems to be "correcting" Melnikov's work, much as he corrected the Maisons Jaoul at Ham Common; the theaters at Sheffield become more systematic, more rational, more orderly then their Melnikovian precedent. This is a very different

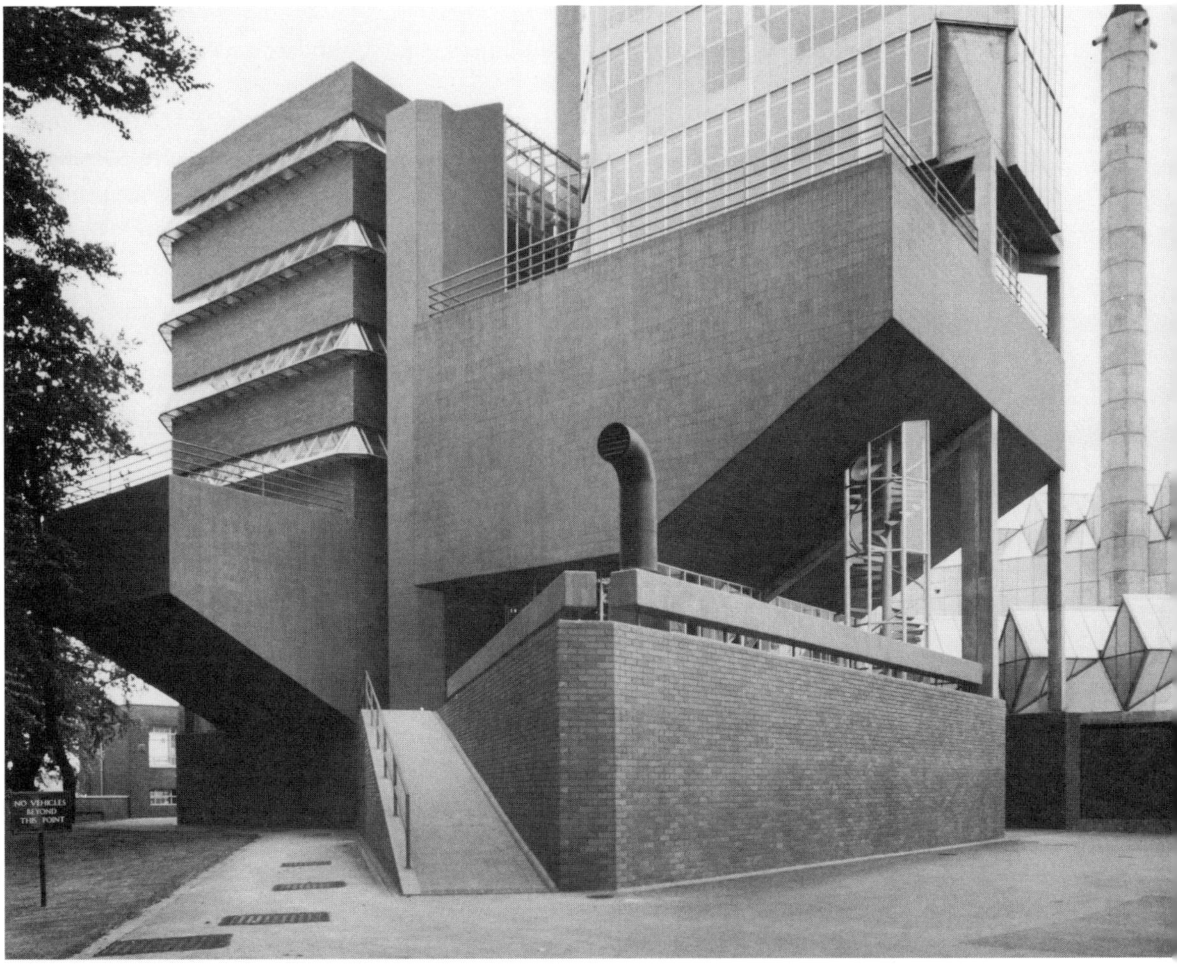
NO VEHICLES BEYOND THIS POINT

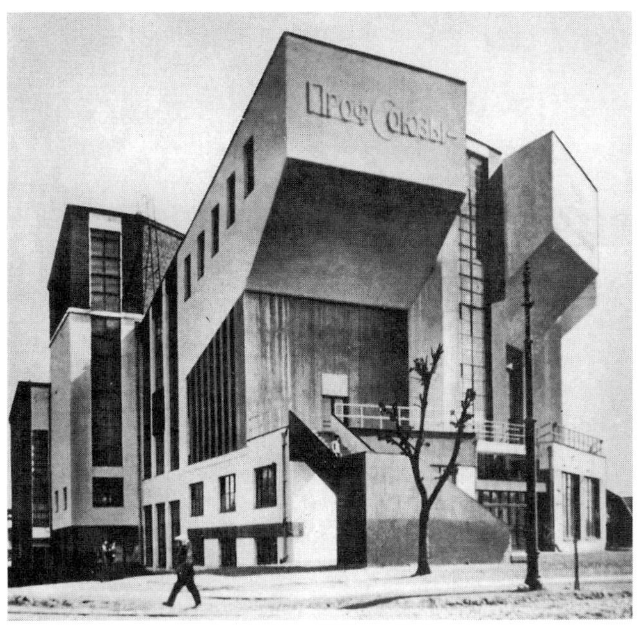

ПрофСоюзы

treatment from that of Leicester's emphatic, freestanding lecture halls, which propose an extension and fulfillment—not a standardization or rationalization—of the original version.

This analytical lens of revisioning can be applied equally to the other sources, including the Johnson Wax Building. Again the visual reference is unmistakable (though perhaps less glaringly so), but the specific means through which Stirling revisions Wright have not been fully explored by critics or historians (figs. 74, 75). As Frampton notes, Wright's influence can be registered in the use of interior tiling (the "glazed bridge links") and the brick podium, and he convincingly situates Stirling and Gowan's use of the podium at Leicester as a continuation of a Wrightian strategy that reinforces horizontality, particularly at the entrance.[77] Jacobus develops a more direct comparison between the towers of the two projects, noting that "both buildings offer the play of a vertical against a horizontal volume" but that Wright's tower is "all one thing" whereas Stirling and Gowan's "visibly articulates its circulation."[78] Indeed, the singularity of Wright's laboratory tower contrasts with the articulated collection of vertical elements in Stirling and Gowan's tower complex. Wright's tower consists of alternating horizontal bands of brick and translucent glass, with a thin concrete edge at the top and bottom of each brick band, revealing a hint of the concrete construction that supports the cantilevered floor slabs. In Wright's tower, the bands run seamlessly around the building's rounded corners. Leicester's laboratory tower picks up on the horizontal banding but introduces significant modifications—using a chamfered rather than a rounded corner (though only the glass, not the brick, is chamfered), removing the concrete "edge" to the brick bands, and projecting the glass beyond the brick. In the administration tower Leicester is a revisioning of Wright's tower as well; here the alternating glass/concrete banding is visible mainly at night—the transparency of the all-glass façade revealing the structural system by a means that recalls Wright's building. In the many night photographs taken of Leicester, the two towers appear as negatives of one another; the thin illuminated glass rings of the laboratory tower echoing the opaque concrete floor slabs of the same width in the administration tower.

At Leicester, the brick and glass play a much more complex volumetric tug-of-war than in Wright's version, particularly in the laboratory building. Here Stirling and Gowan complete the suggestion implicit in Wright's earlier project that glass is becoming "solid," achieved largely through the rounded edge. But because of the flush façade, at Johnson Wax there is a more ambiguous reading between glass and brick, both visually and in terms of which piece registers as structurally dominant. In the laboratory tower at Leicester, this glass/brick battle is played out in more deliberate terms; the glass penetrates the brick exterior "cube," and the laboratory tower appears to have two façades—a glass one layered behind the brick "box," which escapes at the horizontal cuts.

A final example of Stirling's historical revisionings can be seen in the glass stair tower beneath the large lecture hall, which penetrates the under-

Figure 74
Stirling and Gowan, Leicester Engineering Building. At night, the horizontal banding of glass and brick in both the laboratory and administrative towers is highlighted.

Figure 75
Frank Lloyd Wright, Johnson Wax Building, Research Tower, Racine, Wisconsin, 1951. Wright's singular tower also alternates glass and brick bands.

side of the lecture volume (fig. 76). The stair has been compared to Walter Gropius's factory building in Cologne (1914), and Stirling himself compared it to Ellis's Cook Street Building. In the Gropius example, a glazed circular stair at the corner of the factory reveals the serpentine stair wrapped around a central core. Ellis's stair, similarly glazed, occupies the courtyard space at the back of his building and seems to have no central core but instead to be cantilevered from individual floors. In both earlier instances the striking glass cylindrical volume is anchored to the building. But at Leicester the stair tower completely breaks free from any adjacencies or connections to other

Figure 76
Stirling and Gowan, Leicester Engineering Building. The free-standing glass stair beneath the large lecture hall offers an entrance for latecomers.

parts of the program—even more dramatically so than the lecture halls. Its structural and visual independence distinguish it from the Gropius or Ellis precedents, and, as with the lecture theaters, force us to see both of the earlier examples as less complete iterations of the "glazed stair idea." Stirling's stair becomes even more resonant in that it seems to be holding aloft the lecture theater—not only is it stripped from its parasitic relationship to other structural members, it now appears to be structurally inverted, with glass as "support."

Rather than simply repeating Melnikov's lecture theaters or Wright's tower or Gropius's stair, Stirling and Gowan radicalize and revision them. In the case of the Melnikov towers, Stirling and Gowan's exaggerated cantilevers and disassociation—both material and structural—from the rest of the project suggest that Melnikov didn't go far enough with his original form, that it could have been taken to a greater and more profound extreme. Melnikov's theaters begin to seem a weaker, milder version; the full volume of the lecture halls, which, thanks to Leicester, are now perceived as three-dimensional objects, seem to be buried within the Melnikov building, almost as if they desired to break free. Similarly, Gropius's glass stair appears trapped within the building envelope rather than exalted and freestanding, as the stair at Leicester. And the glass/brick dichotomy in the Johnson Wax Building appears somehow less clear than the pair of towers at Leicester, each of which seems to explore a functional and material logic of glass and brick.

None of these revisionings represents a "swerve" from the original, or even a "generalizing away of uniqueness," but rather a "completion," or what Bloom terms "tessera."[79] In this scenario, the later poet "provides what his imagination tells him would complete the otherwise 'truncated' precursor poem."[80] For Bloom this "antithetical" use of the precursor's work suggests that the original work would be "worn out" if not "redeemed as a newly fulfilled and enlarged" work by the later poet. Perhaps the most provocative aspect of tessera is the suggestion that the later work isn't simply a copy or even a correction but a "redemption" of the earlier work. For some critics, the familiarity of the early modernist references at play, the seeming regression, suggested that Leicester was nostalgic, or even naïve, in its allusions to earlier modernist icons. In his otherwise favorable review of the building when it was first completed, Jacobus writes that Leicester "takes us back, embarrassingly, to the adolescence of contemporary design."[81] Bloom's framework, however, allows us to see the referential gestures at Leicester as "forward." Revisioning, in this case, fundamentally alters the way we understand the "original" and introduces the possibility that the later version could, in fact, supersede it. To say that another way: we begin to read Leicester as the originary moment—as the "stronger" version of the idea. To return to Banham's provocation, Leicester did indeed "invent modernism all over again," but not simply through its own novelty or radicality: Leicester engaged modernism's canonical works and "rewrote" them in such a way that modernism itself was forever changed.

CHAPTER 4

ONE ENORMOUS GESTURE

FLOREY BUILDING (1971)

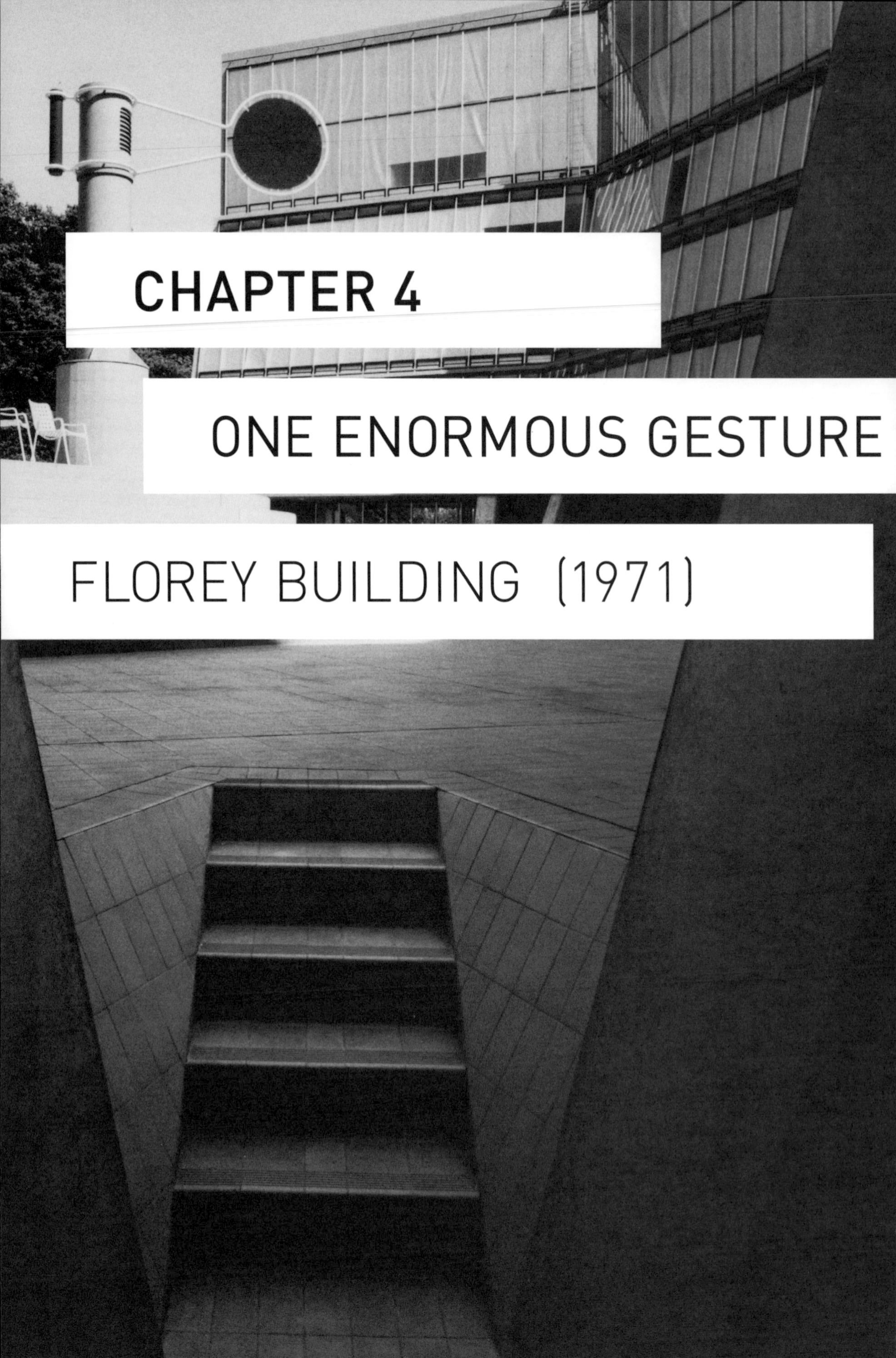

The mid-1960s and early 1970s, following the completion of the Leicester Engineering Building, were some of the most prolific and critically acclaimed years in Stirling's career. During this period—the only time he practiced alone rather than in a partnership—Stirling completed the Cambridge University History Faculty Building (1967), Students' Residence at St. Andrews (1968), and the Olivetti Training School at Haslemere (1971).[1] He also designed urban redevelopment studies for New York City and Lima, Peru (1968 and 1969–70, respectively), as well as three well-known and extensively published, though unbuilt, projects: Dorman Long Headquarters (1965), Siemens AG Headquarters (1969), and Derby Civic Centre (1970). The diversity of these works attests to a range of influences and explorations; historians and critics have discussed them in relation to technology, prefabrication, monumentality, urbanism, and a burgeoning classicism.[2]

In the various considerations of this period, however, the Florey Building at Queen's College Oxford, begun in 1966 and completed in 1971, has been largely overlooked (fig. 77). When it is discussed, Oxford is typically linked with Leicester and Cambridge, the three presented as a trio of university

Figure 77
James Stirling (firm), Florey Building, The Queen's College, University of Oxford, England, 1971.

buildings that followed the "Corbusian" work of the 1950s and preceded the "museum" or "German" series of the later 1970s. Mark Girouard begins his 1972 review of the newly completed Florey Building: "Leicester Engineering, Cambridge History Faculty and now Oxford Florey; three buildings of similar size in similar materials for similar patrons and based on the same approach," stating that the buildings were "based on exactly the same design strategy."[3] Robert Maxwell, also writing on the completion of Florey, says that it "seems to be the last of a series" in the "red-tile style."[4] Joseph Rykwert, in his 1972 article, echoes his fellow critics: "Stirling's latest building . . . belongs in the sequence of Stirling's executed buildings with the Cambridge History Faculty or even with the Leicester Engineering Building."[5] A 1968 exhibition at the Museum of Modern Art in New York—"Three University Buildings"—solidified the trinity, and a collection of essays on this "Red Trilogy" further cements the connection.[6] Stirling himself seemed to validate the temporal grouping of the works, and of his projects more generally, stating in 1980: "I think our projects have tended to come in series. Brick buildings in the '50s, glass skin and tile buildings in the early '60s."[7] He reiterated the characterization in 1990, calling the buildings "variations on a theme, all low cost buildings, comprised of industrial glazing, engineering bricks and external tiles."[8]

Indeed, what Maxwell called Stirling's red-tile style is markedly different not only from the architect's earlier or later work but also from contemporaneous projects, such as St. Andrews, Runcorn, and Olivetti, which employed techniques of prefabrication (in concrete and plastic), or the more monumental/megastructural steel-and-glass work of Dorman Long or Siemens. Leicester, Cambridge, and Florey were all designed within a ten-year span, were built on university campuses, and, perhaps most importantly, share a seemingly identical material palette: concrete frame infilled with patent glazing, clad with a mixture of red brick and ceramic tile.

This grouping, however, has, in most accounts, identified Florey as a watered-down version of its predecessors—particularly of Leicester, one of the most critically and popularly lauded buildings of this era.[9] In his Stirling biography *Big Jim,* Mark Girouard dedicates an entire chapter to the "Leicester Explosion," while Cambridge and Oxford follow in a chapter tellingly titled "After Leicester." The description of Oxford receives only two paragraphs of the nearly three-hundred-page book.[10] In his introduction to the 1984 monograph *James Stirling: Buildings and Projects,* Colin Rowe calls Oxford "little more than a repetition, just a bit more of the pseudo-aggressive same of Leicester and Cambridge."[11] And in his essay "Real and English," Peter Eisenman is even more explicit in valorizing Leicester at the expense of its successors: "Despite recent critical pronouncements, which would have us place Leicester, Cambridge and Oxford in an historical continuum, it is my contention that Leicester remains seminal and singular in this context." He continues, even more forcefully, "Cambridge and Oxford are not polemical. They seem to be merely borrowing on the iconic charge given by the use of similar materials and building methods developed at Leicester."[12]

My argument in this chapter runs counter to these pronouncements. Rather than seeing Florey as a "lesser" Leicester, or a recapitulation of its motifs, I find Florey a culmination not only of the red-brick group but of Stirling's work as a whole up to that point. Florey is in fact the "seminal and singular" project. Unlike the "exploded" articulation of Leicester, Florey is a contained and immediately comprehensible entity—"one enormous gesture," to borrow a phrase from Vincent Scully.[13] Although Florey's highly sculptural and unprecedented form is seemingly untethered from historical influences, in fact it sublimates an array of references. The result is a functionally derived yet semantically rich form that Stirling called "functional-symbolic."[14] At Florey, Stirling continued and advanced his investigation into the idea of type, an inquiry begun at Churchill College, by isolating and revisioning specific components of the "Oxbridge" courtyard while overlaying additional typological "roots." The project is unified and multivalent, semantic and syntactic—in short, Stirling's most dialectical project and a synthesis of his investigation into an historically informed modernism.

STIRLING'S FLOREY SCHEME: REVISIONING COURTYARD ELEMENTS

The idea to construct a new residential building for Queen's College originated in the early 1960s in response to an expanding student population at Oxford. The project was largely the initiative of Lord Howard Florey, elected provost of the college in 1962, who pushed for a new, signature building rather redevelopment of existing sites.[15] This new building would provide residences for graduates and undergraduates, but the majority of their life at the university—including classes and meals—would remain at the college proper. Thus the Florey Building, as it became officially known, was never meant to be a self-contained community, as was Stirling's Churchill College, but rather a satellite dormitory for the principal campus.

The Florey Building was Stirling's earliest solo commission after his breakup with James Gowan in 1963.[16] His selection by Queen's College was controversial from the beginning, as a number of members of the building committee disliked his style—both personal and architectural—and as a group they remained "irretrievably divided on choice of a new architect."[17] Opposition to his appointment was not a result of his identity as a "modern" architect, as might be expected; by the mid-1960s Oxford and Cambridge had effectively accepted modernism as the language of its building campaigns, marking a radical shift from the early 1950s, when, as J. M. Richards wrote in 1952: "There seems not to be, in either of the two old universities, any awareness of what is happening in the arts in the contemporary world . . . even more in architecture."[18] Beginning in the late 1950s, however, modern architecture became widely utilized, if not the norm. At Oxford, specifically, buildings such as The Architects' Co-Partnership's "Beehives" for St. John's College (1958), Powell and Moya's Brasenose College Staircases (1961), Aarne Jacobsen's St. Catherine's College (1964), and Leslie Martin's Manor Road Library Group (1964) signaled a willingness to build in the "new" style.[19] Stirling's Florey Building, then, could develop and extend a modernism that already existed at Oxford, a factor that

Figure 78
Stirling, Florey Building. Site plan. Florey, at lower right, is physically separated from but typologically related to the traditional courtyard buildings of Oxford at left.

Figure 79
Stirling, Florey Building. Axonometric.

undoubtedly enabled a scheme more progressive than would have been accepted even five years earlier.

The site for the new building, along a branch of the Cherwell River in an area northwest of the university known as St. Clement's, comprised largely nondescript buildings and a municipal car park (fig. 78).[20] The site was chosen as part of a larger deal between the city and the university, which intended to build additional dormitories in the area and create a kind of mini residential district, with buildings linked by a public walkway along the Cherwell. The walk was never executed, a fact that proved a great disadvantage for the Florey Building, as many of its design features were predicated on this larger development; the building became a singular episode on what was envisioned as a continuous promenade.

The initial program brief called for an all-male undergraduate dormitory to house as many student rooms as possible given the height restrictions, along with accommodations for a resident bachelor fellow and research fellows, lodging for a porter, and a flat for the caretaker.[21] Although a communal breakfast room and kitchen were to be included, it was stressed that students would still be taking their main meals and all of their classes at the main campus: "Nothing should be done which would encourage the building to become a social centre in competition with the main college buildings in the High Street."[22]

Though Stirling was hired in July 1964, the Florey project did not begin in earnest for nearly another three years as the university wrestled with legal and financial issues. Stirling presented the first design in September 1966 and the site was handed over to the contractor in February 1968, with an estimated construction period of twelve months. Ultimately the building took more than three years to complete, with the first students occupying their rooms in April 1971.[23] At the official opening ceremony in May the provost declared the building "distinctive and uncompromising. . . . We do not doubt that it will be regarded by our successors as a striking example of twentieth-century architecture."[24]

Stirling's "distinctive" scheme responds to the site constraints and programmatic requirements with a relatively simple parti: a roughly U-shaped building surrounding an open courtyard. Rather than a foursquare or even orthogonal plan, the building's layout is semi-octagonal and open to one side. The entire structure is heroically raised one story on eleven oversized concrete A-frame struts that encircle the base of the five-story structure, which steps back at each of the first three levels, leaning onto its concrete "legs" (fig. 79).

Although the building bears little resemblance to its immediate Oxford neighbors, Stirling emphasizes that the courtyard at Florey "tries hard to make connections to the courtyards of the Oxbridge College."[25] In a 1974 lecture he paired photographs of various elements of the Florey Building with their counterparts in traditional Oxbridge buildings, writing: "It was intended that you could recognize the historic elements of: courtyard, entrance gate towers, cloisters; also a central object replacing the traditional fountain or statues of

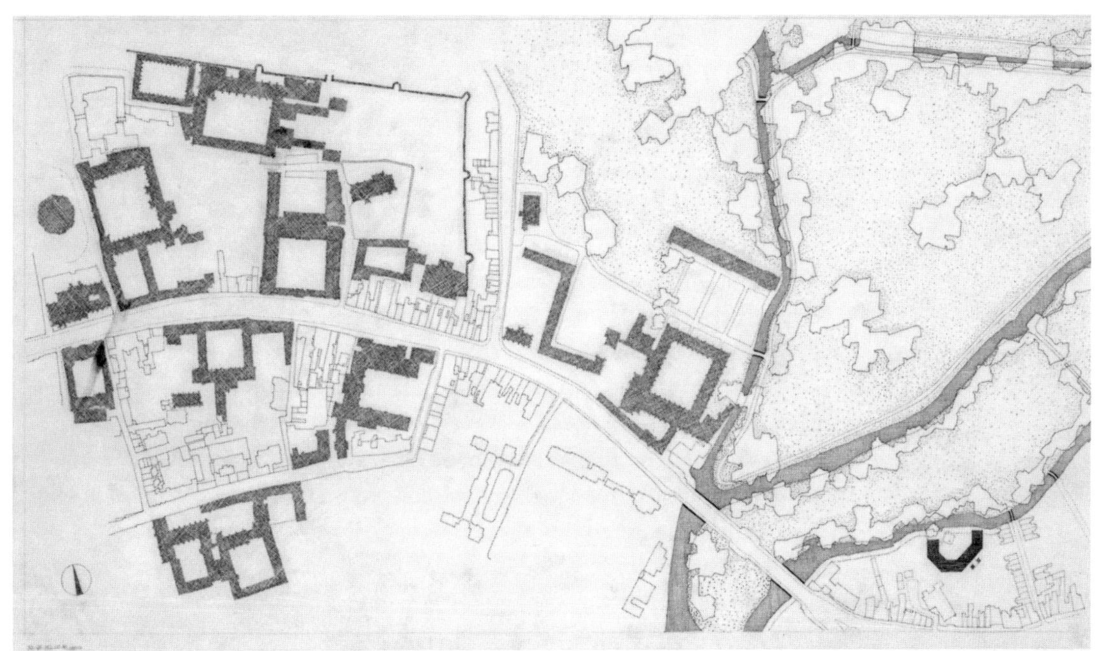

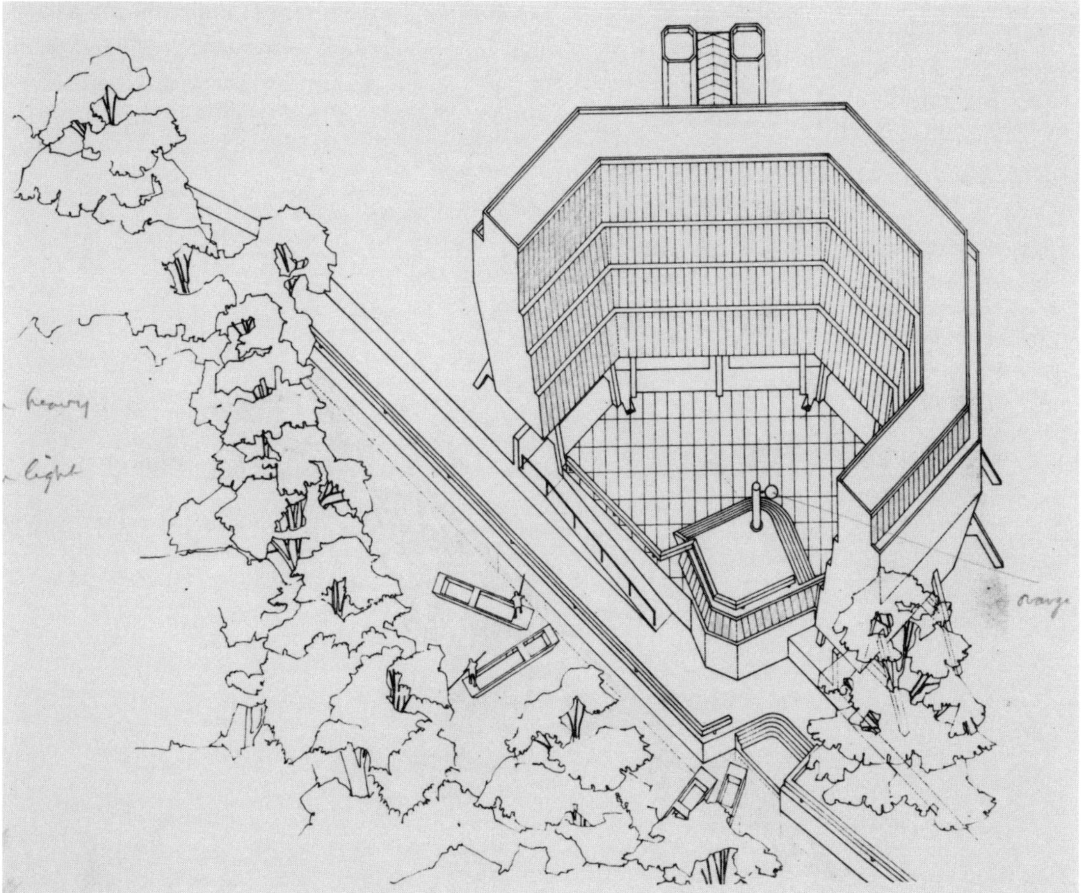

the college founder. In this way we hoped that students and public would not be dis-associated from their cultural past."[26] Like Churchill, Florey retains the core aspects of a typical Oxbridge college—above all, the open courtyard encircled by a ring of student rooms—but Florey's revisionings of the courtyard type are decidedly more radical. Rather than creating an "ideogram" of the college quadrangle as he had at Churchill—distilling the courtyard type to its typological essence—Stirling isolates various components of the type and recasts them after interrogating the core properties of each one.

The most dramatic example of this revisioning of the traditional courtyard model can be seen in the faceted, semi-enclosed shape of the project—a shape that defines enclosure much more loosely than do the fully sealed courtyards of traditional Oxford colleges. Earlier sketches demonstrate a clear directive to work through some version of a courtyard plan from the outset: this is the first project for which substantial process documentation is available, and in Stirling's undated "doodles" we see myriad plans and axonometrics (all in Stirling's distinctive Lilliputian scale) of various courtyard iterations; in some the courtyard is formed by three orthogonal bars in a true U-shape, in others by more irregular shapes, and in still others by splayed bars (similar to the dormitories at St. Andrews). Some are curved, some are rectilinear, some are faceted (fig. 80). Some lean in, some don't. None of them display the distinctive A-frame struts of the final design, or pilotis of any kind—suggesting that the notion to elevate the building was a later development. Regardless

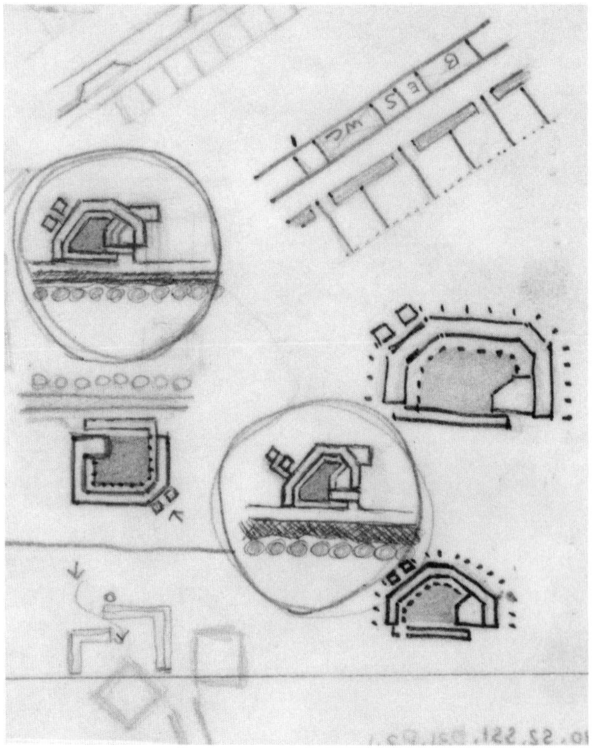

Figure 80
Stirling, Florey Building. An early undated sketch explores variations of a faceted, linear building surrounding a courtyard, open to the side facing the Cherwell River.

Figure 81
Stirling, Florey Building. Stairs between the concrete A-frame struts lead to the paved courtyard half a level above.

of its specific form, however, the idea of the courtyard, enclosed except on the side facing the river, is evident throughout. The persistent investigation into the courtyard and the variability in its shape throughout these early sketches reveal Stirling's interest in testing the *idea* of an enclosed courtyard space rather than an adherence to any particular formal solution.

In the final design the courtyard is raised half a level above grade and paved with ceramic tiles rather than covered in the traditional grass—a gesture allegedly meant to encourage a more democratic use of the space (fig. 81).

Figure 82
Stirling, Florey Building. The cloister surrounding the courtyard.

Figure 83
Stirling, Florey Building. The river entrance was intended to be primary, as illustrated by Leon Krier's famous perspective of a punter approaching the building.

Certainly a paved surface is no more democratic than a grass one (in fact, the opposite might convincingly be argued), but the tiled surface carried a different set of associations than did the traditional grass courtyards that are reserved solely for Oxford dons, and the unexpected material was meant to encourage "everyone to walk."[27] A raised platform in one corner of the courtyard—actually the roof of the breakfast room below—offers a further modification to the traditionally flat courtyard surface. An exhaust vent emerging from the center of the platform is further elaborated as a weathercock that rotates with the winds and delivers an impish nod to the traditional statue at the center of the college courtyard (as well as an update of the Leicester "snorkel").

Access to the courtyard is from a cloister encircling its perimeter (a traditional arrangement) but sunk half a level below with connections possible only through four short stairs, each at one of the building's interior "corners" (a decidedly untraditional solution) (fig. 82). In another modification of the type, the Florey cloister does not provide direct access to student rooms via staircases (something that Stirling maintained, albeit in a highly modified form, at Churchill). Instead, rooms are entered from corridors that run along the backside of the building on each floor and connect to the main elevator and stair towers. The cloister at Florey, then, loses its conventional function as the principal circulation route to the student rooms but retains its function as perambulation around the center court; this is made even more pronounced by its vertical difference from the courtyard.

In fact, with the loss of its identity as an access point to the student rooms, the cloister becomes largely an urban passage through the project, from St. Clement's to the river side, or vice versa. The river entrance, Stirling wrote in the architect's report, was "intended to have almost equal importance as the main entrance, particularly when the river walk is extended and there are other college buildings in the St. Clement's area."[28] A series of ramps lead directly from the river walk to the cloister, slipping past the sunken breakfast room, whose clerestory windows peer out onto the river walk. One of the most published perspectives of the project (redrawn later by Leon Krier) is from the vantage point of the river, showing a punter approaching the building (fig. 83). The drawing reveals the significance of this entrance in the architect's eyes; no similar drawings were ever made from the St. Clement's side.

This river emphasis was evident in other Oxford projects of the era as colleges began to expand into formerly rural areas. Powell and Moya's Wolfson College, begun just after the Florey Building was completed, in 1972, mimicks the building, its arms splayed open to the river. And the Smithsons' contemporaneous Garden Building for St. Hilda's (1971) just a few minutes down the Cherwell, is also oriented to the river. Stirling's response to the riparian site at Florey was unique in that the building literally captures the river as a part of the plan. Stirling intended the "wall of trees" directly across the river as the fourth wall of the courtyard, the "missing" side of the project. Tellingly, in the published site plan the river is rendered black, like the building, marking it as another "figure" in the composition. Not simply a boundary or an edge to the project, it was enveloped and internalized within the plan. The river also inflects the plan geometry—one arm of the building reaches out slightly farther than the other to accommodate the bend in the river—and provides justification not only for the northern orientation of the scheme, questioned for its poor sun exposure, but also for the fact the building turns its back on St. Clement's (though a lack of desirability of the St. Clement's context might equally be cited).

Opening the project to the river generates a building that relates to the rest of campus through views of the spires and monuments of the college beyond. "Every resident will be able to see from his room across the river and through the trees the skyline of Oxford above the meadow."[29] Here an attempt is made to visually link the project to the rest of campus as a substitute for its physical distance, and to rectify what Frampton termed the project's "nostalgia for the centre" in its status as an "isolated object," removed from the "honorific threshold of Magdalen."[30] Again the site plan is telling. Florey is rendered as a solid black figure along with the scattering of the traditional colleges—no buildings on the St. Clement's side appear in black, and the river seems to link Florey to the rest of campus rather than divide it. As a comparison, the Smithsons' St. Hilda's Building, also allegedly oriented across the Cherwell and toward the gardens beyond, is a solid, cubic volume with no adjustments that reflect any orientation to the river; one critic called it "plain, square and dumpy" (fig. 84).[31] Although student rooms all face outward and are given large glazing panels, the building itself is in no way modified to account for the river view or access—the Smithsons simply transplant the center-core office structure from their Economist building of 1964, replacing offices with dormitory rooms.

If the river approach was considered an important access point to the Florey building, the approach from the parking lot on the St. Clement's side never-

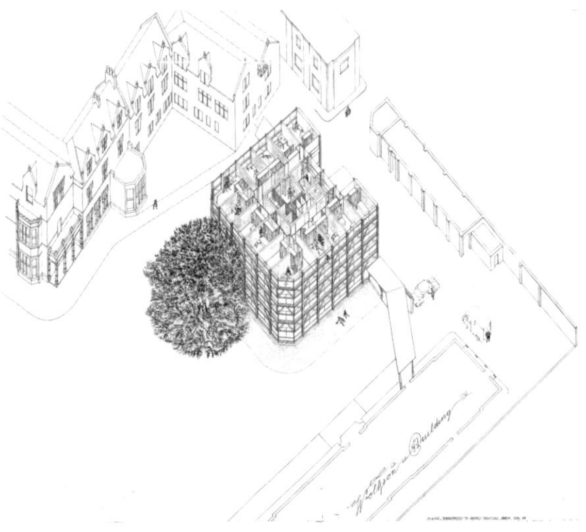

Figure 84
Alison and Peter Smithson, Garden Building, St. Hilda's College, University of Oxford, England, 1971.

Figure 85
Stirling, Florey Building. The "back" of the building at St. Clement's, with the pair of red-tile-clad stair towers.

theless remained the "main" entrance. Stirling reuses the chamfered brick towers he had employed at Leicester and at Cambridge, here placing them side by side to define an updated "entrance tower gate." The towers are pulled away from the building proper and connected by glass-encased walkways at each level, a decidedly less expressionistic version of the "crystalline" glass towers at Leicester, which are now subordinate to the red towers (fig. 85). Subverting the expected entry point between the two towers, Stirling slides the entry around and to the side of the towers, and then slips it beneath the elevated building (fig. 86).

Elevating the project was arguably the boldest gesture in the scheme, and it at first seems to suggest the greatest swerve from the traditional type. But the massive red-brick shape, hovering somewhat perilously on its slender concrete legs, is only a slight exaggeration of the foreboding, protective walls of the traditional Oxbridge college. In both cases the inner sanctum of the courtyard is protected, though at Florey Stirling elevates the building so that it no longer serves as the boundary between inside and out; for this Stirling inserts a low brick wall beneath the building, tracing the back edge of the cloister. This brick wall remains visually subservient to the building volume

Figure 86
Stirling, Florey Building. Ground-floor plan.

Figure 87
Stirling, Florey Building. Upper-floor plan. Student rooms line the interior courtyard while circulation corridors and services are placed along the outer edge.

above it. Here Florey's elevated structure becomes analogous to the earth berm at Churchill; although the former is raised up and the latter is rooted into the ground, both create what Stirling called an "internal environment, private, enclosed and protected."[32]

All student rooms are single-loaded along the building's interior façade, with a corridor behind. The corridor provides access to the two stair towers, one at each end of the building, as well to the toilets, sinks, and showers, which are inserted in a thickened band at the "back" edge of the building along St. Clement's (fig. 87). The corridor plan reflected a significant shift from the traditional staircase model and was generally frowned upon by university administrators not only as inappropriate for the college setting, as suggested in a 1957 report, but also for compromising a "sense of individuality and independence."[33] From a planning perspective, however, the corridor allowed the courtyard façade to be totally given over to rooms, unlike the traditional staircase model in which the stair towers necessarily defined vertical elements on the interior courtyard façade. More importantly, the corridor was meant to engender social space. Stirling originally intended to construct small communal areas or "by-ways" at each bend in the corridor, with small kitchens where students could gather over tea, but these were never carried out, for budgetary reasons as well as for the perceived threat to the importance of socializing at the main Queen's campus. These mini communal facilities, which were also a prominent feature in Stirling's design for the Students' Residence at St. Andrews, reflected the influence of the Smithsons' "streets-in-the-air" from their Golden Lane competition, one of the most influential projects of the early 1950s.[34] Unlike the Smithsons' version, however, Stirling's corridors are enclosed and occupy the "back" of the building; they also introduce a "bend" that Stirling felt would help eliminate the corridor's "institutional" associations and enable social interaction at each of the building's levels.[35]

TYPE: NEUTRALIZING THE PAST

Stirling's use of the corridor at Florey was one of the few true divergences from the model of the "typical" Oxbridge college. The stair towers, courtyard, cloister, even the "statue" at the center, are all forms that rely on and yet reconfigure core "principles" of the courtyard type. As he had at Churchill College, Stirling relied on his deep knowledge of this type, but the typological investigation went beyond his personal biography or interests. Stirling's investigation into the courtyard type was informed by a larger typological discourse emergent at the time.

Though the concept of type is a longstanding one in architecture, it achieved new relevance and became an important locus of criticism and debate in the 1960s and 1970s, particularly in Britain.[36] Italian architect Giulio Carlo Argan is generally credited with reintroducing the subject in his article "On the Typology of Architecture," originally published in German in 1962 and translated into English by Joseph Rykwert for *Architectural Design* in December 1963.[37] Relying principally on Quatremère de Quincy's definition of type

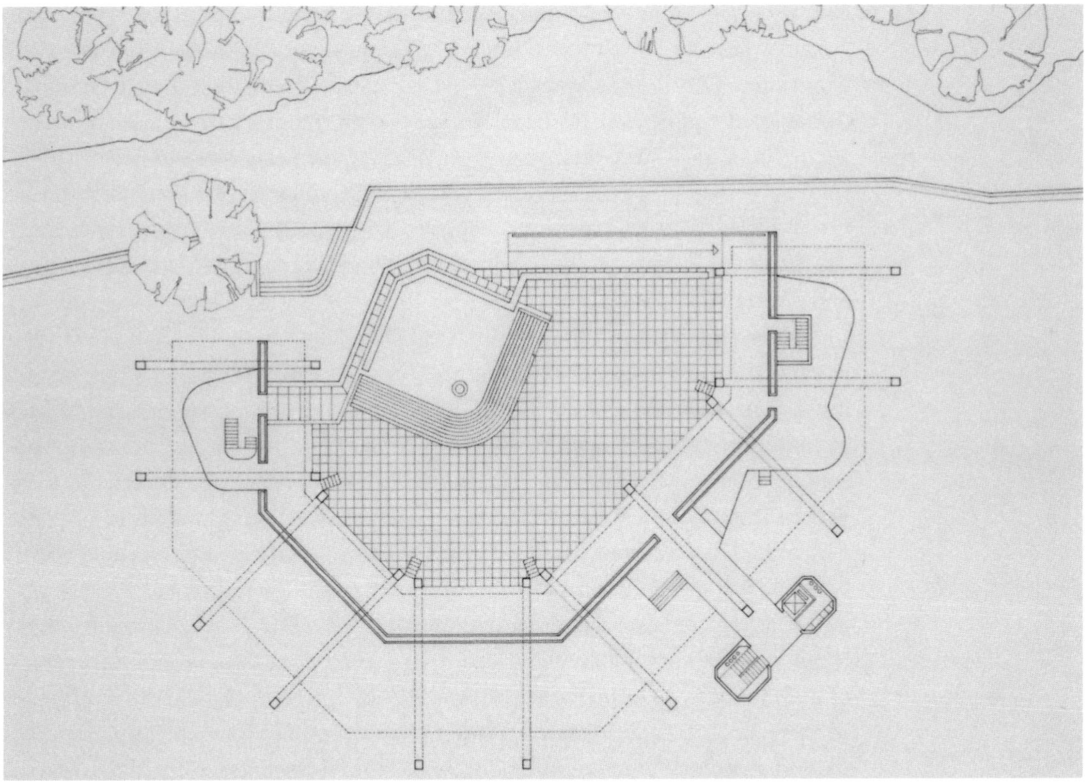

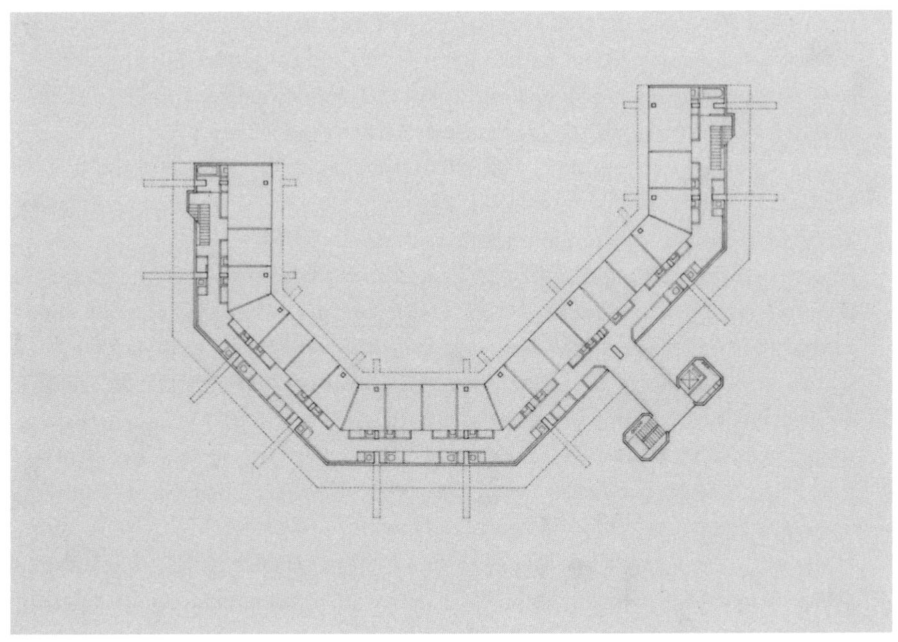

as a "process of reducing a complex of formal variants to a common root form," Argan argues for its relevance in modern architectural culture.[38] Following Quatremère, he distinguishes between the idea of "type" and that of "model." "All is exact and defined in the model; in the 'type' everything is more or less vague," he writes, suggesting that type, in its "vagueness," allowed for architectural invention.[39] Argan puts forth type as a "schema" or "grid" within which the artist or architect intervenes. Through an engagement with type, he argues, the artist "frees himself from being conditioned by definite historical form and neutralizes the past."[40]

In his 1967 article "Typology and Design Method" Alan Colquhoun furthers Argan's discussion of typology, calling for a return to the idea of type, or, more accurately, for an end to its prohibition, which lingered as a byproduct of functionalist dogma.[41] Architects of the modern movement, Colquhoun argues, professed allegiance to scientific methods and ostensibly rational practices, yet at the root of their belief system lay a highly *irrational* foundation, a "teleological doctrine of techno-aesthetic forms."[42] As an antidote to this process of "intuition in a cultural vacuum," Colquhoun posits the notion of type, "which has been rejected again and again by modern theorists." An understanding of typological models, he argues, provides a way to theorize and ground the act of architecture, as opposed to the untheorized, "bio-technical determinism" of early modern functionalism. Rather than rejecting history as antithetical to modern architecture he instead suggests that tradition is necessarily invoked with every formal act, and that to deny this is to deny creativity as well as communicative power. "Not only are we not free from the forms of the past, and from the availability of these forms as typological models, but . . . if we assume we are free, we have lost control over a very active sector of our imagination and of our power to communicate with others."[43]

Argan's and Colquhoun's concept of type is distinct from, though not unrelated to, the traditional understanding of the term as any group of a similar kind of building—a notion perhaps most associated with Nikolaus Pevsner's *History of Building Types* (1976).[44] In this understanding of type, each iteration relates to all of its predecessors, and, most importantly, must respect the formal vocabulary associated with its type: a church has certain characteristics, which are different from a library's, which are different from a prison's, and so on. Unlike Pevsner's fundamentally formalist reading of type, however, Colquhoun's and Argan's definition of type is meta-formal, so that the "common root form" has no particular formal manifestation but is indebted to any number of previous forms. Perhaps more important than its relation to form, however, is type's relation to history. Every architectural act, Colquhoun argues, relies on a history; architecture, like a language, is dependent on a structure of meaning to function and be understood.

Embedded in this formulation of type as it was discussed in the 1960s are two key ideas. First, type does not preclude individual creativity but in fact enables it. "The typological and the inventive aspect of the creative process are continuous and interlaced."[45] This links to the notion that the type prescribes no specific form and in fact encourages formal inventiveness in its "vagueness." Second, the use of historical type, though it relies on past examples, in fact *dehistoricizes* historical precedent; to borrow Argan's term, the past is "neutralized." Argan and Colquhoun suggest a methodology through which history can be utilized but its historical specificity removed—a means to generate new forms from the principles embodied in the historical past. This concept of a neutral or vague but nevertheless essential historical past would provide postwar architects, including Stirling, a way to fold historical sources into their modern designs through the neutral filter of typology. In other words, typology allowed history to reenter modernism, partly through the backhanded argument that modernism was unknowingly and uncritically incorporating "tradition" already.

Michael Hays has argued that the idea of type represents the "desire"—never to be fulfilled—of relating the singular architectural incarnation to a larger system from which is it always, necessarily, apart. Type, in Hays's terms, acts as a "mediator" between the single architectural "instance" and the "substratum of codes, categories, customs, and conventions."[46] He singles out Aldo Rossi's architecture as exemplifying a typological reduction of elements to a fundamental urquality, an act that for Rossi is necessarily tainted with melancholy: "The originality of Rossi's work may well be its capacity to convey, alternately with melancholy or unblinking disenchantment, that the traditional European city—which in some sense means architecture itself—is forever lost, and that the architectural avant-garde has reached an end."[47] And indeed Rossi is the architect of the 1960s and 1970s most associated with the discourse around type—a result of his own writings and projects as well as the writings of others, most notably Rafael Moneo.

Stirling, however, is a worthy subject as well. He clearly understood the courtyard type as still functionally relevant; as he notes in his description of the Churchill College scheme, "The working of a residential college has changed only slightly in the last few centuries."[48] And, as we have just seen, he retained the core components of the type—courtyard, tower, "statue," cloister—albeit in a highly revised form. So on the one hand he is dissecting the type and then reimagining each of its pieces while respecting the original principles governing their forms (the cloister still provides circulation around a courtyard, the dormitory rooms still encircle the open space). More broadly, however, Stirling employs the notion of type as a springboard for invention, using the investigation into the underlying principles to generate hybrids, contaminating the base notion of "courtyard type" with other typological models. It was crucial, however, that each of the other typological models remained subservient to the overall reading of the courtyard building; this coincident, multiple reading of the additional overlaid types is ultimately what gives the project its semantic depth.

The most immediately recognizable of these additional laminates is the amphitheater. The reading of the building as an amphitheater is supported not only by the roughly semicircular plan of the building but also by the stepping

Figure 88
Stirling, Florey Building. View to the courtyard and the roof of the breakfast room from one of the double-height rooms on the top floor.

back at each level, which creates a kind of enlarged seating ring surrounding the central courtyard. The elevated "stage"—the roof of the semisubmerged breakfast room and kitchen—enforces the reading. Although student rooms facing onto the courtyard are a standard aspect of the traditional college, at Florey their voyeuristic function is enhanced through the building's small scale, which defines a direct visual confrontation with rooms across the courtyard, and also through the use of floor-to-ceiling patent glazing. Students are confronted with the gaze of their counterparts across the court (fig. 88). In this way Florey recalls the panoptic, surveillant plan of the Cambridge History Faculty Building, where the entire semicircular reading room is designed to be seen from the librarian's desk at the center.[49] At Florey, however, the panoptic model is inverted, the gaze shifted from the center to the periphery; student rooms are no longer under the watch of any central figure but instead of one another.

Another important typological overlay is the more prosaic but significant notion of the bar building. Florey can be interpreted as part of an entirely different lineage from the Churchill College courtyard model if we consider the building as a linear building wrapping a central space rather than as a central space carved out of a solid block. The most important project from this competing trajectory was Selwyn College—a linear dormitory designed eight years earlier for Cambridge University but never executed (fig. 89).[50] At Selwyn Stirling proposes a linear, S-shaped building that snakes along one edge of the college's garden—with an interior glass façade that leans "in"

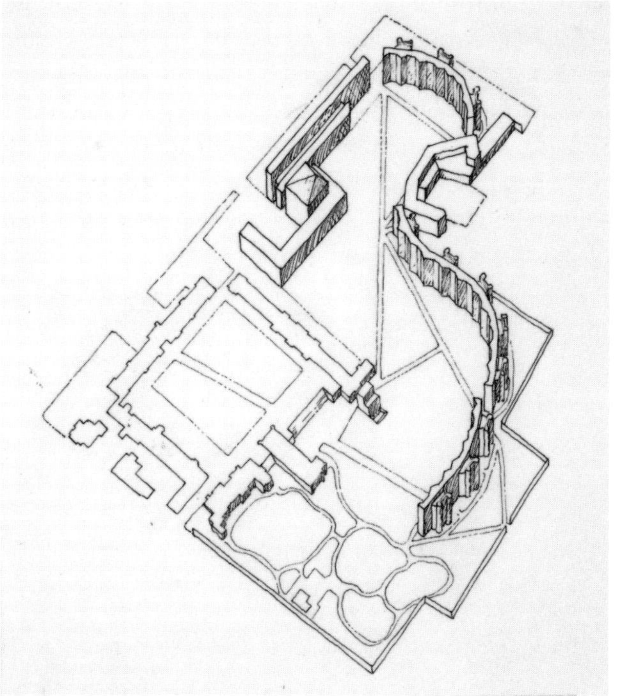

Figure 89
Stirling and Gowan, Selwyn College, University of Cambridge, England, 1959. Axonometric.

rather than Florey's "out"—a shape resonant with Aalto's Baker dormitory at MIT (1948). In 1965 Stirling wrote that the "project for extending Selwyn College was an important move in the direction of our present designs," by which he meant a move away from the "articulated" designs of Leicester and Ham Common to "wrapped glass" buildings, such as Cambridge and Dorman Long.[51] Given the Leicester/Cambridge/Florey triad described at the opening of the chapter, Stirling's own differentiation between Leicester and Florey is here significant. For him they represented two typological directions: the "expressed" or articulated building and the linear bar building.

The key point regarding Selwyn is that the bar building begins to *bend*, and in so doing it defines enclosure; the linear building is transformed from marking an edge to defining a space. Here we are again confronted with the influence of Le Corbusier—in this case, the bent slabs or *redents*. Stirling's Old People's Home of 1966 is another important work in this trajectory—a building in which a series of straight segments are rotated around a central courtyard space (fig. 90). Unlike the sinuous plan of Selwyn, the faceted, rotational form of the Old People's Home lends a geometric precision and systematic quality to the "bend." Florey, then, is a conflation of the faceted form of the Old People's Home—now unhinged to open one side—and the stepped sectional shape of Selwyn.

The significance of this "bent" bar concept at Florey is evidenced in Stirling's process sketches, particularly one in which a series of short, linear buildings overlap to create a gentle curve (fig. 91). Although in the final design these segments are faceted rather than overlapping, the early sketches reveal an interest in an aggregation of bar buildings generating a curve. In early hardline drawings, in which the form was tested on the site, the building is rendered as a continuous linear building bent into segments of varying lengths to create the roughly U-shaped parti of the final scheme. These early sketches demonstrate the combination of two typological precedents—the courtyard building and the linear building—with neither dominating. This idea is significant in that it shifts the reading of Florey from a static, centralized plan (like Churchill), out of which a piece has been extracted, to a dynamic plan formed from a linear element wrapping a courtyard space. We might also argue that it generates a misreading of the traditional courtyard as well. In the same way

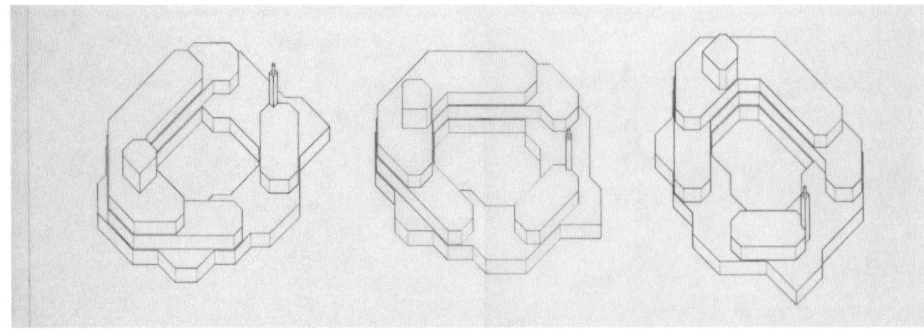

Figure 90
Stirling and Gowan, Old People's Home, London, 1964. Axonometric.

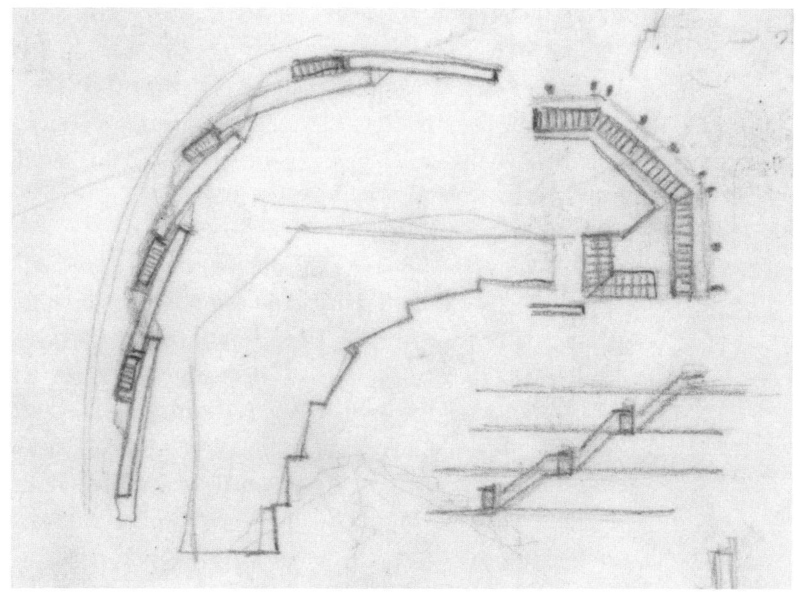

Figure 91
Stirling, Florey Building. The plan sketch at upper left shows overlapping bar buildings used to generate a curving wall.

that the expressed lecture theaters at Leicester shift our reading of Melnikov's "original," Florey's design alters our interpretation of the typical Oxford courtyard building—which is now understood potentially as a bent bar, with the bend at 90 degrees.

Certainly Florey is much further from the typological "root" than Churchill, in its manipulation of specific elements (the entrance tower, the central statue, the cloister) and in the overall form of the building, as well as in the conflation of multiples types (theater, panopticon, "bent" bar). Yet even with this increased formal latitude Florey remains undeniably tied to its typological foundations. Rather than a desire to "essentialize" the precursor, as at Churchill, here is an effort to condense a number of typological ideas into a singular instance. Stirling creates a highly singular object that seems to encapsulate myriad principles of "courtyardness" rather than one which harks back to its most basic and fundamental qualities. This is fundamentally congruent with the typology argument as put forth by Argan, Moneo, and Colquhoun at this same moment: With Florey, Stirling looks to the "vague" notion of type and generates a specific example. He particularizes the general. In Hays's terminology, he negotiates between the "instance" and the "substratum." Stirling's strategy stands in marked contrast to the work of Rossi, whose architecture enacts a kind of negation and simplification of type—a "bleaching out," to use Hays's term—in which the singular building represents a reduction to its bare minimum, which is deeply invested with the cultural memory embedded in the type. Stirling seems to take this for granted; he is interested not in the ur-quality of the type but instead in its potential as a springboard for invention. His hybridizing and recombining of various elements create a formal exquisite corpse of the college courtyard.

Figure 92
Stirling, Florey Building. Plan diagram. The breakfast room is aligned at one half of the controlling forty-five-degree geometry.

Figure 93
Peter Eisenman, House III, Lakeville, Connecticut, 1970. Axonometric. Like Stirling's Florey Building, Eisenman's house is controlled by a forty-five-degree geometry, though Eisenman's system is both more explicit and more dominant.

The geometric system at Florey is one example of this inventive hybridizing. As discussed in Chapter 2, at Churchill Stirling regularizes the typically haphazard Oxbridge plan by creating a perfect square, with bisecting paths and four quadrants, to suggest a generalization or purification of the courtyard plan—what an Oxbridge college *would* look like if it could be planned ex novo and on a tabula rasa. Other schemes of the period, including Martin and Wilson's Harvey Court, similarly regularize the rectilinear geometry of the "quad." Florey, by contrast, abandons the square, but the geometry is equally if not more rigorous. Each segment of the plan is rotated at forty-five degrees to its adjacent segment. A second angle of twenty-two and one-half degrees (one-half of the controlling forty-five-degree geometry for the building facets) is introduced as the controlling axis for the placement of the breakfast room, and bisects the central pair of A-frame struts (fig. 92). This axis allegedly corresponds to the tower at Magdalen College across the river—in one drawing a somewhat doubtful dashed line connects this angle to the very edge of the tower—and sets up the seemingly haphazard placement of the breakfast room as a deliberate move, almost as a kind of arrow pointing back to campus. The tiles in the courtyard, running north-south, reinforce the "control" grid against which the breakfast room seems to "float" off-axis. And at the very center of the scheme, the weathercock on the breakfast room terrace is placed at exactly the centerline of this twenty-two-and-a-half-degree axis. The geometric system is reinforced in section as well, with the angle of the struts mirroring the backward-leaning angle of the building.

This overlay of two grid systems at forty-five degrees to each other was a deliberate gesture on Stirling's part to generate variability while reinforcing "order"—a notion that we can trace back to his Village Housing project. Stirling: "There is a liberation and a greater number of planning choices available when more than one geometry is integrated into the design."[52] At Village Housing, Stirling used roof angles in multiples of thirty degrees; at Leicester, two overlapping grids at forty-five degrees underlie the geometric scheme; at Florey, Stirling ups the ante by introducing a third grid—which is itself a fraction of the second. The overlaid grids become a means to reinforce the logic of the quad, since they coalesce around the central open space, but also, as suggested in the discussion of type, a way to particularize the general. With its faceted angles and complex geometries, Florey is a more specific and idiosyncratic version of a "generic" Oxbridge court. Compare this with Peter Eisenman's manipulation of the grid in his contemporaneous House III project of 1970 (fig. 93). In both cases the conflation of an initial grid and a second grid rotated at forty-five degrees in relation to it generates the underlying geometry for the scheme. For Eisenman the registration of the clash of the competing grids is the primary focus, whereas for Stirling the geometry is subsumed within the overall form. It becomes a means rather than an end, a method for making "planning choices," as Stirling suggests, but is ultimately suppressed within the reading of the specific object. Eisenman's final form, by contrast, expresses the syntactic battle between two grids as a means to

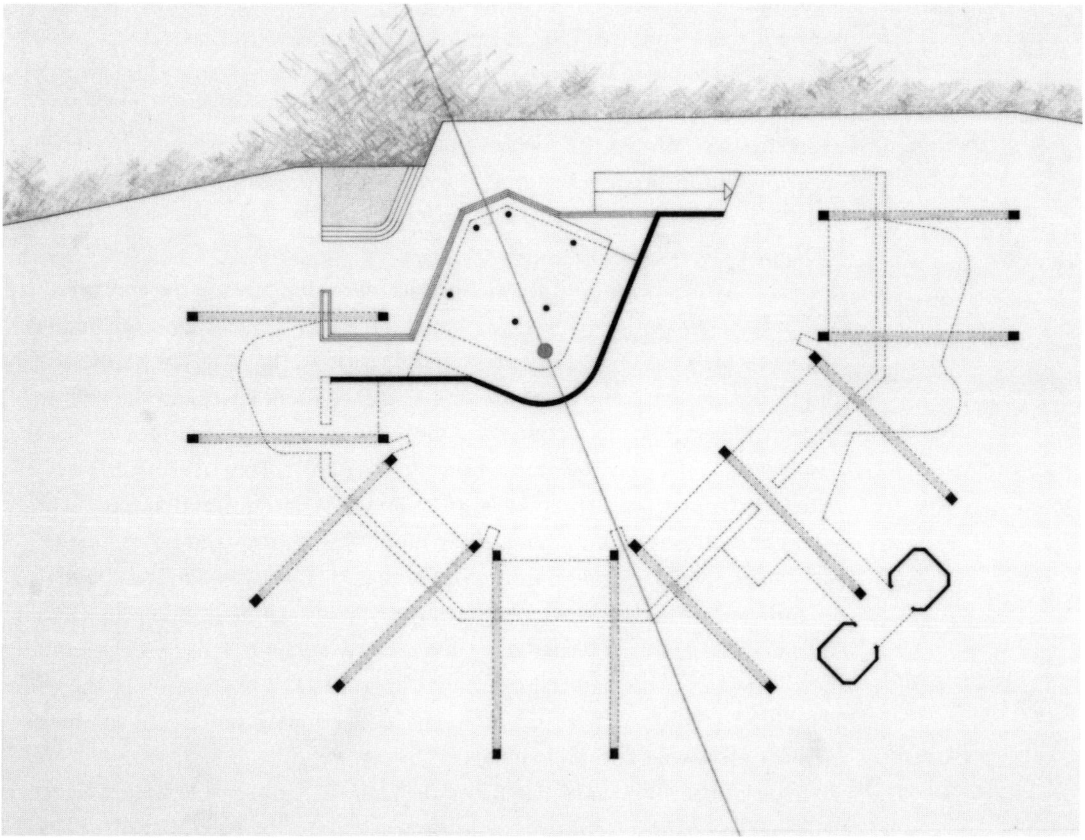

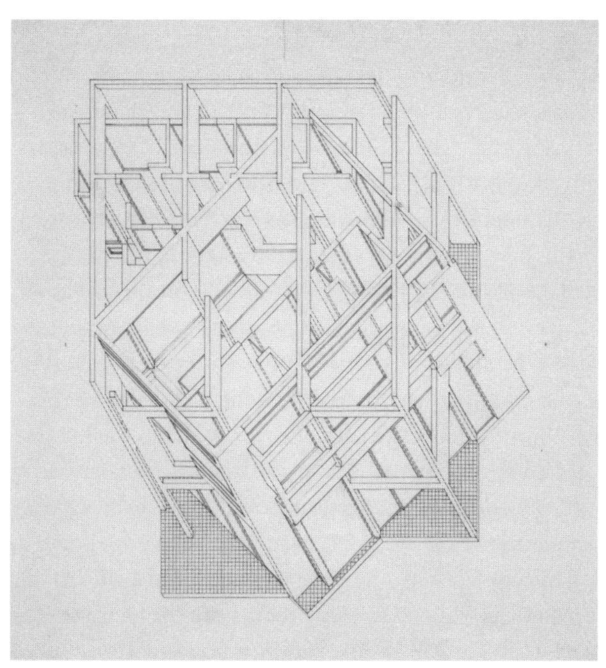

highlight a geometric process, a fascination that would continue into his later built work, such as the Wexner Center. Unlike Eisenman, Stirling is unafraid to include as counterpoints elements that seem to break the rules of the geometric system—notably the Corbusian piano curve in the caretaker's house and even the rounded bullnose of the breakfast platform. For Stirling geometry is a vehicle—a means, as he says, for making "planning choices"—but is not an end in itself. Within the overarching parameters of the type, geometry enables variation, but ultimately the type as a constraint prevails.

MATERIAL SIGNIFICATION

Florey is a two-sided building; the interior elevations facing the courtyard are clad in floor-to-ceiling patent glazing, and the exterior elevations facing St. Clement's are in red tile. The two materials express the different nature of the functions they enclose: student rooms along the inner edge, and the meeting spaces and services supporting them along the outer edge. In other words, the glass signifies the private domain, and tile the public. This treatment is consistent with Stirling's interest in an "expressive" functionalism as seen at Leicester, being able to understand in a building the "various component parts where people are doing different things."[53] The two-sided solution was a significant shift from Leicester, however, where each programmatic volume had a distinct material language—tiled lecture halls, brick base, glass workshops. At Florey the material signification occurs as a bifurcation of the overall building volume, rather than between a collection of "functional volumes," each with its own material language.

This "glazed vs. opaque" paradigm was identified in the work of Le Corbusier by Kenneth Frampton, who dates its appearance to the Pavillon Suisse—a formative influence on Stirling's early thinking, particularly in the community center designed for his thesis, and a site he listed as one of the "buildings visited" for his thesis. Colquhoun similarly describes the use of the two-sided bar building in Le Corbusier's work, emphasizing the shift from his prewar city plans, in which the bars "cut through a uniform and undifferentiated spatial continuum" and are "oriented in both directions" (in other words, the same on both sides), to those in the postwar projects such as the Palais des Nations or Centrosoyuz, in which the bars "have two aspects, one facing the public realm . . . the other the private realm."[54] Stirling's two-sided volume at Florey, though resonant with Le Corbusier's earlier projects, proposes a more nuanced treatment of materials within the apparently simplistic overall gesture of glass interior/tile exterior. The tile cladding which predominantly appears on the St. Clement's exterior in fact proliferates throughout the project, covering the stair and elevator towers, sliding over the chamfered corners of the courtyard stairways, wrapping around the edges of podiums, and spilling over from the terrace, down the stairs, and onto the courtyard; it even wraps the underside of the elevated structure. This continuous tile connects all of the surfaces of the project *except* the patent glazing of the student rooms, further emphasizing the distinction between the student rooms and the public spaces—the

Figure 94
Stirling, Florey Building. The St. Clement's entrance.

interior courtyard, the interior hallways and stairs—on both horizontal and vertical surfaces.

Brick is used only in a series of walls located at the edges of the river walk and the courtyard, and along the back of the cloister. Unlike at Leicester, there is no longer a deliberate ambiguity between brick and tile, and Stirling seems to be putting forth a more explicit commentary on its structural properties as distinct from the nonstructural nature of tile—tile is used as a cladding, brick for load-bearing walls. Here again, however, Stirling plays with this literalist functionalist interpretation. The brick wall at the back of the cloister stops short of the structure above, deferring to the *actual* structural member—the horizontal concrete beam of the A-frame strut (fig. 94).[55] Aside from its self-supporting role, the brick wall is given a new or secondary functional justification as a continuous hollow duct housing the various services for the project—the slender pipes emerge from the top of the wall to slip into the underside of the looming structure above. In addition, the wall serves as the back edge of the cloister, physically and visually securing the courtyard from the parking lot at the rear of the building.[56]

The brick walls illustrate Stirling's complex play with functionalist justification—a game that arguably began with the insertion of the concrete upstands at Ham Common, in which concrete panels beneath the windows were added to give the concrete a greater presence on the façade. Stirling and Gowan saw this as a means to more "truthfully" express the actual ratio of concrete to brick in the project, to create the correct visual register of the proportion of concrete. The desire for the expression or articulation of the materials trumped their necessity. At Leicester this expressive functionalism was a critical aspect of the project, as we saw in the last chapter. Despite Pevsner's and others' condemnation of the expressive tendencies of the building, Stirling never saw its expressive quality as a challenge to its functionalist credentials. At Florey this relation between function and expression—more specifically a challenge to their alleged antipathy—remains. Mark Girouard begrudgingly admits that although Stirling's projects of the 1960s, including Leicester and Florey, are first and foremost "beautiful toys," they are beautiful toys that "work."[57]

This dichotomy between the necessary structure and the expressive function of the structure is nowhere more clear than in the concrete A-frame struts that encircle the building. In Stirling's own work we can see these as a development of the canted concrete supports on the backside of the Leicester workshops, in which the forty-five-degree struts supported the cantilevered workshops of the second floor and enabled heavy machinery to be lifted directly to its underside. But the struts at Florey also represent a more general continuation of the precarious stability at Leicester; Stirling often joked that Leicester would collapse if a piece was removed, and at Florey there is a sense that if one kicked the slender concrete strut hard enough it would snap and the entire project topple over in its wake. The active sense of imbalance pervades Florey in a much more dramatic way than at Leicester—the entire building is propped on splayed, spindly, knock-kneed legs. Although they are certainly not derived from any purely functional characteristic, and are clearly expressive, even in Pevsner's terms, they are also an integral structural component, not simply a visual or decorative flourish.

In the bound book accompanying his thesis of 1950, Stirling includes a "statement of aesthetics" which reads, "Only forms like a slab on its side, a table top, can be placed on posts and hover." He further argues that putting a "box on edge" or constructing a building taller than it is wide is "to contradict its verticality"; vertical forms should "plunge into the ground like a spear." This is a direct critique of Le Corbusier's Unité, which is a vertical slab elevated on pilotis—in other words, a box on edge—and an endorsement of the prewar work, in particular the Villa Savoye at Poissy, which, though also elevated on pilotis, is a horizontal mass, or a "table top." Predictably, Stirling's thesis project is a table top and thus able to "hover." The administration tower at Leicester is also an elevated box, though that reading is compromised somewhat given the lecture hall below and the brick base. Florey occupies a peculiar place in this horizontal/vertical divide since it is arguably more of a box on edge than a table top, but it also leans back, removing the purely vertical characteristics of a building like the Unité. Perhaps because of this unwillingness to elevate slabs, none of Stirling's sketches for Florey, even ones made once the clamshell shape was in place, show the project as elevated. In addition to its visual dissonance the elevated box on edge presents real structural questions, particularly in relation to lateral loads. The final solution at Florey offers a more vigorous structural and visual solution for elevating a slender building. By making the building oblique rather than vertical, the box no longer "contradicts its verticality" because it leans back.

Stirling's work of the 1960s seemed, to Banham, an answer to his call for the architect to "discard his whole cultural load" and embrace technological culture.[58] In his review of the Cambridge History Faculty, Banham compares the building to a giant machine that the occupants would need "mechanical literacy and competence" to operate, going so far as to suggest that it would ultimately need to be torn down, since it, like any technology, had only a limited "useful life."[59] Banham extolls not only the technological mastery of the building (the ceiling in the reading room in particular) but its "visual qualities" as well. "It will present a continuously interesting overhead spectacle . . . only interesting is an inadequate word for this spectacular roof," he said, going on to compare it to Scheerbart's Glassarchitekture.[60] The "spectacular" quality of the machine was as important to Banham as its function; his "purely" technocratic position was both ideologically, historically, and aesthetically biased.[61]

Stirling's attitude toward function at Florey was in many ways distinct from Banham's; he was explicitly critical of what he perceived to be the "banal and arrogant" technocratic solutions of his contemporaries.[62] Where he did concur with Banham, however, was in the credence given to the "spectacular"—we might also say expressive—aspects of technology as over and above its purely functionalist ones. Recall Stirling's statement that functionalism alone was "not enough," that it must also be expressive.[63] At Florey the "mechanistic" aspects of the building are transformed into formal and figural solutions. The window-cleaning mechanism offers perhaps the best example. Beginning with Leicester, Stirling developed a fascination with enormous window-cleaning gantries. There is one atop the Leicester administration tower, its basket cantilevered over the building edge, as well as a smaller one over the laboratory tower, and both appear in Stirling's chosen photographs—analagous, perhaps, to the automobile "machines" that Le Corbusier would carefully situate for photographs outside his purist villas. Both gantries are parasitic machines attached to the building form, which remains essentially unaffected by their presence. The scale of the gantry atop the administration tower even begins to approximate one of the "functional volumes" of the project. Stirling includes a similar gantry on the roof at Cambridge, and at Olivetti Haslemere the gantry slides along the upper ridge of the glass atrium to become a spectacle in its own right. At Florey, however, the building itself assumes the role of the cleaning machine; the slope of the glass walls and their stepped profile allow for a walkway at each level for window-cleaning access; all that's required is a sliding library-style ladder (featured in early photographs but absent in later documentation). Florey, then, answers more fully than Leicester or Cambridge Banham's call for architecture to perform as a machine rather than simply symbolize one. The building itself becomes a machine; it no longer needs to be served by one.

FLOREY'S IMAGE: USES OF AXONOMETRY

John Summerson described Florey as Stirling's first building "in which imagery was concentrated in one emphatic formal statement."[64] Girouard similarly stated that Florey "is immediately and convincingly there, a single coherent, glistening, precise and totally convincing object. The main image . . . is simple and memorable."[65] This "coherent" reading distinguishes Florey from its predecessors in Stirling's oeuvre. It is a building in the legacy of what Rowe termed the modern movement's "object-fixation."[66] It is also notably different from the multivolumetric composition of Leicester or the dueling glass and brick volumes at Cambridge; Florey is condensed to a single form. In 1963 Stirling wrote that each of a building's "component parts" should "express" its function, but Florey, unlike Leicester or Cambridge, is essentially one giant "part."[67] Rather than a series of volumes lashed together or a juxtaposition of two distinct volumes, there is instead one figure. This brings Florey in line with the "unified" tendency in Stirling's work, to use Colquhoun's characterization, exemplified by Churchill, that runs counter to the "exploded" projects (such as Leicester). We can also connect this to his writings of the 1950s in which he articulated a desire to create projects that were "one idea buildings," or of the "'one dominating space' species."[68]

Florey's status as a single, comprehensible object was intimately connected with the techniques used to represent it, particularly the axonometric. The Florey Building was the first of Stirling's projects to be drawn in a worm's-eye axonometric, from below—the so-called Choisy method in acknowledgment of the nineteenth-century architect who pioneered the technique. The Choisy axonometric is distinguished by a plan drawing, rotated some amount (often forty-five degrees), with elevation lines projected vertically, giving the viewer the sense of being "below" the building, looking up from beneath the plan. Judging from its frequent appearance in magazines and other publications, the Choisy drawing of Florey became a favorite of Stirling's. After its appearance in the early 1970s, the worm's-eye axonometric would become a consistent trope used to document portions of a building sequence.

Choisy's two-volume *Histoire de' l'Architecture,* with its seventeen hundred illustrations, all drawn by Choisy and nearly all of them axonometrics, had been a leading instructional nineteenth-century text. Le Corbusier included a number of Choisy's axonometric drawings (uncredited) in *L'Esprit Nouveau* and *Towards a New Architecture,* solidifying their place in modern architectural discourse.[69] In the mid-1950s and 1960s Choisy was again revisited, particularly in England, as a key figure relating to the modern movement and its principles. Julius Posener published an article on Choisy in the *Architectural Review* in

1956, responding to a resurgent interest in his work and in French rationalism more broadly. Posener highlights Choisy's influence on key figures of the modern movement, asserting that he was the "father of Perret's and even of Le Corbusier's doctrines." He also cites the didactic and explanatory power of his drawings, calling him a "magician of logic."[70] In his 1960 book *Theory and Design in the First Machine Age,* Banham devotes the entire second chapter—subtitled "Rationalism and Technique"—to Choisy. Like Posener, Banham singles out the highly simplified axonometric drawings as a crucial aspect of Choisy's contribution. "Detailing is suppressed and one is left with an elegant and immediately comprehensible diagram." He continues with a quote from Choisy that they are the "careful and learnedly drawn representation of fact."[71]

Stirling's use of axonometry is also associated with other important modernist proponents, notably the de Stijl painters and architects of the 1920s, who are generally credited with the "modern revival" of axonometry, as well as El Lissitzky's prouns, which, as Yves-Alain Bois notes in his article "Metamorphosis of Axonometry," had already written the official "birth certificate" of axonometry in 1919.[72] Axonometrics were used extensively in Alberto Sartoris's *Encyclopédie de l'Architecture Nouvelle*—a book that Stirling listed as one of the most important in his student days (more important, in fact, than Le Corbusier's *Oeuvre Complète*). And axonometry was a principal tool of purist painting, particularly the ninety-degree or "straight up" axonometric, a projection angle that tends to emphasize the distortion possible with the technique rather than its "synthetic" potential. Le Corbusier's still lifes with their "flattened" bottle tops are perhaps the best example. Stirling's use of the axonometric, then, was intimately tied to these earlier modernist associations, and part of a resurgent interest in the technique in 1960s Britain, evidenced by its use in numerous contemporaneous publications, notably Kenneth Frampton's *British Buildings, 1960–64* of 1966.

As Bois notes, axonometry as a representational technique carries with it a distinct ideology, particularly when compared to perspective. Axonometry, he writes, "abolishes the fixed viewpoint of the spectator and creates several possible readings of one and the same image," as opposed to perspective, which places the eye in a specific place and makes for a "petrified" view.[73] Axonometry, also unlike perspective, allows for geometrical "truth" since dimensions are measured equally, and it provides "synthetic representation"—in other words, an object (or building) can be seen in its apparent entirety, plan and front view simultaneously. It is only a small step from Bois's argument that the axonometric offers a synthetic representation to the claim that the axonometric isn't so much a means of representation as it is a design tool. Charles Jencks describes Stirling's axonometrics as tools that enable him to "work out the space, structure, geometry, function and details altogether and without distortion," a "magic wand," a way to "resolve" the design.[74] "Stirling's work is rooted in the technique of draughting; the method leads to the form. Without such a technique, sophisticated constructions would be impossible. A whole aesthetic and way of life comes from the logic and articulation possible with such a

Figure 95
Auguste Choisy, axonometric of Santa Sophia, Constantinople, reproduced in Le Corbusier's *Towards a New Architecture*, 1927.

Figure 96
Stirling, Florey Building. Worm's-eye axonometric.

method."[75] Banham disagrees. In his introductory essay to a catalogue of Stirling's drawings he takes pains to argue that Stirling's use of the axonometric was simply an expedient tool, an easy method for "disciplining the presentation of widely differing buildings."[76] For Banham, unlike for Jencks and others, Stirling's choice of drawing technique "implies nothing about their mode of design," and he goes on to state that his axonometrics were simply a means to produce clarity, comparing them to the machinery drawings to which they were exposed during the war: "Those instruction manual drawings, intended to make it possible to strip, reassemble, and above all, understand, sophisticated and enigmatic items of machinery, were not necessarily elegant but they had to be clear at all costs."[77]

This explanatory power might more easily be argued for the use of the "traditional" axonometric (with a view from above), which does seem to explain or clarify the project components and even its assembly. But the use of the worm's-eye axonometric at Florey can hardly claim to be "clear at all costs." Instead, it gives a highly biased and disorienting reading of the project—largely because the viewer occupies an impossible position beneath the ground; the building seems to float above. The sense of gravity is lost, or denied. This is a visually unforgiving technique, one that requires a fair amount of work on the part of the reader in deciphering the images as architectural objects.

As suggested in the last chapter, axonometry was critical to Stirling's ability to define a "particulate" architecture comprising various volumetric components of "solidified space" at Leicester. In both Leicester and Florey the axonometric gives an understanding of the totality of the project, largely because of the "synthetic" quality of the axonometric and its ability to render the project in its entirety even as it highlights the distinct pieces.[78] But the axonometric also introduces a scalar ambiguity, particularly given its more familiar use in describing machinelike products. With the worm's-eye axonometric, Florey is stripped of scalar clues. There are neither figures nor traditional architectural markers (doors, windows, stairs) or contextual factors (trees, walkways, roads) to betray its size. It becomes an object rather than a building. Colquhoun writes that Stirling's "volumes" are conceptualized "as if they could be held in the hand and physically manipulated," a statement that echoes Posener's description of Choisy's axonometrics: "He seems to take into his hand the individual stone, or piece of timber, and from them builds up the wall, the pier, the column, the vault, the roof, following their vicissitudes throughout the project."[79] Girouard describes Florey as a "beautifully finished toy."[80] The worm's-eye axonometric reinforces this diminutive reading; because of the disorienting viewpoint and its lack of context or relationship to the ground, the "architecturalness" of the project is minimized.

In a worm's-eye axonometric the plan is the dominant figure, typically rendered in solid black poché, with elevation lines projecting vertically. When Le Corbusier reprints Choisy's worm's-eye axonometrics in *Towards a New Architecture*—one of Santa Sophia in Constantinople and one simple diagram of a portion of the Palace in Amman in Syria—he places them in his section

THREE REMINDERS TO ARCHITECTS 47

abstraction; it is nothing more than an algebrization and a dry-looking thing. The work of the mathematician remains none the less one of the highest activities of the human spirit.

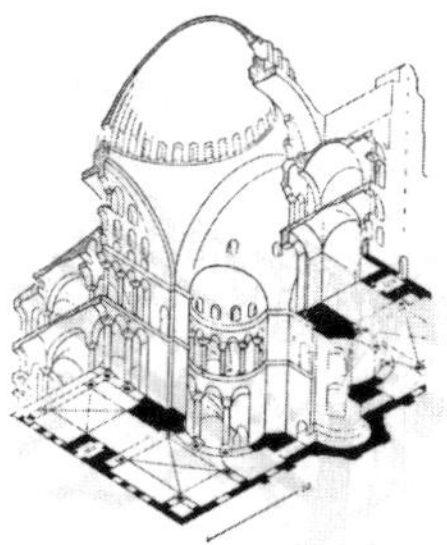

SANTA SOPHIA, CONSTANTINOPLE

The plan influences the whole structure: the geometrical laws on which it is based and their various modulations are developed in every part of the building.

Arrangement is an appreciable rhythm which reacts on every human being in the same way.

The plan bears within itself a primary and pre-determined rhythm: the work is developed in extent and in height following the prescriptions of the plan, with results which can range from the simplest to the most complex, all coming within the

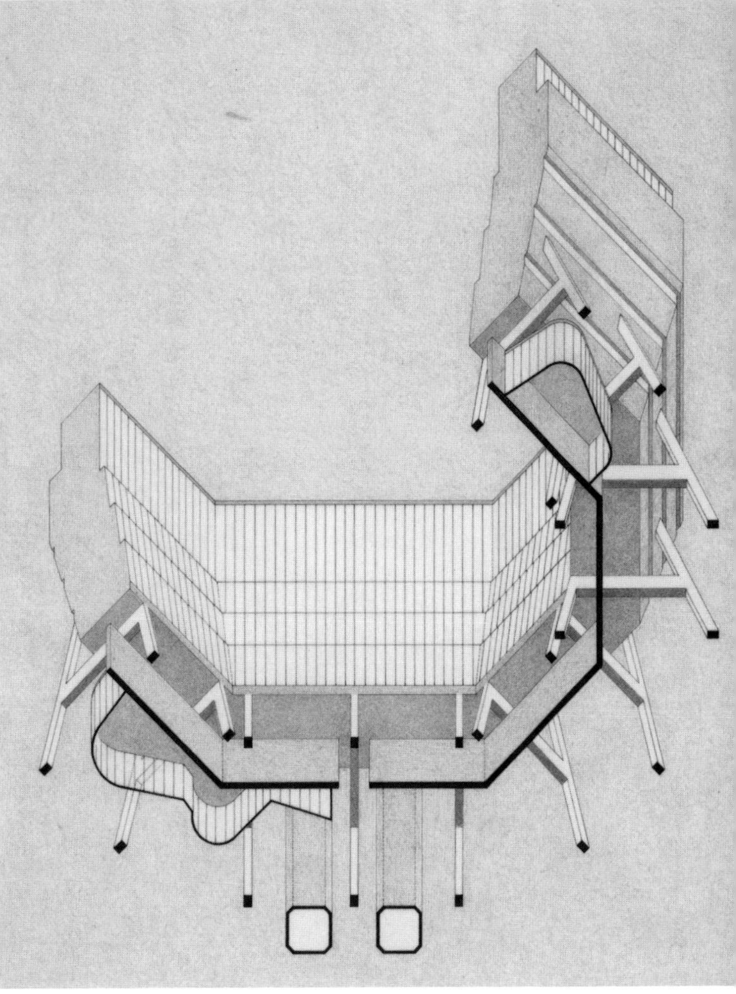

"reminding" architects of the importance of the plan (fig. 95). These drawings, in combination with an aerial axonometric of the temple at Thebes and the plan of the Acropolis, are used to illustrate his well-known adage that the plan is the "generator." "The plan is what determines everything; it is the decisive moment."[81] In the worm's-eye Florey axonometric, the plan—the portion of the building that actually touches the ground where the cut is taken—is in fact quite minimal. The only building elements that engage the ground are the brick wall bounding the courtyard, the bases of the A-frame struts, and the pair of entrance towers (fig. 96). Like the Gothic cathedrals and Greek temples in Choisy's *Histoire de l'Architecture,* Florey is supported by point loads. The use of the worm's-eye axonometric highlights just how *lightly* the building treads on the ground, how little "plan" there really is, and further enhances the "floating" quality of the project.

The worm's-eye axonometric has repercussions in section as well as in plan. In most of Choisy's drawings (including those that Le Corbusier

includes in *Towards a New Architecture)* the building is cut away at particular places to reveal aspects that would otherwise remain hidden and to emphasize construction techniques. In the Santa Sophia worm's-eye, for example, the section is cut through the center of the dome and the adjacent side chapels. By contrast, in Stirling's axonometrics of Florey, in both the views from above and below, nothing is cut away; the building is represented in its entirety, reinforcing the desire to represent a coherent object. Nevertheless, the building *appears* to be cut away at the two ends facing the river. The flat, unarticulated edges register as apparent section cuts of the building, as if they were the shaded gray poché in a Choisy axonometric. An earlier series of perspective sketches support this reading (fig. 97). In two sketches the building appears literally sliced in half, while another sketch depicts an actual section cut of the building and reinforces the reading of the building edge as apparent section cut as well. Florey, in this case, can be interpreted as a fulfillment of the axonometric technique; the building actualizes the convention of cutting away portions to enable a more comprehensible picture of the entire building to emerge. But in this case there is no "complete" building—the apparent building fragment as represented in the drawing is in fact the entirety of the project. Our mind completes the portion of the building that appears to be missing, the part of the structure that would circle around to completely enclose the courtyard.

As it was with the Leicester axonometric drawing—which prioritized the approach to the building along its forty-five-degree geometry—the specific view angle of the Florey axonometric is important. In both the traditional and worm's-eye axonometrics of Florey the vertical axis of the drawing is coincident with the entry axis to the project, centered between the two towers. The drawing, in other words, is lined up with the entrance to the building. Because of this chosen angle, in both the aerial and worm's-eye axonometrics the bottoms of the two towers appear flattened. They take on the same quality as the bottle tops in Le Corbusier's purist still lifes; we read them as the distorted portion, particularly since the rest of the project seems more truthfully three-dimensional. In addition to reinforcing the controlling geometry of the scheme, the choice of view angle renders the idiosyncratic geometry of the

Figure 97
Stirling, Florey Building. Early perspective studies in which the building appears to be "cut," as in a section drawing.

breakfast room more pronounced—it seems off-kilter, loose in the otherwise ordered composition. If the axonometric drawing had taken as its centerline the breakfast room axis, it would have been the towers that seemed askew. Compare this with Leicester, where the view angle of the axonometric is always aligned with the controlling forty-five-degree grid of the project, giving a similarly flattened quality to portions of the image, particularly the workshop roof, while also reinforcing the comprehensiveness of the grid system. Nothing is askew, everything aligns.

This possibility for distortion and ambiguity in the axonometric's "truthful" presentation was one of the qualities that most interested the de Stijl artists and architects. As Bois demonstrates, the "convenience" and efficiency of being able to show an entire building synthetically, which was an important aspect of the axonometric in its uses in military drawing and other fields, gave way for de Stijl and to some extent for Constructivist and Suprematist artists, who instead capitalized on the "perceptive ambiguity" of the drawing type—in other words, where the figure seems to shift from concave to convex form, and where lines alternately recede and project from the page, a quality epitomized by Joseph Albers's well-known later engravings. While Stirling's axonometrics never take on the "undecidable" or "vertiginously ambivalent" qualities of an Albers drawing or a Lissitzky proun, a degree of fundamental disorientation indeed occurs. The constructedness of the drawing is immediately legible; the unfamiliarity of the view angle displaces focus from the building to its representation, rendering the project as an object more than a building.

To its ability to simultaneously clarify and obfuscate we can also add the axonometric's role in portraying the "image" of the architectural object in question. In both his initial 1955 essay and his 1966 book documenting the New Brutalism's ethic and aesthetic, Banham listed "image" as a key component not only of the burgeoning British "style" but also in contemporary aesthetics more generally. Reflecting the legacy of Erwin Panofsky's writings on iconology, with his definition of image as "secondary meaning," Banham describes "image" not simply as the way that something appears but as that which allows a building to be grasped in its totality, as containing an idea, as *embodying* an idea—the effect of the object.[82] Image was that which captured an emotion, which made the building "memorable."[83] "It requires that the building should be an immediately apprehensible visual entity, and that the form grasped by the eye should be confirmed by experience of the building in use. Further, that this form should be entirely proper to the functions and materials of the building, in their entirety."[84] Stirling's axonometric drawings are what truly launch the building into the status of "image"—not only by rendering the building as a totality, as something "to be held in the hand," but also by elucidating the principles behind the project, elevating architecture above mere "building."

Finally, the use of the axonometric had important connotations in terms of Stirling's attitude toward history. William Jordy singled out the axonometric drawing—a tool born of modernism's "revolutionary" period—as a tool for reintroducing history into modern architecture. The axonometric, he writes, "presented past buildings as complex objects assembled of simple shapes."[85] He writes in 1963 that the axonometric had begun to appear again, in depictions of buildings like Kahn's Salk Institute, with its Beaux-Arts–influenced plan meets Hadrian's villa, and that the "elemental quality of the shapes . . . represent a symbolic objectification of past monuments which extends ideals born of the twenties."[86] Through the axonometric the "past is literally re-born in its objectification." These "ideals" were deliberately evoked in Stirling's use of the technique at Florey, but for Stirling, this reborn past was no longer medieval cathedrals or Renaissance palazzos, as it had been for Choisy (or even Le Corbusier), but modernism itself. Stirling used the the axonometric—the modernist technique for depicting the past—to depict modern architecture's own historical status. Not unlike his use of Moretti's plaster casts, what was born as an analytical tool became a generative one. In other words, the axonometric wasn't simply a depiction of the architecture but an analytical presentation of the critical ideas embedded within it.

SUBLIMATING REFERENCE

Unlike Leicester, where the historical references are immediate and inescapable, and where the desire to identify the various precedents and antecedents has controlled much of the discourse and criticism surrounding the building, Florey seems somehow to have escaped the "death grapple" with influence.[87] While the project deliberately connects to the typological tradition of the college courtyard, no specific or obvious precedents, like Melnikov's Rusakov Club or Wright's Johnson Wax, jump to the forefront. Florey prompts more of a suspicion, a lurking feeling, perhaps, that the influences are there but buried more deeply. The concrete A-frame struts are a good example. They do not offer a "completion" of any single precedent as, say, the lecture halls at Leicester do for Melnikov's theaters, or even a "swerve" from a predecessor, as Ham Common vis-à-vis Maisons Jaoul. Instead, the sources for these megastructural concrete elements are more myriad and more muted. There are remnants of the awkward structural gymnastics of Viollet-le-Duc, particularly the diagonal cast iron supports in his concert hall of 1854. We can see Archigram's Walking City with its giant elevated structures on splayed, telescoping "legs," as well as the diagonal framing system of Plug-in City. The diagonal struts also evoke Louis Kahn's City Tower project of 1958, with its external frame of diagonal struts. We might even be tempted to cite a generalized "diagonal craze" in the mid- to late 1960s, just as Frampton identified an "octagonal" craze a few years previous.[88] But in both the Kahn and Archigram examples the diagonal informs a system that overtakes the reading of the project as an object; in Stirling's case the diagonals serve to hold up the object—they are closer to Corbusian pilotis than to Archigram's grid. Perhaps the most striking visual resonance comes from a Constructivist project illustrated in Banham's *Theory and Design*—El Lissitzky and Mart Stam's Wolkenbügel project. Again we see the influence of the Russian Constructivists on Stirling's work, with a specific precedent being revisioned, much as he had with

Melnikov's Rusakov Workers' Club at Leicester. Although we might also cite the Russian Constructivists' general fascination with the oblique—think of Tatlin's tower and Lissitzky's Lenin Tribune—as an important influence at Florey, the Wolken-bügel project offers a more specific example of a precedent that is reconfigured and accommodated within Stirling's project. Like Florey, Lissitzky and Stam's building is supported by giant cantilevered legs—which also splay in plan as well as in section—with an administrative block placed atop a lift tower that also leans back to create a similar juxtaposition of contrasting geometries and a sense of a controlled fall (figs. 98, 99).

These references are harder to identify and certainly less definitive than their more obvious counterparts in a project like Leicester. Our interest, however, is not in identifying sources but rather in the means through which they are revisioned. Florey represents a shift away from the projects considered thus far in this book—Ham Common, Churchill College, and Leicester—in that its legibility as a singular figure overrides the registration of influence. In Bloom's terminology it represents a kind of "self-purgation and solipsism"—in other words, the burden of influence *seems* to be cast off. If the life of the poet/architect is marked by a constant dialectical movement between guilt and freedom, between acknowledging influence and willing oneself free of it, only to be drawn back in again, then Florey is perhaps the purest moment of release—Stirling's "wildest" moment, in which he strays further from anything else in either his own work or the work of others.

But, of course, the object is itself dialectically constructed; this "freedom" is only illusory, a false freedom. The achievement of the Florey Building is its sublimation of precedent rather than freedom from it. This is the project's greatest contribution: its dual reading as *both* an autonomous form—self-contained and internally consistent—and an historically embedded and dependent object. The specificity of the end result, which is legible as a singular image rather than a collection of quotations, carries within it the traces of specific architectural precedents as well as generalized architectural principles. This strategy of condensing or subsuming references into a singularity results in an architectural language in which any single formal gesture (the A-frame struts, for example) evokes not one but many precedents (Kahn, Archigram, Viollet-le-Duc). The single architectural "word" takes on multiple meanings.

If sublimation, in Freudian terms, suggests a translation of unfilled desires into a productive capacity—the only productive defense mechanism—then at Florey we can see the influence anxiety translated into arguably the most "excessive," which is to say novel, work of architecture. As a specific object that has subsumed a wide range of historical precedents, Florey becomes a kind of stand-in, a synecdoche, for modernism itself. Paradoxically, this culmination of the modernist "object-fixation" is also the moment at which the object, as a result of its objectness and therefore its repeatability, becomes a part of history. With Florey, Stirling generates a universal ahistorical idea that can then itself be revisioned. Tellingly, after Florey, Stirling moves away from the "building as object" to more embedded, contextual, and funda-

Figure 98
Stirling, Florey Building. The building "leans" back onto the concrete A-frame struts.

Figure 99
El Lissitzky and Mart Stam, Wolkenbügel project, 1924, reproduced in Reyner Banham, *Theory and Design in the First Machine Age*, 1960.

mentally urban projects. This was partly a result of the sites that he was given—in the historic centers of Düsseldorf, Cologne, Rome, and eventually Stuttgart—but it cannot simply be explained through circumstance, suggesting that, after Florey, Stirling's historical revisions are made more complex as his own work is accepted as part of the historical past.

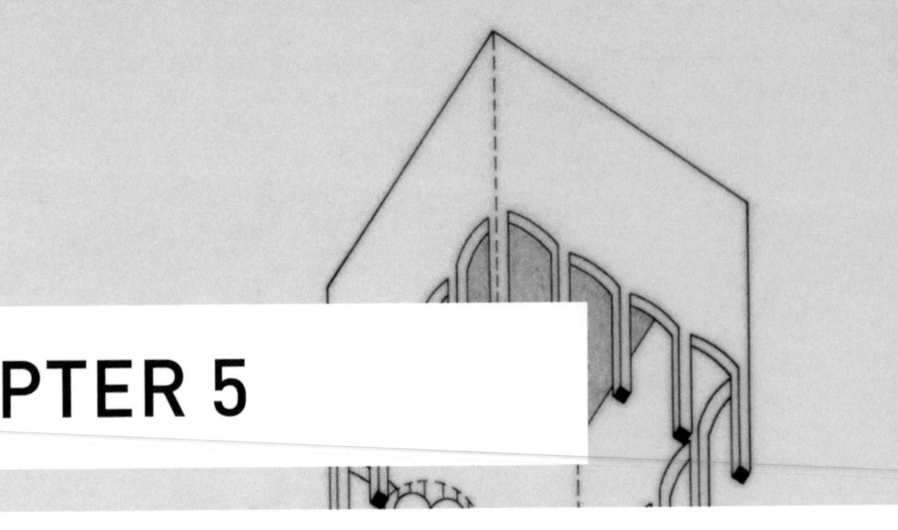

CHAPTER 5

RECOLLECTING FORWARD

DÜSSELDORF (1975)

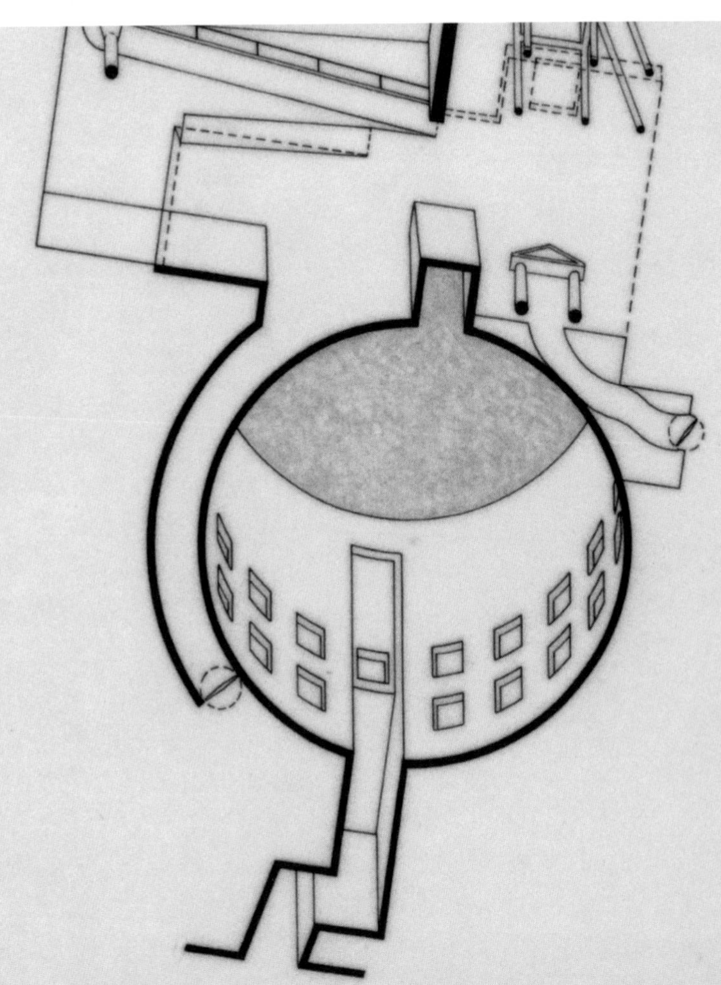

Beginning in the late 1960s and continuing through the mid-1970s, Stirling designed a series of projects in historic European city centers. Critics and historians have highlighted this period as a turning point in Stirling's career, as his work seemed to move in a new direction, one with an increasingly Neoclassical tendency. Although the two projects most often cited in this shift are the Derby Civic Centre (1970) and the Arts Centre at St. Andrews University (1971), in this chapter I consider a slightly later project that similarly engages with the historical city but advances a more complex relation to it: Stirling's competition entry for the North Rhine–Westphalia Museum, Düsseldorf (1975).[1] Completed in partnership with Michael Wilford, Düsseldorf stands as a critical project in Stirling's oeuvre in terms of its formal language and compositional technique (fig. 100). It marks the beginning of another of Stirling's tripartite series—in this case the "German series," which includes the Wallraf-Richartz Museum competition for Cologne of the same year, and the Neue Staatsgalerie in Stuttgart, begun in 1977, which is effectively a version of Düsseldorf adjusted to new site constraints. As the inaugural moment in this series, Düsseldorf is particularly significant in that it marks Stirling's move away from designing singular, discrete, and totalized objects—a quality that reached its apotheosis at Florey—toward projects that are collections of

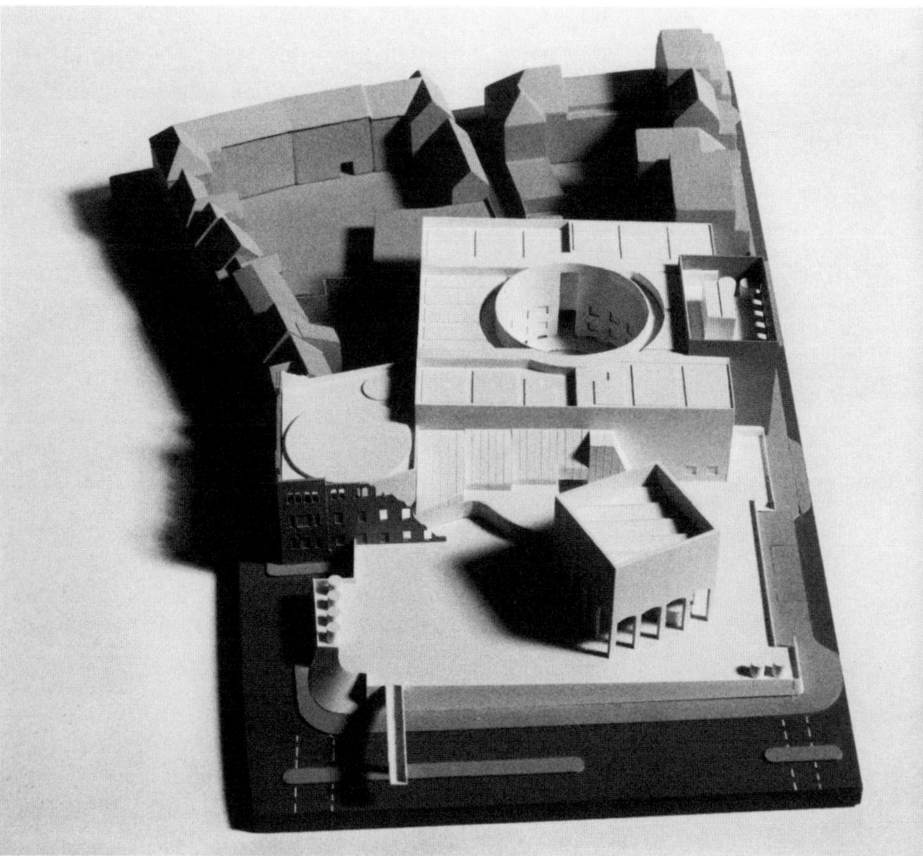

Figure 100
James Stirling and Partner, North Rhine–Westphalia Museum, Düsseldorf, Germany, 1975.

objects. Rather than "generalizing away the uniqueness" of historical precedents to create a neutralized typological figure, as he had in the "great court" at Churchill or the "amphitheater" at Florey, Stirling combines various building fragments in the overall building design.

The deployment of this more fragmented compositional technique at Düsseldorf was indebted to the discourse surrounding Colin Rowe and Fred Koetter's seminal text *Collage City,* published in August 1975 (the same month Stirling submitted his Düsseldorf competition entry).[2] As applied to architecture in the 1970s, collage was a strategy for combining various historical "set pieces" in fragmented, piecemeal compositions while also promoting a "contextual" urban strategy—a term with a complex meaning, as will be discussed, and a bias toward a Neoclassical language. Stirling's response to the collage discourse at Düsseldorf, however, was neither capitulation to Rowe and Koetter's techniques of historicist pastiche, nor was it a rejection of his continually evolving modernist ideals. As Alan Colquhoun convincingly argued, the twin formal instincts of "fragmentation/explosion" and "unification/implosion" had always existed in Stirling work, and Düsseldorf can be seen as a continuation, with substantial modifications, of both of these compositional techniques evident from his earliest projects.[3] For Düsseldorf Stirling indeed employs specific historical quotations, and he embeds the project directly into the fabric of the traditional city. This "turn" to history, however, represented a development of, not a divergence from, his earlier explorations into the functional principles behind historical precedents. By 1975, Stirling's architecture was already deeply embedded in history, and Düsseldorf represented his continuing quest to "persist and extend" the vocabulary of modern architecture with an ever-expanding formal arsenal.[4]

STIRLING'S MUSEUM DESIGN

In August 1974 Stirling received a letter from the finance minister of the Land of North Rhine–Westphalia, inviting him to participate in a competition for a museum of twentieth-century painting in Düsseldorf, Germany; he was one of only four international architects included in the competition, which was otherwise open to all German architects.[5] Stirling received final competition requirements at the end of January 1975 and a submission deadline of August 1 of the same year; the results were announced in early December.[6] The mid-1970s was a difficult time for many architectural offices, but particularly for Stirling's; with the exception of the second stage of the Southgate Housing Project in Runcorn New Town (completed in 1976) there was little work in the office.[7] Given this lack of work Stirling had significant time to dedicate to the project, and numerous accounts from employees at the time emphasize his commitment to the Düsseldorf competition.[8]

Founded in 1961, the Museum for North Rhine–Westphalia had originated with the purchase of nearly one hundred drawings and paintings of Paul Klee, and, under the direction of Werner Schmalenbach, had been slowly adding to the collection in the nearly fifteen years since. In addition to the Klee collection, the museum held one hundred works of the painter Julius Bissier. Having outgrown its space in the Schloss Jägerhof in the Hofgarten (which allowed for only a partial viewing of the collection), the museum sought to expand on a site in central Düsseldorf. The site was in the Grabbeplatz, in the center of historic Düsseldorf; it had suffered heavy bomb damage during World War II and was being used as a parking lot. A number of "important existing buildings"—including the Land Court Building to the west and the bombed-out shell of the town library to the north—surrounded the platz, and the committee requested that they be integrated into the design.[9] The program for the new museum called for nearly 70,000 square feet of program space, which, in addition to galleries, included an auditorium, a library, an education department, administrative offices, workshops, and stores.

Stirling and Wilford's design knits into the existing city fabric a group of building elements that contain the various museum functions: a solid museum block, square in plan, with a circular courtyard extracted from its center; an adjacent circular gallery space housing the Klee/Bissier collection, a cubic entrance pavilion at the center of the redesigned Grabbeplatz, and a series of enclosed and articulated circulation elements among them. The entrance pavilion is "attached" to the museum block through an undulating, patent-glazed vestibule. A public walkway, mandated in the competition brief, passes through the building, reinstating an historic connection to the Ratinger Mauer at the north. The walkway begins beneath the entrance pavilion, continues along a sinuous stone wall meant to evoke the former town wall at or near its original location, dips below the museum block, passes through the centralized open-air courtyard at the heart of the scheme, and exits at the rear into an exterior gallery-like space lined with shops and restaurants.

This courtyard is a response to the original competition brief's call for a "second square" in the "internal area of the city block," although Stirling's courtyard is arguably more of a garden than a square.[10] Four planted cypress trees are arranged symmetrically, one in each corner of the courtyard, and holes in the pavement "could be left for planting and eventually almost the entire surface could have a covering of shrubs, ivies etc."[11] The idea of placing a garden at the center of the scheme might well have originated with Norman Reid, director of the Tate Gallery; sometime in early 1975 Stirling had asked Reid for advice on the project, and in particular "what sort of gallery Schmalenbach might have in mind." Reid responded with a handwritten note in which he suggests that the design "have an *in* and an *out,* but in between should allow the visitor a choice of direction now and again, something like visiting a garden perhaps."[12] While it doesn't allow an explicit "choice of direction," Stirling and Gowan's walkway splits as it ramps up and around the courtyard. Importantly, the "garden" courtyard remains inaccessible from the museum itself; it is possible to enter it only from the public walkway. Although there are windows onto the courtyard from the surrounding galleries, there is no door. It is a completely public space embedded within the physical structure of the museum (figs. 101, 102).

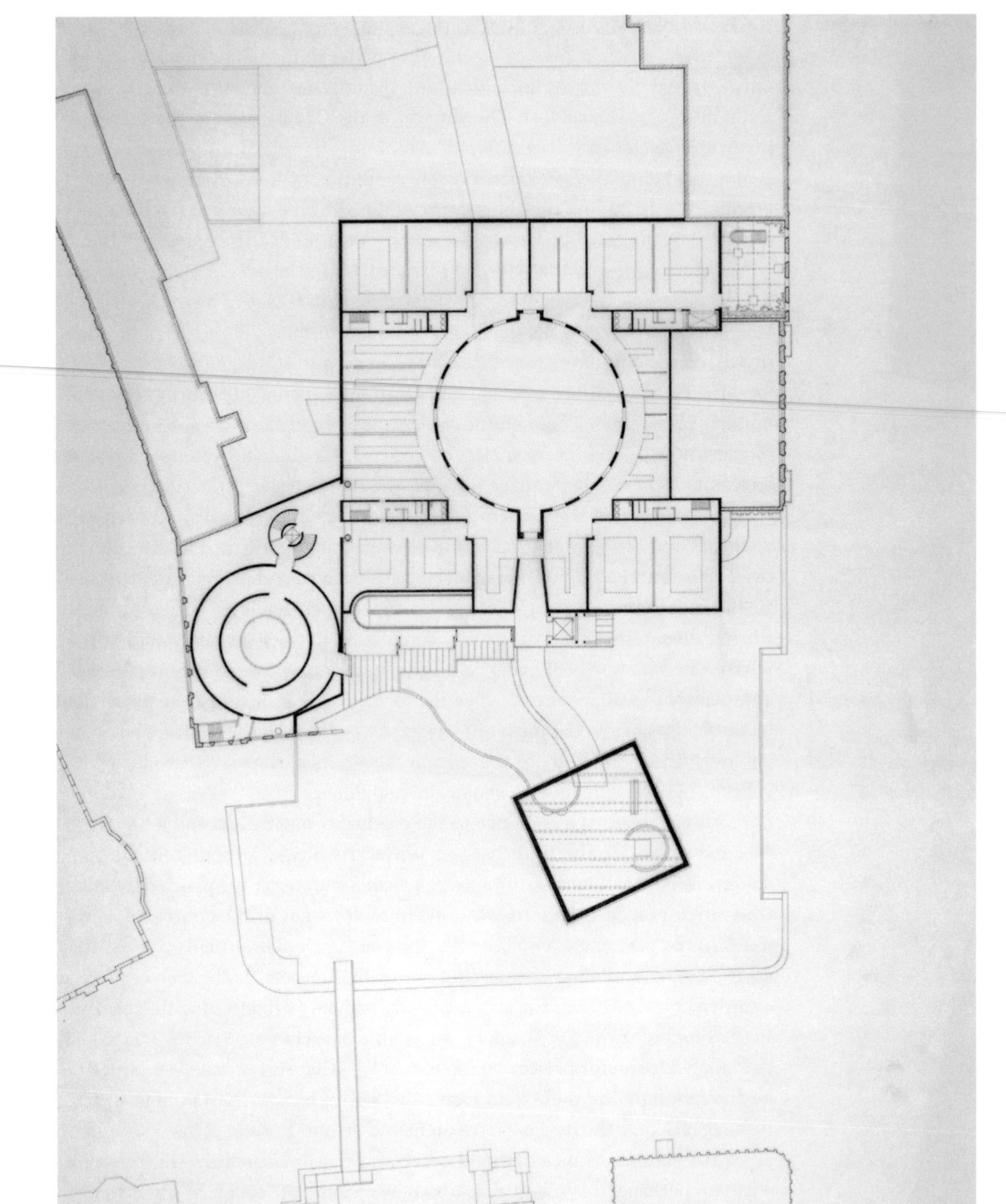

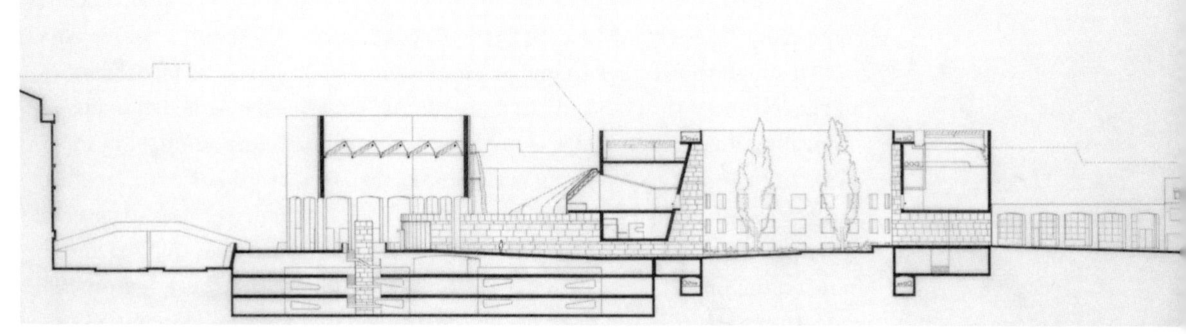

Figure 101
Stirling and Partner, Düsseldorf. First-floor plan.

Figure 102
Stirling and Partner, Düsseldorf. Section. The public thoroughfare begins at the entrance pavilion in the elevated plaza, passes beneath the museum block into the central open-air courtyard, and exits at the rear into a gallery-like space lined with shops and restaurants.

The circular void of the rotunda/garden finds its counterpoint in the solid cubic entrance pavilion placed within the elevated plaza in the Grabbeplatz. Square in plan, the glass-roofed, open-air pavilion is circumscribed by sixteen columns. Beyond its function as a kind of overscaled folly it serves as an inaugural moment for the three possible routes into and through the museum: the public walkway to the Ratinger Mauer (which follows the curving stone wall that slips beneath the pavilion), the entrance to the museum proper (accessed via revolving doors to the entrance vestibule), and a connection to the parking garage below (through a circular elevator and stair core in its southeastern corner). It was also intended to serve as a shelter for people waiting for the bus, or simply as a place to congregate—"a much smaller scale alternative to the entrance steps of the Metropolitan Museum (New York) or the portico of the British Museum (London)."[13]

Within the museum, the main gallery spaces are arranged between the circular courtyard and the roughly square building perimeter, with exhibition walls running perpendicular to the exterior walls. The principal circulation route encircles the interior courtyard; a "bump" in the wall directly above where the walkway passes indicates the shift from the pre- to postwar work in the collection. In the Klee/Bessier block another circle defines the gallery space; here, by contrast, works are displayed on curving walls, which are lodged within the irregular shell of the existing library building.[14] All of the exhibition spaces in the main gallery are on the upper floor, where they could be top-lit with natural light, as was required by the committee; the Klee/Bessier galleries, however, were to be artificially lit and could therefore occupy two stories. The lower floors of the project are given over to offices, a four-hundred-person lecture theater, library, administration, and "refreshment room." The entire scheme is raised on a platform that serves a purpose similar to that of its Churchill predecessor—elevating the project from the surrounding context and leveling out the uneven terrain—with the additional urban function of isolating pedestrians from the three traffic routes surrounding the plaza and providing space for parking beneath with minimal excavation. Stirling also felt that the raised plaza would increase the possibility for outdoor uses, including exhibitions, and it made more feasible the proposed bridge across the Mühlenstrasse (not required by the brief, and a clear precursor to Stirling's proposed bridge connecting his Sackler Museum to the Fogg Museum at Harvard a decade later).

Although the sixteen-member jury—composed of architects, academics, and government officials, all German—found that Stirling's design made an "appealing impression," he was not awarded a prize.[15] The commission was awarded to Dissing + Weitling, a Copenhagen-based studio of Arne Jacobsen successors whose black granite rectangular block razed all existing structures; other prizes went to German architects.[16] Of Stirling's design (judged anonymously) the jury expressed doubts as to its attitude toward preservation: "The aspects of architectural heritage are dealt with in a fashion which is in no way satisfactory and leads to doubts about the point or sense of preservation."[17]

"ALMOST 100 PERCENT PRESERVATIONIST"

However unsatisfactory the jury found his preservationist response, Stirling's Düsseldorf project was deeply and intentionally imbricated with its historic context and aimed to preserve at least some portion of it. In 1970 Stirling wrote that he was "almost 100 percent preservationist," especially if the alternative was "meaningless, anonymous and inefficient places" created by contemporary architecture.[18] His strategy at Düsseldorf, however, was neither simply to reiterate the language of the existing fabric nor to provide a "restrained" modernist building in the vein of Dissing + Weitling. Instead, Stirling retained select portions of existing buildings and engaged specific exigencies of the Grabbeplatz site and its surrounding buildings and monuments. His efforts at preservation are neither prosaic nor retardaire; he revisions the historic city in both material and compositional terms, articulating a critical position vis-à-vis the past and its relationship to the present.

The most complex example of his preservationist attitude is his treatment of the existing library façade. In the competition report it was suggested that "parts of the façade of the former town library . . . may be integrated into the new building or moved to some other location."[19] Stirling retains the library façade completely along the Neubruck Strasse at the western edge of the site but selectively carves away the most prominent face of the library on the Grabbeplatz to create a more dramatically "ruined" appearance. The wall feigns disintegration as it slopes toward the center of the plaza, the jagged, artificially destroyed edge dominating the profile (fig. 103). Characteristically, Stirling's solution was derived from a seemingly literalist interpretation of the brief—to reuse "parts of the façade" in the design. Rather than grafting or blending the old and the new, however, or even deferring to the bombed-out structure, he further decimates the shell. Stirling described the overall project strategy at Düsseldorf as "infill and preserve," and here he literally infills the ruin with building while preserving the ruined shell as a screen through which to glimpse the new Klee/Bessier gallery behind. This gesture no doubt provoked the ire of the committee, which objected to the use of "alienated bits of façade of historic buildings," a practice they saw as antithetical to a true attempt to "preserve" them.[20]

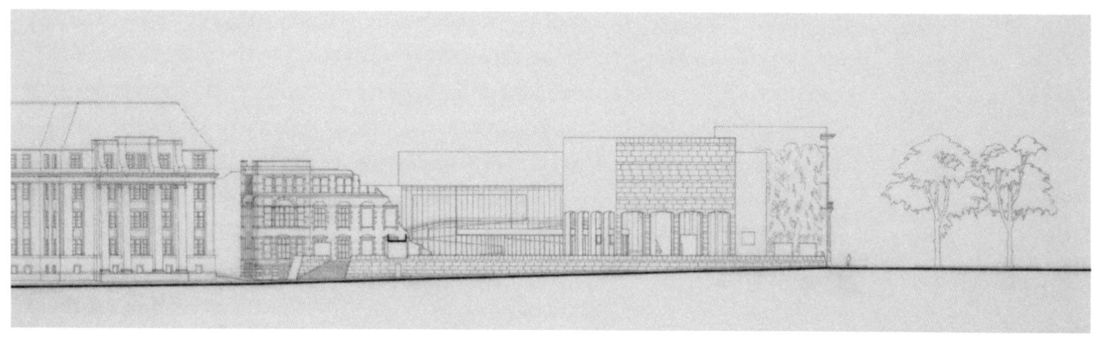

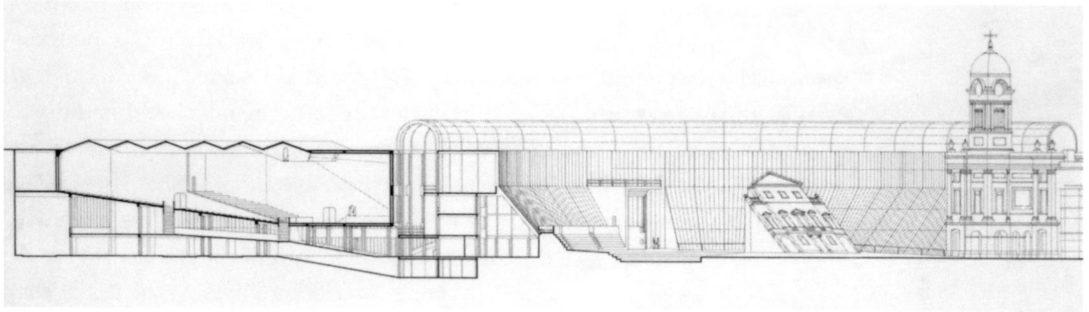

Figure 103
Stirling and Partner, Düsseldorf. Elevation with the "ruined" library façade at left.

Figure 104
James Stirling (firm), Derby Civic Centre, England, 1970. Sectional elevation. The rescued Neoclassical façade is tilted to define a stage backdrop within the redefined urban space.

We might compare Stirling's treatment of the Düsseldorf library façade to his reuse of the Town Hall façade at Derby, in which an existing eighteenth-century façade is tilted forty-five degrees to become the proscenium for a new theater space (fig. 104). In both cases he "preserves" the existing façade, in part (Düsseldorf) or whole (Derby), but in so doing he deprives the remaining fragment of its original function. Although the reuse of the façade at Derby is more radical (and more clever) as an oblique backdrop, at both Düsseldorf and Derby Stirling's preservationist attitude runs counter to any received notion of a deference to the status quo, and in both cases the repurposing of the retained fragment is a critical aspect of its imagined reuse. It becomes a strictly two-dimensional element, one which loses its original coherence as enclosure to become either a roof (Derby) or a screen (Düsseldorf). In both cases the remaining fragment loses its "architecturalness" and becomes a commentary on the presumed qualities of a façade: that is, something that is necessarily vertical or that necessarily defines enclosure.

Echoes of this "ruined" gesture reappear at Stuttgart, though in a more subtle way than in the monumental, crumbling façade of Düsseldorf. As at Düsseldorf, Stuttgart sits on a giant stone plinth, and also as at Düsseldorf, this plinth conceals a parking lot. At Stuttgart the edge of this stone base forms the street edge against which the project rises dramatically into the hillside. At one point in the wall a few stones have been selectively removed and appear to have tumbled to the ground, where they lay strewn about the grass (fig. 105). Like the jagged edge of the library façade at Düsseldorf, these fallen stones reveal the materiality of the wall even as they undermine its structural significance. At Stuttgart the wall is, of course, newly constructed rather than repurposed, and here the act of ruination is more mischievous than critical—perhaps more comparable to James Wines's contemporaneous BEST warehouses, with their crumbling façades, than to the slightly uncomfortable reminder of war's devastation in Düsseldorf's fragmented edge.

We might compare Stirling's treatment of the library façade at Düsseldorf with Kahn's well-known fascination with ruins around this same time period. For example, Kahn wrapped his National Assembly Building at Dhaka (1962) and the Exeter Library (1972) in brick screens to evoke the two-dimensionality of building shells (fig. 106). Kahn never literalizes the act of ruination, however, as Stirling does; his "ruins" are always intact, their power suggestive and eternal. They evoke the passage of time and architecture's desire for permanence and immutability. Stirling's ruined façade at Düsseldorf, by contrast, or even at Stuttgart evokes the very opposite, the impermanence and fragility of architecture. At Düsseldorf we might extend that commentary to the devastating effects of the Allied bombers. What Kahn and Stirling share here is an insistence on the materiality of the building fragment. Stirling's eroded library façade is deliberately positioned as a remnant of the real, as having material and weight. The jagged cut along its edge emphasizes the thickness of the original stonework; in every orthographic drawing of the project the diagonal cut is carefully stippled to show its materiality.

Venturi, too, engages the notion of the ruin around this time, but with a decidedly different emphasis that bypasses the question of materiality altogether. In his Franklin Court Project of 1976 the "ghost" of Benjamin Franklin's original house (razed in 1812) is defined through a steel-frame structure that becomes a diagram or outline of the former structure (fig. 107). An "imagined" house is substituted for the "real," unlike at Düsseldorf, in which the real

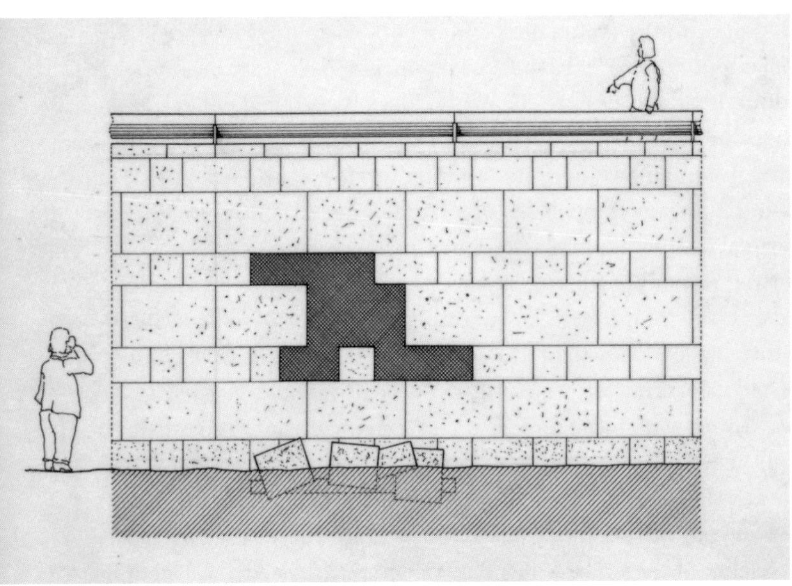

Figure 105
James Stirling, Michael Wilford and Associates, Staatsgalerie, Stuttgart, Germany, 1984. Elevation. "Fallen" stones in the perimeter wall construct a more mischievous "ruin."

Figure 106
Louis Kahn, Library, Phillips Exeter Academy, New Hampshire, 1972. Kahn's brick façade evokes the two-dimensionality of ruined building shells.

Figure 107
Venturi Scott Brown and Associates, Franklin Court, Philadelphia, 1976. The steel frame structure outlines the "ghost" of Franklin's former home.

is actively preserved. Although they begin with different conditions—the memory of a structure long vanished (Franklin's house) vs. the reality of a useless "real" structure (the library façade)—their attitudes toward history differ as well. Venturi's project is ultimately deferential toward the "archival" evidence—the archaeological remnants (an "extremely rare Bristol punch-bowl") are carefully framed in glass vitrines beneath grade—while Stirling appears frankly heretical in his willingness to selectively demolish portions of the structure.

This treatment of the ruined library building—whether mischievous or somber or both—was but a piece of the project's relationship to the existing city fabric, and I do not want to suggest that Stirling omits more traditionally preservationist gestures at Düsseldorf. In fact, this is one of the most frequently commented-upon aspects of the scheme, following in the trajectory of St. Andrews and Derby and their engagement with European historical centers. Girouard describes Düsseldorf as "fitted carefully into the centre of a city." He continues: "Its mass is broken up by the retention of existing buildings, and it is responsive to the existing street plan."[21] And indeed, the entire museum block is buried within the existing fabric and finished with slabs of natural or reconstructed stone, not only "as relief from the greyness of many modern buildings in Düsseldorf" but also to correspond to the Neo-classical buildings in its immediate vicinity. Stirling wrote that the building was meant to "harmonize" with the surrounding buildings, to become an "integral element in historic Düsseldorf," and he would later describe the contextual quality of his projects during this period as opposed to his earlier works: "Most of our early buildings were out beyond the suburbs, on the margin. The Leicester building was in the back of the university. You can do anything you want, out there, but with Munich, Cologne and Düsseldorf, I found myself in the center of the city, with an identity that shouldn't be disturbed. In these historical centers . . . I should allow the context to influence me."[22] The project, however, is by no means a purely conciliatory gesture toward the existing city, and it begs the question of what Stirling meant by allowing himself to be "influenced" by context.

CONTEXTUALISM: OBJECT VS. URBAN

The term contextualism came into common usage in architectural history only in the late 1950s and early 1960s, and it was born of a critique of modernist practices. Like other discursive phenomenon (functionalism, regionalism, and so on), distinct strands of contextualism developed with varying geographic and ideological affiliations and subtleties.[23] In Italy the discourse centered around the figures of Richard Rogers and Vittorio Gregotti and was articulated largely through the pages of *Casabella* (where Rogers was editor) and through the projects and writings of Aldo Rossi. In its Italian iteration contextualism was intimately tied to the historical city (typically, and unsurprisingly, an Italian historical city) and its attendant cultural associations and historical memories. As Adrian Forty has shown, the consistent mistranslation of *ambiente*—the term used by both Rossi and Rogers—as "context" missed the original term's emphasis on environment or atmosphere and a dialectical relationship to the past. Significantly, this understanding of contextualism was deeply reliant on the individual object—think of the iconic shape of Rossi's floating Teatro del Mundo of 1979—as the repository of cultural memory and as constitutive of the city itself.

By contrast, context as it came to be developed and understood in America focused primarily on an architectural object's relationship to the spaces of the city rather than on the object itself. Under the teaching and writings of Colin Rowe at Cornell, this version of contextualism (which had many overlaps with collage, as will be seen in the following section) foregrounded mappings of the city (again Italy loomed large, particularly eighteenth-century Rome) and on the inherent ambiguity in the figure/ground diagram that emerged from gestalt psychology, with a particular emphasis on the manipulation of the object in relation to its surrounding context.

Linking the two discourses was a broader desire to situate the architectural object in relation to *something*—to move away from the isolated modernist object, perhaps best exemplified by Le Corbusier's purist villas of the 1920s. In his own writings during this period Stirling often uses the term "contexturalism" (with the added "r"), a seeming malapropism which was in fact a neologism—an intentional provocation and swerve of the "correct" term.[24] "Contexturalism" was meant to imply a conflation of "context" and "texture," with "texture" referring to the urban fabric and further distinguishing the idea from contextualism as it was being developed in literary criticism as the "act of setting a poem or other work in its cultural context."[25] Stirling's use of the term "contexturalism" (which he always placed in quotation marks) suggests his privileging of the physical and formal context over an historical or a cultural one.

Stirling's understanding and articulation of "contexturalism," like much of his earlier intellectual formation, was indebted to the writings and teachings of Rowe, though he did not align exactly with his mentor and teacher. If contextualism à la Rowe was typified by the Hôtel de Beauvais in Paris—an example in which "idealized forms" were fitted within an irregular site, resulting in a series of strategic deformations to accomplish the fit—Stirling's contextualism at Düsseldorf is striking for the *lack* of deformation in the formal components. The square plans of the entrance pavilion and museum block, the circular forms of the central courtyard and Klee/Bessier gallery all remain pure. There are no skewed geometries, no circles squeezed into ellipses as at Beauvais; rather than accommodating the historic context, each building component maintains its geometric integrity. Stirling's insistence on the relative immutability of geometric forms seems to veer slightly away from Rowe and the American version of contextualism, which focused primarily on an architectural object's relationship to the spaces of the city, rather than the object itself, and suggests instead an allegiance with the Italian school of contextualism, with its insistence on the autonomous object. But Stirling's contextualism was no more synonymous with Rossi's than it was with Rowe's. In Stirling's work we see an inherently dialectical understanding of contextualism, at once relating to the historical city around it and at the same time insisting on a distinction from it.

The entrance pavilion perhaps best embodies this dialectical contextualism. On the one hand it responds directly to its site conditions and the immediate urban surroundings; it is oriented to the axis of the Mühlenstrasse and positioned to offer a view of the Burgplatz—an important urban square on the river containing the Schlossturm tower—as well as to be seen from it (fig. 108). The shallow arches of the pavilion mimic the adjacent library façade. Its colonnades and overall cubic volume are an explicit reference to the pair of Neoclassical gatehouses that mark the entrance to the park nearby and which would have been visible from Stirling's entrance pavilion given the site lines of the project. The pavilion was also meant to refer to the original art gallery that had once stood on the site but had been destroyed; Stirling would include images of this building, also a freestanding pavilionlike structure, in publications of the projects. As a freestanding object in the plaza (at least perceptually) Stirling's entrance pavilion also relates to the Schlossturm in the middle of the Burgplatz. Stirling is careful to include both the Neoclassical gatehouses and Schlossturm in the site plan to reinforce the new pavilion's triangulation between the existing monuments (fig. 109). Significantly, the axis of the drawing is oriented neither north-south nor according to the overall geometry of the museum block but to the axis of the pavilion. The pavilion is the center of the city.

On the other hand, the pavilion is also arguably the most *out* of place object in the scheme. It floats seemingly adrift in the plaza, misaligned with the rest of the project and attached through the convoluted geometry of the glass entrance. In some of the first plan sketches for the project this entrance pavilion indeed truly floats across the plaza (fig. 110). Stirling marks the axis from the Burgplatz along the Mühlenstrasse with a diagonal line bisecting the pavilion; one version shows the pavilion anchored to the entrance pavilion, but in a second sketch it is pulled away and drifts closer to the pedestrian bridge. This second version would have given the pavilion an even greater prominence in the view from the Mühlenstrasse, as well as a more disembodied relationship to the rest of the scheme. Also contributing to the strangeness of the pavilion is the proportion and provenance of the colonnade that circumscribes its base, which seems equally to be derived from Le Corbusier's pilotis and from the Neoclassical gatehouses. These columns/pilotis elevate the top-heavy structure above with an "entablature" taller than the columns themselves. The pavilion is overscaled in relation to the rest of the project—in fact it is taller than the museum block itself—yet feels somehow diminutive. Here perhaps we have the inverse of Stirling's well-known interest in the "monumentally small"—he would often describe his favored Thomas Hope chair, for example, as a small object with a large presence—in the "diminutively large," in other words, that which is physically imposing in scale but proportioned as a small object.[26] Like the Florey building, the pavilion feels more like an object than a building.

Figure 108
Stirling and Partner, Düsseldorf. Model. View of the entrance pavilion from the Mühlenstrasse.

Figure 109
Stirling and Partner, Düsseldorf. Site plan.

The project, then, is at once embedded within and respectful of the city fabric, as well as resistant to it. Although much of the scheme indeed "harmonizes" with the city—in the choice of materials, the retention of portions of the existing structure, and the largely concealed quality of much of the museum block—the pavilion offers a more complex commentary on the surrounding fabric: a foreign object seemingly dropped from the sky yet resonant with nearby monuments and reminiscent of previous structures on the site. This strangeness is perhaps intentional if not inevitable for an English paratrooper building in a German city on a site destroyed by Allied

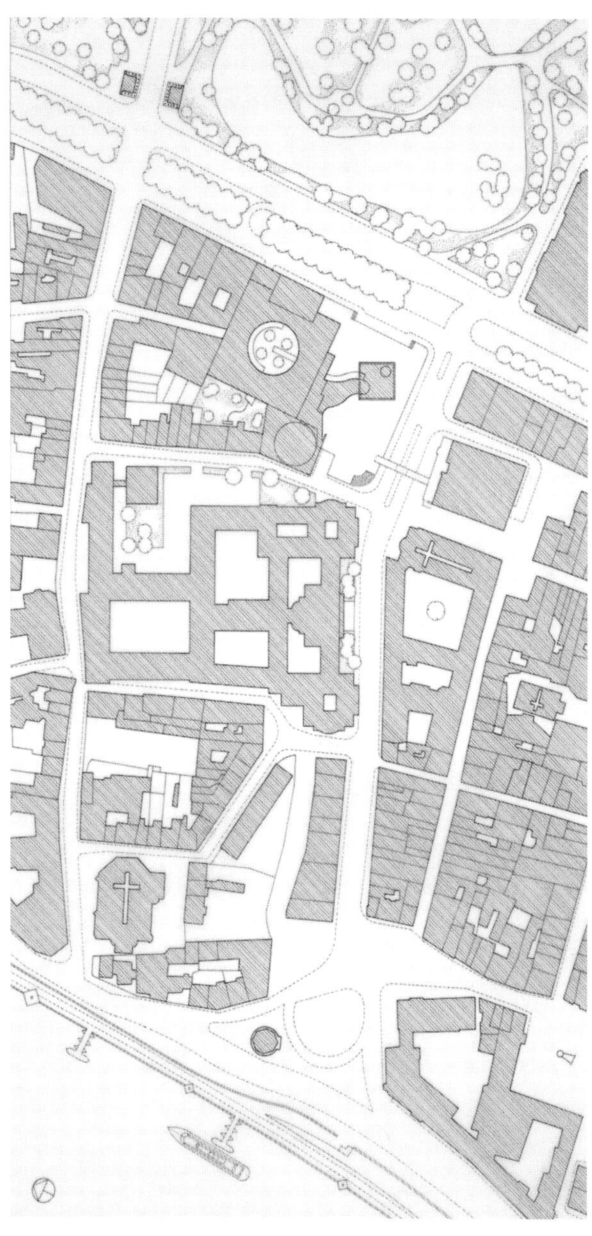

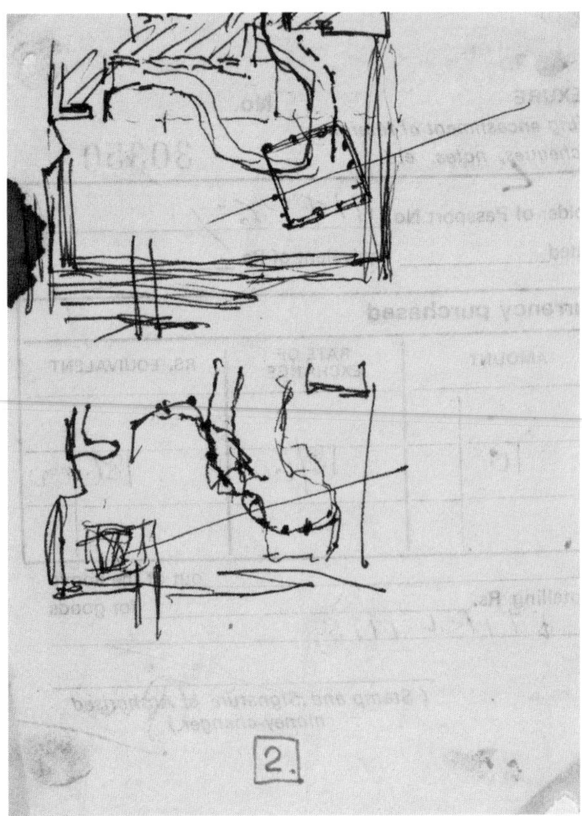

Figure 110
Stirling and Partner, Düsseldorf. Development sketches of the entrance pavilion. Note its complete detachment from the museum block in the lower sketch.

bombs. Even leaving aside the relatively recent experiences of the war, so much of Stirling's earlier work was deeply embedded within a British tradition of Oxbridge courtyards, medieval Scottish castles, and Liverpool docks, not to mention London stock bricks and patent glazing. What happens when Stirling is no longer embedded in his own traditions and country? The pavilion provides one answer, a project that is both of the city and foreign to it, which respects its traditions but holds them open for investigation. Here Stirling is perhaps closest to Rossi, tapping into the forms of a collective memory; but for Stirling there is no inherent meaning in this cultural memory. The pieces of the city are retained as fragments, and new elements are reimagined, but there is no attempt to make sense of them.

In the end, perhaps the most contextual gesture at Düsseldorf isn't the preserved elements of the existing building, or the attempt to align and embed the project within the rules of the historical city, but the fact that the building itself becomes a kind of city. Moneo writes that, beginning with Düsseldorf, Stirling desires "architecture and the city to be one and the same thing."[27] Indeed Düsseldorf's contextualism—or "contexturalism"—is arguably most powerful not in its conciliatory urban gestures or in its desire to "harmonize" with the city but in the fact that the project itself, with its aggregation of buildings and its creation of urban spaces, is in itself a miniature city.

THREE-DIMENSIONAL COLLAGE

In his RIBA Gold Medal Acceptance speech of 1980 Stirling made explicit his debt to Rowe, "my good friend then as now," stating that his latest projects (including Düsseldorf) were "a *collage* of old and new elements, Egyptian cornices and Romanesque windows, but also Constructivist canopies, ramps and flowing forms—a union of elements from the past and present."[28] The influence of Rowe is here made explicit, and particularly of Rowe and Koetter's essay *Collage City,* one of the most influential texts of the era. The essay, written in 1973, first appeared in partial form in the August 1975 issue of the *Architectural Review,* and the book of the same title—an extended version of the essay—was published in 1978.[29] By the time the essay (and certainly the book) was published, the ideas surrounding collage had already been widely circulated in architectural culture, largely through Rowe's urban design courses at Cornell, which he began teaching in 1963, resulting in numerous students who subsequently proliferated and published his ideas and methods.[30] Rowe himself wrote in 1975 that the ideas in *Collage City* dated back to a lecture given in Alvin Boyarsky's London summer school of 1970.[31] The term collage had, of course, existed in art history much longer: Clement Greenberg's seminal text "Collage" was first published in 1958, with the technique dating back to Picasso and Braque in the early twentieth century.[32] Stirling had been exposed to various artistic explorations of collage not only through his relationship with Rowe but through his general art historical knowledge of cubism, as well as of such figures in the Independent group as John McHale and Eduardo Paolozzi (a number of whose collages hung in Stirling's living room).[33]

Following anti-Hegelian critic and philosopher Karl Popper—"the critic of utopia and the exponent of tradition's usefulness"—Rowe and Koetter reject any totalizing schema, suggesting instead "piecemeal utopias." They advocate an approach as a "bricoleur" (a term borrowed from Claude Lévi-Strauss), putting together a range of objects across time periods: "It is suggested that a collage approach, an approach in which objects (and attitudes) are conscripted or seduced from out of their context is—at the present day—the only way of dealing with the ultimate problems of either or both Utopia and tradition."[34] Rome—both Imperial and Papal—serves as the dominant model for *Collage City,* but an arguably more powerful precedent is Hadrian's Villa—a "miniature Rome"—which, in Rowe and Koetter's terms, "attempts to dissimulate all reference to any single controlling idea," as opposed to Versailles, a "sketch for total design."[35] "It is better to think of an aggregation of small, and even contradictory set pieces (almost like the products of different regimes) than to entertain fantasies about total and 'faultless' solutions which the condition of politics can only abort."[36]

The reading of Düsseldorf as collagist, in Rowe and Koetter's terms, is seemingly supported by the project's juxtaposed geometries and axes, as well as an array of geometric shapes. Like Hadrian's Villa, Düsseldorf appears to be an aggregation of buildings that have accumulated over time rather than been designed at once. The solid museum block, the glazed entrance hall, and the colonnaded entrance pavilion are not only of varying shapes and placed in contrasting relationships on the site, they also represent different formal types (cubic, circular, curvilinear) and material languages (stone, concrete, glass). In response to Stirling's entry to the Düsseldorf competition, the jury wrote that it contained "too great a number of heterogeneous elements," a critique that supports the reading of the project as collagist.[37]

But we might ask whether these collage techniques—specifically the "collision" of "set pieces"—were truly new at Düsseldorf. Surely Leicester was "collagist," with its series of volumes lashed together in an orchestrated figural play. Indeed, Stirling wrote of Leicester, the "total building could be thought of as an assemblage of everyday elements."[38] Was Düsseldorf simply a scalar shift from Leicester—with the "elements" now at the scale of building volumes (museum block, entrance hall) rather than programmatic elements (a lecture hall or stairway)? Was collage circa 1975 simply an extension of assemblage circa 1959?

While true to some degree, in that both describe a compositional strategy for arranging a series of discrete elements into a fragmentary whole, the comparison elides critical differences between Leicester and Düsseldorf, the first of which is the fact that the assemblages at Düsseldorf are organized in plan rather than in section. This larger shift in Stirling's work from an emphasis on section to plan, as noted by Moneo and others, is certainly supported by a comparison between Leicester and Düsseldorf (though of course earlier "plan-based" projects such as Churchill contradict this theory).[39] The plan is undoubtedly the organizing device at Düsseldorf, particularly since much of the building had to be one story to allow for top-lighting. Perhaps a more critical distinction between Leicester and Düsseldorf in their strategies of assemblage/collage is that in the former, the collection of elements remains subservient to the reading of the singular form. Even with its clearly "explosive" tendency, Leicester's components are contained within an overall image of a unitary building. However complex it may be, the "centripetal" pull, as Eisenman described it, keeps the various volumes together along the vertical axis. At Düsseldorf, however, the building elements break free of any unitary reading and disaggregate across the site. The building is no longer a singular object but a collection of objects—an important distinction not only from Leicester but from Stirling's later projects at St. Andrews or Derby, both of which are also singular objects.

This reading of the project as both assemblage and collage appears most clearly in Stirling's axonometric drawings for the project. As discussed in previous chapters, it was the axonometric drawings that gave Florey its "object-like" quality, and it was the axonometrics of Leicester that enabled the legibility of the various components of the project that could only be be understood, in some sense, through the these drawings. At Düsseldorf Stirling explores a new type of axonometric in which select portions of the building are isolated from the project as a whole and rendered as discrete sequences. One of the most reproduced of these drawings depicts the circulation axis from the

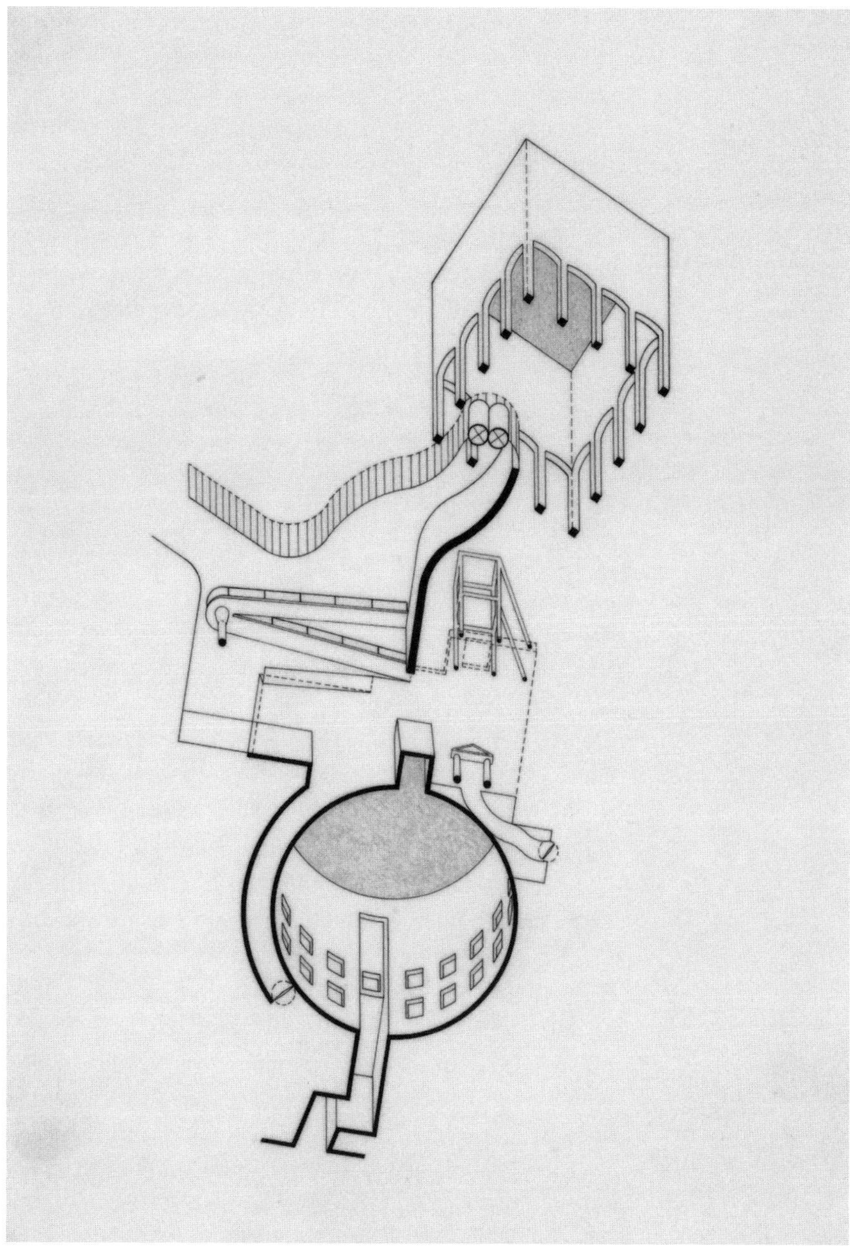

Figure 111
Stirling and Partner, Düsseldorf. Worm's-eye axonometric of the entrance pavilion, circular courtyard, and the circulation elements between them.

entrance pavilion to the Ratinger Mauer. It illustrates the collage mentality in the juxtaposition of the various "set pieces" along the sequence: the entrance pavilion, the entrance hall, the circular courtyard (fig. 111). In a related drawing, Stirling isolates the various "objects" associated with the circulation; the stairs and elevator from the parking lot below, the double revolving doors into the entrance vestibule, the scissor ramp and elevator to the galleries, the walkway to the Kunsthalle (fig. 112). As Ireneé Scalbert notes, these circulation axonometrics do little to explain the circulation, given their disembodied and frag-

Figure 112
Stirling and Partner, Düsseldorf. Axonometric of the entrance lobby and its associated circulation elements: stair, ramps, elevators, and revolving doors, along with the Doric portico that marks the passage to the Kunsthalle.

Figure 113
Le Corbusier, Salvation Army, Paris, 1954. Photograph by James Stirling.

mented quality (particularly the former, in which Stirling uses a worm's-eye angle), and he calls them a "study in topography."[40] In both drawings Stirling demonstrates a *local* logic of assemblage/collage rather than an overall project strategy; the circulation components are extracted from their place within the building, enabling the project to achieve much more completely a collagist sensibility of various components or "as found" elements. Significantly, each of these components (stair, ramp, lift, and so on) retain their autonomy and completeness, even as everything else in the project is removed or cut away.

It is often argued that circulation—specifically the promenade architecturale—was a defining aspect of Stirling's architecture at Düsseldorf.[41] While this is true, circulation was a highly considered aspect of many of Stirling's earlier projects. In describing his Poole competition entry in 1965 he wrote that it was necessary "to re-think the role of circulation (corridors, lifts, staircases, etc.) and to re-state it as the dynamic and motivating element of the building. It was essential to create not merely corridors in the institutional sense but to construct something of a fundamental organizational significance, like an armature or skeleton on to which rooms fastened."[42] Similarly, at Leicester the vertical stair and elevator towers act as visible armature around which the rest of the project revolves, and in both the Old People's Home and Florey the corridor is an organizing element of the design. In none of these earlier examples, however, is the circulation modeled with the same volumetric complexity as at Düsseldorf.

More importantly, in none of these earlier projects does circulation become the primary compositional technique. At Düsseldorf the hierarchy between the circulation armature and the principal building "elements" is effectively disintegrated if not reversed. The axonometric drawings, in particular, insist on circulation as more than the leftover or residual areas of a project that fall between the "real" program spaces. The circulation spaces are no less important than the gallery space or the rotunda; they become equivalent as volumetric objects. If anything, they become more significant, and the "real" program spaces appear to be residual or secondary. This is achieved in part because the circulation takes on the quality of a figure and also because it encapsulates the sectional complexity—moving up and down and over and under the city and the different building elements—while the program pieces remain static. This reversal of the dominant building elements to foreground circulation is achieved most strikingly within the drawings in which only the circulation organs are drawn, without their attendant body. The "static" spaces—in particular the courtyard and the entrance pavilion—are coopted as portions of the circulation sequence, but remain a secondary element. Tellingly, nowhere but in plan or elevation do we see the gallery spaces represented; instead, nearly all of the three-dimensional drawings are given over to representing the circulation sequence.

As others, most recently Vidler, have demonstrated, the circulation sequence at Düsseldorf can be thought of as a revisioning of the entrance sequence to Le Corbusier's Salvation Army building, comprising multiple pavilions—first

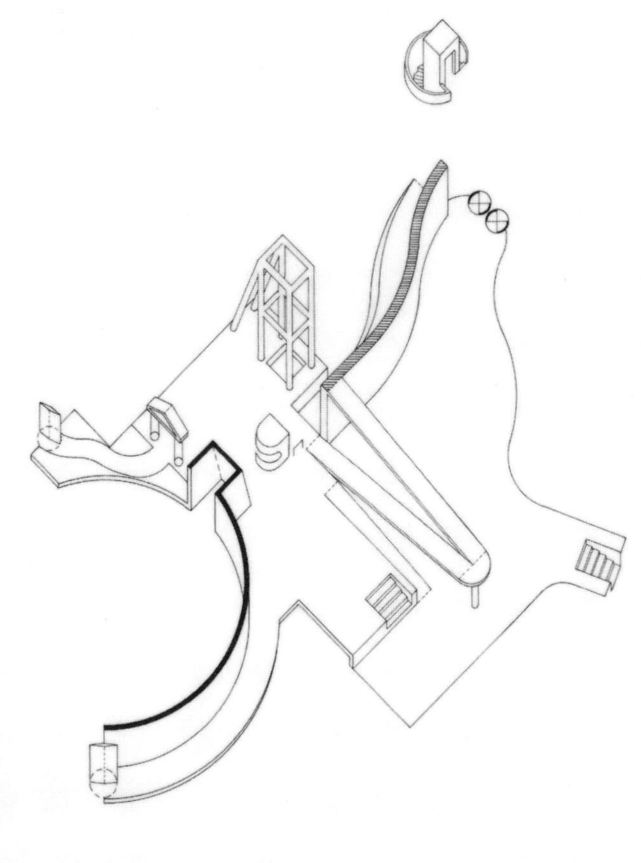

cubic, then circular—attached by a short, enclosed walkway and terminating in an entrance hall (fig. 113). The entire sequence runs parallel to the project itself, and Le Corbusier memorably refers to the group of buildings as a "kind of *hors d'oeuvre,* disposed in front of the great hostel building."[43] In the 1950s Stirling himself described the Salvation Army entry sequence as "disemboweled machine parts" pulled away from the "neutral backdrop of the slab."[44] Although they are disposed parallel to the building, Le Corbusier's appetizers nonetheless lead dutifully to the entrance of the building proper. Stirling's collection of circulation elements, on the other hand, pass right through the building. The entrance sequence has no conclusion or logical endpoint in the building itself; instead, it leads one to the alley in back and through to the city again. And as the axonometric drawings emphasize most clearly, these circulation pieces are now completely "disemboweled," detached from any secondary or subservient relationship to the "architecture" to become in effect their own distinct project.

Another important distinction between Stirling's entry volumes and their Corbusian predecessors is that the elements along Stirling's promenade alternate between solid and void, interior and exterior. This oscillation between positive and negative figures can also be traced to the impact of *Collage City,* which stressed, in addition to the compositional strategy of "collision," a balance between the "continuous solid" of the traditional city and the "continuous void" of the modern one. At its core *Collage City* is an investigation of figure/ground drawing techniques and a testament to the influence of gestalt theory. This interest in gestalt-based manipulations was evident in much of Rowe's earlier thinking; as Rowe and Koetter write in their essay "Transparency: Literal and Phenomenal" of 1963, the key operation of the gestalt diagram is the reversal, the activating of the ground as a figure. "While figure is generally seen as figure by reason of its greater closure, compactness, density and internal articulation and while ground is generally seen as ground by reason of its lack of these qualities, in the figure-ground relationship the ground, although it may at first appear anonymous, is neither subservient nor passive" continuing that this reversal gives the ground "figural significance."[45]

This manipulation of the figure/ground relationship at Düsseldorf is clear from the earliest sketches for the project.[46] The first sketch (drawn on the back of a boarding pass while Stirling was en route to visit Le Corbusier's Chandigarh) contains two small plans and a schematic elevation, all done in black ink marker (fig. 114). Both plans show the museum block with an open, circular courtyard at its center and the entrance pavilion, askew in the center of the Grabbeplatz, connected to the central courtyard. In these initial drawings there is a clear delineation of the museum block as a "continuous solid" (hatched to distinguish it from the open areas of the courtyard and surrounding streets), out of which the central courtyard is carved and the entrance pavilion ejected as an object in the "continuous void" of the plaza. In subsequent axonometric sketches the museum block is rendered as a volumetric solid from which both the central courtyard and the Ratinger Mauer walkway appear to be extracted.

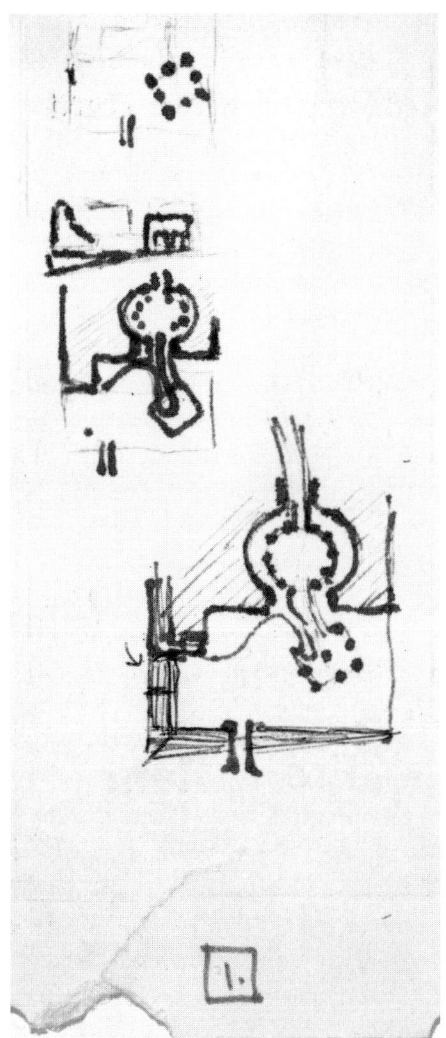

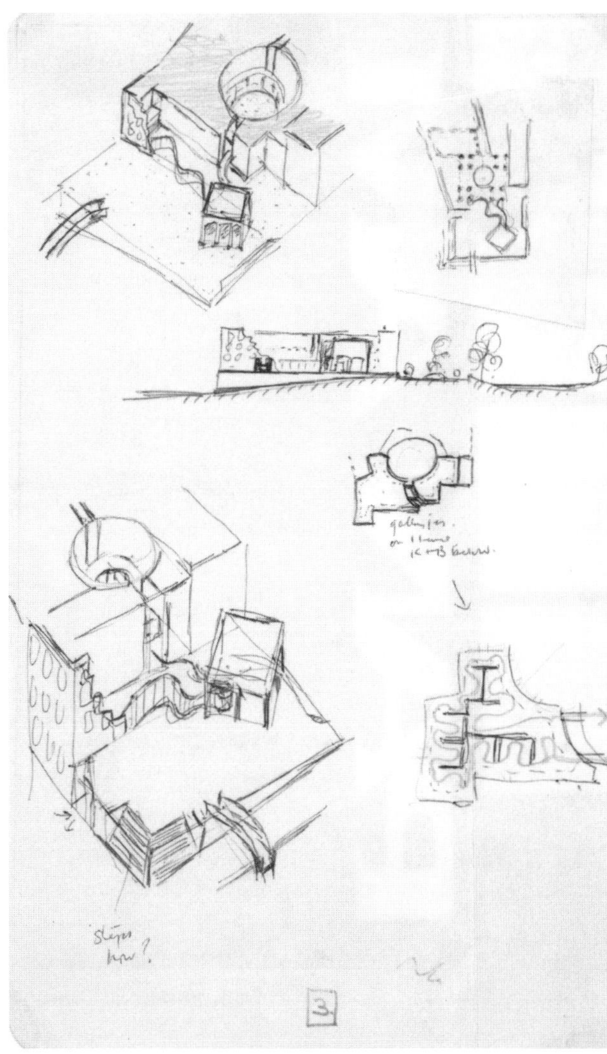

Figure 114
James Stirling, Düsseldorf. Sketch "1."

Figure 115
James Stirling, Düsseldorf. Sketch "3."

In these sketches the positive cubic figure of the entrance pavilion is clearly set against the negative of the courtyard—as if the "solid" was in fact reconstituted from the "void" (fig. 115). Although the extracted cylinder is formally transformed into a solid cube, the transformation seems less a betrayal of the original shape and more a modification according to additional criteria (aligning with existing street lines, references the previous cubic museum, and so on). In other words an active revision of the cylindrical form according to a new set of constraints.

The circular courtyard is arguably the most complex formal device in this figure/ground relationship; although it is a primary "figure" in the composition, it is a negative rather than a positive space. As a positively articulated void it creates what Rowe and Koetter call in *Collage City* the "gestalt condition of ambivalence"—an ambivalence between figure and field, between that which is bounded and that which bounds.[47] Throughout the project there exists a play between building as texture vs. building as object, space as "occupier" vs. space as "definer," in which, as Rowe and Koetter describe, "both buildings and spaces exist in an equality of sustained debate," but this dialectical reading is most convincing and forcefully articulated in the courtyard space.[48] The worm's-eye axonometrics, in particular, obscure what's inside and what's outside, what is "carved away" and what is "added." Although the central courtyard is allegedly a "void" and the pavilion a "solid," in the axonometric drawings they become equivalent as volumetric objects.

As the pavilion makes clear, Stirling never gave in to the primacy of the "figural void," and if anything his fixation on the "object" remained.[49] But the complexity, and ultimately the ambiguity, at Düsseldorf comes from the fact that the project oscillates between reading as "continuous solid" and "continuous void." There is a tension and sustained contradiction between the museum block as a solid, out of which the circular courtyard is extracted, and the plaza as a void, on which the entrance pavilion is inserted, with the patent-glazed entrance hall as a mediating hinge between them. At Düsseldorf, Stirling sets up a "sustained debate" between the "all black" of the historical city and the "all white" of the modern one. The plaza-as-ground is further activated by the pavilion such that there are spaces framed positively between it and the plaza edges—in other words, ground activated as figure.

This solid/void play represents a different technique than the commonly held understanding of collage as defined by Picasso or Braque—pasting material on the surface of the canvas to call attention to the flatness of the picture plane itself—or as extended by Rowe and Koetter—"colliding" various elements "conscripted" out of their context. Düsseldorf cannot be understood simply as a "pasted paper" technique because the pieces of the composition are defined as much by negative space as by positive form. The boundaries and legibility of an individual component are inseparable from adjoining pieces;

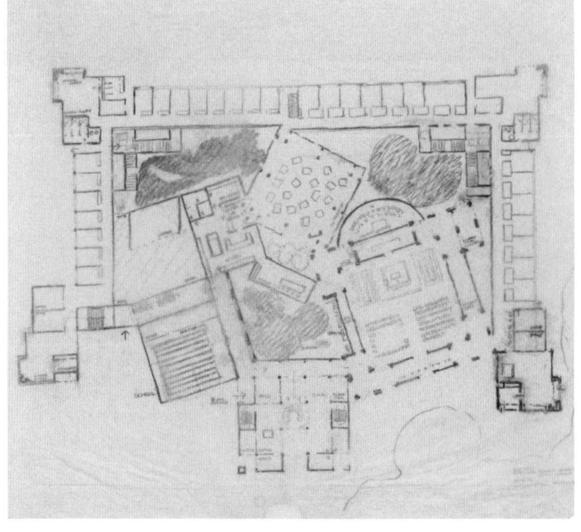

Figure 116
Louis Kahn, Dominican Motherhouse, Media, Pennsylvania, 1969. Plan. Kahn's "room-buildings" are scattered within the orthogonal three-sided perimeter.

the pavilion isn't simply added to the plaza, it is extracted from the museum block, and its entrails remain in the curving form of the entrance lobby. This is a very different compositional strategy than, say, Kahn's Dominican Motherhouse of 1969, in which the various program pieces—what Kahn called "room-buildings" (for example, chapel, refectory, school rooms)—are literally moved around on the page as paper cutouts (fig. 116).[50] At the Dominican Motherhouse the uniformity and boundedness of the individual figures enable the reading of their juxtaposition and skewed angles to take precedence, especially as they are set against the regularized three-sided buildings composed of cellular rows. Stirling's "set pieces," by contrast, are articulated as both positive and negative elements, and reading of the solid/void precludes an easy understanding of the individual pieces.

While undoubtedly indebted to the discourse surrounding collage, this solid/void dialectic can also be connected to Luigi Moretti, the figure so central to Stirling's understanding and manipulation of volumetric figures in his earlier work, particularly Leicester. As discussed in previous chapters, Moretti's essay "The Structures and Sequences of Spaces" exerted a profound influence on Stirling; Moretti's plaster casts made from models of the interiors of historic buildings informed Stirling's understanding of building volumes as registrations or translations of their interior spatial conditions.[51] As Stirling described the impact of Moretti's casts in 1960, if space could be "imagined as a solid mass determined in shape and size by the proportion of a room or the function of a corridor," then "various elements of the programme could be plastically assembled."[52] Moretti, like Rowe, shifts focus from the object to the space in and around the object. The key distinction between Moretti's and Rowe's understanding of space, however, is that Moretti's is volumetric rather than planometric. Rowe himself acknowledged that the figure/ground technique "will lend itself to the description of cities mostly on flat sites and, mostly, with a ceiling of about five stories and, apart from that, it doesn't work."[53] While Stirling's manipulations at Düsseldorf are undoubtedly plan based, they are also three-dimensional, and here Moretti provides a critical overlay to collage's inherently two-dimensional bias. Both the extracted volumes (the circular courtyard) and the solid figures (the cubic entrance pavilion) at Düsseldorf are legible as "solidified space," which in turn defines a more complex, three-dimensional understanding of the figure/ground dialectic of Rowe—the "gestalt condition of ambivalence." The importance of the void, as well as the act of assemblage—the two critical components of *Collage City*—are already evident in Stirling's reading of Moretti, long before Rowe and Koetter's text.

There are, of course, moments in *Collage City* that wrestle with volume rather than simply plan, notably Rowe and Koetter's well-known juxtaposition of the voided interior gallery space of the Uffizi as the negative volumetric equivalent or "jelly mould" for the Unité, which is turned "inside out."[54] The comparison deliberately if somewhat unconvincingly biases the Uffizi, which they claim to be "much more completely a 'collective' structure" and a "two-faced" building (though more likely they simply prefer it as a subtracted "ground" project rather than an additive "figural" one). Nevertheless, this solid/void discussion enacts a misreading similar to Moretti's, in which solid form is understood as an inverse of negative space. Perhaps the clearest articulation of this technique is Stirling's Wallraf-Richartz Museum in Cologne, under way at the same moment as Düsseldorf. On an even more complex site abutting the railway yard, the Hohenzollern Bridge, and the cathedral, Stirling inserts a grouping of solid and voided objects, though in this case the objects are literally subtracted—particularly the sunken sculpture court, a miniaturized version of the cathedral looming above it, which is "removed" from the plaza floor. A much-reproduced freehand drawing of the project renders it as a composition of solid and void elements, with the voided sculpture court as the base of the drawing—reminiscent of a Moretti plaster cast (fig. 117).

This notion of "solidified space" is significant beyond its ability to see solid as void or void as solid, as it offers a more precise tool for understanding Stirling's volumetric "expression" of function. As at Leicester, in which the volumetric pieces, particularly the lecture halls, articulate a distinct programmatic function, at Düsseldorf each building "fragment"—whether "positive" or

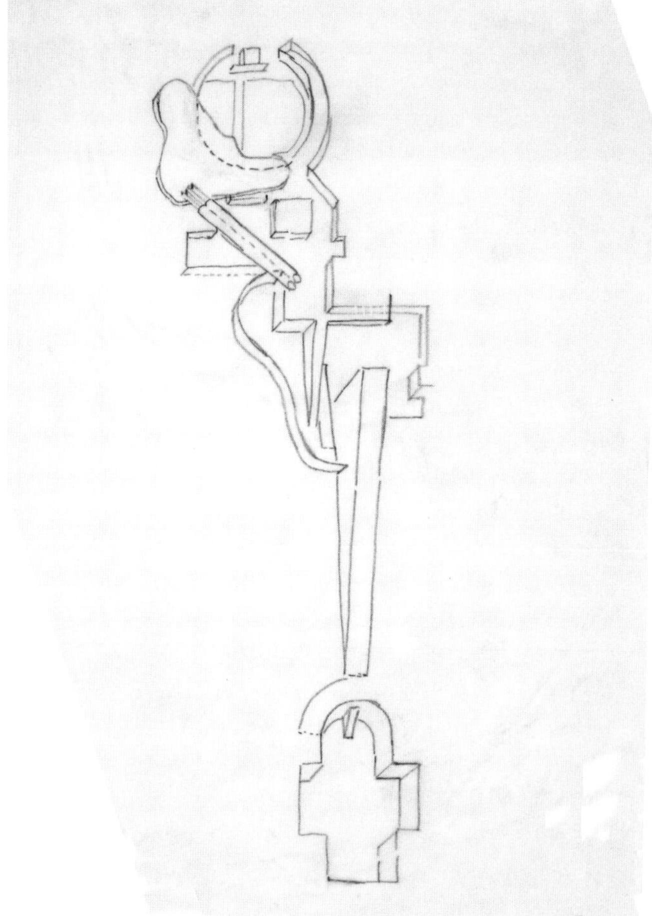

Figure 117
James Stirling and Partner, Wallraf-Richartz Museum, Cologne, 1975. The axonometric sketch highlights solid and void elements.

"negative"—is tied, through its figural articulation, to a specific and recognizable use. The cubic pavilion defines the entry; the solid block houses the museum; the adjacent block and cylinder hold the Klee/Bessier galleries; the curving glass vestibule provides entrance to the galleries. In general there are no double codings, à la Venturi, or mixed metaphors; each shape is articulated as distinct from another precisely because it performs a different function. This too is an important distinction from Rowe, for whom each of the "fragments" deployed is meant to be understood only as a compositional piece.

"NEOCLASSICAL INTENT": AN EMPTYING OUT

We have seen that collage suggested a compositional strategy of "collision" and aggregation, as well as a figure/ground exploration, but as Stirling's RIBA remarks illustrate, collage also came to be understood as a license to mix and match a deliberately heterogenous collection of architectural elements from various historical time periods and formal languages. As a critique of modernist utopian practices, collage was associated with the resurgence of a classical vocabulary, as both a symptom and an initiator of postmodern architectural Neoclassicism.[55] Rowe and Koetter's "city of composite presence" is made up almost exclusively of a premodern history, and Stirling's Düsseldorf must be understood as a negotiation with this burgeoning Neoclassical language as it emerged in the architectural context of the mid-1970s.

In 1974 Stirling wrote that he always considered himself "more neo-classical than art nouveau."[56] In 1977 John Summerson described Stirling's architecture as returning to "Neo-Classical soil" though "less as a recessional than an inspirational act."[57] In *The Language of Postmodern Achitecture* Charles Jencks labels Stirling a "still-modernist," but he singles out Düsseldorf as a project that "represents a new stage in Post-Modern urbanism, because it shows a modern architect acting with the kind of sensitivity towards the historical context one would expect of a traditionalist, with the freshness and invention of a Renaissance architect."[58] Whether or not we label Stirling circa 1975 as a proto-postmodernist, a full-fledged postmodernist, a Neoclassicist, or a modern-day Renaissance architect, he does use historical forms and quotations overtly at Düsseldorf. How do we reconcile this vocabulary with the sensibility of a committed modernist? How does his use of classicism become "inspirational" rather than "recessional?"

Perhaps the best example of Stirling's "inspirational" reworking of the classical past is in the centralized rotunda, which appears at both Düsseldorf and Stuttgart and serves as the most overt reference to the nineteenth-century museum, particularly Schinkel's Altes museum in Berlin (figs. 118–120). Stirling would frequently cite the Düsseldorf/Stuttgart/Altes connection, referencing the plan of Schinkel's famous museum in which a circular courtyard is similarly fitted within the cubic museum block. This circular space at the center of the Düsseldorf scheme was evident from Stirling's first sketches; in the earliest ones made on the back of his Chandigarh boarding passes, the centralized space is encircled by a colonnade (which would disappear soon after),

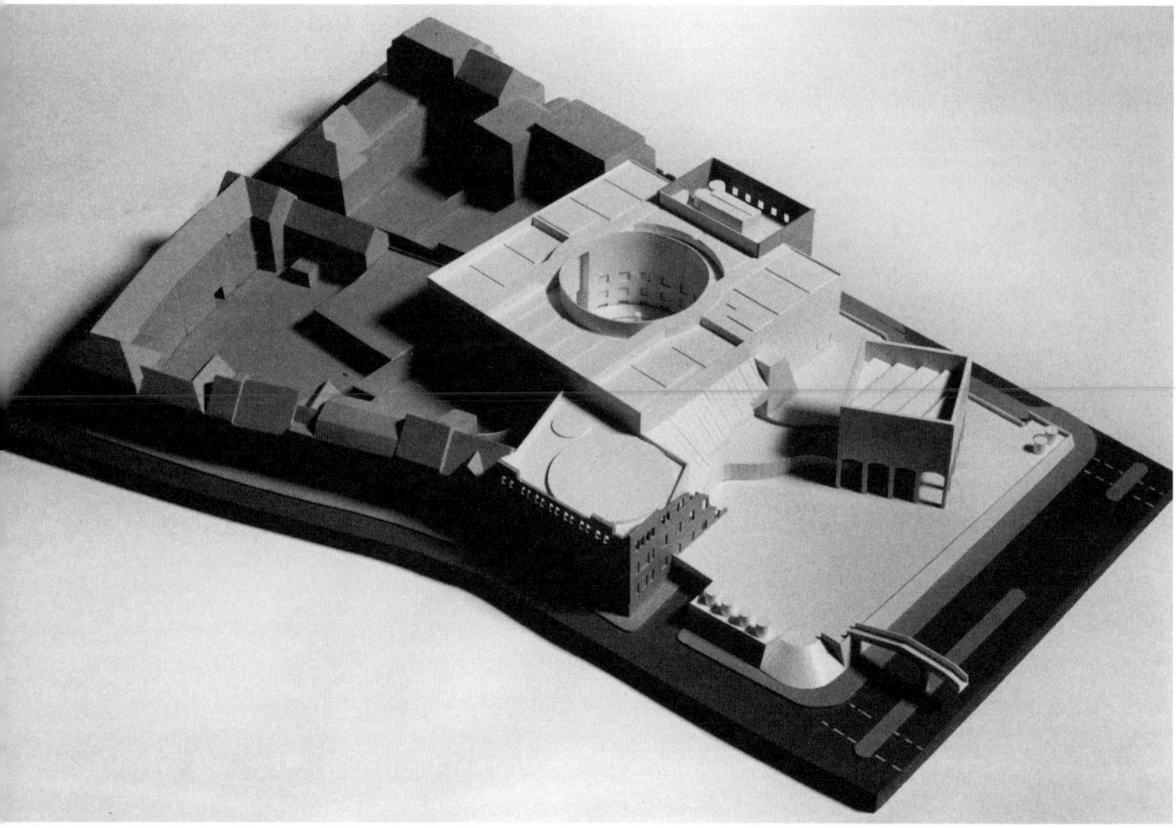

Figure 118
Stirling and Partner, Düsseldorf. Model.

Figure 119
Stirling, Wilford and Associates, Staatsgalerie. Model.

making the Altes connection, or at least a more Neoclassical intent, even more explicit. Stirling's misreadings and corrections to the original, however, are equal to the alignments. For one, he decapitates the original, creating an open-air courtyard rather than an enclosed space. He removes the continuity between the rotunda and the rest of the museum by making it accessible only to the public walkway, unlike Schinkel's rotunda, which is accessed both at the second level, as a climax to the grand entrance stair, as well as at the ground floor. At Stuttgart, the courtyard is also open to above, but here it is made accessible from the museum rather than from the public thoroughfare, which now snakes up and around its interior walls. In both of Stirling's revisionings of Schinkel's rotunda, he strips the source of its classical, symmetrical, and climactic role at the center of the scheme (not to mention its overt reference to the Roman Pantheon) to become instead a negative compositional piece in the overall design. Of the rotunda at Stuttgart, Stirling writes: "It is no longer acceptable to do classicism straight and in this building the central pantheon, instead of being the culminating space is but a void—a room like a non space; instead of a dome open to the sky."[59]

Of course the circle-in-the-square has a long history in architecture and can hardly be isolated to the influence of just one building, even one as significant as the Altes Museum. There are numerous photographs in the archive that suggest additional historical precedents, including an eighteenth-century Mausoleum at West Wycombe—an open-air hexagonal "shell"—as well as a massive, open cylindrical drum included in his series of photos of the Liverpool docks. Additionally, we can recall that in the anthologized 1974 version of "Mathematics of the Ideal Villa," Rowe adds a comparison between the plan of the Altes Museum and of Le Corbusier's Palace Assembly at Chandigarh (fig. 121). The fact that Stirling's initial sketches were made en route to Chandigarh reinforces this connection to Le Corbusier's project, in which a circular auditorium sits within a rectangular building framework. At Chandigarh the auditorium is cut loose from its centralized position and drifts to the east of center of the project; although Stirling restores the rotunda to its

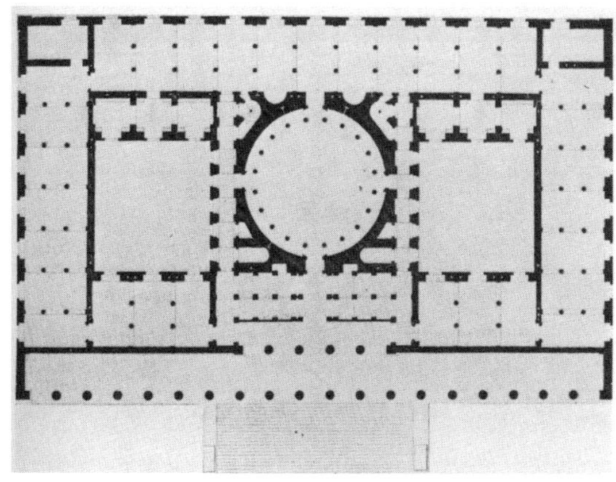

Figure 120
Karl Friedrich Schinkel, Altes Museum, Berlin, 1830. Plan. Both Düsseldorf and Stuttgart take as a starting point Schinkel's centralized rotunda and surrounding museum block.

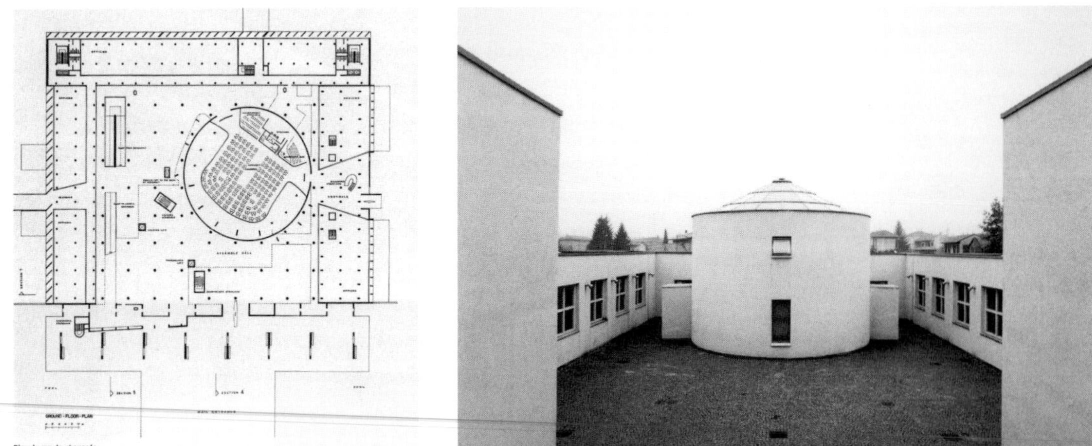
Plan du rez-de-chaussée

more classically correct position at the center of the scheme in both Düsseldorf and Stuttgart, the asymmetry of the Corbusier plan reappears in other places; the entrance pavilion at Düsseldorf, in particular, assumes a similar skewed geometrical position.

To the circular rotunda can also be ascribed a more generalized, nonspecific, typological role in architectural history. In the first publication of Venturi's essay "Complexity and Contradiction," which appeared in *Perspecta* 9/10 in 1965, he traces the evolution of a series of "spaces within spaces" and in particular circular courtyards within rectilinear buildings, noting that these "dominant-shaped courtyards make the primary space; the rooms within the contrasting perimeter become residual." Venturi juxtaposes an image of Kahn's first scheme for the Unitarian Church and Charles I's palace at Granada, suggesting not only two additional "circle-within-a-square" sources but also a sensibility about grafting and merging historical precedents, and in particular about collapsing history through the use of plan homologies.[60] In Stirling's first sketches for Düsseldorf the interior colonnade of the rotunda creates what Venturi terms a "'lining'—that is, a space within a space analogous to its frame."[61]

In Stirling's historical revisionings in the Düsseldorf courtyard, none of the "original" sources is directly legible or predominant; instead, the generalized recollection of their sum total defines the design. A broad and diverse range of precedents are subsumed by the courtyard form, "generalizing away the uniqueness" of any one particular source. In this way the Düsseldorf courtyard, as a compilation of myriad historical references, achieves the status of "neutralized" form, as the Florey Building had nearly ten years earlier. In both projects the embeddedness of a range of historical precedents within the realized form removes any historical specificity. A key distinction, however, is that at Düsseldorf the rotunda is just one element in the composition while at Florey there is effectively only one element—"one enormous gesture." Every piece of the composition at Düsseldorf (the pavilion, the walkway, the reused library façade) is *also* a product of historical condensation. The project thus

Figure 121
Le Corbusier, Assembly Building, Chandigarh, 1955. Plan. Le Corbusier abandons Schinkel's symmetry even as he retains the centralized rotunda and U-shaped exterior.

Figure 122
Aldo Rossi, Fagnano Olona Elementary School, Italy, 1976. Rossi's centralized, circular rotunda is a resilient solid as compared to Düsseldorf's void.

embodies multiple typological narratives; each component brings its own multivalent collection of references which then become an element in the collage.

Rossi's nearly contemporaneous Fagnano Olona Elementary School (1976) also deploys a rotunda as the central element in the composition, and, like Stirling's courtyard, Rossi's school evokes historical associations and traditions (fig. 122). But Rossi's rotunda (a resilient solid to Stirling's void) serves as a kind of proto-architecture; it evokes something before precedent, retreating to what Hays describes as a "bleached-out" language of a kind of primitive or ur architecture. Hays further writes that the reading of the central library rotunda at Fagnano Olona is achieved only once it can "negate its origins as baptistery or theater," with its typological associations of theater, church, and so on, and that Rossi achieves this by stripping the form down to its most elemental, most basic.[62] The rotunda at Düsseldorf, by contrast, is a layering rather than a peeling away; it conflates and hybridizes forms. Stirling sources many different versions in order to create a singular iteration, while Rossi attempts an essentialization that returns each act of architecture to the originary moment, to its most basic and primal forms. Both end up with a typologically universal form though born of different operational means; for Stirling, a kind of cataloguing and conflating of sources à la Durand; for Rossi, an essentializing of precedents in the vein of Quatremère de Quincy.

The story becomes more complex when Stirling repeats the central circular courtyard almost verbatim at Stuttgart, though with the changed museum access and relationship to the public pathway. His revision to the courtyard certainly reflects the more complex topography of the hillside Stuttgart site versus the flat Düsseldorf one, but more importantly it suggests the development of Stirling's self-referential practice. Unlike the repeated stair towers of Leicester/Cambridge/Oxford, which appear more or less verbatim as they pass from one project to the next, the courtyard at Düsseldorf is redeployed at Stuttgart with modifications that advance or revision the original in much the same way that Bloom discusses a later poet modifying an earlier one. Here Stirling is both the "early" and the "late" as he is modifying his own work, refining it as a typological element that can assume variation.

Beyond the reference to the Altes rotunda—or even to the more generalized notion of a rotunda as a classical element—Düsseldorf also includes specific historical forms: a Tuscan portico frames a passageway to the Kunsthalle; a Doric portico marks the entrance to the Klee/Bissier collection; a Gothic bay window provides views from the upper level of the Klee/Bissier gallery down to the entrance hall. Each of these isolated quotations marks a threshold or a passageway into the "sacred" realm of the art object. They are arranged as a kind of progressive narrative—from one historical "stage" to the next—Tuscan/Doric/Gothic—a more fragmented version of Schinkel's didactic sequence from Greek Stoa to Roman Pantheon at the Altes museum. Unlike Schinkel's stoa or rotunda, however, Stirling's classical elements are never integrated into the building as a whole. Like Venturi's lone Ionic "symbolic column" at the 1973 Allen Art Museum in Oberlin, which is placed "on display" in the museum, Stirling's quotations are meant to be viewed as art objects themselves, separate from the building structure and from their architectural "function." In both cases the isolated classical element becomes intentionally acontextual. In this inversion, the classical piece becomes the "other" in the context of the modern museum, even as the museum itself attempts to become integrated with the historic city. Beyond their overall disjunction within the museum, the classical quotations are used subversively, much like Stirling's treatment of the historical façade at Derby. The Tuscan portico that marks the entrance to the Kunsthalle leads to a confined, curving hallway, a perverse use of the salutatory entrance. Even more aggressively, the Doric portico leading to the Klee/Bessier gallery is split in two pieces as it spans the stair and elevator core, leaving half a pediment on either side. This misuse of the historic object deliberately disassociates it from any historical meaning, performing a quintessential Bloomian misreading. Although the scale and relative "correctness" of the classical elements are left intact (unlike Venturi's inflated column, with its overscaled and abstracted volutes and wood "fluting")—one still walks through the portico and looks through the window—each is also subverted.

Simon Sadler argues that the only difference between the "imminent postmodern historicism" of Derby and the "projective modernism" of Florey is that in the former Stirling quotes completed historical projects—"the Renaissance façade, the Regency arcade, the nineteenth-century glasshouse"—while in the latter he quotes the "unfinished work of the Soviet avant-garde."[63] The suggestion is that in referencing unfinished historical sources Stirling maintains the possibility for an "unfinishable" and therefore projective modernity, whereas the closed referential systems at Derby are inherently postmodernist.[64] But Stirling's treatment of the reference at Düsseldorf, as at Derby, elides this easy contrast, since the classical elements are presented in a decidedly anticlassical and even heretical way.

Stirling referred to himself as more a Neoclassical than an Art Nouveau architect. But perhaps he was in fact closer to the Renaissance mentality. Alan Colquhoun described the distinction between the Renaissance and Neoclassicist architect as such: the former maintained a "strong faith in the contemporary world"—the classical language was used because it seemed "more modern than recent medieval culture"—while the Neoclassicist, at least in the eighteenth century, was drawn to classicism by a sense of "poetic reverie, nostalgia, and a sense of irretrievable loss."[65] Stirling's use of specific classical elements (the Doric portico) and generalized "classic" forms (the rotunda) were employed in this vein—as means to extend the vocabulary of modern architecture as something, perhaps, "more modern" than the stale regurgitations of the International Style. To be sure, Stirling was never a classicist—an important distinction from Leon Krier, for whom the classical language retained a self-evident ontological value, or even Mies, whose classicism reflected a belief in eternal values such as symmetry and order. For Stirling the reference to Schinkel was a conscious break with, rather than a continuation of, classicism, which allowed him to manipulate the various elements of the classical system. Again we might compare this to Mies, who was also influenced by Schinkel, as demonstrated by Philip Johnson and others, but for whom Schinkel represented the deeper values of classicism rather than a set of formal and compositional tropes.

The use of the classical fragment was, for Stirling, always a rich and deliberate play with myriad associations, as well as a deliberate acknowledgment of the *lack* of ontological meaning. Here Tafuri's interpretation of the 1970s avant-garde remains critical; the loss of meaning of the "discarded battle remnants" of modernity, as Tafuri observed, was indeed the tool with which Stirling and others were free to experiment within the postwar "boudoir." By 1975 that repertoire of tools had extended to include classical remnants as well, but classical remnants that were equally mute, equally voided of any "meaning" or significance in the terms that a classicist would understand. Stirling's alleged Neoclassicism, then, is really no different from his adoption of collage techniques. In both cases he proposes a recombination of architectural elements at the service of invention. Along these lines Vidler has argued the similarity between Churchill—one of the most "unitary" of Stirling's type-forms—and the "sprawling miniature city" of Düsseldorf; both are in the end inventions, "empirically formulated and constructed with a combinatorial skill reminiscent of Vanbrugh, Soane or Schinkel."[66]

In his discussion of Kenosis, the revisionary ratio of "repetition and discontinuity," Bloom introduces Kierkegaard's notion of "recollecting forward." "Repetition and recollection are the same movement, only in opposite directions; for what is recollected has been, is repeated backwards whereas repetition properly so called is recollected forwards."[67] Kierkegaard goes on to say that repetition leads to happiness, while recollection leads to unhappiness. Within the very definition of the notion of repetition, Bloom suggests via Kierkegaard, is a necessarily progressive notion, and through this we can reframe Stirling's seemingly mimetic gestures as "recollecting forward." In Bloom's terms, Stirling's operations on Schinkel's rotunda or his misuse of the Gothic window or the Doric portico represent an "emptying out" of the original. No longer correcting, generalizing, or completing his precursors, Stirling instead seems to reference more directly these classical sources; but his directness voids them of their original meaning, thereby remaking history in his own terms. In Kenosis, although the poet seems to be emptied of creativity, the act of "humbling" oneself before the precursor in fact "empties" the precursor as well. Repetition in fact advances the precursor's work; although the poet seems to "simply" reuse historical forms, no longer attempting "originality," in fact "this 'emptying' is a liberating discontinuity and makes possible a kind of poem that a simple repetition of the precursor's afflatus or godhood could not allow"—in essence an "undoing" of the precursor's "strength."[68] Recollecting forward and emptying out are the tools of the bricoleur who enacts a deliberate loss of continuity—in Stirling's case, going "back" to the historical fragments as a means to move forward.

CHAPTER 6

THE REMAINS OF MODERNISM

ROMA INTERROTTA (1978)

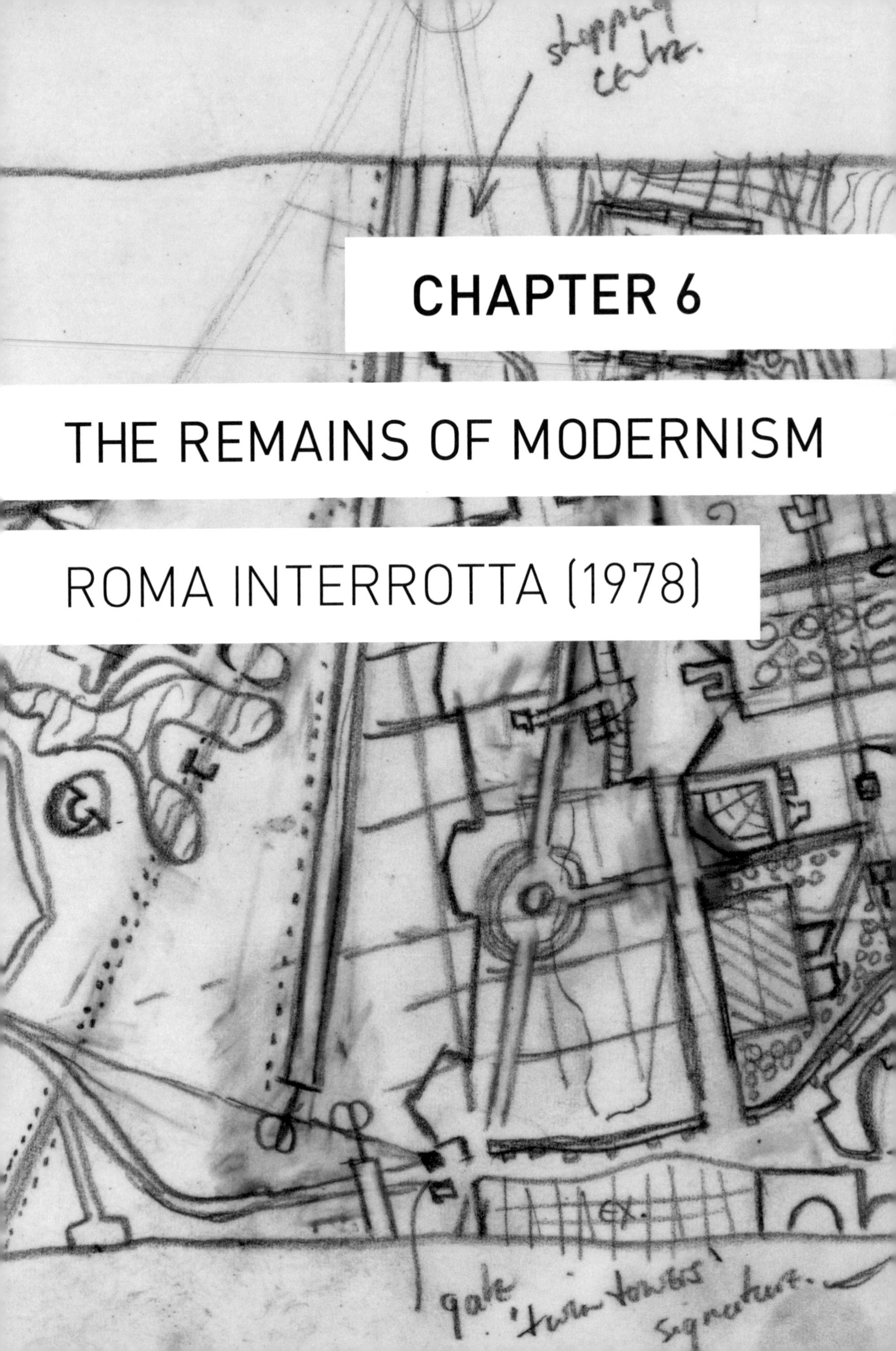

Stirling's lectures in the 1970s and 1980s followed a more or less predictable format: a didactic and untheorized description of a select group of projects, beginning in the 1950s (usually with his thesis) and stretching to his most recent work. The choice of projects would sometimes vary, depending on the audience or the context, and he would alter the introductory remarks to thank the particular group to whom he was speaking, but he almost always retained the chronological framework.

On a lecture circuit that began in November 1981 at the Yale School of Architecture and continued into 1982 with stops across the United States (Columbia University, the Graham Foundation in Chicago, the University of Illinois Architecture School in Urbana-Champaign) as well as Europe (the AA in London, Paris, Bergamo, Munich, Darmstadt, and the American Academy in Rome),[1] Stirling revisited this well-trodden formula with one significant exception—he began not with his most recent work, nor his most distant, but with an unbuilt exhibition project from 1978—Roma Interrotta (fig. 123).

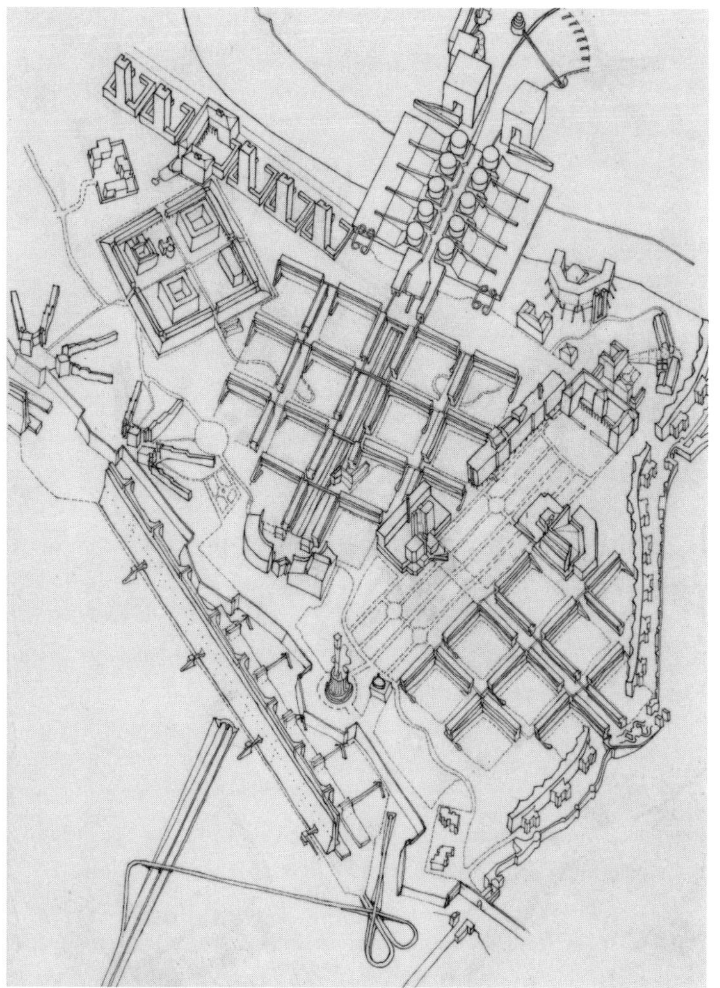

Figure 123
James Stirling and Partner, Roma Interrotta Exhibition, Italy,1978. Axonometric.

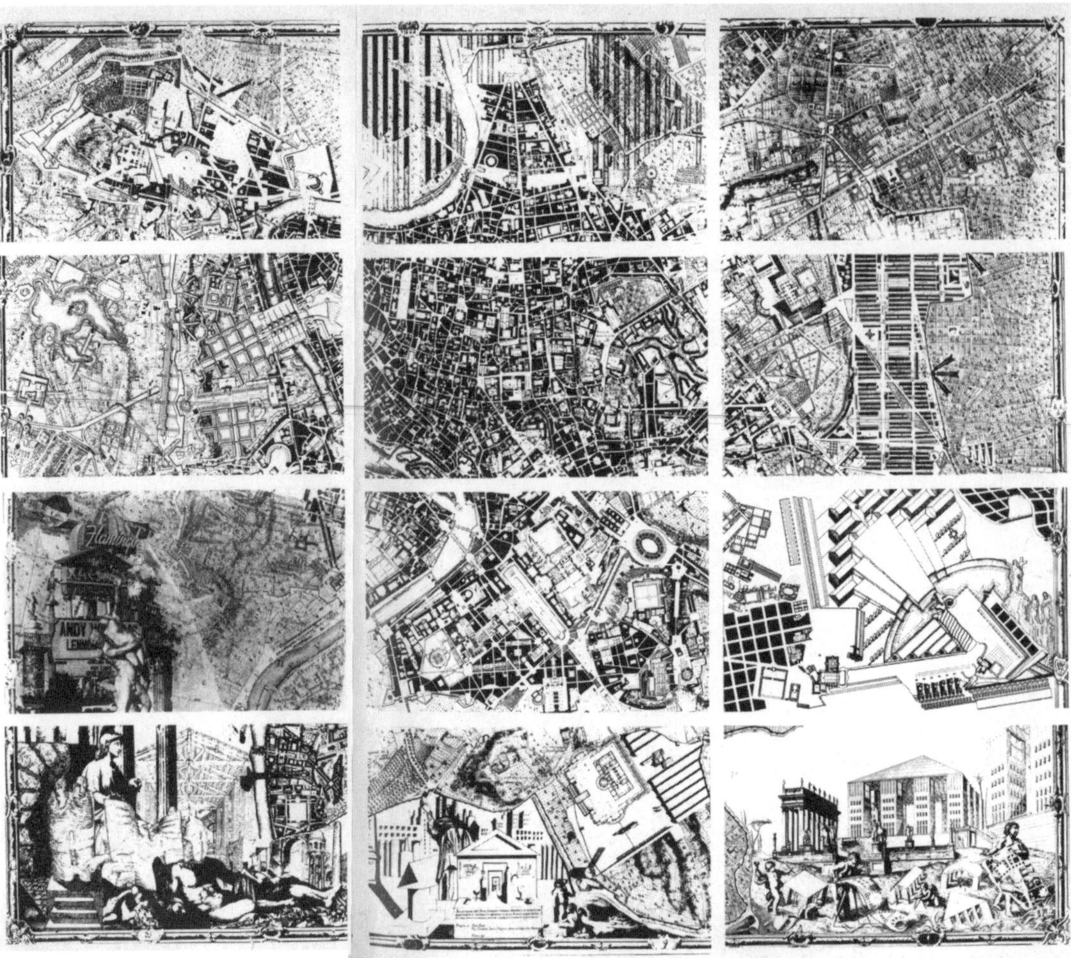

The choice of Roma Interrotta as the lead-off in these lectures, inconsistent with the otherwise chronological format, tells us not only about the importance that he placed on the project but also that he saw it as an introduction to his career as a whole, as something outside the "history" of his own practice. In this chapter I argue that this little-studied work, seemingly whimsical in nature, was in fact ideologically significant within Stirling's oeuvre. My claim is that Stirling's entry to the Roma Interrotta, like each of the projects considered in this book, marks a critical turning point in his career and a significant articulation of his historical revisioning.

A "CONTEXTURAL-ASSOCIATIONAL" PROJECT

In 1977, twelve teams of European and American architects were invited by the Incontri Internazionale d'Arte in Rome to submit a proposal to "redesign" a portion of Nolli's 1748 plan of Rome (fig. 124). Roma Interrotta, or Rome Interrupted, was the brainstorm of Piero Sartugo and Michael Graves (both of whom would participate in the exhibition), among others, and was sponsored

Figure 124
Roma Interrotta. Plan of all twelve entries. Stirling's Sector IV is in the left column, second from top.

by the mayor of Rome, art historian Carlo Argan. In addition to Stirling, Graves, and Sartugo, the invited architects were Constantino Dardi; Antoine Grumbach, Paolo Portoghesi, and Vittorio Gigliotti; Romaldo Giurgola; Robert Venturi and John Rauch; Colin Rowe; Rob Krier; Aldo Rossi; and Leon Krier. All participants were given one of the twelve portions or "sectors" of Nolli's map, which, though equal in size, were not always equal in content—the lower corners, for example, contain virtually no cartographic information, while the central sectors are dense with medieval building fabric. Stirling's Sector IV, northwest of the historic city core, contained Trastevere, portions of the Aurelian walls, and a few significant architectural monuments, including Donato Bramante's Tempietto and Giulio Romano's Villa Lante at Bagnaio.

The twelve designs were exhibited in Trajan's Market from May to June 1978, at the AA in London in spring 1979, and at the Cooper-Hewitt Museum in New York in summer 1979. An accompanying catalogue, published in English and Italian, provides the principal documentation of the exhibition, with select introductory essays and documentation of each project by the chosen architects.[2] Some of the participants took only a few pages—Venturi and Rauch's passages from *Learning from Las Vegas* and collaged images of Caesar's Palace occupy just six—while others, including Stirling, elaborated on their design with textual and supporting graphic material. A mockup for Stirling's portion of the catalogue survives in the archive and includes nearly exact replicas of each of the fifteen pages, complete with sketches for the included images.[3] This mockup, along with the numerous sketches held by the archive and Stirling's exhaustive text—a rarity at this stage of his career—attest to the attention that he gave to the project.

The goal of Roma Interrotta, as stated by the organizing agency, was to provide a "critical examination of the process of change in the urban fabric" of Rome and ultimately "to create a vehicle for curing the ills of the city and its historical center."[4] In his introduction to the catalogue, Argan emphasizes the very real problems faced by the "bloated and disfigured" city, which had been "fragmented" by speculation and development. The city "interrupted" was a way to sweep away two hundred years of "mistakes," to attempt a return to an idyllic beginning as a place to invent and reconfigure. However, Argan admits, the exhibition was not intended to offer "real" solutions. "The Roma Interrotta exhibition . . . is comprised not of proposals for urban planning, naturally, but of a series of gymnastic exercises for the imagination. The contributions to this exhibition are a group of adventurous, fantastic research studies on the urbanistic womb of Rome."[5]

Indeed, the entries appear as "fantastic" proposals, by turns playful and grandiose, whimsical and maniacal. Given the "unreal" quality of the map, and the fact that it documented a city that no longer existed, it would be difficult to imagine anything less. What might a true urban planning proposal resemble in such an absurd proposition as this one? Nevertheless, Argan's statement seems to make light of what were, in many cases, genuine attempts to engage very real aspects of the city, both past and future. Rossi, for example, doesn't propose any "hypothetical alternative" but instead delineates a plan for the Baths of Caracalla (which occupy the majority of his Sector XI) by equipping them with modern heating and cooling systems, and the result, perhaps unsurprisingly, looks remarkably like his Modena Cemetery. Rowe's comprehensive redesign of Sector VIII offers a different sort of contextualism, importing Roman precedents from various time periods to "rebuild" the Palatine Hill. Some projects seem to ignore their "original" Roman site altogether. Leon Krier designs a series of monumental sheltered piazzas and employs a number of Piranesi drawings to suggest additional locations for these piazzas throughout the city (of course his particular "site," at the lower right-hand corner, had virtually no cartographic information to begin with). Others interpret "site" somewhat more wryly. Venturi and Rauch's scheme for Sector X overlays a photomontage of the Las Vegas Strip—the photo of Caesar's Palace replacing Piranesi's original etching of the Temple of Castor and Pollox—on the section beyond the Janiculum wall, although here again the original sector was largely scenographic.

The projects are difficult to group according to their ambition, much less their style, particularly given their range in the scale of intervention. Some of the proposals are relatively "modest," at least in relation to the others—Portoghesi, in Sector V, initially argued that "no intervention was either necessary or appropriate" but ultimately inserted an infill project whose organic form, completely at odds with the eighteenth-century context, is metaphorically connected to the site's "original" geological formation. Others were heroic and grandiose, such as Sartugo's violent diagonal gashes to completely disaggregate Sector I—which comprises the entirety of the Vatican complex—generating what Alan Chimacoff, in his review in the 1979 issue of *AD* that was dedicated to the Roma Interrotta exhibition, dubbed "mindless destruction and confusion" in the guise of "constructivist Haussmann."[6] In the case of Rowe's scheme, the scale extends beyond the image or even the architecture. In addition to completely reconstructing Sector VIII his team inserts a fictionalized narrative (fabricated footnotes, too!) to accompany the comprehensive figure-ground proposal.

Much of the commentary following the exhibition found fault with the highly personal and idiosyncratic nature of each solution, and the inherently disjointed and cacophonous response of the proposals as a whole. Chimacoff laments the "absence of communication between adjacent participants" and is dismayed by the "jarring" "juxtapositions" of projects. In the end he finds their diversity "so great" that he relegates his commentary solely to individual entries—though he does allow that Stirling's was one of the most "skillfully made."[7] The desire for consistency or at least cohesion is perhaps the necessary bias of any reviewer, but what consistency might have been expected from an exhibition such as this?

Chimacoff is explicit about where he thinks "value" might emerge in such a "questionable enterprise": on the one hand, it could provide cultural commentary, whether contemporary and historical, and on the other, it could offer more prophetic ideas about the city's future and its past—"how it should be, how it might have been." Roma Interrotta would appear to be oriented to this latter utopian aim, although in Argan's mind "Utopia has never set foot in Rome," and for him the proposals in Roma Interrotta were ones of "imagination" rather than utopic thinking: "Hypotheses on the Rome which would have resulted had man continued to imagine it and not to plan it (badly)."[8] This insistence on imagination and memory, on freedom from any limiting constraints, would inform all of the entries; there was of course no program, and the "site" that each architect was given, though based on a geographically verifiable portion of Rome, was frozen nearly 230 years prior. Although Stirling took part in numerous competitions over his career, many of which served as testing grounds for new ideas and often served as turning points (for example, Churchill and Düsseldorf), none was as purely speculative as Roma Interrotta.

Which makes it all the more surprising, then, that this is arguably the most "contextural" —the term he used to conflate "contextual" and "texture"— of all Stirling's projects, albeit a radical, even heretical, form of "contexturalism." His proposal is unique among the twelve entries in that Stirling doesn't attempt to redesign the eighteenth-century city or any of its attendant structures, à la Rossi, nor does he insert large-scale urban-planning gestures in the vein of Sartugo, nor even does he propose a new contextual urbanism, as did Rowe. Instead, he inserts thirty of his own projects from throughout his oeuvre—both built and unbuilt—into his Nolli sector (figs. 125, 126). In the "rigorous method" through which he situates each of these projects in the eighteenth-century fabric of Rome, projects serve as a "confirmation and a complement to that which exists," in much the same manner that Düsseldorf responded to its location within the block at the Grabbeplatz.[9] "Wall buildings," such as Selwyn or Doha, trace the contours of the Aurelian walls. Similarly, "hill buildings" and "river edge" buildings find their counterpart in Nolli's Rome: the Florey Building, placed along the Tiber rather than the Cherwell, opens its amphitheater shape to face the river and a distant view (now Franceso Borromini's Oratorio dei Filippini rather than Magdalen College), while Cologne straddles the Tiber rather than the Rhone. The St. Andrews dormitory is situated on the Janiculum Hill, the splayed-bar buildings opening to provide views of the Eternal City, rather than the Scottish mountains. Other projects find their place in relation to "existing" buildings in Nolli's plan rather than through site characteristics. Olivetti Haslemere becomes an extension to the Villa Farnesina rather than the Queen Anne mansion of the original. St. Andrews Arts Centre now encloses a forecourt in front of Romano's Villa Lante. The eventual location of each of the projects was anything but given; dozens of process sketches in the archive demonstrate that Stirling worked through various placements and densities of the projects, in relation both to one another and to the Nolli plan.

Projects were also grouped to create districts within his plan. For example, Stirling defines a university area near the river (which includes Cambridge, Oxford, and Leicester, along with Selwyn and Sheffield) and a residential area

Figure 125
Stirling and Partner, Roma Interrotta. Thirty of Stirling's own projects are inserted into Sector IV of Nolli's 1748 map of Rome.

to the northwest, in which a number of his early projects (Expandable House, Village Housing, House on the Isle of Wight, and Stiff Dom-ino) are placed as "follies" around an artificial lake and are connected by a footpath. In other cases he creates new relationships between two or more of his own projects—the Düsseldorf entrance pavilion replaces the tilted assembly hall façade in the Derby Civic Centre project. And some seem purely fanciful; Stirling replaces the equestrian statue of Giuseppe Garibaldi with his own likeness, modeled after his fiftieth birthday cake, and inserts the new "vacuum strada," a roadway beneath the Janiculum that connects to the city center and "sucks up the overload of cars from off the streets of Rome."[10] (Stirling includes a photo of an everyday vacuum cleaner in his catalogue entry, adjacent to one of the Oratorio).[11]

The overarching idea of this "contextural-associational" planning method, as Stirling states in his catalogue text, "Revisions to the Nolli Plan of Rome (The MFA Solution)," is to achieve the same "density of environment to that evolved via history," and he describes the method as "akin to the historic process." Stirling's Rome, in other words, should approximate Rome as it had in fact evolved over time—he invites comparison by including a contemporary "tourist" map and describes his "alternative" city as containing a "not dissimilar quantity of working and living areas, institutions and public spaces, etc."[12] Stirling's "utopian" vision appears, strangely enough, to offer an essentially self-similar or at least comparable counterpart to the existing city. This

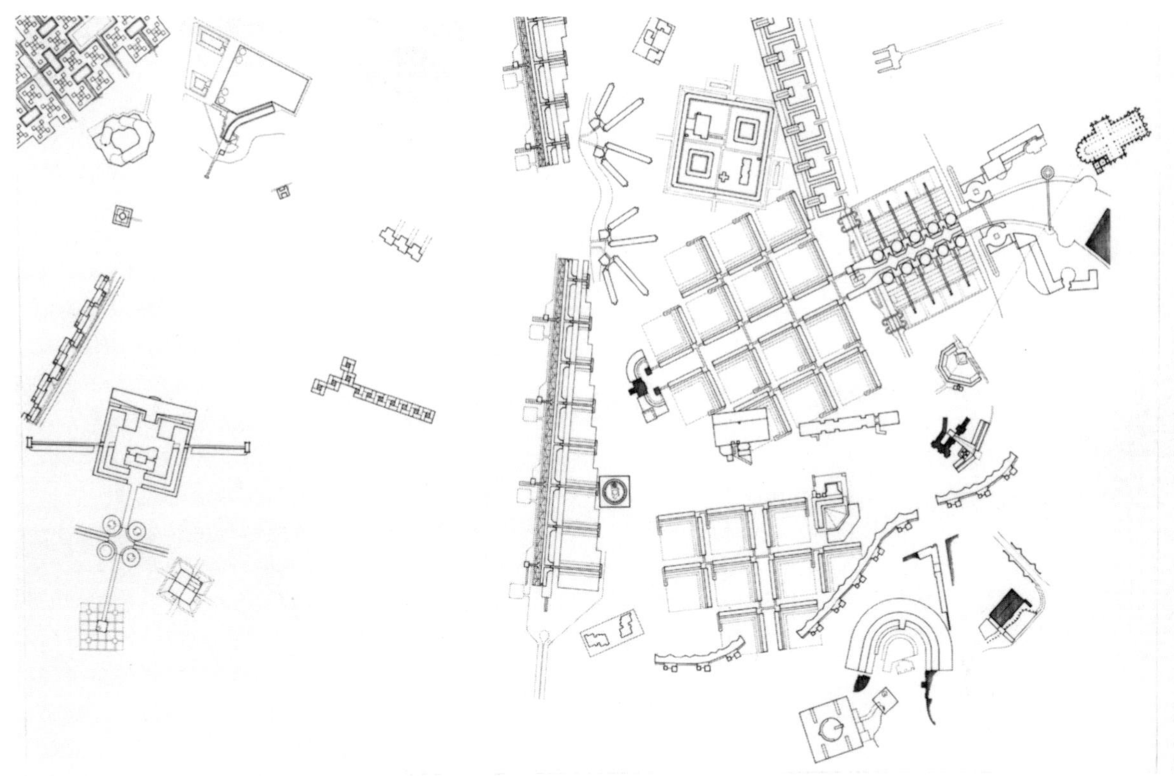

Figure 126
Stirling and Partner, Roma Interrotta. With the Nolli background removed, the collection of Stirling projects is made apparent.

seemingly paradoxical notion—a utopia of the status quo—is made more logical once we understand it as a reaction to postwar utopian planning. Stirling ends his introductory text with a forceful critique of "rational planning" (going so far as to call for the "disbandment of the planning profession in the U.K."), listing its devastating results in cities such as Liverpool and Glasgow.[13] Against the disastrous urban effects of this notion of "progress," then, he articulates a city steeped in memory, one which attempts to respect and even mimic the "historic process." He would later write that his goal in the project was to see if it was possible, using only his own work, to "establish the fragment of a city; to see if our collected works in any theoretical way added up to a tentative urbanism."[14] Nevertheless, despite his critique of "rational planning"—by which he means modernist "object" urbanism and the likes of British New Town planning—his project is essentially an exercise of the "mostly white" of the tabula rasa modernist planning, with implanted objects, rather than the "mostly black" of the traditional city, as Rowe had dubbed it in *Collage City.*

Stirling makes an explicit link with *Collage City,* writing that his "contextural-associational" method was similar to that used in Rowe and Koetter's book, and he singles out the influence of the "teaching of C. Rowe."[15] The way Stirling arranges his projects within the Nolli map—the variety of angles and correspondences, the lack of any axial or gridded planning, except as it exists in his own projects, and the seeming "collision" between various projects—is certainly resonant with the "chaotic" language of collage, of local logics and assemblies. On one of the project's archival notes pages is transcribed the final passage from *Collage City:* "Collage deriving its virtue from irony, a method for using things and simultaneously disbelieving in them, it is also a strategy which can allow utopia to be dealt with as *image,* to be dealt with in fragments without our having to accept it *in toto.*" The collage connection was made explicit by others as well, including Chimacoff, who links Stirling's entry with Rowe's as similarly controlled by the "collision of planimetric grids and the juxtaposition of clear fragments."[16] Bruno Zevi singles out Stirling's project as "masterly 'collage.'"[17] And indeed the entire exhibition must be situated within the expanding collage discourse at the moment, including Rowe and Koetter's book, which was published in the same year, 1978. Terms like "collision" and "fragment" populate nearly every entrant's text, and to Rowe must be attributed a resurgent interest in the Nolli plan, which he and Koetter describe, in *Collage City,* as a "model which might be envisaged as alternative to the disastrous urbanism of social engineering and total design."[18] Further, the idea to have twelve architects each design a piece of the city, absent coordination among them, was itself a collagist notion.

Anthony Vidler disputes the notion that Stirling's entry was collage and instead links the entry with Rossi's "belief in articulated typologies."[19] It is true that, unlike Rowe's scheme, Stirling's comprises totalities rather than fragments. Each of his projects is presented as a complete entity. But even if we disregard the project's compositional language I would argue that the more powerful connection with collage comes in Stirling's "conscription" of his projects from out of the original context—a component of collage as critical as the formal language of collision and fragment. Through the insertion of his own works into a foreign context—the Nolli map—Stirling achieves a misreading of the city as well, ultimately, a reflexive revisioning of his own architecture.

ANOTHER WICKED ARCHITECT

Stirling begins his Roma Interrotta somewhat enigmatically with a description of megalomania. "Megalomania is the privilege of a chosen few. Piranesi who made his plan in 1762 was surely a Megalomaniac Frustrated Architect (MFA) as also Boullée, Vanbrugh, Soane, Sant'Elia, Le Corbusier, etc. and it is in this distinguished company as an MFA . . . that we make our proposal. The Megalomaniac Frustrated Architect . . . is at his most frustrated in regard to projects designed but not built."[20] The plan of 1762 is a reference to Piranesi's Campo Marzio scheme, a similarly fictional reconstruction of a sector of Rome in which Piranesi attempts an "accurate" reconstruction of the Campo Marzio section, based on the Severin marbles, while inserting his own invented moments (fig. 127). Campo Marzio, then, was a hybrid of invention and reconstruction, of truth and fiction, and offered a kind of dialectical staging between Piranesi's Roman vedute, in all their attempts at verisimilitude, and his imaginative capricci such as the Carceri series or his Collegio Romano project.

The Campo Marzio scheme was a touchpoint for others in the exhibition

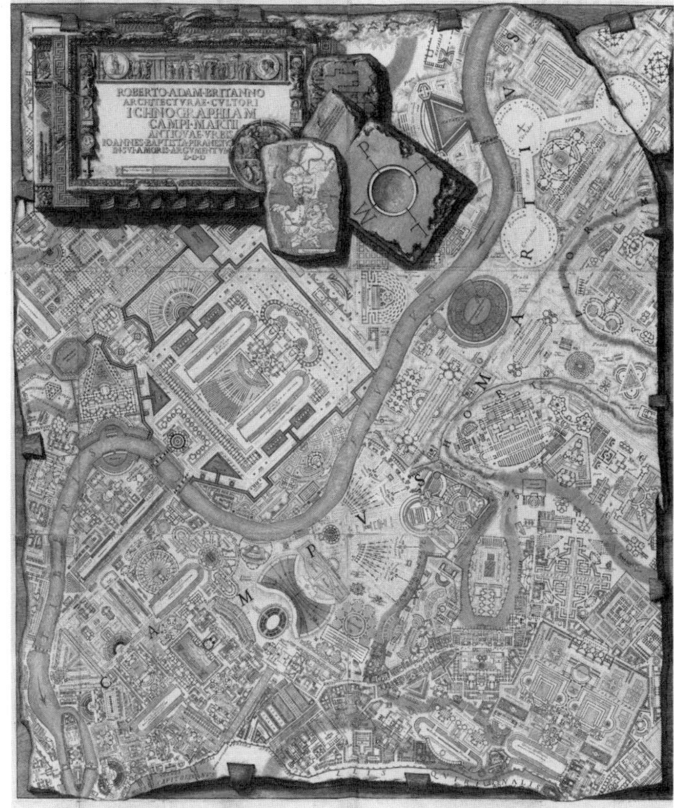

Figure 127
Giovanni Battista Piranesi, Campo Marzio plan, eighteenth century. Like Stirling at Roma Interrotta, Piranesi offers a fictional reconstruction of a sector of Rome.

as well. Dardi begins the description of his entry with a comparison between Piranesi's scheme and Nolli's plan which, he notes, are separated by only thirteen years—the former "projective and ideological," the latter "descriptive and philological."[21] In his introduction to the *AD* issue on Roma Interrotta, Michael Graves also compares Nolli's plan to Piranesi's. "One is a composition of mutually adjusted set pieces, and the other involves the mutual modification of figure and ground, providing a comprehensible equity between figural object and figural space."[22] Though his distinction frankly obscures more than it clarifies, it is meant to highlight Nolli's emphasis on the "fragment" as opposed to Piranesi's interest in an overall figure/ground totality of the city. By 1978, Campo Marzio clearly had taken on a polemical role as an exemplary project, not only of a collage sensibility but also of an avant-garde position, a position elaborated most fully in the writings of Manfredo Tafuri. In his 1973 text *Architecture and Utopia,* Tafuri singles out Piranesi's Campo Marzio scheme as a "colossal piece of bricolage" and a "prophetic" project in which his reconstituted city of Roman "fragments" offers a glimpse into the contradictions and complexities of the dialectical relationship between the city and architecture, "between the demand for order and the will to formlessness."[23] For Tafuri, Piranesi is the foundational figure of the architectural avant-garde—the original "wicked architect" (and therefore a direct precursor for Stirling)—

a radical claim that he would develop in his 1980 book *The Sphere and the Labyrinth,* which begins with Piranesi and more or less ends with Stirling.

It was at Campo Marzio in particular, a "formless heap of fragments colliding one against the other," that the epic battle between architecture and the city was initiated, Tafuri suggests, a battle in which architecture, though it might attempt to retain its "completeness and preserve itself from total destruction" was in the end "pitilessly absorbed and deprived of any autonomy."[24] With its cacophony of architectural fragments, Campo Marzio represents for Tafuri the moment at which the possibility of architecture's communicative possibility is called into question. Through the incessant multiplication of Roman fragments, a "monstrous pullulation of symbols devoid of significance," Campo Marzio ultimately renders architectural language meaningless. "Formal invention seems to declare its own primacy, but the obsessive reiteration of the inventions reduces the whole organism to a sort of gigantic 'useless machine.'"[25] Architecture, by "dissolving into the uniformity ensured by preconstituted formal systems"—in other words, by relying on the language of Roman antiquity—announces the impossibility for communication. It was thus in Piranesi's seemingly "rational" reconstruction of the city, Tafuri suggests, that the fundamental "irrationality" of architectural language is exposed.

These are almost exactly the same terms that Tafuri uses to describe Stirling's architecture in his 1973 essay "L'Architecture dans le Boudoir: The Language of Criticism and the Criticism of Language."[26] Though the period under investigation had shifted more than two hundred years, Tafuri's conception of the avant-garde remained consistent—a culture forced to operate with the "degraded means" of architectural language. For Tafuri, the neo-avant-garde architects of the 1970s had no choice but to recombine the "mute" pieces of a regurgitated language of the modern movement, pieces that had lost any ability to communicate "meaning." The result of these "salvage operations" with modernism's "discarded battle remnants" was ultimately the relegation of their formalist exercises to the "boudoir" in the face of an all-consuming capitalist system (though he did allow—at least in this stage of his career—a certain pleasure to be gained from such formal play).[27] Tafuri singles out Stirling among his peers in the 1970s as the architect who had most fully ingested this lesson of architecture's inherent muteness; for Tafuri, Stirling had "'rewritten' the 'words' of modern architecture, building a true 'archeology of the present.'"[28] As Tafuri describes it, Stirling's architecture, particularly the Derby Civic Centre, "demonstrates the consequences of reducing the architectural object to a syntax in transformation, to a linguistic process that wishes, nevertheless, to challenge the tradition of the Modern Movement."[29]

This connection between Stirling and Piranesi, and more specifically between Roma Interrotta and Campo Marzio, is worth exploring further. Although Tafuri never discusses Stirling's Roma Interrotta competition (both *Architecture and Utopia* and "L'Architecture dans le Boudoir" were published earlier), Tafuri's theoretical framework suggests an interpretive tool through which to understand Roma Interrotta as more than fancy or even archaeology and instead as an elaboration of a crisis of the architectural object and ultimately as an ideological proposal. Aside from their obvious, but not insignificant, similarity as simultaneous inventions and archaeologies for the city of Rome, in both Stirling's and Piranesi's projects the "incessant" multiplication of architectural form breaks down communicative possibility. The repetition of a displaced formal language, out of sync with its "proper" context and meaning, calls into relief the artifice of the language itself—whether the language was Roman antiquity or Stirling's own works.

At Leicester and Derby, it was Stirling's recollection of modernism's forms as "empty signs" that made Stirling exemplary in Tafuri's eyes in that he seemed to grasp the break between signifier and signified, the inherent impossibility of meaning in architectural form. Stirling's shift to a classical language at Düsseldorf, by this logic, was simply an extension of this exercise, with Doric porticos substituting for pilotis, but both, in the end, reinforcing the arbitrary choice of the architectural sign. In each of these works the "origin" of the revisioned fragment was relatively clear—recall the reference to Melnikov's Rusakov Workers' Club at Leicester or Schinkel's Altes Museum at Düsseldorf. Certainly there were multiple referents within a given project (again, Leicester is a useful example—with Melnikov and Wright and others at play), but each was unquestionably understood as a *fixed* moment in architectural history to which architecture could look back; this fixity in fact enabled revision, as the contours or outlines of the original form were stable. In some cases there was a second-level referent—Le Corbusier's Maisons Jaoul, for example, was itself a revisioning of vernacular sources, and the rotunda at the Altes Museum was derivative of the Roman Pantheon. Though these forms carried historical roots, there was still an identifiable source, even if it was layered or modified. The *act* of revisioning was the critical act, but the source itself was never up for critique. This position was complicated to some degree if the referent was a typological idea rather than a specific precedent—recall the investigation of the "Oxbridge" college type at Churchill College, and again at the Florey Building. In both cases this typological referent was mixed with more specific and generalized precedents: reference to medieval earthworks, Kahn, Le Corbusier, Archigram, and Viollet-le-Duc, to name but a few. But here again the origin, though now a typological idea rather than a singular building, was still legible and stable.

In choosing his *own* work as the referent at Roma Interrotta, however, Stirling violates the entire system of influence and revision and most importantly the stability of the referent. What does it mean to revision yourself? And what does it mean to revision yourself if the project to which you are referring is itself already a revision of something else? At Roma Interrotta the "language" at play is Stirling's own invented formal accumulation rather than a specific reference or an invented form. How does this change the status of language? On a certain level, we have already answered this question, at least on a smaller scale, since the entirety of Stirling's oeuvre was one of self-quotation. Elements were reused verbatim from one project to the next: the pair of stair towers, for example, which first appear at Sheffield and which reappear consistently throughout his work in the 1960s and 1970s, or the earth berm that first appears at Churchill and is then reconstituted surrounding Camberwell and again as a stone plinth at Cambridge. Certainly Roma Interrotta can be seen as an extension of this self-referentiality. Indeed, one of most emblematic and revelatory sketches of Roma Interrotta is a thumbnail sketch, appearing in the margins of one of the countless Roma Interrotta iterations, in which the tile-clad stair towers are rearranged as a hinge point between Florey and Cambridge (fig. 128). The self-consciousness of the repetitive trope is here called into relief, but this is only a slight exaggeration of Stirling's consistent play with formal repetition throughout his oeuvre, a repetition, recalling Bloom's formulation via Kierkegaard, that "recollects forward."

The obvious distinction between Roma Interrotta and these earlier works is that at Roma Interrotta Stirling reuses entire projects rather than project elements, such as a stair or a platform. In both cases the relative autonomy and immutability of the form is critical; the elements must remain recognizable if we are to understand their carryover, just as the project must remain unchanged if we are to "get" the reference. And indeed the stair towers change almost imperceptibly in both material and scalar terms from Leicester to Florey—the edges are still chamfered, the windowless volumes are still clad in brick. Similarly, Stirling leaves his projects more or less unmodified when redeploying them in the Nolli map. This consistency is necessary for recognition. But there is a distinction between these two systems of self-quotation that exceeds simply a question of scale.

Each of Stirling's projects, as we have seen, is a repository of condensed historical allusion. Each already has a distinct history embedded in its form, and to modify the form would be to lose this embedded history. Referencing his own works, unlike an "outside" reference, whether classical or modern, destabilizes the originary moment. This may seem a paradoxical statement given that the references—Stirling's own projects—are so clearly put forth; they appear to be the most stable choices as precursors and are in almost all cases incorporated into the Nolli plan completely unmodified. But in "generalizing away the uniqueness" of historical precedents in each of his earlier projects Stirling creates a repertoire of metahistorical or ahistorical forms. Given their layered, already-revisioned quality, they cannot simply be recalled as "natural" precedents. They can no longer be understood as an origin point in the way that a Melnikov or a Wright building—or even a repeated stair tower—can be, because the act of self-quotation opens up an endless chain of references. So although they initially appear "full" of meaning—we recognize them as projects from Stirling's past—that meaning disintegrates once we realize that his own past is being inserted into a fabricated site and history. Here another "crisis" of language is articulated when the "word" spoken is a self-defined one.

This is another way of saying that Stirling's own buildings and projects are employed at Roma Interrotta as historical types. And the few projects that

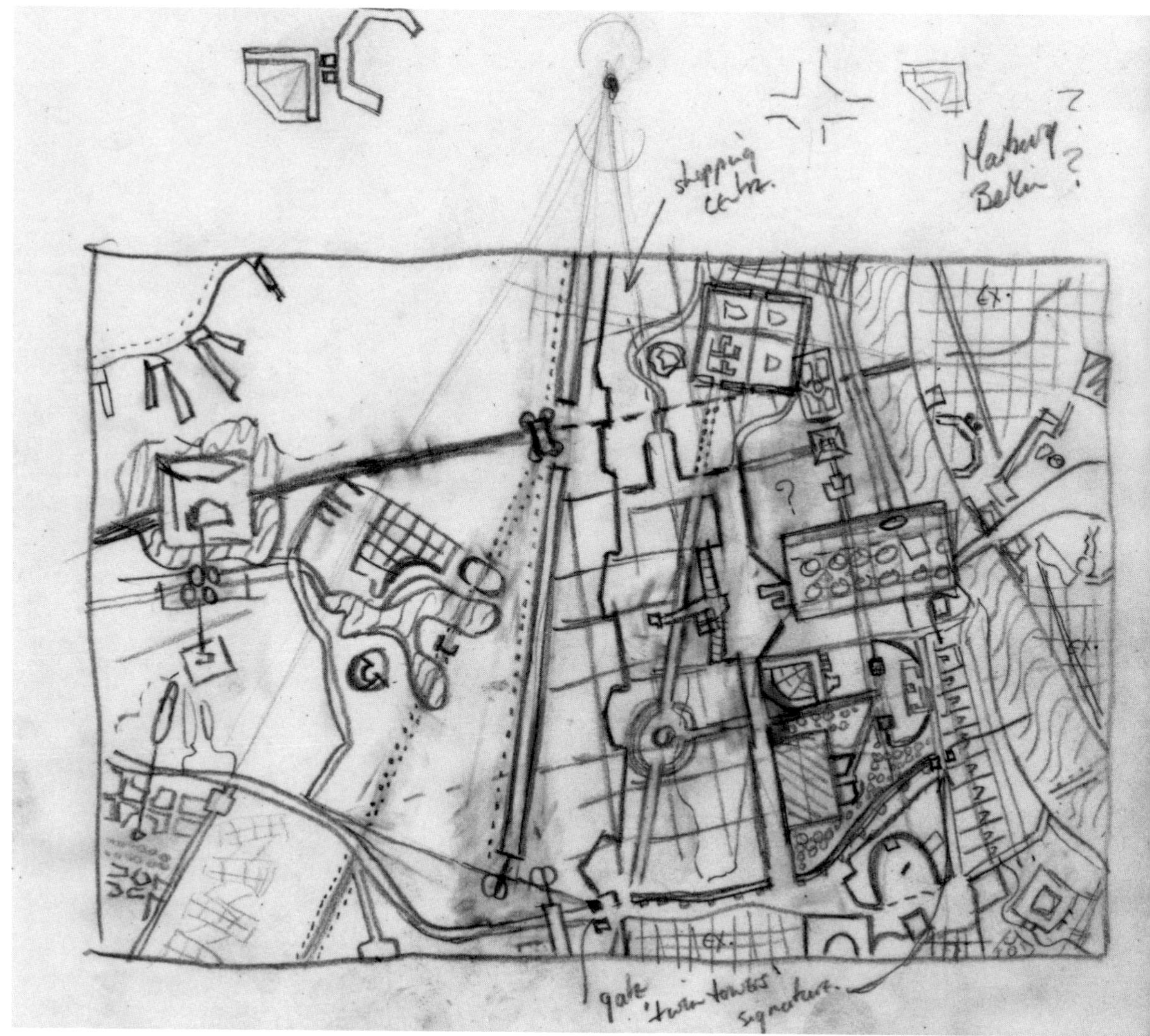

Figure 128

Stirling and Partner, Roma Interrotta. One of the many sketches testing various locations of Stirling's projects in the Nolli map. A detailed plan sketch at the upper left shows Florey and Cambridge linked by their shared stair towers.

Figure 129
Peter Eisenman, Cannaregio, Venice, 1978. Eisenman's scheme achieves a self-referentiality similar to that in Stirling's Roma Interrotta by inserting multiple versions of his unbuilt House 11a into the Venice site.

are modified are so treated to become "purer" examples of the type. Selwyn is extended as a continuous wall, for example, and Stirling is able to build all eight fingers of the St. Andrews dormitory rather than the two that were built. In both cases the mandate of the type, the set of rules that predates formal specificity, allows for its extension as a fulfillment of the original typological aim. In these cases the project as a singular element is displaced by the project as a type, which enables invention and completion and other modifications to the original without violating its definitional terms. Further, Stirling is able to articulate and realize his original aims for the project; we see how he would have wanted each project to appear in an "ideal" world.

This act of self-quotation, and the articulation of a crisis of architectural language, is explored with equal if not greater intensity—if also a more pronounced obliqueness—in Eisenman's Cannaregio project of exactly the same historical moment (fig. 129). Although it doesn't share the same "genus loci" as the Campo Marzio and Roma Interrotta, Eisenman's project, like Stirling's, is an exploration of the technique of self-quotation. Cannaregio proposes a fictionalized layering of Venice as an inquiry into the question of "site" itself—an "artificial excavation," to use Eisenman's terminology, of the archeology of the site. To the "real" topography he adds not only Le Corbusier's unbuilt Venice Hospital project as part of the site's "past," but his own House 11a, arranged within the Venice Hospital grid that now blankets the site, as yet another layer in this constructed topography.

Both Eisenman's and Stirling's projects emerge from investigations into certain logics of the site, and from a desire for some kind of slippage between the "real" city, its own history, and the specific architectural instances that constitute that history. In Eisenman's project, Le Corbusier's Venice Hospital project disappears into the medieval city to become a part of its past. There is no attempt to distinguish between the two. Similarly, Stirling's own work is carefully drawn on par with the existing projects in the Nolli plan; the first impression is of seamlessness, of the blend between his projects and the Nolli map. But the drawing techniques reveal important differences in their attitude toward the past and how it relates to the present; Eisenman renders both the Venice Hospital and the medieval fabric as single line drawings, while Stirling "sets off" his own projects using shadowed roof plans. Had he truly desired his projects to be "contextual" within the Nolli plan he would have employed plan cuts as Rowe and others did.

At Cannaregio, versions of Eisenman's House 11a are repeated across the site, infilling the "holes" inscribed by the Venice Hospital grid. Each arrangement of "el" pieces is scaled and twisted and manipulated to different effect, and each is deliberately out of place within both the existing Venetian fabric and the fictional Corbusian one—their voided cubic forms in contrast to the irregular geometries of the city fabric. In this case iterability engenders what Hays terms a complete "nullification of the confiscated object's semantic qualities."[30] In Stirling's project, on the other hand, the semantic qualities of the object are decidedly maintained—each borrowed project is located within the map according to "contextual-associational" factors, in a "logical" setting, and each retains its original form. Unlike Eisenman's projects, set apart from their context, Stirling's projects seem to strive instead for a kind of urban camouflage.

Despite these differences, both projects articulate a related attitude vis-à-vis architecture's relationship to the city. Stirling manages to slip his projects into the city fabric with minimal damage, and both the architecture and the city survive unscathed as the object is subsumed within the urban mapping. This would seem to be an echo of Piranesi's Campo Marzio, in which the city is ultimately "victorious" over the architecture. Unlike Piranesi, however, Stirling balances the autonomy of the architectural with the significance of the urban pattern. Eisenman's Cannaregio city/architecture dialectic achieves a similarly sustained tension between object and fabric; although the inserted Corbusian grid controls the placement of each House 11a, within these prescribed, localized moments the objects are allowed complete freedom—scalar, volumetric, and so on. Wherever they land—in other words, wherever the grid allows them to be—the object destroys and displaces the "real" city. Similarly, Stirling's projects, even as they seem to obey the logic of the existing city, to find their "natural" place in the historic city, then achieve a reversal and engender new readings of Nolli's city through their insertion. In other words, both seek an ideological position somewhere between the "victory" of the urban as at Campo Marzio or in Rowe's *Collage City,* and the victory of the object in "rational planning" or modernist tabula rasa schemes. For Stirling this is an extension of the urban position articulated at Düsseldorf in which he balanced the "object" of the pavilion with the "fabric" of the museum block, achieving a dialectic between the two urban models that Rowe claimed to support in *Collage City* but in fact could never achieve given his predilection for the "all black" of the historical city. In both Stirling's and Eisenman's projects the object of architecture retains its autonomy and yet is ultimately controlled by the city; Stirling's object responds through accommodation while Eisenman's actively resists. Nevertheless, both achieve this sustained dialectic.

THE RETURN OF THE DEAD

The Roma Interrotta competition came after a difficult time in Stirling's practice. Since completing the Florey Building's in 1971 Stirling had received no commissions, and the Florey Building, along with the Cambridge History Faculty Building and other of his earlier works, were under considerable public scrutiny given their high-profile mechanical failures. Whether because of or perhaps in spite of this lack of built work, the office was in the midst of an intensive publication and exhibition schedule. The Royal Institute of British Architects organized an exhibition of Stirling's drawings in spring 1974, the catalogue for which included an introductory essay by Reyner Banham and was published that fall (the second edition followed in 1976).[31] In 1975 Stirling was selected for the "9 Architects" exhibition, and an exhibition of his own work, "19 Projects," traveled to Naples, Rome, Brussels, Zurich, Lausanne, Trieste, and Tehran. The following year he participated in the Venice Biennale.[32] And in 1977 he was one of seven architects featured in the acclaimed "Architecture 1" show at the Leo Castelli Gallery in New York,[33] and he had his own show, "James Stirling—Four Projects," at the Walker Art Center, Minneapolis. Stirling also frequently lectured at schools and conferences internationally.[34]

The most significant of the publication endeavors was the monograph for Gerd Hatje titled *James Stirling: Buildings and Projects, 1950–74,* which had been in progress since the late 1960s but which was reengaged at the end of 1973 and worked on extensively until its publication in 1975. The book, a deliberate reference to Le Corbusier's *Oeuvre Complète* in both layout and graphic content, contained the most extensive documentation at the time of Stirling's work. Leon Krier redrew many of Stirling's early projects, as well as more recent ones, to not only unify the work but also reflect a more Corbusian aesthetic—unshaded line drawings, with a particular emphasis on axonometrics.[35]

The mid- to late 1970s, then, were a strange period of increasing international notoriety coupled with decreasing professional achievement. Given this publication and exhibition intensity, the period also became, by default, one of retrospection for Stirling. Through the process of putting together the publications, lectures, and exhibitions he was forced to consider his own work as history, to cull his by then considerable output, to eliminate some materials and redraw others. Krier wrote that of all of Stirling's gifts he found his ability as an editor to be his most impressive quality. "He taught me how to publish. Publishing is very different from building. You need to produce special drawings, and very, very special views. He was fantastic at editing."[36] Although Krier was referring to his ability to edit drawings for a publication, this role as editor carried over to the presentation of his oeuvre more broadly, across a range of media, and Roma Interrotta was, at its core, an extension of this retrospective moment and a demonstration of Stirling's exemplary editing skills. The project was a collection and an exhibition of Stirling's own oeuvre complète. It was the designed counterpart to the Hatje book, a carefully edited collection of his works.

Stirling's role as a collector is often mentioned in the same breath as his gift as an editor. With Thomas Hope chairs and Regency items displacing or at least coexisting with Aalto and Corbusier furniture in the late 1960s and early 1970s, Stirling's personal collecting seemed to mirror his shifting architectural interests. Rowe claimed that once he began collecting early nineteenth-century furniture (around 1967), this "exercised quite a bit of influence upon his behavior as an architect," particularly his burgeoning "Neo-Classical propensities."[37] With Roma Interrotta we can see the architect as a collector in a different light, in this case "collecting" his own projects in lieu of furniture or paintings. Perhaps a better term would be curation, for the act of compiling was carried out with a particular aesthetic aim; it enabled a reframing of the content (his earlier projects) and an extension or fulfillment of the original aims of each project (completing the wall at Selwyn, for example, or locating Florey on the Tiber with views across the Tiber rather than the Cherwell). Krier recalled that sometime between the late 1960s and the mid-1970s Stirling destroyed nearly all of his early drawings and sketches. Stirling was curating his oeuvre in reality as well as in representation.

In his review of the Hatje monograph in 1975, Reyner Banham noted the recent hiatus in architectural production for Stirling's office, a problem that the book, to his mind, would do little to remedy: "With its black dust-jacket and Alfred-Roth revival layout and typography, it is more likely to suggest that the architect is already dead!" The exclamation mark here indicates Banham's irritation with Stirling's unnecessary assumption of the "martyr's crown of persecuted avant-gardism" given that "Stirling is still very much alive."[38] Or was he? Was presenting his earlier projects in the context of a "new" and "visionary" project in fact a kind of death?

"Apophrades," or the "return of the dead," the last of Bloom's revisionary ratios, is marked by precursors who come back to haunt the living poet. This is possible only once the living poet has reached the proper "strength" (though he is never clear that the ratios must happen in sequence). The critical distinction between the strong poet's engagement with the "dead" and a less mature poet's use of influence is that the strong poet now holds his poem "open" to the precursor's in a way that enacts a seeming historical reversal. According to Bloom, the "uncanny effect" of this return of the dead is a kind of historical inversion: "The new poet's achievement makes it seem to us, not as though the precursor were writing it, but as though the later poet himself had written the precursor's characteristic work."[39] Bloom suggests this as a way of rewriting the past, so that the past becomes the "influenced" or "later" work. Rowe seems to be channeling Bloom in his description of Stirling's St. Andrews Arts Centre, which he calls "'antecedent' fantasy," by which he means that it reverses the sense of "early" and "late," since the original building, to which Stirling adds two glass wings, appears as "not the original but rather the 'degenerate' Baroque result . . . the existing building (also italicized) is now supported by additions which, conceptually, can only seem to predate it."[40]

Stirling's Roma Interrotta, as a literalized "return of the dead," indeed enacts this historical inversion whereby the "later poet" appears to have written the earlier work—in this case, Stirling's twentieth century projects rewrite Nolli's seventeenth-century Rome. But in using his own work as "precedent" the project complicates the identification of the precursor. To phrase that another way, what is "alive" within this project, and what is "dead"? Here Eisenman's Cannaregio provides little guidance, since his inserted House 11as are so violently transformed in their adopted Venetian context, unlike Stirling's projects which remain very much themselves in their Roman one. Rossi's analogous city, however, does offer a related idea of the city comprising pieces that are recognizable yet inconceivable. Rossi's well-known description of Canaletto's "imaginary" Venice is perhaps most telling; he describes Canaletto's painting of a Venice made up of Palladian buildings transposed from other parts of Italy: "The geographical transposition of the monuments within the painting constitutes a city that we recognize, even though it is a place of purely architectural references."[41] For Rossi, this suggests a design method through which "preestablished and formally defined" elements, each carrying its own history and meaning, can be brought together to define a "significance" greater than the individual elements. In his own work, such as the Modena Cemetery, this led to the notion that a building could itself stand as an analogy for the city.

I do not mean to suggest that at Stirling's Roma Interrotta each project becomes analogous to the city as a whole. Instead, to return to Rossi's analysis of Canaletto's Venice, each project stands for something outside itself, each project is understood to encapsulate an entire history and other set of associations *even as* it becomes something new— it "means" something different once it is "conscripted" into a new setting. But this depth of meaning, and the "delirium of typological chaining" it suggests (a phrase that appears in the notes accompanying Stirling's Roma Interrotta entry, in reference to Piranesi), is put forth simultaneously with a flattening of historical meaning. In employing his own projects as history's "battle remnants" Stirling effectively equalizes history. His projects are the "remains of modernism," strewn about the battlefield of the historical city. His dead fragments speak only to themselves—and to an irrecoverable past.

Stirling's retreat into his own history, however, marks another protean self-reinvention. This "death," like all deaths, is also a rebirth. Roma Interrotta marks the moment at which the distinction between the past, present, and future dissolves. Just as he was able in his earlier works to release modernism's stranglehold by reimagining its forms, at Roma Interrotta, Stirling opens the door to all of history by revisioning his own projects. Unlike Rossi's evocation of the dead, which suggests a sense of loss and ultimately of melancholy, Stirling's use of his own work as precedent lays bare the pretense of quotation, unlocking the excitement of seemingly endless recombinatory possibilities. The *act* of revisioning assumes priority and ultimately supersedes the anxiety over the choice of the source. Once the distinction between quoting himself and quoting others is eliminated, all of history can be "seen again." Continuing the investigation of historical forms and "principles" developed in his work of the 1950s and 1960s, at Roma Interrotta Stirling arrives at a kind of endgame in which historical differences are effectively collapsed. As Tafuri said of the "gigantic architectural dreams" of Enlightenment architects such as Boullée (one of Stirling's "Megalomaniac Frustrated Architects"), they were "not so much unrealizable dreams, as experimental models of a new method of architectural creation."[42]

CONCLUSION

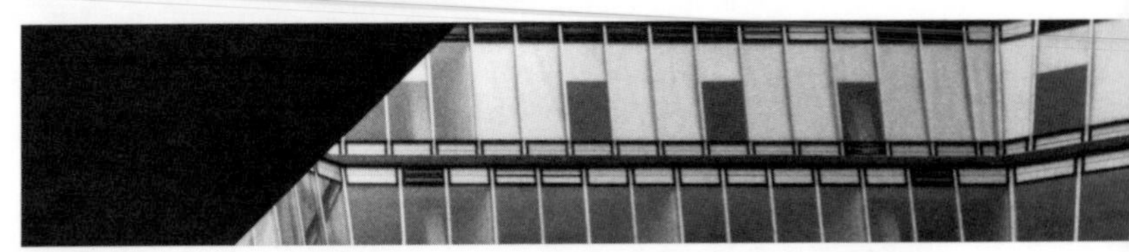

In 1963, Stirling wrote, "I believe that modern architecture has nothing to do with the past. . . . While I enjoy past architecture in itself I do not accept that you can carry it over into our time as a lesson to assist you. It lacks relevance."[1] Here we are reminded of Bloom's description of Nietzsche, whom he characterized as one of the great deniers of influence. Nietzsche was the rare exception, the artist who possessed a "strangely optimistic refusal to regard the poetical past as primarily an obstacle to fresh creation" and saw it instead as "vitalization."[2] Somehow Nietzsche was able to escape the "anxiety" surrounding influence to make it productive. The Nietzsche example, though not developed significantly in Bloom's text, is important in that it problematizes Bloom's insistence on melancholy as constitutive of the creative personality—as a necessary byproduct of the realization of the artist's own "death" and the impossibility of escaping influence—to offer instead a glimpse of the idea that, perhaps, the recognition of the inevitability of influence might lead not to despair but to inspiration.

Like Nietzsche and other of Bloom's "strong poets," Stirling seems to have escaped this melancholic disposition. As Claire Zimmerman has stated, "Here was someone who loved the positive potentials of the work that he did."[3] John Summerson memorably characterized Stirling as "Vitruvius Ludens," or the architect at play. By "play" he meant not simply the manipulation of forms or spaces in the vein of Le Corbusier's famous definition of architecture as the "magnificent play of volumes brought together in light."[4] Instead, Summerson employs play in the much more common sense of having fun; more specifically he found Stirling's play to be a reaction to the previous generations' "dogged seriousness." "I see Stirling as the architect who, more than any other in this country, or perhaps anywhere, has . . . turned the old seriousness back to front and re-engaged it as play. He is essentially a great player—even something of a gambler—an architect cast more distinctly than most in the role of homo ludens."[5]

Indeed, as Stirling's capacity for and seeming delight in this play increased over the span of his career, his early denial of the "lessons" or "relevance" of past architecture would fade. Later he acknowledged myriad influences with a wry smile, an irreverent, contrary and often humorous disposition, and without any attendant apologies or qualifications. In a 1974 lecture at the Second Annual Iran International Congress of Architecture in Persepolis, Stirling presented pairs of slides in which he grouped one of his own projects with a "source" image. The precedents encompassed the range of architectural history, as well as its periphery: classical buildings (Villa Giulia), Neoclassical ones (Hawksmoor, Blenheim), paintings (de Chirico), anonymous structures (castles, Inca stonework), and technologies/engineering (Oakland Bridge, Olivetti typewriter factory).[6] Similarly, in his RIBA address upon receiving the Gold Medal in 1980—titled, tellingly, "Architectural Aims and Influences"—Stirling named a dizzying range of architects who he claimed had influenced him at various times, going all the way back to his student days. He mentions "Stiff art nouveau designers" like Charles Rennie Mackintosh and Josef Hoffmann, then Le Corbusier and the Italian rationalists, on to Nicholas Hawksmoor, the English Baroque (particularly in bombed-out London after the war), Thomas Archer, and John Vanbrugh. He writes of learning about the Russian Constructivists and a particular book on Gunnar Asplund "which I devoured." He details his interest in the vernacular, but also the Victorians—William Butterfield, George Edmund Street, and George Gilbert Scott. Later he notes the influence of the English Neoclassicists—John Soane, William Playfair, Henry Goodridge—and their German counterparts—Friedrich Gilly, Friedrich Weinbrenner, Leo Von Klenze, and, of course, Schinkel. He writes that he was particularly interested in the transition from Neoclassical to Romantic in the first half of the nineteenth century—a "move from that sparse abstraction which somehow carried a maximum of emotive association to the break up of classicism with the incoming language of realism and naturalism was a fascinating circumstance which I think has parallels in architecture today."[7]

It did not matter, he seemed to suggest, what the precedent was or where it came from. There was no sacred meaning embedded in any one period (whether it be modern or premodern) or in the relationship between the former and the latter, or even in architecture with a capital "A" as a necessary influence or precedent. Perhaps the best example of this blasphemous attitude was his inclusion of the vacuum cleaner as one of the sources images for Roma Interrotta, on par with Romano's Villa Lante. Although he acknowledges the potential pitfalls of these glib juxtapositions—"an interaction between the design for a new building with association to the past is a dangerous tightrope to walk, with compromise and sentimentality on either side"—the pitfalls seemed less dangerous when "association with the past" was freed from its more staid and well-worn tropes and brought into the world of typewriters and vacuum cleaners.[8] He emphasizes that there must be some kind of "connexion," be it in "material, constructional method, or association," between the new building and its source, a notion that freed him from any allegience to "proper" architectural references. We can see this as an extension of his "discovery" of history at Churchill, whereby any historical precedent (from medieval earthworks to Cambridge colleges to Corbusian masterworks) became available for reconfiguration and reapplication once its "principles" were understood and could be translated into contemporary terms. The extension in this case was to take this argument past architecture and into the realm of everyday objects. Most intriguingly, this extension or expansion in the notion of the referent was at the same time a return to the foundational modernist notion of architecture's relationship with both the principles and the aesthetics of the machine—Le Corbusier's steam liner now replaced by a vacuum cleaner, but both embodying the advanced technology of their day.

The contrast between his "history doesn't influence me at all" statement of 1963 and the litany of acknowledged "aims and influences" in his RIBA address of 1980 marks the transition from the "ephebe" to the mature poet. As Stirling became more confident in his own ability to remake history—to surpass, even, these earlier examples—he was able to discuss them as influences.

Importantly, Stirling mentions that he wasn't trained under a "master," as in a traditional system, so he didn't have to worry about "getting out from under the influence of one."[9] Although Le Corbusier may have been the closest approximation of such a master, his influence was always filtered through a generational gap as well as the analytical lenses and interpretations of figures like Rowe. And, perhaps most importantly, the influence of Le Corbusier would become increasingly entangled and enmeshed with various other sources and ideas. Even at Ham Common, in which we see the most direct influence of Le Corbusier, Stirling's "rationalization" of Maisons Jaoul also includes layers of British industrial vernacular and various regional precedents. The influence of Corbusier, in other words, was never pure or unmediated.

This seeming shift in Stirling's attitude toward history suggests more than simply maturation. William Jordy once ascribed the lasting influence of Le Corbusier and Mies—as compared to J. J. P. Oud or Walter Gropius—to the fact that they had not rejected their starting point but understood it.[10] We see a similar desire on Stirling's part to revisit and understand his beginnings, both in his writings and lectures and in his buildings. Stirling's consistent lecture format, discussed in the last chapter, in which he would begin with his earliest projects and move chronologically through to his most recent ones, reframing and reworking them into a coherent narrative, can be seen as a part of this continuous self-analysis and critique. Further, his attempt to identify his influences as his career progressed represented a desire to understand his own origins in a broader sense.

Stirling's willingness to cite a laundry list of influences, however, tells us nothing about the *way* he revisioned those sources, and this, ultimately, is Stirling's greatest contribution to architectural history—his capacity to revision, not to quote. As an obvious but useful comparison, consider the fact that the modern references that Stirling frequently incorporates—Le Corbusier, Constructivism, de Stijl, chief among them—are *exactly* the same sources we see in Eisenman, Rossi, and Bernard Tschumi around this same time, none of whose work "looks" like Stirling's, nor like each other's. Ultimately it matters less what the sources are than how they are manipulated. And although there was a certain continuity to these "neo-avant-garde" practices—if nothing else, a group of "sons" wrestling with the same "fathers"—their differences are equally if not more pronounced, as the same set of sources is revisioned in highly diverse ways.

This comparison also begins to suggest an answer to the question of what distinguishes Stirling's use of the past from what Hays termed the "over and over again" repetition of the neo-avant-garde practices of the 1970s such as the New York Five—with their "empty numbing repetition of forms left over from the presumed authentic historical avant-garde."[11] For one, Stirling's repertoire of sources is both broader and deeper. In other words, he is "repeating" different forms—the Neoclassical rotunda rather than the white cube or, better, the Neoclassical rotunda *and* the white cube. Here again, though, it is the act of revisioning—rather than the choice of the source—that suggests the specificity of Stirling's practice. The series of strategies developed throughout this book—correcting, completing, generalizing, emptying out, and so on—are what set his designs apart from his peers'. His willingness to reconfigure and reinvent sources, to hybridize and even violate their original terms, stands in profound contrast to the hagiographic attitude apparent in the work of, say, Richard Meier, which is, at its core, a refinement, not a revision, of Le Corbusier's work.

Further, Stirling was always interested in the artifact, in architecture first, rather than the discursive formation—a key distinction from someone like Eisenman, or even Rossi. In the end, Stirling developed a more diverse set of methods for revisioning an initially more diverse set of historical sources than the "presumed authentic historical avant-garde." To use Hays again, Eisenman, Hejduk, and Tschumi "peel the language off from the real, repeating the same already reified forms but transforming them into a self-enclosed, totally structured system of signs."[12] But Stirling *connects* to the real, insisting on architecture's materiality—its brick and stone and glass.

And yet this veers dangerously close to calling Stirling a kind of glorified builder, a gifted formmaker blind to the larger implications or ideological import of his work, a role that Stirling often claimed for himself—the unsophisticated Liverpudlian against the Londonite effetes. To the contrary, I would propose that Stirling was acutely aware of and engaging discourse. Vidler has recently suggested, as have others before him, that although Stirling put forth no "theory" à la Eisenman or Rossi or Venturi—in other words, no written articulations of the ideas driving or underlining his work—his theory emerged from the work itself.[13] And while I don't disagree that Stirling was less a theorist than were many of his contemporaries, there were also crucial moments of self-critique, particularly ones where he looked for contradictions, or what he termed "oscillations," in his practice. I would also stress that for Stirling the discourse and the architecture object were both enlisted in the service of creating a new architecture. It wasn't about creating a new theory, in other words, any more than it was "merely" about building. Stirling devoured the discourse and the object equally in the service of design. Again this is a critical distinction from Rossi or Eisenman, and perhaps a modification to Vidler's argument in that Stirling's projects weren't self-consciously set up to feed back into the discourse but were the endpoint in themselves. For Stirling, the project was the means and the end.

To return, then, to our initial question—was Stirling a modernist or postmodernist?—we must reply that Stirling remained a committed modernist but that his practice redefined the term itself. The "derevolutionizing" of modernism that Stirling identified after the war—"the creation of a pluralist architecture in dialogue with architectural tradition"—was an idea to which Stirling was not only indebted but also helped bring about.[14] For Stirling, modernism was never a set of forms or stylistic ideas from the past or the present or the future. Instead, it was a way of operating, and as such it required continual work and modification. In Stirling's own work, modernism was constantly being produced and was therefore constantly reimagined and revisioned. This operation of remaining modern enabled the inclusion of historical references; once the revolutionary rhetoric had dissipated, the fundamental similarities between modernism's logics and those embedded within buildings throughout history—from medieval earthworks to nineteenth-century museums to postwar Corbusian projects—could be identified and capitalized on. These modern qualities could be found equally in a building from the immediate past or in a more remote one. Beyond simply "allowing" history into modernism, Stirling's architecture revealed modernism's instability within history and the possibility—the necessity—that it be continuously produced.

Stirling was someone who strove to revision, to "see again," the architecture of the past, to make it modern—to "aim correctively," in Bloom's terms. Bloom's theory of influence applies to the creative act as well as to the critical interpretive one. In our own consideration of Stirling we must now also attempt to see again his work, to revision simplistic categorizations of his work as either modernist or postmodernist, and to understand how his architecture reveals fundamental ideas about the role of influence and the possibilities for rethinking precedent.

NOTES

INTRODUCTION

1 Martin Filler, "Cultural Centering," *Architectural Record* (September 1984): 142.

2 James Stirling, from "The Black Notebook," in Stirling, *James Stirling: Early Unpublished Writings on Architecture*, ed. Mark Crinson (New York: Routledge, 2010), 24.

3 Harold Rosenberg, *The Tradition of the New* (London: Thames and Hudson, 1959), 9.

4 Letter dated October 26, 1988, interview for *Ambiente* magazine, DRCON2000:0027:846, James Stirling/Michael Wilford Fonds, Canadian Centre for Architecture, Montréal (CCA).

5 William Jordy, "The Symbolic Essence of Modern European Architecture of the Twenties and Its Continuing Influence," *Journal of the Society of Architectural Historians* 22, no. 3 (October 1963): 179.

6 DRCON2000:0027:846, James Stirling/Michael Wilford Fonds, CCA.

7 See Mark Crinson and Jules Lubbock, eds., *Architecture: Art of Profession. Three Hundred Years of Architectural Education in Britain* (Manchester: Prince of Wales Institute of Architecture, Manchester University Press, 1994), esp. chapter 3. Stirling would later write: "The school of architecture was in tremendous ferment as the revolution of modern architecture had just hit it (1945) secondhand and rather late." Stirling, "An Architect's Approach to Architecture," *Royal Institute of British Architects Journal* 72 (May 1965): 231.

8 Colin Rowe, "James Stirling: A Highly Personal and Very Disjointed Memoir," introduction to *James Stirling: Buildings and Projects*, ed. Peter Arnell and Ted Bickford (New York: Rizzoli, 1984), 10–13.

9 Stirling, "Architect's Approach to Architecture," 231.

10 Mark Girouard, *Big Jim: The Life and Work of James Stirling* (London: Chatto and Windus, 1998), 36.

11 James Stirling, "Architectural Aims and Influences," *RIBA Journal* (September 1980): 134.

12 Robert Maxwell, introduction to Stirling, *James Stirling: Writings on Architecture* (Milan: Skira, 1998), 9.

13 Harold Bloom, *A Map of Misreading* (New York: Oxford University Press, 1975), 12.

14 Interview (not broadcast) with Tony Russell of the BBC, July 5, 1986, http://www.bbc.co.uk/bbcfour/audiointerviews/profilepages/stirlingj1.shtml.

15 Girouard, *Big Jim*, 36.

16 James Stirling, undated postcard, DDR2006:0022, James Stirling/Michael Wilford Fonds, CCA.

17 Stirling, *Early Unpublished Writings*, 75.

18 Adrian Forty, "Le Corbusier's British Reputation," in *Le Corbusier: Architect of the Century* (London: Arts Council of Great Britain, 1987), 35–41.

19 James Stirling, "Retrospective Statements," *Independent Group: Postwar Britain and the Aesthetics of Plenty*, ed. David Robbins (Cambridge: MIT Press, 1990), 95.

20 Anthony Vidler, *Histories of the Immediate Present: Inventing Architectural Modernism* (Cambridge: MIT Press, 2008), 62. Vidler ends his chapter on Rowe with a discussion of Stirling.

21 Ibid., 68.

22 Joan Ockman, "Form Without Utopia: Contextualizing Colin Rowe," *Journal of the Society of Architectural Historians* 57, no. 4 (December 1998): 450.

23 Girouard claims that the first time Stirling visited the Unité was in summer 1955. See Girouard, *Big Jim*, 82.

24 Stirling, "Architect's Approach to Architecture," 231.

25 Rowe, "Highly Personal Memoir," 19.

26 Ibid., 18. He added that it probably owed as much to the Eameses as to Mies.

27 James Stirling, "Plan of Town Centre and Development of Community Centre for Newton Aycliffe Co. Durham" (thesis, Liverpool University, 1950), 22.

28 Paula Young Lee, "Modern Architecture and the Ideology of Influence," *Assemblage* 34 (December 1997): 34.

29 Bloom's ideas have been imported to architectural criticism before—in two very different contexts if not on opposing "teams." Vincent Scully traces the influence of the Shingle Style of the late nineteenth century on the architecture of the 1970s, particularly Robert Venturi, in Bloomian terms. Vincent Scully, *The Shingle Style Today; or, The Historian's Revenge* (New York: Braziller, 1974). Peter Eisenman, on the other hand, employed Bloom's notions of "misreading" and the "swerve" in the mid-1970s. Peter Eisenman, "Misreading Peter Eisenman," in Eisenman, *Houses of Cards* (New York: Oxford University Press, 1999). In neither case, however, was there an attempt to understand the role of influence more deeply in a single figure. While Scully convincingly traces the Shingle Style's influence on Venturi and his peers, and weaves an equally compelling web of influences from the Shingle Style via Wright and European modernists, his adoption of Bloom's notion of influence is employed more directly to resuscitate the Shingle Style from the historical dustbin. And Eisenman uses Bloom largely to support his own design strategies.

30 Bloom, *Map of Misreading,* 10.

31 Ibid., 7.

32 Ibid. Stirling, "Black Notebook," 19.

33 I do not claim that Stirling read Bloom—although he was likely aware of Bloom's work through his concurrent teaching at Yale. An archival note alludes to a more direct awareness of *The Anxiety of Influence;* Charles Jencks wrote to Stirling in the early 1970s: "The whole question of influence really is a problem—legal, practical, spiritual and internal—as Scully has argued in his 'a shingle style today or the historian's revenge' (i.e., H. Bloom's *The Anxiety of Influence: A Theory of Poetry,* 1973). I hope we can discuss this later." DRCON2000:027:849, James Stirling/Michael Wilford Fonds, CCA.

34 Robert Maxwell presented a large (though by no means comprehensive) selection in Stirling, *Writings on Architecture.*

35 Excerpted from a letter dated April 18, 1991, addressed to an assistant editor at *Blueprint,* and offered as an explanation for why he could not write an article on Schinkel for the magazine. DRCON2000:027:847 2-2, James Stirling/Michael Wilford Fonds, CCA.

36 Rafael Moneo, "On James Stirling: Buildings and Projects," book review, *Oppositions* 7 (Winter 1976): 90.

37 In his memorial essay to Stirling, Colin St. John Wilson writes: "Stirling operated a magpie avidity to steal whatever he liked while yet turning it into his own—and that is a freedom which is only possible to someone who belongs to no school." *Architectural Review* 91, no. 1150 (December 1992): 20.

38 *James Stirling: Buildings and Projects, 1950–74,* ed. John Jacobus (Oxford: Oxford University Press, 1975), and *James Stirling: Buildings and Projects,* ed. Peter Arnell and Ted Bickford (New York: Rizzoli, 1984).

39 See *ANY* 1, no. 2, "A Tribute to James Stirling" (September–October 1993).

40 Mark Crinson has undertaken the most thorough investigation of the Stirling and Gowan partnership. See his article "Picturesque and Intransigent: 'Creative Tension' and Collaboration in the Early House Projects of Stirling and Gowan," *Architectural History* 50 (2007): 267–95, and his book *Stirling and Gowan: Architecture from Austerity to Influence* (London: Yale University Press, 2012).

41 Walter Benjamin, "The Work of Art in the Age of Mechanical Reproduction," orig. 1936, in *Illuminations,* ed. Hannah Arendt, trans. Harry Zohn (New York: Harcourt, Brace and World, 1968).

42 Craig Hodgetts, "Big Jim," *Architect* (December 2010): 49.

43 Anthony Vidler, *James Frazer Stirling: Notes from the Archive* (Montreal: Canadian Centre for Architecture; New Haven: Yale Center for British Art and Yale University Press, 2010).

44 Though too numerous to list comprehensively, two important examples are Reinhold Martin, *The Organization Complex: Architecture, Media, and Corporate Space* (Cambridge: MIT Press, 2003); and Sarah Goldhagen, *Louis Kahn's Situated Modernism* (New Haven: Yale University Press, 2001).

45 Philip Johnson, "A Tribute to James Stirling," *ANY* 1, no. 2 (September–October 1993): 48.

46 Rafael Moneo, *Theoretical Anxiety and Design Strategies in the Work of Eight Contemporary Architects* (Cambridge: MIT Press, 2005), 3.

47 Claire Zimmerman, "James Stirling Re-assembled," *AA Files,* no. 56 (2007): 37.

CHAPTER 1
RATIONALIZING JAOUL

1 Reyner Banham, *New Brutalism: Ethic or Aesthetic?* (New York: Reinhold, 1966), 88.

2 James Stirling, "Black Notebook," in Stirling, *James Stirling: Early Unpublished Writings on Architecture,* ed. Mark Crinson (New York: Routledge, 2010), 24, 43.

3 Ibid., 53.

4 James Stirling, "Retrospective Statements," *Independent Group: Postwar Britain and the Aesthetics of Plenty,* ed. David Robbins (Cambridge: MIT Press, 1990), 195.

5 James Stirling, "Garches to Jaoul: Le Corbusier as a Domestic Architect in 1927 and 1953," *Architectural Review* 118 (September 1955): 145–51.

6 Ibid., 151.

7 Mark Crinson, "L'Architecte Anglais," in Stirling,

Early Unpublished Writings, 124.

8 James Stirling, "Ronchamp: Le Corbusier's Chapel and the Crisis of Rationalism," *Architectural Review* 119 (March 1956): 155–61.

9 Ibid., 161.

10 Ibid., 160.

11 Stirling, "Garches to Jaoul," 151.

12 Ibid., 147.

13 Stirling, "Ronchamp," 156.

14 Stirling, "Garches to Jaoul," 151.

15 Stirling's use of the term rationalism here is distinct from its use to describe Italian architecture of the 1930s. Stirling would later write that he had discovered the work of Giuseppe Terragni and Pietro Cataneo as a student, and that during the mid-1950s he held a general "enthusiasm" for the Italian rationalists. Stirling, "Retrospective Statements," 195.

16 J. M. Richards, "Towards a Rational Aesthetic: An Examination of the Characteristics of Modern Design with Particular Reference to the Influence of the Machine," *Architectural Review* (December 1935): 211–18.

17 Ibid., 215.

18 Stirling, "Garches to Jaoul," 151.

19 Stirling, *Early Unpublished Writings*, 53.

20 Nikolaus Pevsner, *Outline of European Architecture*, 6th ed. (Baltimore: Penguin, 1960), 700.

21 Nicholas Bullock, *Building the Post-War World: Modern Architecture and Reconstruction in Britain* (London: Routledge, 2002), 219.

22 The contents page of the September 1955 issue of *Architectural Review* pokes fun at Stirling, writing that he performed the "shortest stay on record—5 weeks—in the LCC Planning Department."

23 A decade earlier a panel at RIBA, which included John Summerson and Sir Charles Reilly, former head of the Liverpool School of Architecture, decried the "evil time" they were experiencing in which the individual architect, rather than "sink his personality" into a larger group or toward a great collective good, was instead unduly emphasized. "So long as that existed no great work could be done." "What Is Modern Architecture," report of a MARS group meeting on December 13, 1944, *Builder* (December 29, 1944): 510.

24 John Summerson, "The Case for a Theory of Modern Architecture," *RIBA Journal* (June 1957): 307–10, originally delivered as a lecture at RIBA on May 21, 1957. Also published in abbreviated format in *Builder* 192 (May 24, 1957): 947–48.

25 For a more detailed analysis of Summerson's relationship to the modern movement, see Alan Power, "John Summerson and Modernism," in *Twentieth-Century Architecture and Its Histories*, ed. Louise Campbell (London: Society of Architectural Historians of Great Britain, 2000), 153–76.

26 Alina Payne, "Rudolf Wittkower and Architectural Principles in the Age of Modernism," *Journal of the Society of Architectural Historians* 53, no. 3 (September 1994): 328, 340.

27 Banham, *New Brutalism*, 15n7.

28 James Stirling, "Architectural Aims and Influences," *RIBA Journal* (September 1980): 134.

29 Stirling took the job at Lyons Israel Ellis in 1952 after his brief stint at the London County Council. See Mark Girouard, *Big Jim: The Life and Work of James Stirling* (London: Chatto and Windus, 1998), 86–89, for a general description of this period. See also Stirling's own recollections in "Conversation between Alvin Boyarsky and James Stirling, Alan Forsyth, and David Gray," in *Lyons Israel Ellis Gray: Buildings and Projects, 1932–1983*, ed. Alan Forsyth and David Gray (London: Architectural Association, 1988), 204–5. Leonard Manousso was chairman of Maybrook Properties, a development firm that completed projects in England, Belgium, and France. Manousso's son Paul, a former AA student whom Stirling befriended through London circles (in particular, Sam Stevens and Alan Colquhoun), suggested Stirling for the project. See Girouard, *Big Jim*, 73–74.

30 Mark Crinson, "Picturesque and Intransigent: 'Creative Tension' and Collaboration in the Early House Projects of Stirling and Gowan," *Architectural History* 50 (2007): 271.

31 Caroline Benton traces the development of the L-shaped windows in Maisons Jaoul, noting that their shape emerged only after larger, glazed windows had been deemed in violation of privacy bylaws and a building permit withheld. Although this doesn't account for the particular shape of the window, it does go some way toward explaining the reduced opening of the L-shaped window vs. a traditional window, and the fact that the window was pushed up beneath the concrete floor slab to allow for the greatest possible privacy while also admitting light. Caroline Benton, *Le Corbusier and the Maisons Jaoul* (New York: Princeton Architectural Press, 2009), 65.

32 Previous examples of the type existed mainly in garden cities, which had replaced existing urban "slums"; examples include the two-story maisonettes at Alton East, Roehampton (1956), and the more traditional terraced houses at Woodyard Square by Tayler and Green (1951). For a discussion of Roehampton and low-rise housing more generally, see Bullock, *Building the Post-War World,* 89–90. See also John Summerson, introduction to *Ten Years of British Architecture '45–'55,* Arts Council Exhibition 1956 (London, 1956), especially 42–46. For comprehensive treatments of postwar housing production in Britain, see Anthony Jackson, *The Politics of Architecture: A History of Modern Architecture in Britain* (Toronto: University of Toronto Press, 1970), chapter 8, as well as Bullock, *Building the Post-War World,* chapters 3 and 4.

33 In typical London County Council low-rise housing projects of the early 1950s, such as Alton East, the "people's detailing" included pitched roofs and picturesque planning. This was especially prevalent in slightly earlier postwar projects, including Churchill Gardens, London, by Powell and Moya (1950), and Spa Green, Finsbury, by Tecton (1950), both of which were mixed-use developments with "modern" high-rise flats.

34 James Stirling and James Gowan, "Flats at Langham House, Ham Common, Richmond," *Architectural Design* (November 1958): 448.

35 James Stirling, "An Architect's Approach to Architecture," *Royal Institute of British Architects Journal* 72 (May 1965): 233. "Flats at Ham Common," *Architectural Review* (October 1958): 222. See also ibid.

36 Jackson, *Politics of Architecture,* 186.

37 Stirling, *Early Unpublished Writings,* 104.

38 James Stirling, "Regionalism and Modern Architecture," *Architects Yearbook* 8 (1957): 65. Stirling wrote that despite their "will to modernity," the Hertfordshire schools "do not set a standard either in conception or style."

39 "Flats at Ham Common," 219.

40 Ibid.

41 Nikolaus Pevsner and Bridget Cherry, *The Buildings of England: London, South,* vol. 2 (New Haven: Yale University Press, 1983), 473.

42 Kenneth Frampton, "Transformations in Style: The Work of James Stirling," *A+U* 50 (1975): 135.

43 Alison and Peter Smithson, *Ordinariness and Light: Urban Theories, 1952–60, and Their Application in a Building Project, 1963–70* (London: Faber and Faber, 1970), 169.

44 Stirling, "Garches to Jaoul," 146.

45 Benton, *Maisons Jaoul,* 140.

46 Stirling, *Early Unpublished Writings,* 104.

47 Henry-Russell Hitchcock, *Modern Architecture in England* (New York: Museum of Modern Art, 1969), 35. He notes Tecton's use of brick and the rough stone walls of Marcel Breuer and F. R. S. Yorke's pavilion at the royal show in Bristol, which was featured in the exhibition and in the accompanying publication.

48 Ibid.

49 Stirling, *Early Unpublished Writings,* 83.

50 Stirling, "Garches to Jaoul," 147.

51 James Stirling and James Gowan, "Afterthoughts on The Flats at Ham Common," *Architect and Building News* (May 1959). Reprinted in James Stirling, *James Stirling: Writings on Architecture,* ed. Robert Maxwell (Milan: Skira, 1998), 77.

52 Le Corbusier was always placed above Mies in Stirling's writings and lectures notes. Stirling would later write that he found Miesian grids lacking "integrative potential," and in an undated postcard he describes Mies (along with Frank Lloyd Wright) as "not 20th Cent." and clearly inferior to Le Corbusier—"the specific ultimate master of 20th cent. space and form." DDR2006:0022, James Stirling/Michael Wilford Fonds, Canadian Centre for Architecture, Montréal (CCA).

53 Stirling, "Architect's Approach," 240.

54 "Le Corbusier's Unité d'Habitation," *Architectural Review* 109 (May 1951): 293–300.

55 Reyner Banham, "Plucky Jims," *New Statesman* (July 19, 1958): 83.

56 Stirling and Gowan, "Flats at Langham House, Ham Common," 448.

57 The concrete upstands were not entirely structurally superfluous—they minimized thermal movement in the wall and stabilized the adjacent bricks.

58 These free-span windows are possible because

the two-story buildings' crosswall construction frees up the north and south façades, while in the three-story buildings all walls are structural and therefore all windows are "punched."

59 Stirling, "Garches to Jaoul," 148.

60 Stirling and Gowan, "Afterthoughts on Ham Common," 75.

61 James Stirling, "Notes for a Lecture," in Stirling, *Early Unpublished Writings*, 69.

62 Banham, *New Brutalism*, 88.

63 Alan Colquhoun, "Architecture as a Continuous Text," *ANY* 1, no. 2 (September 1993): 18.

64 Crinson, "Picturesque and Intransigent," 274. Crinson's assessment is based largely on his extensive interviews with Gowan.

65 Banham, *New Brutalism*, 357.

66 Peter Cook, "Regarding the Smithsons," *Architectural Review* (July 1982): 37.

67 Harold Bloom, *The Anxiety of Influence: A Theory of Poetry*, 2nd ed. (London: Oxford University Press, 1997), 14.

68 Vincent Scully, *The Shingle Style Today; or, the Historian's Revenge* (New York: Braziller, 1974), 40.

69 Philip Johnson, "The House at New Canaan, Connecticut," *Architectural Review* 108, no. 645 (1950): 152.

70 Colin Rowe, "J. F. S., 1924–1992," Introduction to memorial issue on Stirling, *ANY* 1, no. 2 (September–October 1993): 9.

71 Alison and Peter Smithson, *The Charged Void* (New York: Monacelli, 2001), 40.

CHAPTER 2
DISCOVERING HISTORY

1 James Stirling, "'The Functional Tradition' and Expression," *Perspecta* 6 (1960): 88–97. In the fall of 1959 Stirling was invited by the Art and Architecture School's new dean, Paul Rudolph, to teach a studio at Yale, which led to his article in *Perspecta*. On Stirling's time at Yale, see Mark Girouard, *Big Jim: The Life and Work of James Stirling* (London: Chatto and Windus, 1998), 116–36.

2 Stirling, "'Functional Tradition' and Expression," 89.

3 Ibid., 95. Sigfried Giedion's well-known and similar pairing of the Ronchamp towers with a "primitive" building (in his case, Cycladian towers) in *Space, Time and Architecture* did not appear until the 1967 edition—after Stirling's "Functional Tradition" article was published. Sigfried Giedion, *Space, Time and Architecture: The Growth of a New Tradition*, 5th ed. (Cambridge: Harvard University Press, 1967), 578.

4 This project has been consistently dated to 1958, beginning with the 1975 Jacobus Monograph, and repeated in nearly all subsequent scholarship. In fact, the competition was not announced until January 1959, though the College was founded in 1958. The earlier date for Churchill College created the architectural sequence of Churchill/Camberwell/Selwyn, which may have been desirable.

5 For an overview of the Churchill College competition, see Elain Harwood, "The Churchill College Competition and the Smithson Generation," in *Twentieth-Century Architecture and Its Histories*, ed. Louise Campbell (London: Society of Architectural Historians of Great Britain, 2000): 37–56. For a comprehensive look at university architecture during the post-war years, see Diane Chablo, "University Architecture in Britain: 1950–1975" (Ph.D. diss., Oxford University, 1987), and Stephen Muthesius, *The Postwar University: Utopianist Campus and College* (New Haven: Paul Mellon Centre for Studies in British Art and Yale University Press, 2000).

6 Sussex by Basil Spence (1960); East Anglia by Denys Lasdun (1962); York by Robert Mathew, Johnson-Marshall and Partners (1961); Kent by Lord Holford (1962); Essex by Architects Co-Partnership (1963); Warwick by Arthur Ling, then Yorke Rosenberg and Mardall (1963); and Lancaster by Shepherd and Epstein (1966).

7 William Holford and H. Myles Wright, *Cambridge Planning Proposals: A Report to the Town and Country Planning Committee of the Cambridgeshire County Council* (Cambridge: Cambridge University Press, 1950).

8 Nicholas Taylor and Philip Booth, *Cambridge New Architecture: A Guide to the Post-War Buildings* (Cambridge: Editors at Trinity Hall, 1964), 174–82.

9 It was one of four purchased by the university based on Holford's 1950 report. Harwood, "Churchill College Competition," 38.

10 Gerard Fielden, "Churchill College Cambridge: The Competition Reviewed," *Builder* (August 14, 1959): 4.

11 Powell and Moya declined the invitation. In addition

to Stirling and Gowan, the twenty remaining entrants were: Architects Co-Partnership; Sir Hugh Casson, Neville Conder and Partners; H. T. Cadbury-Brown; Chamberlin, Powell and Bon; Brett & Pollen; James Cubitt & Partners; David Aberdeen & Partners; Erno Goldfinger; Howell, Killick & Partridge; Lyons, Israel & Ellis; Robert Matthew, Johnson-Marshall & Partners; Yorke, Rosenberg & Mardall; Norman & Dawbarn; David Roberts; Richard Sheppard, Robson & Partners; Alison & Peter Smithson; Frederick Gibbert & Partners; Fry, Drew, Drake & Lasdun; and Tayler & Green.

12 Stirling and Gowan were not among the initial list of four recommended firms that Martin submitted to the committee. Harwood, "Churchill College Competition," 39.

13 Lasdun at East Anglia; Matthew, Johnson-Marshall at York; Architects Co-Partnership at Essex; and Yorke, Rosenberg and Mardall at York. Note that two assessors from the competition—Holford and Spence—also designed New Universities (Kent and Sussex, respectively).

14 Fielden, "Churchill College Cambridge," 4.

15 From the original program brief provided by the jury, as excerpted in Colin Boyne, "Churchill College: A Science College, But Is Its Design Based on Scientific Principles?" *Architects' Journal* (September 3, 1959): 119.

16 Ibid.

17 Colin Rowe, "The Blenheim of the Welfare State," *Cambridge Review* 81, no. 1964 (October 31, 1959): 89–92.

18 Richard Sheppard, Robson and Partners, "Competitors Report," in "Competition for Churchill College, Cambridge," *Architects' Journal* (August 13, 1959): 8.

19 "Competition for Churchill College, Cambridge: The Assessors Report on the Final Stage," *Architects' Journal* (August 13, 1959), 7.

20 A number of contemporary reviews chastised the committee for failing to nominate Howell, Killick and Partridge's scheme. Fielden wrote that it was "distinctive, imaginative and consistent," the "most stimulating scheme showing what can be done by the *avant guarde* of the profession" ("Churchill College Cambridge," 5). R. Furneaux Jordan was even more explicit, describing the firm's plan as the only one to create both a "break-through" to a "new monumentality" as well as "romantic landscape." Their inexperience served as an advantage since they were as yet "un-aware of how little the Establishment can really 'take.'" R. Furneaux Jordan, "Churchill Memorial College: The Price of Greatness," *Architect and Building News* (August 12, 1959): 15.

21 "Assessors Report," 7.

22 James Stirling and James Gowan, "Competitors Report," in "Competition for Churchill College, Cambridge," *Architects' Journal* (August 13, 1959): 27.

23 "Assessors Report," 7.

24 Fielden, "Churchill College Cambridge," 5.

25 Stirling and Gowan, "Competitors Report," 27.

26 Kenneth Frampton, "Transformations in the Style: The Work of James Stirling," *A+U* 50 (1975): 135.

27 Rowe, "Blenheim of the Welfare State," 91.

28 Stirling, "Competitors Report," 27, and "'Functional Tradition' and Expression," 95. Stirling's interest in monumentality would become more pronounced in the 1970s and 1980s, reflecting shifts in architectural discourse, as well as in the increasing scale of his projects, particularly museums, during this same time. See James Stirling, "The Monumental Tradition," *Perspecta* 16 (1980): 32–43.

29 José Luis Sert, Fernand Léger, and Sigfried Giedion, "Nine Points on Monumentality," in Joan Ockman, ed., *Architecture Culture, 1943–68: A Documentary Anthology* (New York: Rizzoli, 1993), 29.

30 Ibid., 30.

31 A. E. Richardson, *Monumental Classic Architecture in Great Britain and Ireland* (London: Batsford, 1914), 6.

32 James Stirling, *James Stirling: Early Unpublished Writings on Architecture*, ed. Mark Crinson (New York: Routledge, 2010), 23.

33 Ibid., 31.

34 Ibid., 26.

35 James Stirling, "Regionalism and Modern Architecture," *Architects Yearbook* 8 (1957): 62.

36 This drawing appears on the cover of the Churchill College competition submission.

37 Fielden, "Churchill College Cambridge," 4.

38 As paraphrased in Giulio Carlo Argan, "On the Typology of Architecture," trans. Joseph Rykwert, *Architectural Design* 33 (December 1963): 565.

39 Harold Bloom, *The Anxiety of Influence: A Theory of Poetry*, 2nd ed. (London: Oxford University Press, 1997), 15.

40 James Stirling, "Architectural Aims and Influences," *RIBA Journal* (September 1980): 135.

41 Ibid. As Sarah Ksiazek (now Sarah Williams Goldhagen) established, these photos are nearly identical to a series of slides in the personal collection of Louis Kahn, presumably taken by both architects when they traveled together in the English countryside sometime in the late 1950s. Sarah Ksiazek, "Architectural Culture in the Fifties: Louis Kahn and the National Assembly Complex in Dhaka," *Journal of the Society of Architectural Historians* 52 (December 1993): 421–23.

42 Stirling's Village Housing scheme was in fact submitted to the CIRPAC meeting at La Sarraz in September 1955. Theo Crosby, "Contribution to CIAM 10," *Architects' Yearbook* (1956): 37. Crosby's information is corroborated by the date on the Village Housing Drawing itself—June 1955. Stirling's entry was then submitted on behalf of the MARS group to the CIAM X meeting in Dubrovnik. Stirling neither attended CIAM X nor was he invited to participate in any of the preparatory meetings. His invitation to submit came from the Smithsons. He would later write that the "beginning of my break with the Smithsons" came after hearing that they had presented his work at CIAM as "from the school of the Smithsons," noting that it had since become a "definite break." "James Stirling in Tokyo, Interviewed by Arata Isozaki," A+U (August 1971), republished in Stirling, *James Stirling: Writings on Architecture,* ed. Robert Maxwell (Milan: Skira, 1998), 197.

43 Stirling's description of the project, in *James Stirling: Buildings and Projects,* ed. Peter Arnell and Ted Bickford (New York: Rizzoli, 1984), 43.

44 The modules were seven feet and ten and one-half feet, and roof planes were angled at either thirty or sixty degrees.

45 James Stirling, "Lecture '81," in *Architecture in An Age of Skepticism: A Practitioner's Anthology,* ed. Denys Lasdun (London: Heinemann, 1984), 193.

46 Stirling, "Regionalism," 68.

47 Ibid.

48 "New Empiricism: Sweden's Latest Style," *Architectural Review* (June 1947): 199–204. Eric de Mare, "The New Empiricism: The Antecedents and Origins of Sweden's Latest Style," *Architectural Review* 103 (January 1948): 9–22.

49 Stirling, "Regionalism," 65.

50 Ibid.

51 J. M. Richards, *The Functional Tradition in Early Industrial Building* (London: Architectural Press, 1958).

52 *Architectural Review* (July 1957): 4 (frontispiece).

53 Stirling, "'Functional Tradition' and Expression," 89.

54 Zurko deemphasizes the modern movement's claim to functionalism, offering instead a historical survey of the term from the ancient Greeks through to the nineteenth century, with the intention of debunking the notion that functionalism was solely the property of the twentieth century, specifically the modern movement. Edward Robert de Zurko, *Origins of Functionalist Theory* (New York: Columbia University Press, 1957).

55 Colin Rowe, *The Mathematics of the Ideal Villa and Other Essays* (Cambridge: MIT Press, 1987), 9.

56 James Stirling, interview with Tony Russell, BBC, July 5, 1985 (recorded but not broadcast) http://www.bbc.co.uk/bbcfour/audiointerviews/profilepages/stirlingj1.shtml

57 The permit reads: "To take photographs and/or make sketches on the Dock estate until June 1968. Granted by the Mersey Docks and Harbour Board of Liverpool." DR2006:0022, Folder I-Liverpool, James Stirling/Michael Wilford Fonds, Canadian Centre for Architecture, Montréal (CCA).

58 Francesco Passanti, "The Vernacular, Modernism, and Le Corbusier," *Journal of the Society of Architectural Historians* 56, no. 4 (December 1997): 438–51, 537.

59 James Stirling, "Ronchamp: Le Corbusier's Chapel and the Crisis of Rationalism," *Architectural Review* 119 (March 1956): 161.

60 Girouard, *Big Jim,* 79–80.

61 Stirling, "Regionalism," 65.

62 Murray Fraser with Joe Kerr, *Architecture and the "Special Relationship": The American Influence on Post-War British Architecture* (London: Routledge, 2007), 10.

63 As Girouard notes, his attitude shifted, at least in retrospect, over the course of his career. Girouard quotes extensively from a letter Stirling wrote to Robin Bell six weeks after he'd arrived in America (sometime in August 1948), in which he writes of a "superficial" intellectual culture and "priggish" and "hard as nails" American families. He describes New York City as a "ghastly monstrosity." By contrast, in a comment many years later he wrote of his "amazement" on "seeing the bright chrome buildings and spotless pavement of New York. People forget how clean and bright and shiny New York was back then." Girouard, *Big Jim*, 40–45, passim.

64 James Stirling, "Garches to Jaoul: Le Corbusier as a Domestic Architect in 1927 and 1953," *Architectural Review* 118 (September 1955): 146.

65 James Stirling, "Black Notebook," in Stirling, *Early Unpublished Writings*, 53.

66 Ibid. Stirling goes on to describe both Chandigarh and the Palace of the Soviets as "regional" in this way; the former as it was "indebted to the history and traditions of a native Indian culture," and the latter as it "makes considerable reference to Russian constructivism."

67 Stirling, "Regionalism," 65.

68 Frampton, "Transformations in Style," 135.

69 Stirling, "'Functional Tradition' and Expression," 92. At La Tourette, two rows of single rooms, stacked one atop another, project from the exterior wall; at Churchill, this notion is modified so that only the upper row of rooms projects (the lower is set flush with the exterior wall).

70 Ibid.

71 James Stirling, "Notes for a Lecture," in Stirling, *Early Unpublished Writings*, 72.

72 Robert McCarter, *Louis Kahn* (New York: Phaidon, 2005), 176.

73 Stirling, "Architectural Aims and Influences," 135.

74 Nikolaus Pevsner, "Modern Architecture and the Historian, or the Return of Historicism," *RIBA Journal* 68 (April 1961): 236.

75 John Summerson, "Viollet-le-Duc and the Rational Point of View," from *Heavenly Mansions* (New York: W. W. Norton, 1963), 141.

76 Rafael Moneo, *Theoretical Anxiety and Design Strategies in the Work of Eight Contemporary Architects* (Cambridge: MIT Press, 2005), 317.

CHAPTER 3
AN "EXPRESSIVE" FUNCTIONALISM

1 Reyner Banham, "The Word in Britain: Character," *Architectural Forum* 119 (August–September 1964): 125.

2 "Ten Buildings That Point to the Future," *Fortune* (October 1964), and James Stirling, "An Architect's Approach to Architecture," *Royal Institute of British Architects Journal* 72 (May 1965): 233.

3 John Jacobus, "Engineering Building, Leicester University," *Architectural Review* (April 1964): 254.

4 Stirling, "Architect's Approach to Architecture," 233.

5 E. W. Parks, "Leicester University Engineering Laboratory, 16th August, 1959," AP140.S2.SS1.D23.P22, James Stirling/Michael Wilford Fonds, Canadian Centre for Architecture, Montréal (CCA).

6 E. W. Parks, "Leicester University Engineering Laboratory: A Preliminary Note on Buildings and Staff," AP140.S2.SS1.D23.P22, James Stirling/Michael Wilford Fonds.

7 James Stirling, "Royaumont Talk," in Stirling, *James Stirling: Early Unpublished Writings on Architecture*, ed. Mark Crinson (New York: Routledge, 2010), 91.

8 Stirling, "Architect's Approach to Architecture," 233.

9 Frank Newby, "Notes on the Structure," *Architectural Design* (February 1964): 69.

10 James Stirling, "Anti-Structure," slide talk given at Bologna University, November 1966, *Zodiac* 18 (November 1966): 57.

11 Stirling, *Early Unpublished Writings*, 92.

12 "The Work of Stirling and Gowan," *Architect and Building News* (January 7, 1959). Reprinted in RIBA catalogue 17.

13 Stirling, *Early Unpublished Writings*, 106.

14 Stirling, "Architect's Approach to Architecture," 231.

15 Stirling, *Early Unpublished Writings*, 22

16 Stirling, "Anti-Structure," 57.

17 Alan Colquhoun, "The Strategies of the Grands Travaux," in *Modernity and the Classical Tradition: Architectural Essays, 1980–87* (Cambridge: MIT Press, 1989), 125.

18 Claire Zimmerman, "James Stirling Re-assembled," *AA Files*, no. 56 (2007): 40n6.

19 Reyner Banham, *Theory and Design in the First Machine Age* (New York: Praeger, 1960), 16.

20 Ibid., 20.

21 Peter Eisenman, "Real and English," *Oppositions* 4 (October 1974): 5–33.

22 Ibid., 19.

23 Ibid., 9.

24 Alan Colquhoun, "Architecture as a Continuous Text," *ANY* 1, no. 2 (September 1993): 18.

25 Although no preparatory sketches for Leicester

(or any early Stirling projects) survive, the tiny axonometric was a favorite if not the preferred design tool for Stirling in later work.

26 Reyner Banham, introduction to *James Stirling,* catalogue of exhibition held at the Royal Institute of British Architects, Heinz Gallery, 21 Portman Square, London, April 24–June 21, 1974, 4.

27 Ibid., 14.

28 Le Corbusier, *Towards a New Architecture,* trans. Frederick Etchells from 13th ed. (New York: Dover, 1986), 40; William Jordy, "The Symbolic Essence of Modern European Architecture of the Twenties and Its Continuing Influence," *Journal of the Society of Architectural Historians* 22, no. 3 (October 1963).

29 Zimmerman, "Stirling Reassembled," 34.

30 Stirling, *Early Unpublished Writings,* 34.

31 Ibid., 9.

32 James Stirling, "'The Functional Tradition' and Expression," *Perspecta* 6 (1960): 91–92.

33 Luigi Moretti, "The Structures and Sequences of Spaces," trans. Thomas Stevens, in *Oppositions* 3 (October 1974): 109–39.

34 Ibid., 138.

35 Stirling, "Architect's Approach to Architecture," 233.

36 Ibid., 236.

37 Stirling, "Anti-Structure," 57.

38 Stirling, "Architect's Approach to Architecture," 233.

39 James Stirling, "Seven Keys to a Good Architecture," *20th Century* (Winter 1963): 151.

40 Stirling, "'Functional Tradition' and Expression," 89.

41 Lewis Mumford, "Function and Expression in Architecture," *Architectural Record* 110 (November 1951): 106.

42 Nikolaus Pevsner, *Outline of European Architecture,* 6th ed. (Baltimore: Penguin, 1960), 700.

43 Nikolaus Pevsner, "The Anti-Pioneers II," "Architecture in Our Time," *Listener* (January 5, 1967): 7.

44 "Some Thoughts on the New Building of Stirling & Gowan at Leicester University," Remark by David Usborne, Student, *Architecture Association Journal* (December 1963), 146.

45 Banham, "Word in Britain: 'Character,'" 118.

46 James Stirling, "Architecture in Our Time," Letters to the Editor, *Listener* (January 12, 1967), 58.

47 Stirling, "Seven Keys," 151.

48 Stirling's article "'Functional Tradition' and Expression," in which he describes his strategy for working with Moretti's notion of "solidified space," was at some point subtitled a "design strategy"—the original title remains in the photo credits.

49 Charles Jencks, *Modern Movements in Architecture* (New York: Anchor, 1973), 261.

50 Manfredo Tafuri, "L'Architecture dans le Boudoir: The Language of Criticism and the Criticism of Language," *Oppositions* 3 (May 1974), reprinted in K. Michael Hays, ed., *Architecture Theory Since 1968* (Cambridge: MIT Press, 1998), 149.

51 Ibid., 151.

52 Eisenman's essay "Real and English" appeared in *Oppositions 4,* directly following the issue in which Tafuri's article was published; in Frampton's introduction to "Real and English" he makes Eisenman's debt to Tafuri explicit, more or less setting up Eisenman's piece as a rehashing of Tafuri's ideas (though Eisenman himself never credits Tafuri within the article).

53 Zimmerman, "Stirling Re-assembled," 56.

54 Irénée Scalbert, "Cerebral Functionalism: The Design of Leicester University Engineering Building," *Archis* (May 1994): 74.

55 Eisenman, "Real and English," 10.

56 Ibid., 11.

57 Stirling, "Architect's Approach to Architecture," 240.

58 Jordy, "Symbolic Essence," 179.

59 Ibid., 182.

60 Ibid.

61 Peter Bürger, *Theory of the Avant-Garde,* trans. Michael Shaw (Minneapolis: University of Minnesota Press, 1984), 70.

62 Banham, "Character," 121.

63 Ibid., 72.

64 Frampton, "Leicester University Engineering Laboratory," *Architectural Design* 32 (February 1964): 61. Kenneth Frampton, "Transformations in Style: The Work of James Stirling," *A+U* 50 (1975): 135.

65 Jacobus, "Engineering Building," 260.

66 Colin Rowe, "James Stirling: A Highly Personal and Very Disjointed Memoir," introduction to *James Stirling: Buildings and Projects,* ed. Peter Arnell and Ted Bickford (New York: Rizzoli, 1984), 26.

67 Ibid., 20.

68 Joseph Rykwert, "Episodio Inglese," *Domus* (June 1964): 1.

69 Tafuri, "L'Architecture dans le Boudoir," 295. The Italian for this feature is terribly translated as "porthole."
70 Frampton, "Leicester," 61.
71 Scalbert, "Cerebral Functionalism," 78.
72 Reyner Banham, "The Style for the Job," *New Statesman* 67 (February 14, 1964): 98.
73 Ibid.
74 Banham, "Character," 125.
75 Frampton, "Leicester," 61.
76 Ibid.
77 Ibid.
78 Jacobus, "Engineering Building," 260.
79 Bloom borrows the term from psychoanalyst Jacques Lacan, for whom (according to his translator Anthony Wilden) it signifies a "token of recognition or 'password.' The tessera was employed in the early mystery religions where fitting together again the two halves of a broken piece of pottery was used as a means of recognition by the initiates." Harold Bloom, *The Anxiety of Influence: A Theory of Poetry,* 2nd ed. (London: Oxford University Press, 1997), 67.
80 Ibid., 66.
81 Jacobus, "Engineering Building," 254.

CHAPTER 4
ONE ENORMOUS GESTURE

1 After Stirling's partnership with James Gowan dissolved in 1963, following the completion of Leicester, he practiced under the title of James Stirling (Firm) from 1963 to 1971. Michael Wilford began working with Stirling as an assistant on the Cambridge History Faculty Building; he became an associate partner in 1971, and in 1980 the firm became James Stirling, Michael Wilford and Associates, which would last until Stirling's death in 1992.
2 While Leicester's relationship to functionalism was a touchstone in Stirling historiography in the 1960s, by 1971 much of the discussion had shifted to the role of classicism (with the Derby Civic Centre and St. Andrews Art Gallery the most often-cited projects). See Colin Rowe, "James Stirling: A Highly Personal and Very Disjointed Memoir," introduction to *James Stirling: Buildings and Projects,* ed. Peter Arnell and Ted Bickford (New York: Rizzoli, 1984).
3 Mark Girouard, "Florey Building, Oxford," *Architectural Review* (November 1972): 266–68, 277.
4 Robert Maxwell, "A Rakish Dorm Confronts Oxford," *Architecture Plus* 1, no. 1 (February 1973): 30.
5 Joseph Rykwert, "Florey Building, Queen's College, Oxford," in "James Stirling 4 Progetti," *Domus* (November 1972): 12–13.
6 Alan Berman, ed., *Jim Stirling and the Red Trilogy: Three Radical Buildings* (London: Frances Lincoln, 2010).
7 James Stirling, "Acceptance of the Royal Gold Medal in Architecture 1980," *Architectural Design* 7–8 (1980): 7.
8 James Stirling, "Design Philosophy and Recent Work," *Architectural Design* 7–8 (1980): 7.
9 Leicester is one of the few Stirling projects to which a book-length study is dedicated. John McKean, *Leicester Engineering Building: James Stirling and James Gowan* (London: Phaidon, 1994).
10 Mark Girouard, *Big Jim: The Life and Work of James Stirling* (London: Chatto and Windus, 1998).
11 Rowe, "Highly Personal Memoir," 21.
12 Peter Eisenman, "Real and English," *Oppositions* 4 (October 1974): 30.
13 Scully's description of McKim, Mead and White's Low House: "The Low House, rediscovered, was like the chronic apparition of a tremendous and hitherto unsuspected local force: a giant out of this earth. It was one enormous gesture, one fundamental act." Vincent Scully, *The Shingle Style Today; or, The Historian's Revenge* (New York: Braziller, 1974), 4.
14 James Stirling, "Stirling Connexions," statement made at the second Iran International Congress of Architecture in Persepolis, 1974, *Architectural Review* 157, no. 939 (May 1975): 275. Also published in *Casabella* 399 (March 1975): 22.
15 Before WWII, Oxford had 4,391 students; by 1961 there were 7,396, a nearly 170 percent increase. For a thorough and highly biased history of the design and construction of the Florey Building, see A. A. Williams, "The Florey Building: A Narrative Account of the Project" (February 28, 1981), Queen's College Archive, 2W135. According to Williams, the college had originally planned to redevelop the college at Queen's Lane—the Smithsons were among those who submitted a scheme—but a 1960 repair showed that the building was in need of an entire reconstruction. Williams,

formerly bursar of the college (1958–77), was a clear opponent of Stirling's. Here is just a glimpse into his vitriolic criticism of the scheme: "The result has been the disfigurement of the best building site Oxford would see for a century or more by a structure revolting and unhuman in its hideousness and defective in practically every aspect of its functioning" (Williams, "Florey Building," VI: 35).

16 Stirling and Gowan had together received the commission for the History Faculty Building at Cambridge in the spring of 1963, but by December Stirling had informed the university that "Mr. Gowan and I are dividing the practice." Girouard, *Big Jim,* 138.

17 Williams, "Florey Building," I: 2. The other two architects interviewed were Downson, who "made little impression," and Howell and Partridge, who alienated one of the committee members during their interview by contradicting him. Williams, "Florey Building," II: a, 10.

18 J. M. Richards, "Recent Building in Oxford and Cambridge," *Architectural Review* 112 (August 1952): 78.

19 Powell and Moya, especially, would define a new language of exposed concrete, augmented in the later 1960s and early 1970s by Ove Arup's more technologically motivated concrete-and-glass solutions.

20 The site was purchased from the city in 1968 after more than three years of negotiations, largely because a public car park and boathouse were on the site. The city required the college to make accommodations for public punting elsewhere, though this was ultimately dismissed. The original site Stirling had been given was farther from the college, on Iffley Road.

21 Although the original target was between one hundred and one hundred thirty residents, the committee would later reduce its requirements, and Stirling would ultimately include seventy-four rooms.

22 Architect's summary of the brief, "Student's Hall of Residence, Queen's College, Oxford," *Architectural Review* 152 (November 1972): 260.

23 See Williams for an extended account of the building's construction history. There was no time to solicit bids from various contractors; W. H. Chivers and Son were chosen with a fixed-sum contract. See Girouard, *Big Jim,* 156–60, for a further account of the problems surrounding the building's construction.

24 To the great embarrassment of the college, the formal opening of the building, which included a scheduled visit from the Queen and the Queen Mother, had to be rescheduled due to construction delays. The provost at the time was Robert Normal William Blake. Williams, "Florey Building," IV: 32.

25 Stirling, "Acceptance of Royal Gold Medal," 8.

26 Stirling, "Stirling Connexions," 275. An image of the Florey court is paired with a view of the Trinity College courtyard; Florey's twin stair and elevator towers with the Trinity Gate Towers, and the Florey cloister with the Trinity cloisters. Stirling is careful not to assign any direct causality between the two images: "Nevertheless, there is, I hope, a connection, be it in material, constructional method, or association" (276).

27 The courtyard was later covered with grass.

28 James Stirling, "Architect's Report To Be Read in Conjunction with Drawings," October 10, 1966, Queen's College Archive, Architect: General File, FB1788: 1967–76.

29 Ibid.

30 Kenneth Frampton, "Stirling in Context: Buildings and Projects, 1950–75," *Royal Institute of British Architects Journal* 83, no. 3 (March 1976): 103.

31 Stephen Gardiner, "Eyeful in Oxford," *Listener* 86 (September 30, 1971): 442. Nikolaus Pevsner wrote, "Its calculated bluntness determines the appearance." Nikolaus Pevsner and Jennifer Sherwood, *The Buildings of England: Oxfordshire* (U.K.: William Clowes and Sons, 1974), 246. The Smithsons' site was set back from the river and lacked the same immediacy to the river of the St. Clement's site.

32 James Stirling, "'The Functional Tradition' and Expression," *Perspecta* 6 (1960): 92.

33 From Niblett Report of 1957, as quoted in Diane Chablo, "University Architecture in Britain, 1950–75" (Ph.D. diss., University of Oxford, 1987), 154.

34 For a discussion of the Golden Lane scheme, see Alison and Peter Smithson, *Ordinariness and Light: Urban Theories, 1952–60, and Their Application in a Building Project, 1963–70* (London: Faber and Faber, 1970), 53–61.

35 Of the Old People's Home of 1966 he wrote that since the corridor was "always bending there are never long institutional views down it." James Stirling, "An Architect's Approach to Architecture," *RIBA Journal* (May 1965): 233.

36 For a discussion of the typology discourse of the 1960s and 1970s, see Werner Oechslin, "Premises for a Resumption of the Discussion of Typology," *Assemblage* 1 (October 1986): 37–55. Oeschslin's "resumption" of the typology discourse was a reaction to what he perceived as a flattening of the term as it had begun to be appropriated by architectural postmodernism. Important articles on typology during this period (in addition to the Argan and Colquhoun articles discussed) were Rafael Moneo, "On Typology," *Oppositions* 13 (Summer 1978): 23–45, and Anthony Vidler, "The Third Typology," *Oppositions* 7 (Winter 1976–77): 1–4.

37 Giulio Carlo Argan, "On the Typology of Architecture," trans. Joseph Rykwert, *Architectural Design* 33 (December 1963): 564–65. In his accompanying notes Rykwert writes, "It seemed to the translator to approach a subject which is central to speculation about architectural theory both in this country and in America—but to do so from a rather unfamiliar standpoint and so contribute a new element to current discussion."

38 Ibid., 565.

39 Ibid., 564.

40 Ibid.

41 Alan Colquhoun, "Typology and Design Method," *Arena: Architectural Association Journal* 83, "Meaning in Architecture" (June 1967). Republished in *Perspecta* 12 (1969): 71–74.

42 Ibid., 72.

43 Ibid.

44 Nikolaus Pevsner, *A History of Building Types* (Princeton: Princeton University Press, 1976).

45 Argan, "On the Typology of Architecture," 565.

46 K. Michael Hays, *Architecture's Desire* (Cambridge: MIT Press, 2009), 29.

47 Ibid., 9.

48 Stirling "'Functional Tradition' and Expression," 96.

49 All of the student rooms at Florey are single rooms, as is the custom at Oxford, which further reinforces the "cell" idea.

50 For a discussion of the development of the "chain" building form see Chablo, "University Architecture in Britain, 1950–75," 85. Chablo links Selwyn's chainlike form to the Howell, Killick and Partridge scheme for Churchill College of 1959, noting that the model was also applied by Ahrends, Burton and Koralek in their "snake-like" plan for Keble College, Oxford (1976), Howell, Killick and Partridge at St. Anne's Oxford (1969), and by Powell and Moya at the Cripps Building at St. Johns (1966).

51 Stirling, "Architect's Approach to Architecture," 233.

52 Stirling, "Anti-Structure," 116.

53 Stirling, "Seven Keys to a Good Architecture," 151.

54 Alan Colquhoun, "The Strategies of the *Grands Travaux*," in *Modernity and the Classical Tradition: Architectural Essays, 1980–87* (Cambridge: MIT Press, 1989), 134.

55 This nonstructural brick wall, running beneath the building on pilotis, had a long lineage in Stirling's oeuvre; in his student projects, Organic Chemistry Laboratories for a Northern University, England, a one-story theater block was placed beneath the elevated tower; and in his thesis of 1950, he also infilled the ground plane beneath the building on pilotis with a series of programs encircled by a rough stone wall. In each of these early projects his desire for a Corbusian structure on pilotis was clearly in conflict with a need to "ground" the building overall.

56 The main electrical and water supply are routed through the building to the duct stacks on the south façade.

57 Girouard, "Florey Building," 267.

58 Reyner Banham, *Theory and Design in the First Machine Age* (New York: Praeger, 1960), 330.

59 Reyner Banham, "History Faculty, Cambridge," *Architectural Review* 144 (December 1968): 333.

60 Banham wrote that it was the "least boring luminous ceiling in the whole of recent architecture." Ibid., 332.

61 See Gillian Naylor, "Theory and Design: The Banham Factor," *Journal of Design History* 10, no. 3 (1997): 241–52; Nigel Whiteley, *Reyner Banham: Historian of the Immediate Future* (Cambridge: MIT Press, 2002).

62 Stirling, "Stirling Connexions," 275. Newby's influence is here significant, particularly knowing that one of his most important contributions at Leicester was the willingness to transfer loads across diagonal braces into the "Y" beam.

63 Stirling, "Seven Keys," 151.

64 John Summerson, "Vitruvius Ludens: James Stirling," *Architectural Review* 173 (March 1983): 29.

65 Mark Girouard, "Florey Building," 266.

66 "There is something in Modern Architecture called

'object-fixation,' probably at no other time in the 20th century have people been so concerned with making significant objects, and at the same time as making them they have great guilt about making these objects and wish them to go away. A complete ambivalence in reaction to 'the object.''' Colin Rowe, "On Conceptual Architecture," lecture delivered at the Artnet conference on Conceptual Architecture, January 17–18, 1975, *Net* 3: 9.

67 Stirling, "Seven Keys," 151.

68 Stirling, *Early Unpublished Writings,* 31.

69 Le Corbusier's best known Choisy appropriation—the drawing of the Acropolis in Athens—is one of the few instances of perspective used in Choisy's book. Le Corbusier includes only two Choisy, or worm's-eye, axonometrics in *Towards a New Architecture*—one of Santa Sophia and the other of the Palace in Amman. Both are cutaway, in plan and section. In his own projects that he features in the book, Le Corbusier never uses the worm's-eye axonometric.

70 Julius Posener, "Choisy," *Architectural Review* (1956): 235.

71 Banham, *Theory and Design,* 25.

72 Yves-Alain Bois, "Metamorphosis of Axonometry," *Daidalos,* no. 1 (1981): 42.

73 Ibid., 46.

74 Charles Jencks, *Modern Movements in Architecture* (New York: Anchor/Doubleday, 1973), 263.

75 Ibid., 267.

76 Banham, Introduction, *Catalogue of an Exhibition Held at the Royal Institute of British Architects, Heinz Gallery, 21 Portman Square, London, 24 April–21 June, 1974* (London: RIBA Publications for the RIBA Drawings Collection, 1974), 10.

77 Ibid., 14.

78 Alan Colquhoun, "Architecture as a Continuous Text," *ANY* 1, no. 2, "A Tribute to James Stirling" (September–October 1993): 18.

79 Posener, "Choisy," 236.

80 Girouard, "Florey Building, Oxford," 267.

81 Le Corbusier, *Towards a New Architecture,* trans. from 13th ed. by Frederick Etchells (New York: Dover, 1986), 46.

82 See Laurent Stadler, "'New Brutalism,' 'Topology,' and 'Image'": Some Remarks on the Architectural Debates in England Around 1950," *Journal of Architecture,* 13: 263–81.

83 Reyner Banham, "The New Brutalism," *Architectural Review* 118 (December 1955): 358.

84 Ibid.

85 William Jordy, "The Symbolic Essence of Modern European Architecture of the Twenties and Its Continuing Influence," *Journal of the Society of Architectural Historians* 22, no. 3 (October 1963): 186.

86 Ibid.

87 Scully's memorable phrase to describe Robert Venturi's "death grapple" with McKim, Mead and White in *Shingle Style Today,* 26.

88 The overall shape reflects a general penchant for terraced projects at this time—the University of East Anglia, with its massive Ziggurat housing blocks as perhaps the best example. Claire Zimmerman has also noted the resemblance to the Smithsons' Terrace Housing of 1957. Zimmerman, "James Stirling Reassembled," *AA Files,* no. 56 (2007): 33.

CHAPTER 5
RECOLLECTING FORWARD

1 For Colin Rowe, St. Andrews was a "manifesto piece" in its contextual strategy and historical quotations set in "italics." Rowe, "James Stirling: A Highly Personal and Very Disjointed Memoir," introduction to *James Stirling: Buildings and Projects,* ed. Peter Arnell and Ted Bickford (New York: Rizzoli, 1984), 21. For Kenneth Frampton it was Derby, not St. Andrews, that represented Stirling's growing interest in a "broad cultural context" and increasing Neoclassical tendencies. Kenneth Frampton, "Stirling in Context: Buildings and Projects, 1950–75," *Royal Institute of British Architects Journal* 83, no. 3 (March 1976): 104.

2 Colin Rowe and Fred Koetter, "Collage City," *Architectural Review* 158 (August 1975): 66–91.

3 Alan Colquhoun, "Architecture as a Continuous Text," *ANY* 1, no. 2 (September 1993): 18.

4 James Stirling, "Influence of Corb on Me Now and When I Was a Student," in Stirling, *James Stirling: Early Unpublished Writings on Architecture,* ed. Mark Crinson (New York: Routledge, 2010), 74.

5 "Letter from Finance Minister, *Landes Nordrhein-Westfalen,*" August 8, 1974, "Düsseldorf Competition," DRCON2000:0027:0818:0819, James Stirling/Michael Wilford Fonds, Canadian Centre for Architecture,

Montréal (CCA). Only the international entrants were paid. This was the first project in which Stirling was in full partnership with Michael Wilford, and the competition team consisted of Russell Bevington, Robert Livesey, and Crispin Osborne (Leon Krier had left the office after finishing the Hatje book in 1974).

6 Mark Girouard, *Big Jim: The Life and Work of James Stirling* (London: Chatto and Windus, 1998), 190.

7 Stirling had recently finished putting together the Hatje book with Leon Krier, and the dust was just settling on the controversy around the technical failures of the Florey Building, completed in 1971.

8 Girouard, *Big Jim*, 198–99.

9 "Building Competition," in "Düsseldorf Competition," James Stirling/Michael Wilford Fonds, CCA.

10 Ibid., 293.

11 James Stirling, "Architect's Competition Brief," in "Stirling in Germany," 2 "Düsseldorf: Re-Design of the Grabbeplatz and a Building for the North Rhine–Westphalia Art Collection," *Architectural Review* 160 (November 1976): 296. His arrangement recalls a drawing published by Stirling in the 1975 monograph *James Stirling: Buildings and Projects, 1950–74*, depicting a Provençal courtyard containing a symmetrical grid of nine cypress trees. Though the drawing is dated 1950, Leon Krier said that he saw Stirling draw it in 1974. Girouard, *Big Jim*, 195.

12 "I think the fact that he has invited you must mean that he wants some new and imaginative approach to the question of presenting works of art. Caution! So far the best architects have produced buildings which can bear hardly on their contents (Wright, Mies van der Rohe, et al.). It must have an *in* and an *out*, but in between should allow the visitor a choice of direction now and again, something like visiting a garden perhaps." Handwritten letter from Norman Reid, "Düsseldorf Competition." James Stirling/Michael Wilford Fonds, CCA.

13 Stirling, "Architect's Competition Brief," 293.

14 Archival sketches show that Stirling developed this space as a labyrinthian form, formally similar to Le Corbusier's Mundaneum and, in some of the sketches, nearly identical to the contemporaneous labyrinth work of artist Joe Tilson.

15 Though it was one of the final ten. The jury was composed of nine "expert judges"—architects and professors from Stuttgart, Düsseldorf, Hanover, Offenbach, and Zurich—as well as five additional judges and two advisors.

16 Dissing and Weitling's scheme was completed in 1986.

17 Competition Report, English trans., "Düsseldorf Competition," James Stirling/Michael Wilford Fonds, CCA.

18 James Stirling, "A Conversation with Some American Students," *JA: The Japan Architect* 45, no. 7 (July 1970): 32.

19 Stirling, "Architect's Competition Brief," 292.

20 Ibid.

21 Girouard, *Big Jim*, 199.

22 James Stirling, quoted in Douglas Davis, "Master of Inconsistency," *Newsweek* (June 29, 1981): 74.

23 Adrian Forty, *Words and Buildings: A Vocabulary of Modern Architecture* (New York: Thames and Hudson, 2000), 133.

24 Specifically, he described his Roma Interrotta project of 1978 as "contextural-associational." James Stirling, "Revisions to the Nolli Plan of Rome (The MFA Solution)," in Jennifer Franchina, trans. and ed., *Roma Interrotta* (Rome: Officina, 1978), 84. See Chapter 6 for a more complete discussion of this project.

25 This definition of contextualism comes from the Oxford English Dictionary, 3rd ed. The term first appeared in philosophy in 1920s and was adopted by literary criticism in the mid-1950s. "Contexturalism" as an invented term seems to have emerged from the students of Colin Rowe at Cornell, specifically Stuart Cohen, though Rowe himself never used the term: "The interesting thing is that the term [contextualism] was really coined to describe the strategy of urban design that was being worked out by Colin and the students in the urban design studio. Originally, I had wanted to call it 'contexturalism,' which is context and texture, with texture referring to the idea of urban fabric. Colin kept saying no, no, no, you can't do that, it's not a real word, you must call it 'contextualism.' That was a word that was starting to appear in literary criticism. Colin hated the word; he never used the word in writing or anywhere, except to say offhand that what we were doing in the studio was referred to by Hurtt and Cohen and Schumacher as contextualism." "Oral History of Stuart Earl Cohen." Interviewed by Betty J. Blum, Chicago Architects Oral History Project.

http://www.artic.edu/aic/libraries/caohp/cohen.html. Accessed on May 15, 2007, 29.

26 "Small can be beautiful—and monumental—it is not a matter of size but rather a matter of *presence*—a chair can be monumental." James Stirling, "Acceptance of the Royal Gold Medal in Architecture 1980," *Architectural Design* 7–8 (1980): 10.

27 Rafael Moneo, *Theoretical Anxiety and Design Strategies in the Work of Eight Contemporary Architects* (Cambridge: MIT Press, 2005), 36.

28 Stirling, "Acceptance of the Royal Gold Medal," 6.

29 Colin Rowe and Fred Koetter, *Collage City* (Cambridge: MIT Press, 1978). The book maintained the structure of the original essay, divided into five sections: "Utopia: Decline and Fall," "After the Millennium," "Crisis of the Object: Predicament of Texture," "Collision City and the Politics of 'Bricolage,'" and "Collage City and the Reconquest of Time." A thirty-page "Excursus" is appended to the book. All references herein are to the 1978 edition unless otherwise noted.

30 See Colin Rowe, introduction, *As I Was Saying: Recollections and Miscellaneous Essays,* vol. 3: *Urbanistics* (Cambridge: MIT Press, 1996). Rowe republished a number of these projects in his 1996 memoirs; of special importance seemed to be Wayne Cooper's thesis of 1967, which was a virtual catalogue of figure/ground plans of premodern cities (indeed, Rowe had tried to persuade him to publish them). It was Cooper's plan of Wiesbaden that appeared (uncredited) on the frontispiece of the book edition of *Collage City.* See also Steven Hurtt, "Conjectures on Urban Form: The Cornell Urban Design Studio, 1963–82," *Cornell Journal of Architecture,* no. 2 (Fall 1983): 54–141, for a more comprehensive survey of this studio work.

31 "Collage City: Rowe Replies," *Architectural Review* 158 (November 1975): 322. Rowe's letter a response to Nathan Silver's letter, in which he complained that the ideas in *Collage City* were stolen from his and Jencks's book *Adhocism.* Nathan Silver, "Letter to the Editor," *Architectural Review* 158 (October 1975): 192. For brief historicizations of *Collage City,* see K. Michael Hays, introduction to "Collage City" in *Architecture Theory Since 1968,* ed. K. Michael Hays (Cambridge: MIT Press, 1998), and Joan Ockman, "Form Without Utopia: Contextualizing Colin Rowe," *Journal of the Society of Architectural Historians* 57, no. 4 (December 1998): 448–56. See also the issue of *ANY* dedicated to Colin Rowe's influence, "Form Work: Colin Rowe," *ANY,* no. 7–8 (1994), and George Baird, "Oppositions in the Thought of Colin Rowe," *Assemblage* 33 (1997): 22–35.

32 Clement Greenberg, "Collage (The Pasted Paper Revolution)," *Art News* 57, no. 5 (September 1958): 46–49. Greenberg traced the development of collage in both Picasso and Braque.

33 He recalled that he found them "clever and free." James Stirling, "Retrospective Statements," *Independent Group: Postwar Britain and the Aesthetics of Plenty,* ed. David Robbins (Cambridge: MIT Press, 1990), 195.

34 Rowe and Koetter, *Collage City,* 144.

35 Ibid., 91. They reluctantly acknowledge the troubling fact that Hadrian was, of course, "no less autocratic than Louis XIV."

36 Ibid., 81.

37 "Competition Report."

38 James Stirling, "Stirling Connexions," statement made at the second Iran International Congress of Architecture in Persepolis, 1974, *Architectural Review* 157, no. 939 (May 1975): 275.

39 Moneo argues that Düsseldorf was the moment that Stirling shifted from a section-based strategy to a plan-based one, and therefore from a fundamentally modernist orientation to a Beaux-Arts or classical one. This neglects earlier plan-based projects such as Churchill or Camberwell.

40 Irénée Scalbert, "James Stirling," in *OASE* 79: 38.

41 Graham Shane argues that the glass-skinned interstitial circulation spaces are the truly revolutionary aspects of the Düsseldorf project scheme. "These spaces connect the objectives of the brief, which are conceived as functionally well defined and spatially segregated objects." "It is this 'preferred route,' these sentences, this promenade architecturale, that distinguishes Stirling's work as architecture." Shane, "Cologne in Context," *AD* (November 1976): 687.

42 Stirling, "An Architect's Approach to Architecture," *Royal Institute of British Architects Journal* 72 (May 1965): 231.

43 Alan Colquhoun, "The Strategies of the *Grands Travaux,*" in *Modernity and the Classical Tradition:*

Architectural Essays, 1980–87 (Cambridge: MIT Press, 1989), 152.

44 James Stirling, "Garches to Jaoul: Le Corbusier as a Domestic Architect in 1927 and 1953," *Architectural Review* 118 (September 1955): 146.

45 Colin Rowe and Robert Slutzky, "Transparency: Literal and Phenomenal, Part II," in *As I Was Saying,* 103.

46 Stirling and his wife, Mary, traveled in India for three weeks in February and March 1975, as Jim was lecturing for the British Council. He wrote to Alan Colquhoun, "I was much moved by 2 of Corb's buildings at Chandigarh (should have gone to Chandigarh a long time ago)." Girouard, *Big Jim,* 84. Bevington, in an interview with Girouard, said that "Jim made a site visit, and there's a classic sketch made on the back of an airline ticket coming back, of his thoughts about the project." Ibid., 199.

47 Rowe and Koetter, *Collage City,* 78.

48 Ibid., 83.

49 Eisenman in unpublished interview with Emmanuel Petit, February 19, 2010.

50 Robert McCarter, *Louis Kahn* (New York: Phaidon, 2005), 289.

51 Luigi Moretti, "The Structures and Sequences of Spaces," trans. Thomas Stevens, in *Oppositions* 3 (October 1974).

52 James Stirling, "'The Functional Tradition' and Expression," *Perspecta* 6 (1960): 91.

53 Rowe, *As I Was Saying,* 24.

54 Rowe and Koetter, *Collage City,* 68. The resonance with the Uffizi is made even more significant in the early sketches, in which Stirling describes the plan arrangement as "Uffizi plan."

55 In their concluding "excursus" to the book, Rowe and Koetter include a series of examples or "stimulants"—"possible *'objets trouvés'* in the urbanistic collage"—and none among them is modern. Rowe and Koetter, *Collage City,* 151–81.

56 The letter was in response to an earlier letter from Charles Jencks.

57 John Summerson, "Vitruvius Ludens: James Stirling," *Architectural Review* 173 (March 1983): 20–21.

58 Charles Jencks, *The Language of Postmodern Architecture* (New York: Rizzoli, 1981), 111.

59 Stirling, "Writings on Architecture," 156.

60 The two images are taken from Venturi's 1966 essay "Complexity and Contradiction," which first appeared in this issue of *Perspecta,* though the juxtaposition of the two images is Stern's, not Venturi's. Robert Venturi, "Complexity and Contradiction in Architecture," *Perspecta* 9/10 (1965): 29. Venturi analyzed a series of examples across historical time periods, including the Villa Farnese and the two cover images. These precedents are given even greater importance when we examine Stirling's first sketches for Düsseldorf in which the courtyard is rendered with a colonnade around the interior, creating what Venturi called a "'lining'—that is, a space within a space analogous to its frame." Ibid., 26. Though this colonnade disappeared in the eventual design, it indicated his initial fascination with these more classical renderings of the courtyard space.

61 Venturi, *Complexity and Contradiction,* 26.

62 K. Michael Hays, *Architecture's Desire* (Cambridge: MIT Press, 2009), 43.

63 Simon Sadler, "L'Architecture dans le Salon: The Civic Architecture of a Projective Modernism," in *Neo-Avant-Garde and Postmodern: Postwar Architecture in Britain and Beyond* (London: Yale Center for British Art, 2010), 368–69.

64 Ibid.

65 Alan Colquhoun, "Three Kinds of Historicism," *Modernity and the Classical Tradition: Architectural Essays, 1980–87* (Cambridge: MIT Press, 1989), 6.

66 Anthony Vidler, "The Architecture of James Stirling," *Skyline* (November 1981): 18.

67 Kierkegaard, in Harold Bloom, *The Anxiety of Influence: A Theory of Poetry,* 2nd ed. (London: Oxford University Press, 1997), 82.

68 Ibid., 87–88.

CHAPTER 6
THE REMAINS OF MODERNISM

1 James Stirling, "Lecture 81," in *Architecture in an Age of Skepticism,* ed. Sir Denys Lasun (London: Oxford University Press, 1985), 213n1. Stirling noted that he kept a version of this slideshow of the firm's current work on hand, generating a "new version" every two years or so. James Stirling, "The Monumentally Informal," in Stirling, *James Stirling: Writings on Architecture* (Milan: Skira, 1998), 151–52.

2 Jennifer Franchina, trans. and ed., *Roma Interrotta:*

[catalog of an exhibition at Cooper-Hewitt Museum, June 12–August 12, 1979] (Rome: Incontri internazionali d'arte, 1979), 84. The competition was also featured in an issue of *Architectural Design* guest edited by Michael Graves. *Architectural Design* 49, no. 3–4 (1979), 1–104.

3 James Stirling and Partner, "Roma Interrotta" exhibition, page layouts for publication, DRCON-2000:0027:0933:001–005, James Stirling/Michael Wilford Fonds, Canadian Centre for Architecture, Montréal (CCA).

4 Graziella Lonardi, Preface to Franchina, *Roma Interrotta*, 10.

5 Giulio Carlo Argan, Introduction, Franchina, *Roma Interrotta*, 12.

6 Alan Chimacoff, "*Roma Interrotta* Reviewed," *AD* 49: 17.

7 Ibid., 8.

8 Argan in Franchina, *Roma Interrotta*, 12.

9 James Stirling, "Revisions to the Nolli Plan of Rome (The MFA Solution)," in Franchina, *Roma Interrotta*, 84.

10 Stirling in Franchina, *Roma Interrotta*, 87. Stirling celebrated his fiftieth birthday in 1976, consistent with the shift of his birthdate to 1926.

11 Stirling in Franchina, *Roma Interrotta*, 84.

12 Ibid.

13 Ibid., 85.

14 James Stirling, "Lecture '81," in *Architecture in an Age of Skepticism: A Practitioner's Anthology*, ed. Denys Lasdun (London: Heinemann, 1984), 193.

15 Stirling also notes that he was indebted to the "working methods of a few architects (e.g., O. M. Ungers)." Stirling, in Franchina, *Roma Interrotta*, 84.

16 Chimacoff, "*Roma Interrotta* Reviewed," 8.

17 Bruno Zevi, "*Roma Interrotta*," *Cronache di Architettura*, 1978, reprinted and translated in *Piero Sartugo, Nathalie Grenon: Architecture in Perspective* (New York: Monacelli, 1988), 143.

18 Colin Rowe and Fred Koetter, *Collage City* (Cambridge: MIT Press, 1978), 85.

19 Anthony Vidler, *James Frazer Stirling: Notes from the Archive* (New Haven: Yale Center for British Art and Yale University Press, 2010), 213.

20 Stirling's use of "MFA" was in response to a scathing review by Hugh Brogan in the *Cambridge Review* (October 1968), in which Brogan accused Stirling and other "megalomaniac" architects of being "structural fascists," concerned only with their place in the art histories. Stirling includes Brogan's reference as a footnote. Stirling, "Revisions to the Nolli Plan," 84, 97.

21 Constantino Dardi, in Franchina *Roma Interrotta*, 48.

22 Michael Graves, "Roman Interventions," *AD* 49, no. 3–4 (1979): 4.

23 Manfredo Tafuri, *Architecture and Utopia: Design and Capitalist Development* (Cambridge: MIT Press, 1976), 14.

24 Manfredo Tafuri, *The Sphere and the Labyrinth: Avant-Gardes and Architecture from Piranesi to the 1970s*, trans. Pellegrino d'Acierno and Robert Connolly (Cambridge: MIT Press, 1987), 34.

25 Ibid., 15.

26 Manfredo Tafuri, "L'Architecture dans *le Boudoir*: The Language of Criticism and the Criticism of Language," *Oppositions* 3 (May 1974): 37–62. The essay was first delivered as a lecture in April 1975 at the conference "Practice, Theory, and Politics in Architecture," at Princeton. Reprinted in K. Michael Hays, ed., *Architecture Theory Since 1968* (Cambridge: MIT Press, 1998), 146–73.

27 Ibid., passim.

28 Ibid., 293.

29 Tafuri, "Boudoir," in Hays, *Architecture Theory*, 149.

30 K. Michael Hays, *Architecture's Desire* (Cambridge: MIT Press, 2009), 62.

31 *James Stirling: Catalogue of an Exhibition Held at the Royal Institute of British Architects, Heinz Gallery, 21 Portman Square, London, 24 April–21 June, 1974* (London: RIBA Publications for the RIBA Drawings Collection, 1974).

32 See *Environment, Participation, Cultural Structures: General Catalogue, La Biennale di Venezia* (Venice: Alfieri, 1976), vol. 2. The catalogue features partial axonometric drawings of Cologne and Düsseldorf.

33 The other architects featured were Raimund Abraham, Aldo Rossi, Emilio Ambasz, Richard Meier, Walter Pichler, and Venturi and Rauch. See Ada Louise Huxtable, "Architectural Drawings as Art Gallery Art," Architecture View, *New York Times*, October 23, 1977; and Paul Goldberger, "Architectural Drawings Raised to an Art," *New York Times*, December 12, 1977.

34 Notable was the Iran International Congress of Architecture in Persepolis in September 1974. For a complete list of the symposium, see Laleh Bakhtiar, ed., *Towards a Quality of Life: The Role of Industrialization in the Architecture and Urban Planning of Developing Countries. Report of the Proceedings of the Second International Congress of Architects,* Persepolis, Iran, 1974 (Tehran: Ministry of Housing and Urban Development, 1976). For an excerpt of Stirling's presentation, including his slide pairings, see James Stirling, "Stirling Connexions," statement made at the second Iran International Congress of Architecture in Persepolis, 1974, *Architectural Review* 157, no. 939 (May 1975): 275.

35 Gerd Hatje had approached Stirling in 1969. Krier began work on the book in 1970, but the bulk of the work was done from the end of 1973 until publication in 1975. See Mark Girouard, *Big Jim: The Life and Work of James Stirling* (London: Chatto and Windus, 1998), 187.

36 Krier responding to the question of how Stirling had influenced him: Girouard, *Big Jim,* 187.

37 Colin Rowe, "James Stirling: A Highly Personal and Very Disjointed Memoir," introduction to *James Stirling: Buildings and Projects,* ed. Peter Arnell and Ted Bickford (New York: Rizzoli, 1984), 16.

38 Reyner Banham, "England and America," *Journal of the Society of Architectural Historians* 36 (December 1977): 263.

39 Harold Bloom, *The Anxiety of Influence: A Theory of Poetry,* 2nd ed. (London: Oxford University Press, 1997), 16.

40 Rowe, "Highly Personal and Very Disjointed Memoir," 21.

41 Aldo Rossi, *Architecture of the City* (Cambridge: MIT Press, 1982), 166.

42 Tafuri, *Architecture and Utopia,* 13.

CONCLUSION

1 James Stirling, "Seven Keys to a Good Architecture," *20th Century* (Winter 1963): 151.

2 Harold Bloom, *The Anxiety of Influence: A Theory of Poetry,* 2nd ed. (London: Oxford University Press, 1997), 50.

3 Claire Zimmerman, "James Stirling Reassembled," *AA Files,* no. 56 (2007): 39.

4 Le Corbusier, *Towards a New Architecture,* trans. Frederick Etchells from 13th ed. (New York: Dover, 1986), 37.

5 John Summerson, "Vitruvius Ludens: James Stirling," *Architectural Review* 173 (March 1983): 19.

6 James Stirling, "Stirling Connexions," statement made at the second Iran International Congress of Architecture in Persepolis, 1974, *Architectural Review* 157, no. 939 (May 1975).

7 James Stirling, "Acceptance of the Royal Gold Medal in Architecture, 1980," Architectural Design Profile 29, *Architectural Design* 7–8 (1980): 7.

8 Ibid., 276.

9 James Stirling, *James Stirling: Writings on Architecture,* ed. Robert Maxwell (Milan: Skira, 1998), 134.

10 "Le Corbusier and Mies have consistently re-mained the most influential: this not because they have rejected their starting point, as for example both Oud and (to a lesser degree) Gropius have done, but because they have understood it." William Jordy, "The Symbolic Essence of Modern European Architecture of the Twenties and Its Continuing Influence," *Journal of the Society of Architectural Historians* 22, no. 3 (October 1963): 182.

11 K. Michael Hays, *Architecture's Desire* (Cambridge: MIT Press, 2009), 4.

12 Ibid., 7.

13 Anthony Vidler, *James Frazer Stirling: Notes from the Archive* (New Haven: Yale Center for British Art and Yale University Press, 2010).

14 Letter dated October 26, 1988, interview for *Ambiente* magazine, DRCON2000:0027:846, James Stirling/Michael Wilford Fonds, CCA.

ILLUSTRATION CREDITS

The photographers and the sources of visual material other than the owners indicated in the captions are as follows. Every effort has been made to supply complete and correct credits; if there are errors or omissions, please contact Yale University Press so that corrections can be made in any subsequent edition.

James Stirling/Michael Wilford fonds, Canadian Centre for Architecture, Montréal (figs. 1–5, 7, 9, 10, 14–21, 23–28, 30, 35–37, 39–41 45, 46, 48, 51–64, 69, 71, 72, 74, 76–83, 85–92, 94, 96–98, 100, 101–5, 108–15, 117–19, 123, 125, 126, 128); © 2011 Artists Rights Society (ARS), New York/ADAGP, Paris/F.L.C. (figs. 6, 8, 22, 47, 65, 70, 121); Courtesy of Mary Stirling (fig. 11); Photograph by Michael Wickham (fig. 28); Courtesy of *Perspecta* (figs. 29, 42, 45); Gerard Fielden, "Churchill College Cambridge: The Competition Reviewed," *Builder*, August 14, 1959 (figs. 31–33); Courtesy of the Frances Loeb Library, Harvard Graduate School of Design (figs. 34, 38, 84); Louis I. Kahn Collection, The University of Pennsylvania and the Pennsylvania Historical and Museum Commission (figs. 49, 106, 116); © Richard Einzig, photographer (figs. 53, 58); © Michael Carapetian, photographer (fig. 56); RIBA Library Photographs Collection (fig. 66); © Amanda Reeser Lawrence (fig. 71); Photograph by Yukio Futagawa (figs. 72, 77): Ezra Stoller © Esto (fig. 75); Peter Eisenman fonds, Canadian Centre for Architecture, Montréal (fig. 93, 129); Courtesy of Dover Publications, Inc. (fig. 95); Courtesy Mark Cohn for Venturi Scott Brown and Associates, Inc. (fig. 107); © John Donat photography (fig. 119); Canadian Centre for Architecture, Montréal © Eredi Di Luigi Ghirri (fig. 122); from Jennifer Franchina, trans. and ed., *Roma Interrotta: [catalog of an exhibition at Cooper-Hewitt Museum, June 12–August 12, 1979]* (Rome: Incontri internazionali d'arte, 1979) (fig. 124); Printing and Graphic Arts Department, Houghton Library, Harvard University, 63-368 (fig. 127).

INDEX

Page numbers in *italics* refer to illustrations.